Photoshop® 6 For Dummies

Windows Version

Sheet

Toolbox Shortcuts

Note: To access the tools, press the key(s) listed. If you uncheck the option Use Shift key for Tool Switch in your Preferences, you can eliminate the need to press the Shift key to change tools.

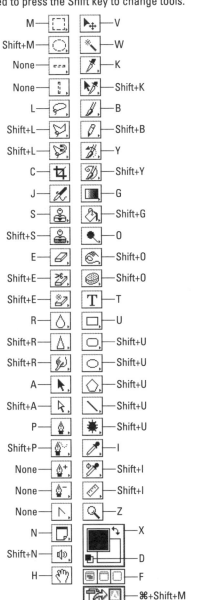

M	V
Shift+M	W
None	K
None	Shift+K
L	B
Shift+L	Shift+B
Shift+L	Y
C	Shift+Y
J	G
S	Shift+G
Shift+S	O
E	Shift+O
Shift+E	Shift+O
Shift+E	T
R	U
Shift+R	Shift+U
Shift+R	Shift+U
A	Shift+U
Shift+A	Shift+U
P	Shift+U
Shift+P	I
None	Shift+I
None	Shift+I
None	Z
N	X
Shift+N	D
H	F
	⌘+Shift+M

Navigation Tricks

Scroll image	spacebar+drag
Zoom in	Ctrl+spacebar+click
Zoom in and change window size	Ctrl+plus
Zoom out	Alt+spacebar+click
Zoom out and change window size	Ctrl+minus
Scroll up or down one screen	PageUp/PageDown
Scroll left or right	Ctrl+Page Up/ Page Down
Move to upper-left corner of image	Home
Move to lower-right corner of image	End
Zoom to 100%	Double-click on Zoom tool
Fit on Screen	Ctrl+0
Cycle through all open image windows	Ctrl+Tab

More Fun with Selections

Fill selection with foreground color	Alt+Backspace
Fill selection with background color	Ctrl+Backspace
Display Fill dialog box	Shift+Backspace
Cut selection	Ctrl+X
Copy selection	Ctrl+C
Paste image last cut or copied	Ctrl+V
Reapply last filter	Ctrl+F
Adjust levels	Ctrl+L
Free Transform	Ctrl+T
Transform Again	Ctrl+Shift+T

For Dummies®: Bestselling Book Series for Beginners

Photoshop® 6 For Dummies®
Windows Version

Cheat Sheet

Daily Activities

Cancel operation	Esc or Ctrl+. (period)
Close image	Ctrl+W
General preferences	Ctrl+K
Display last preferences panel used	Ctrl+Alt+K
Open image	Ctrl+O
Print image	Ctrl+P
Page setup	Ctrl+Shift+P
Quit Photoshop	Ctrl+Q
Save image to disk	Ctrl+S
Save As	Ctrl+Shift+S
Save for Web	Ctrl+Alt+Shift+S
Undo last operation	Ctrl+Z

Palette Shortcuts

Color palette	F6
Layers palette	F7
Info palette	F8
Actions palette	F9
Step forward in History palette	Ctrl+Shift+Z
Step backward in History palette	Ctrl+Alt+Z
All palettes, status bar, options bar, and Toolbox	Tab
Just palettes	Shift+Tab
Raise value in option box	Up arrow
Lower value in option box	Down arrow

Painting and Editing Tricks

Increase brush size	]
Decrease brush size	[
Change opacity of tool in 10% increments	1, ... , 9, 0
Paint or edit in straight lines	Click, Shift+click
Change eraser type	Shift+E
Erase to History	Alt+drag

Layer Tricks

New Layer	Ctrl+Shift+N
Clone selection to a new layer	Ctrl+J
Cut selection to a new layer	Ctrl+Shift+J
Change opacity of layer in 10% increments	1, ... , 9, 0
Activate layer that contains specific image	Ctrl+click
Activate next layer up	Alt+]
Activate next layer down	Alt+[
Hide all layers but one	Alt+click on eyeball
Show all layers	Alt+click on eyeball
Select the contents of active layer	Ctrl+click on layer name in Layers palette

Selection Tricks

Note: All selection tricks are performed with selection tools. (There's a shocker.)

Draw straight lines	Alt+click with Lasso tool
Add to selection outline	Shift+drag
Deselect specific area	Alt+drag
Deselect all but intersected area	Shift+Alt+drag
Deselect entire image	Ctrl+D
Reselect last selection	Ctrl+Shift+D
Select everything	Ctrl+A
Hide extras	Ctrl+H
Move selection outline only	Drag or press an arrow key

Hungry Minds™

For Dummies®: Bestselling Book Series for Beginners

Photoshop® 6 For Dummies®
Mac Version

Cheat Sheet

Toolbox Shortcuts

Note: To access the tools, press the key(s) listed. If you uncheck the option Use Shift key for Tool Switch in your Preferences, you can eliminate the need to press the Shift key to change tools.

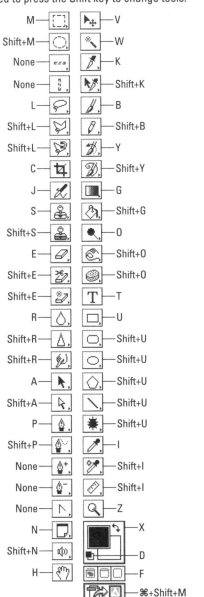

M	V
Shift+M	W
None	K
None	Shift+K
L	B
Shift+L	Shift+B
Shift+L	Y
C	Shift+Y
J	G
S	Shift+G
Shift+S	O
E	Shift+O
Shift+E	Shift+O
Shift+E	T
R	U
Shift+R	Shift+U
Shift+R	Shift+U
A	Shift+U
Shift+A	Shift+U
P	Shift+U
Shift+P	I
None	Shift+I
None	Shift+I
None	Z
N	X
Shift+N	D
H	F
	⌘+Shift+M

Navigation Tricks

Scroll image	spacebar+drag
Zoom in	⌘+spacebar+click
Zoom in and change window size	⌘+plus
Zoom out	Option+spacebar+click
Zoom out and change window size	⌘+minus
Scroll up or down one screen	Page Up/Page Down
Scroll left or right	Ctrl+Page Up/Page Down
Move to upper-left corner of image	Home
Move to lower-right corner of image	End
Zoom to 100%	Double-click on Zoom tool
Fit on Screen	⌘+0
Switch between Photoshop and the Finder or other open applications	⌘+tab

*(**Note:** Keep the CMD key pressed down and click the tab key to toggle through Finder and all open applications)*

More Fun with Selections

Fill selection with foreground color	Option+Delete
Fill selection with background color	⌘+Delete
Display Fill dialog box	Shift+Delete
Cut selection	⌘+X
Copy selection	⌘+C
Paste image last cut or copied	⌘+V
Reapply last filter	⌘+F
Adjust levels	⌘+L
Free transform	⌘+T
Transform again	⌘+Shift+T

For Dummies®: Bestselling Book Series for Beginners

Photoshop® 6 For Dummies®

Mac Version

Cheat Sheet

Daily Activities

Cancel operation	⌘+period or Esc
Close image	⌘+W
General preferences	⌘+K
Display last preferences panel used	⌘+Option+K
Open image	⌘+O
Print image	⌘+P
Page setup	⌘+Shift+P
Quit Photoshop	⌘+Q
Save image to disk	⌘+S
Save As	⌘+Shift+S
Save for Web	⌘+Option+Shift+S
Undo last operation	⌘+Z

Palette Shortcuts

Color palette	F6
Layers palette	F7
Info palette	F8
Actions palette	F9
Step forward in History palette	⌘+Shift+Z
Step backward in History palette	⌘+Option+Z
All palettes, Options bar, and Toolbox	Tab
Just palettes	Shift+Tab
Raise value in option box	Up arrow
Lower value in option box	Down arrow

Painting and Editing Tricks

Increase brush size	]
Decrease brush size	[
Change opacity of tool in 10% increments	1, ... , 9, 0
Paint or edit in straight lines	Click, Shift+click
Change eraser type	Shift+E
Erase to History	Option+drag

Layer Tricks

New layer	⌘+Shift+N
Clone selection to a new layer	⌘+J
Cut selection to a new layer	⌘+Shift+J
Change opacity of layer	1, ... , 9, 0
Activate layer that contains specific image	⌘+click with Move tool
Activate next layer up	Option+]
Activate next layer down	Option+[
Hide all layers but one	Option+click on eyeball
Show all layers	Option+click on eyeball
Select the contents of active layer	⌘+click on layer name in Layers palette

Selection Tricks

Note: All selection tricks are performed with selection tools. (There's a shocker.)

Draw straight lines	Option+click with Lasso tool
Add to selection outline	Shift+drag
Deselect specific area	Option+drag
Deselect all but intersected area	Shift+Option+drag
Deselect entire image	⌘+D
Reselect last selection	⌘+Shift+D
Select everything	⌘+A
Hide extras	⌘+H
Move selection outline only	Drag or press an arrow key

Hungry Minds™

Copyright © 2001 Hungry Minds, Inc.
All rights reserved.

Cheat Sheet $2.95 value. Item 0704-4.

For more information about Hungry Minds,
call 1-800-762-2974.

For Dummies®: Bestselling Book Series for Beginners

Readers Rave about Previous Editions of Photoshop For Dummies:

"Thanks so much for your most enjoyable book, *Photoshop For Dummies*. Not only has it helped me to get through everything, it is even funny."

— Zelia Rosenfeld, Hollis, NH

"This is the first *For Dummies* book I've owned, and it is definitely the most enjoyable and easy to read manual I've ever encountered to date. Thanks for the most useful tool I will probably ever own!"

— Carolyn Deckert, Uniontown, OH

"A quick note to thank you for *Photoshop 4 For Dummies.* You've made me look good even to my all-powerful service bureau."

— Sherra Picketts, Gabriola Island,
British Columbia, Canada

"Easy to use, simple language, starts from scratch. Not just tips and tricks. I bought it to have on hand for those I train."

— Carolyn Boyle, Orlando, Florida

"Great book to start learning a complex program . . . I laughed, I cried."

— Robert G. Kopp, Plano, Illinois

"Sense of humor is right up my alley . . . funnier than Don Rickles at his best moments on the old *Tonight Show.*"

— Ken Funk, New York, New York

"It broke down all of the complicated jargon into simple English. It allowed me to use my program to the fullest extent."

— Jesse Stenbak, Keene, New Hampshire

"This is fun and easy enough to read that I can read it on its own rather than using it only as a reference to solve problems while at the computer."

— Roberta Brenner, Van Nuys, California

Photoshop® 6
FOR
DUMMIES®

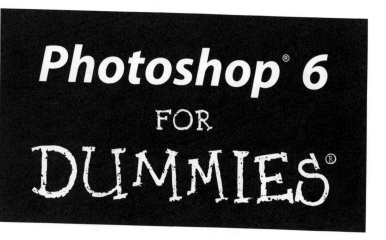

Photoshop® 6 FOR DUMMIES®

by **Deke McClelland**

Revised by Barbara Obermeier

Hungry Minds™

HUNGRY MINDS, INC.

New York, NY ◆ Cleveland, OH ◆ Indianapolis, IN
Chicago, IL ◆ Foster City, CA ◆ San Francisco, CA

Photoshop® 6 For Dummies®

Published by
Hungry Minds, Inc.
909 Third Avenue
New York, NY 10022
www.hungryminds.com
www.dummies.com (Dummies Press Web site)

Library of Congress Control Number: 00-103650

ISBN: 0-7645-0704-4

Printed in the United States of America

10 9 8 7 6 5 4 3

1B/QV/QT/QR/IN

Distributed in the United States by Hungry Minds, Inc.

Distributed by CDG Books Canada Inc. for Canada; by Transworld Publishers Limited in the United Kingdom; by IDG Norge Books for Norway; by IDG Sweden Books for Sweden; by IDG Books Australia Publishing Corporation Pty. Ltd. for Australia and New Zealand; by TransQuest Publishers Pte Ltd. for Singapore, Malaysia, Thailand, Indonesia, and Hong Kong; by Gotop Information Inc. for Taiwan; by ICG Muse, Inc. for Japan; by Intersoft for South Africa; by Eyrolles for France; by International Thomson Publishing for Germany, Austria and Switzerland; by Distribuidora Cuspide for Argentina; by LR International for Brazil; by Galileo Libros for Chile; by Ediciones ZETA S.C.R. Ltda. for Peru; by WS Computer Publishing Corporation, Inc., for the Philippines; by Contemporanea de Ediciones for Venezuela; by Express Computer Distributors for the Caribbean and West Indies; by Micronesia Media Distributor, Inc. for Micronesia; by Chips Computadoras S.A. de C.V. for Mexico; by Editorial Norma de Panama S.A. for Panama; by American Bookshops for Finland.

For general information on Hungry Minds' products and services please contact our Customer Care Department within the U.S. at 800-762-2974, outside the U.S. at 317-572-3993 or fax 317-572-4002.

For sales inquiries and reseller information, including discounts, premium and bulk quantity sales, and foreign-language translations, please contact our Customer Care Department at 800-434-3422, fax 317-572-4002, or write to Hungry Minds, Inc., Attn: Customer Care Department, 10475 Crosspoint Boulevard, Indianapolis, IN 46256.

For information on licensing foreign or domestic rights, please contact our Sub-Rights Customer Care Department at 650-653-7098.

For authorization to photocopy items for corporate, personal, or educational use, please contact Copyright Clearance Center, 222 Rosewood Drive, Danvers, MA 01923, or fax 978-750-4470.

For information on using Hungry Minds' products and services in the classroom or for ordering examination copies, please contact our Educational Sales Department at 800-434-2086 or fax 317-572-4005.

Please contact our Public Relations Department at 212-884-5163 for press review copies or 212-884-5000 for author interviews and other publicity information or fax 212-884-5400.

About the Author

Deke McClelland is a contributing editor for *Macworld* and *Publish* magazines. He has authored more than 50 books on computer graphics and electronic publishing, and his work has been translated into more than 20 languages. He started his career as artistic director at the first service bureau in the United States.

Since winning the Ben Franklin Award for Best Computer Book of 1989, Deke has received two awards from the Society of Technical Communication (1994 and 1999), an American Society for Business Press Editors Award (1995), a Maggie from the Western Publications Society (1999), and a Cool2 Award from *Photo Electronic Imaging* magazine (1999). He is also a five-time recipient of the prestigious Computer Press Award. In 1999, the online column Book Bytes named Deke Author of the Year (*www.mymac.com*).

Deke is the author of the following books published by IDG Books Worldwide, Inc.: *Photoshop 6 Bible,* Gold Edition, *Macworld Photoshop 6 Bible, Photoshop 6 for Windows Bible*, and *Photoshop Studio Secrets*, 2nd Edition. He is also the author of *Real World Illustrator 8* and *Real World Digital Photography* from Peachpit Press. The first edition of *Photoshop Studio Secrets* won the Computer Press Award for the best advanced how-to book of 1997.

Publisher's Acknowledgments

We're proud of this book; please send us your comments through our Online Registration Form located at www.dummies.com.

Some of the people who helped bring this book to market include the following:

Acquisitions, Editorial, and Media Development

Senior Project Editors: Jeanne S. Criswell, Andrea Boucher

(Previous Edition: Melba D. Hopper)

Acquisitions Editor: Michael Roney

Copy Editors: Beth Parlon, Christine Berman

Technical Editor: David Herman

Permissions Editor: Carmen Krikorian

Editorial Manager: Rev Mengle

Media Development Manager: Laura Carpenter

Media Development Supervisor: Richard Graves

Editorial Assistant: Candace Nicholson

Production

Project Coordinator: Nancee Reeves

Layout and Graphics: Amy Adrian, Brian Drumm, Sean Decker, Angie F. Hunckler, Jill Piscitelli, Jacque Schneider, Rashell Smith, Jeremy Unger

Proofreaders: Laura Albert, Corey Bowen, Dwight Ramsey, Marianne Santy, Charles Spencer York Production Services, Inc.

Indexer: York Production Services, Inc.

Special Help
Sarah Shupert

General and Administrative

Hungry Minds, Inc.: John Kilcullen, CEO; Bill Barry, President and COO; John Ball, Executive VP, Operations & Administration; John Harris, CFO

Hungry Minds Technology Publishing Group: Richard Swadley, Senior Vice President and Publisher; Mary Bednarek, Vice President and Publisher, Networking and Certification; Walter R. Bruce III, Vice President and Publisher, General User and Design Professional; Joseph Wikert, Vice President and Publisher, Programming; Mary C. Corder, Editorial Director, Branded Technology Editorial; Andy Cummings, Publishing Director, General User and Design Professional; Barry Pruett, Publishing Director, Visual

Hungry Minds Manufacturing: Ivor Parker, Vice President, Manufacturing

Hungry Minds Marketing: John Helmus, Assistant Vice President, Director of Marketing

Hungry Minds Online Management: Brenda McLaughlin, Executive Vice President, Chief Internet Officer

Hungry Minds Production for Branded Press: Debbie Stailey, Production Director

Hungry Minds Sales: Roland Elgey, Senior Vice President, Sales and Marketing; Michael Violano, Vice President, International Sales and Sub Rights

◆

The publisher would like to give special thanks to Patrick J. McGovern, without whom this book would not have been possible.

◆

Contents at a Glance

Cartoons at a Glance

By Rich Tennant

page 7

page 59

page 289

page 399

page 213

page 137

Fax: 978-546-7747
E-mail: richtennant@the5thwave.com
World Wide Web: www.the5thwave.com

Table of Contents

Introduction

●●●

*W*hy in the world is Adobe Photoshop such a popular program? Normally, graphics software is about as much of a hit with the general public as a grunge rock band is with the senior citizen set. And yet Photoshop — a program that lets you correct and modify photographs on your computer screen — has managed to work its way into the hearts and minds of computer users from all walks of life. What gives?

Wouldn't you know it, I just happen to have a couple of theories. First, when you work in Photoshop, you're not drawing from scratch; you're editing photos. Sure, tampering with a photograph can be a little intimidating, but it's nothing like the chilling, abject fear that seizes your soul when you stare at a blank screen and try to figure out how to draw things on it. Simply put, a photograph inspires you to edit it in precisely the same way that an empty piece of paper does not.

Second, after Photoshop hooks you, it keeps you interested with a depth of capabilities that few pieces of software can match. Unlike so many programs that have caught on like wildfire over the years, but are actually a pain in the rear to use — I won't name any, but I bet you can think of a few — Photoshop is both powerful and absorbing. After several years with the program, I am continually discovering new things about it, and I've enjoyed nearly every minute of it. (Okay, so a couple of stinky minutes sneak themselves in every once in a while, but that's to be expected. Photoshop is a computer program, after all, and we all know that computers are cosmic jokes whose only reason for being is to mock us, ignore our requests, and crash at the least opportune moments. In fact, considering that it's a computer program, Photoshop fares remarkably well.)

About This Book

Just because Photoshop is a pleasure to use doesn't mean that the program is easy to learn. In fact, it's kind of a bear. A big, ornery, grizzly bear with about 17 rows of teeth and claws to match. This program contains so much that it honestly takes months of earnest endeavor to sift through it all. By yourself, that is.

When you go into battle armed with this book, however, Photoshop sucks in its teeth, retracts its claws, and lies down like a lamb. In fact, studies show that if you just hold the book up to the computer screen, Photoshop behaves 50 percent better, even if you never read a single page.

If you do read a page or two, Photoshop not only behaves, it also makes sense. The truth is, I wrote this book with the following specific goals in mind:

- ✓ To show you what you need to know at the precise pace you need to know it.

- ✓ To show you how to do the right things in the right way, right off the bat.

- ✓ To distract you and shove little facts into your head when you're not looking.

- ✓ To make the process not only less painful, but also a real adventure that you'll look back on during your Golden Years with a wistful tear in your eye. "Oh, how I'd like to learn Photoshop all over again," you'll sigh. "Nothing I've done since — whether it was winning the lottery that one time or flying on the inaugural commuter shuttle to the moon with the original cast of *Star Trek* — seemed quite so thrilling as sifting through Photoshop with that crazy old *For Dummies* book."

Okay, maybe that's an exaggeration, but prepare yourself for a fun time. In a matter of days, you'll be doing things that'll make your jaw hang down and dangle from its hinges. And don't worry, it's all perfectly legal throughout the 50 states as well as Puerto Rico, the Virgin Islands, and Guam.

Don't You Have Another Photoshop Book?

While you were browsing the bookstore shelves deciding which book on Photoshop to buy, you may have noticed another book by yours truly: *Photoshop Bible*. There's a version for Windows and one for Macs. That 800-page tome covers just about everything there is to know about Photoshop.

Some folks, though, look forward to reading the 800 pages with the same dread they normally reserve for eating 800 pieces of dry toast. As people who have read the *Bible* know, the pages are anything but dry and laborious; in fact, they're more like 800 tasty cookies. "Make it fatter and throw in a free forklift so that I can tote it around my house" is the typical response I get. But even so, the *Bible* is something that this book is not. It's exhaustive.

Photoshop 6 For Dummies looks at things from a different angle. This book points out the features you need to know and shows you exactly how to use them. You don't want to make Photoshop your life — not yet, anyway — but you don't want the thing to just sit there and beep at you and completely destroy your photograph, either. You'd like to reach a certain satisfying level of comfort, like the one you've recently achieved with your cat now that he's no longer clawing the furniture apart. Becoming comfortable and productive with Photoshop is what this book is all about.

What's in This Book

This book comprises a bunch of independent sections designed to answer your questions as they occur. Oh, sure, you can read the book cover-to-cover, and it will make perfect sense. But you can also read any section completely out of context and know exactly what's going on. Also, this book, unlike previous *For Dummies* editions of Photoshop, is a cross-platform book. You'll notice commands for both PCs and Macs and sometimes text will be specific to one platform or another.

To help you slog through the information, I've broken the book into six parts. Each of those parts contains chapters, and those chapters are divided into sections and subsections. Graphics abound to illustrate things that would take 1,000 words to explain, and you'll even find glorious color plates — 16 pages in all — to show off special issues related to color.

To give you an overview of the kind of information you're likely to find in these pages, here's a quick rundown of the six parts.

Part I: What the . . . ? Aagh, Help Me!

The first stage of using any computer program is the worst. You don't know what you can do, you don't know how good the program is, you don't even know how to ask a reasonably intelligent question. These first three chapters get you up and running in record time.

Chapter 1 introduces you to image editing, explains where to find images to edit, and provides a quick glimpse of what's new in Version 6 of Photoshop. Chapters 2 and 3 take you on a grand tour of the Photoshop interface and image window and give you all the information you need to navigate both.

Part II: The Care and Feeding of Pixels

Before you can edit a digital photograph, you have to know a few things about the nature of the beast. What's a pixel, for example, and why is getting rid of one so dangerous? What's the difference between a color image and a grayscale image — other than the obvious? And how do you save or print your image after you finish editing it? All these questions and many more are answered in Chapters 4 through 7.

Part III: Tiptoe through the Toolbox

Photoshop offers fewer tools — pencils, paintbrushes, and the like — than most graphics programs. But these tools are remarkably capable, allowing you to perform pages and pages of tricks while expending minimum effort. Find out how to smear colors, get rid of dust specks, erase mistakes, and do a whole lot more in Chapters 8 through 11.

Part IV: Select Before You Correct

The selection tools let you cordon off the portion of the photograph you want to edit. Select the face, for example, and Photoshop protects the body, no matter how randomly you drag or how spastic your brushstrokes. Chapters 12 through 14 help you understand how selections work and how to use them to your advantage.

Part V: So, You Say You're Serious about Image Editing

Now you step into the really incredible part of the Photoshop playground. In Chapter 15, I introduce you to layers, a Photoshop feature that adds flexibility, creative opportunity, and security to your image-editing life. In Chapter 16, you find out how to create text effects and add them to your image. And in Chapters 17 and 18, I show you the commands that professionals use to sharpen focus, change brightness and contrast, correct colors, and generally make an image look three times better than it did when you started. Finally in Chapter 19, you take a peek at the world of Web graphics.

Part VI: The Part of Tens

Chapters 20 through 22 contain the ultimate Photoshop Top Ten lists. Find out the most essential Photoshop shortcuts, the most amazing special effects tricks, and the answer to that age-old question, "Now that I've finished mucking up my image in Photoshop, what do I do with it?"

Icons Used in This Book

When you're driving, road signs are always warning you about bad things. Slow, Detour, Stop, Dip — these are all signs that I, for one, hate to see. I mean, you never see good signs like Go Ahead and Speed, No Traffic This Way, or Free Money Up Ahead. This book isn't like that. Using friendly little margin icons, I highlight good things and bad things, and the good things outnumber the bad. So don't shy away from the road signs in this book — welcome them into your reading ritual with open arms. Here's your field guide to icons:

 I hate computer jargon just as much as the next red-blooded computer user. But sometimes, I have to use it because there's no word for this stuff in normal, everyday, conversational English. It's a crying shame, I know, but at least I warn you that something nerdy is coming your way with this icon.

 Photoshop has very few obvious shortcuts and a ton of hidden ones. That's where the Tip icon comes in. It says, "Hey, whoa there; here's a juicy one!"

 This icon calls your attention to special little reminders of things I've mentioned in the past or things I want you to bear in mind for the future.

 Photoshop is a kind and gentle program. But every once in a while, it pays to be careful. The Warning icon tells you when to keep an eye out for trouble.

 This icon points out features or commands that have changed or are new in Version 6. If you're upgrading to Version 6 from an earlier version of Photoshop, pay attention to this road sign because lots of things are different now.

 Now and then, I feel compelled to share something with you that has nothing whatsoever to do with your learning Photoshop or any other computer program. It's just my way of showing that I care.

How to Use This Book

When I was in grade school, I don't think a year went by that our teacher didn't show us how to handle our new books. Open the book once in the center and then open the first quarter and the last quarter, each time gently creasing the spine. Never fold the pages or roll them so that they won't lie flat. And be sure to read the words from the beginning to end, just as the author meant them to be read. A book, after all, is a Special Thing to Be Treasured. Here are a couple of thoughts:

 ✔ Break the spine first thing out. The pages lie flatter that way.

 ✔ When you have a question, look it up in the index. Feel free to shut the book and get on with your life when you're done (though I do my best to snag you and make you read longer).

 ✔ If you're just curious about what the book has to offer, look up whatever topic interests you in the table of contents and read a few pages.

 ✔ If you want to learn everything the book has to offer in what I consider the optimum order, turn the next page and start reading at your own pace.

 ✔ If you come across something important, don't hesitate to fold the page, slap a sticky note on it, circle the text with a highlighter pen, or rip out the page and tack it to the wall.

 ✔ And when you've gleaned everything there is to glean, house-train your new puppy with the pages or use them for kindling.

Feedback, Please

Want to send me a line of congratulations or a complaint? If so, please feel free to visit my Web site at www.dekemc.com and then click on the Contact Deke button to drop me a line. I get a ton of mail these days — a hundred or more reader letters a week — so I can't begin to respond to them all. But I do read and appreciate them.

You can also contact the publisher or authors of other *For Dummies* books by visiting the publisher's Web site at www.dummies.com, sending an e-mail to info@idgbooks.com, or sending paper mail to IDG Books Worldwide, Inc., 10475 Crosspoint Boulevard, Indianapolis, IN 46256.

Part I
What the . . . ?
Aagh, Help Me!

In this part . . .

A lot has been written, spoken, and tapped out in Morse code about the value of information. To hear some folks tell it, information is now the top commodity in the industrialized world. Well, I don't know if that's true or not — personally, you can give me money over information any day of the week. "There's always more room in my billfold than my head," is my saying. But being, shall I say, "unlettered," on any subject is no fun.

If you're not sure how to ask an intelligent question about Photoshop, take heart. These first three chapters answer that most impossible of all questions to express, "What the . . . ? I mean . . . ? You know, if the . . . ? Aagh, help me!" For example, you find out what Photoshop is; take a quick, all-expenses-paid jaunt through its tools and commands; and discover how to open and view images.

By the end of Chapter 3, you won't know everything there is to know about Photoshop — otherwise, I could have dispensed with the 19 chapters that follow it — but you'll know enough to phrase a few intelligent questions. And please remember that as you read these chapters, there's no shame in being as yet uninformed. I mean, it must be more than coincidental that the initials for *Photoshop For Dummies* are Ph.D.

Chapter 1

Meet Dr. Photo and Mr. Shop

· ·

· ·

*A*dobe Photoshop is arguably the most comprehensive and popular photo editor around. In fact, I don't know a single computer artist who doesn't use Photoshop on an almost daily basis, regardless of what other programs he or she may use.

I assume that you've at least seen, if not used, Photoshop and that you have a vague idea of what it's all about. But just so that we're all clear on the subject, the primary purpose of Photoshop is to make changes to photographic images that you somehow managed to get on disk. (For some clever ideas on acquiring such images, see the sidebar "Where do I find images to abuse?" later in this chapter.)

If you've used Photoshop for only a week or so, you may have mistaken it for a fairly straightforward package. Certainly, on the surface of the program, Photoshop comes off as rather friendly. But lurking a few fathoms deep is another, darker program, one that is distinctly unfriendly for the uninitiated, but wildly capable for the stout of heart. My analyst would no doubt declare Photoshop a classic case of a split personality. It's half man, half monster; half mild-mannered shoeshine boy, half blonde-grabbing, airplane-swatting King Kong; half kindly old gent with white whiskers chewing on a pipe, half green-gilled invader from another planet chewing on your . . . well, perhaps you don't want to know. In short, Photoshop has a Dr. Jekyll-and-Mr. Hyde thing going — only it's way scarier.

As you may recall from the last time you saw *Abbott and Costello Meet Dr. Jekyll and Mr. Hyde* — indisputably the foremost resource of information on this famous tale — this Jekyll character (not to be confused with the similarly named cartoon crow) is normally your everyday, average, nice-guy scientist.

Then one day, he drinks some potion or gets cut off in traffic or something and changes into his ornery alter ego, known at every dive bar in town by the surname Hyde. Photoshop behaves just the same way, except that no magical transformation is required to shift between the program's Jekyll half and its Hyde half. Both personalities coexist simultaneously in what you might call harmony.

This chapter explores both sides of the Photoshop brain. It also introduces you to the personality changes found in the latest incarnation of the program, Version 6. Finally, I get you started on the road to image-editing bliss by explaining where to find images to edit in the first place.

The Bland but Kindly Dr. Photo

To discover the benevolent Dr. Jekyll half of Photoshop, you need look no farther than the standard painting and editing tools. Shown in Figure 1-1, these tools are so simple, they're practically pastoral, like the kind of household appliances your great-grandmother would have been comfortable with. The eraser erases, the pencil draws hard-edged lines, the airbrush sprays a fine mist of color, and so on. These incredibly straightforward tools attract new users just as surely as a light attracts miller moths.

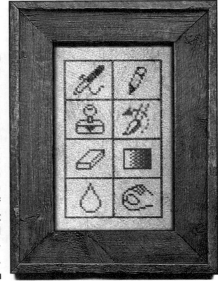

Figure 1-1: Many of the Photoshop tools have an old-world, rustic charm that's sure to warm the cockles of the most timid technophobe.

But you quickly discover that, on their own, these tools aren't super-duper exciting, just like the boring Dr. Jekyll. They don't work much like their traditional counterparts — a line drawn with the pencil tool, for example, doesn't look anything like a line drawn with a real pencil — and they don't seem to be particularly applicable to the job of editing images. Generally speaking, you have to be blessed with pretty major eye-hand coordination to achieve good results using these tools.

The Ghastly but Dynamic Mr. Shop

When the standard paint and editing tools don't fit the bill, you try to adjust the performance of the tools and experiment with the other image controls of Photoshop. Unfortunately, that's when you discover the Mr. Hyde half of the program. You encounter options that have meaningless names such as Dissolve, Multiply, and Difference. Commands such as Image Size and Canvas Size — both of which sound harmless enough — seem to damage your image. And clicking on icons frequently produces no result. It's enough to drive a reticent computer artist stark raving insane.

The net result is that many folks return broken and frustrated to the under-equipped and boring, but nonthreatening, painting and editing tools that they've come to know. It's sad, really. Especially when you consider all the wonderful things that the more complex Photoshop controls can do. Oh sure, the controls have weird names, and they may not respond as you think they should at first, but after you come to terms with these slick puppies, they perform in ways you wouldn't believe.

In fact, the dreaded Mr. Hyde side of Photoshop represents the core of this powerful program. Without its sinister half, Photoshop is just another rinky-dink piece of painting software whose most remarkable capability is keeping the kids out of mischief on a rainy day.

The Two Phunctions of Photoshop

Generally speaking, the two halves of Photoshop serve different purposes. The straightforward Jekyll tools mostly concentrate on *painting,* and the more complex Hyde capabilities are devoted to *image editing.* Therefore, to tackle this great program, you may find it helpful to understand the difference between the two terms.

Painting without the mess

Painting is just what it sounds like: You take a brush loaded with color and smear it all over your on-screen image. You can paint from scratch on a blank canvas, or you can paint directly on top of a photograph. The first option requires lots of talent, planning, and a few dashes of artistic genius; the second option requires an opposable thumb. Okay, that's a slight exaggeration — some lemurs have been known to have problems with the second option — but most people find painting on an existing image much easier than creating an image from scratch.

Notice in Figure 1-2 the rather drab fellow drinking a rather drab beverage. (Though you may guess this man to be Dr. Jekyll armed with the secret potion, most scholars consider it highly doubtful that even Jekyll was this goofy.) I introduce this silly person solely to demonstrate the amazing functions of Photoshop.

Were you to paint on our unsuspecting saphead, you might arrive at something on the order of the image shown in Figure 1-3. I invoked all these changes using a single tool — the paintbrush — and just two colors — black and white. Suddenly, a singularly cool dude emerges. No planning or real talent was involved; I simply traced over some existing details in the image. Better yet, I haven't permanently damaged the image, as I would if I tried the same thing using a real-life paintbrush. Because I saved the original image to disk (as explained in Chapter 6), I can restore details from the original image at whim (the subject of Chapter 11).

Figure 1-2:
The unadorned "I Love My Libation" poster boy of 1948.

Figure 1-3:
A few hundred strokes of the paintbrush result in a party animal to rival Carmen Miranda.

Editing existing image detail

The remade man in Figure 1-3 is the life of the party, but he's nothing compared to what he could be with the aid of some image editing. When you edit an image, you distort and enhance its existing details. So rather than paint with color, you paint with the image itself.

Figure 1-4 demonstrates what I mean. To achieve this grotesque turn of the visual phrase, I was obliged to indulge in a liberal amount of distortion. First, I flipped the guy's head and stretched it a little bit. Well, actually, I stretched it a lot. Then, I further exaggerated the eyes and mouth. I rotated the arm and distorted the glass to make the glass meet the ear. Finally, I cloned a background from a different image to cover up where the head and arm used to be. The only thing I painted was the straw (the one coming out of the guy's ear). Otherwise, I lifted every detail from one of two photographs. And yet, this man's very own mother wouldn't recognize him, were she still alive today.

Mind you, you don't have to go quite so hog-wild with the image editing. If you're a photographer, for example, you may not care to mess with your work to the point that it becomes completely unrecognizable. Call you weird, but you like reality the way you see it. Figure 1-5 shows a few subtle adjustments that affect neither the form nor composition of the original image. These changes merely accentuate details or downplay defects in the image.

Figure 1-4:
Image
editing
has no
respect for
composition,
form, or
underlying
skeletal
structure.

Figure 1-5:
You can
apply more
moderate
edits to your
image.

Just for the record, here are a few common ways to edit photographs in Photoshop:

- ✔ You can *sharpen* an image to make it appear in better focus, as in the first image in Figure 1-5. Generally, sharpening is used to account for focus problems in the scanning process, but you can sometimes sharpen a photograph that was shot out of focus.

- ✔ If you want to accentuate a foreground image, you can blur the focus of the background. The image on the right side of Figure 1-5 is an example.

- ✔ If a photograph is too light or too dark, you can fix it in a flash through the miracle of color correction. You can change the contrast, brighten or dim colors, and actually replace one color with another. Both of the images in Figure 1-5 have been color-corrected.

- ✔ Using the Photoshop selection and move tools, you can grab a chunk of your image and physically move it around. You can also clone the selection, stretch it, rotate it, or copy it to a different image.

And that's only the tip of the iceberg. The book's remaining chapters explore Photoshop as both a painting program and an image editor. Most chapters contain a little bit of information on both topics, but as a general rule, the first half of the book stresses painting, and the second half stresses image editing. Rip the book in half, and you may very well have the makings of a late-night horror flick.

It's New! It's Improved!

 Someday, the folks at Adobe may come out with an upgrade to Photoshop that completely tames the Mr. Hyde half of the program. But Version 6 isn't the upgrade to do it, which is good for me because it lets me continue with my colorful dual-personality analogy. Version 6, it turns out, is one part helpful, unbelievably great upgrade and one part exercise in frustration.

On one hand, Version 6 includes many incredibly useful new features. On the other, Version 6 trashes some time-honored shortcuts and techniques used in earlier versions of the program, a development that is sure to confuse and annoy veteran Photoshop users. One change that may do more than just annoy users is the fact that Version 6 requires a pretty hefty computer system. Version 6 works only on PCs running Windows 98, Windows 2000 Professional, Windows NT 4.0 (SP 4 or later), and later Windows versions (all hereafter referred to as just Windows). Version 6 runs on Macs running OS 8.5

or later. Both platforms require 96MB of RAM, 200MB of disk space, and a CD-ROM. Please note that these are Adobe's *minimum* requirements. If there's one program that benefits from as much RAM as you can throw at it, it's Photoshop. The more you give it, the better the performance.

The good news is that the good side of Version 6 more than compensates for its bad side. So, in the interest of focusing on the positive, here are just some of the improvements Version 6 brings you:

✔ **Extensive type improvements (Chapter 16):** Photoshop finally implements on-canvas type entry and editing. But the improvements don't stop there! You can choose from point or box text. Version 6 offers word wrapping, single character color, character width and height controls, and lots of typographic goodies such as indents, baseline shift, and more. And you can do fun things like warp your text into arcs and bulges.

✔ **Drawing with shape tools (Chapter 8):** A whole new set of tools enables you to create rectangles, ellipses, polygons, stars, or custom shapes either directly on an existing layer or on an exclusive shape layer. You can use the shapes as merely colored pixels or as paths of various sorts. You can also manipulate shapes by using the new Path Component Selection tool and the Direct Selection tool.

✔ **Liquify command (Chapter 9):** You can use this wacky, new command to wreak havoc on your images through interactive warping. Pull, twist, and size your image using brushes of varying widths and pressures. You can also freeze portions to avoid distortion, and if the image gets too bizarre, you can reconstruct your images using various modes.

✔ **Better layer management (Chapter 15):** You can lock and color-code layers and organize them into layer sets. You can drag and drop layer effects between layers and delete linked layers from the palette trash icon. And you are no longer limited to a measly 99 layers. Go to town and add hundreds! Just make sure you have mega amounts of RAM.

✔ **Layer Styles (Chapter 15):** Version 5.5's layer effects got a major makeover and came back under the moniker of Layer Styles. Layer Styles enables you to apply the old shadows, glows, bevels, and embosses but with more variable controls. Also three new styles — overlay, Satin, and Stroke — were added. More extensive blending options and a customizable Styles palette to store all your neat effects round out this new feature.

✔ **Fill layers (Chapter 15):** Adobe has added a new kind of layer called a fill layer. These layers can contain solid color, a gradient, or a pattern. Also, a new kind of adjustment layer called a gradient map has been added.

✔ **Options bar (Chapter 8):** The handy Options bar located under the menu bar replaces the old Options palette. Version 6 has added some new controls, depending on your chosen tool. It also includes the Brushes palette and a new docking well where you can store palettes.

✔ **Better Crop tool (Chapter 9):** The area outside the Crop box is now dimmed for better visualization. You can now apply perspective to the Crop box, which lets you create a non-rectangular crop. And the Crop command under the Image menu now lets you choose non-rectangular and even feathered selections.

✔ **Trim command (Chapter 9):** This command under the Image menu trims away transparency or color from the image's border.

✔ **Improved Extract command (Chapter 13):** The Smart Highlighting option helps the Edge Highlighter to hug the edge of the image. New Cleanup and Edge Touchup tools help in cleaning up those messy edges. Version 6 has many keyboard shortcuts to help you. And most importantly, you can now undo your flubs!

✔ **Slice and Slice Select tools (Chapter 19):** You can now slice and select rectangular sections of your image to which you can apply HTML links and other Web graphic features, such as rollovers and animation. You can also optimize these areas for quick and quality viewing on the Web.

✔ **New printing options (Chapter 7):** Preview, reposition, or resize your image. You can also access Page Setup and Print dialog boxes.

✔ **Add annotations (Chapter 6):** You can add annotations to your image by using the new Notes tool and Audio Annotation tool. Great for reviewing and exchanging files between coworkers, family, and friends.

✔ **Revamped color management (Chapter 5):** All the color settings are now in one handy dialog box. You have multiple color spaces to work in, view in, and print to. This feature also uses the same interface settings as Illustrator 9.

✔ **Enhanced pattern and gradient options (Chapter 14):** You can now define a pattern without a selection. Photoshop just uses the entire image. Multiple patterns can now be stored and accessed via a pop-up swatch menu. Version 6 has a lot of new predefined gradients (called presets) such as noise, pastels, and special effects. Gradient Editor is revamped with stops for opacity and a smoothing control.

✔ **Easier access to files (Chapter 3):** Photoshop adds a Favorites and Recent files submenu in the Open dialog box, enabling you to grab your most popular images. On the Mac, you can find your way around your desktop system or network easily with the Mounted Volumes submenu.

✔ **Enhanced TIFF and PDF file formats (Chapter 6):** The TIFF and PDF file formats now support saving layers. TIFF also supports ZIP and JPEG compression methods.

✔ **Toolbox reorganization (Cheat Sheet):** Some tools have moved and some have new keyboard equivalents. To toggle through the tools, press Shift along with the particular tool's keyboard equivalent. Or set your preferences so that you don't need to press Shift at all.

- ✔ **Save a Copy/Save As combined (Chapter 6):** These two Save commands were combined into one Save As dialog box, which is handy for saving a duplicate image or one with a new name or file format.

- ✔ **Plenty of predefined goodies (various chapters):** Photoshop 6 has a bunch of predefined brushes, gradients, patterns, layer styles, custom shapes, and actions that can be loaded with one click. These preset libraries can also be customized to fit your fancy. Multiple brush and swatch libraries can be loaded simultaneously. Now, if it would just fetch the coffee. . . .

- ✔ **New Swatches palette view (Chapter 8):** You can now view the Swatches palette by list (name) and thumbnail.

- ✔ **Increased values for settings (various chapters):** Many of the settings for selection, filter, and Layer Styles have increased significantly. For example, you can now contract a selection by 100 pixels instead of a maximum of 16 pixels.

- ✔ **Tool feedback (Chapter 2):** If the cursor of your tool shows the Cancel (or No) icon, simply click on the canvas to find the reason why. This feature saves you from having to go to the Help menu.

- ✔ **Show/Hide Extras command (Chapter 3):** The previous Show/Hide Edges command has been revised and now hides selection outlines and also guides, grids, and annotations.

- ✔ **New Guide command (Chapter 3):** This command, located under the View menu, creates a guide at a specific position on the image.

- ✔ **Ruler shortcut (Chapter 3):** Right-click (Control-click on a Mac) on a ruler to access the menu for setting the ruler units.

- ✔ **Improved Stroke dialog box (Chapter 14):** The Stroke dialog box now accepts units other than pixels and also enables you to select your stroke color from within the dialog box. Maximum stroke width has increased to 250 pixels or the equivalent.

- ✔ **Increased flexibility with Automate commands (Chapters 7 and 19):** The Contact Sheet now lets users define font sizes for labels. Picture Package and Web Photo Gallery are now based on templates for easier use.

- ✔ **Better tool labels (Chapter 2):** The tools residing in the flyout menu contain the names and the keyboard shortcuts in addition to just the tool icon.

- ✔ **Improved PhotoCD import (Chapter 3):** The Open dialog box for PhotoCDs is now easier to use. All the options you need to select are within a single dialog box.

Of course, I didn't mention a few little things that you may run across in the book or on your own. A few advanced features were added — improved layer masks and clipping groups, enhanced Actions batch processing, and 16-bit pre-press support. If you just have to know it all, I suggest picking up a copy of the Photoshop 6 Bible, also published by IDG Books Worldwide, Inc. If you're used to working in Photoshop 5.5, some of these changes may confuse you at first. But after you get the hang of using the new features, you discover that they make the editing process much easier. Of course, if you've never used Photoshop, you won't even be aware that Version 6 has a bad side — ignorance is bliss, after all.

Where do I find images to abuse?

We all know how to turn photographs from our cameras into colorful pieces of paper that we can slap into albums or frames. But few of us have scanned a photograph to disk. However, you can find plenty of affordable options if you look in the right places:

✔ You can purchase photos on CD-ROM (prices range from less than 25 cents to several dollars per image). Some of my favorite image vendors are Eyewire (800-661-9410), PhotoDisc (800-979-4413), and Corbis (888-829-0722). These vendors are also online. Check them out at: www.eyewire. com, www.photodisc.com, and www. corbis.com. Prices can be expensive, so be sure to check *before* you download an image.

✔ You can find zillions of photos to download on the Internet or from online services like CompuServe or America Online. The problem is that most of these images are dubious in quality or are pornographic. If you want high-quality, general-purpose images, you have to subscribe to specialized services such as PressLink /MediaStream (www. presslink.com or 800-888-6195).

✔ You can take your own photo into your local Kinko's, or some other copy shop or service bureau, and scan the image to disk. Kinko's charges about $10 per image.

✔ A better (and cheaper) method is to scan images to a Photo CD, which costs between $1 to $3 a shot, plus the price of the CD itself, which is usually in the neighborhood of $10. One CD can hold about 100 images. Check the Yellow Pages under Photo Finishing — Retail. Service bureaus also provide this service. Prices vary widely from vendor to vendor.

✔ Last but not least, digital cameras are becoming less expensive and better in quality. Downloading images from your camera to your computer is also quick and easy. Photoshop accepts the two file formats, JPEG and TIFF, that most cameras utilize. (For more information on formats, see Chapter 6.)

Chapter 2

Canvassing the On-Screen Canvas

*I*f you're brand new to Photoshop — or to computers in general — this is the chapter for you. You get the basic stuff you need to know before you can begin using the program to distort the faces of all your family members.

Even if you're already familiar with the basic interface of Photoshop, give this chapter the once-over to get acquainted with new features in Version 6 and make sure that you and I are speaking the same language. Here, you and I calibrate brains, so to speak.

Giving Photoshop the Electronic Breath of Life

Before you can use Photoshop, you have to start up — or launch — the program. Here's how:

1. **Start your computer.**

2. **Click on the Windows Start button. (Mac users, after you reach the Finder, proceed to Step 4.)**

3. **PC users, choose <u>P</u>rograms⇨Adobe in the Start menu.**

   A submenu appears listing all your Adobe programs.

Why does Photoshop give your computer amnesia?

If your computer says it's out of memory, it just means that a part of the machine is filled to capacity. Memory — known in computer dweeb circles as *RAM* (random-access memory, pronounced *ram,* like the goat) — allows your computer to run programs. Photoshop needs lots of RAM — this version requires a minimum of 96MB and prefers to have even more. If you can't launch Photoshop because of a memory error, you have three options:

✔ Free up RAM by quitting all other programs that are currently running.

✔ Restart your computer by choosing the Shut Down command from the Windows Start menu and then choosing the Restart the Computer option. After your computer restarts, try to launch Photoshop again. (On a Mac, restart the computer by choosing Special⇨Restart at the Finder and try to launch Photoshop after the Finder reappears.)

✔ Buy and install more RAM.

If you've never tried to upgrade the RAM in your machine, seek out expert advice from your local computer guru.

Mac users, locate and activate the Adobe Photoshop 6.0 folder.

Use the mouse to move the arrow-shaped cursor over the icon and press the mouse button. Then choose FileOpen from the menu bar or press ⌘+O. A window labeled Adobe Photoshop opens, containing another eyeball icon and some other icons. You can also launch Photoshop by using a couple of shortcuts. Either double-click — press the mouse button twice in rapid-fire succession — on the program icon or press ⌘+↓.

If you're not sure where Photoshop is located on your hard drive, choose File⇨Find from the menu bar (or press ⌘+F). Then type the word **Photoshop** and press the Return key. A list appears with all files containing the word Photoshop. Locate the program icon and double-click to launch the program directly from this list. If you still can't find the program, cry in anguish and beat your monitor with something soft and squishy.

PC users, if you can't seem to locate Photoshop on your system, choose Find⇨ Files or Folders in the Start menu. Type Photoshop in the Named field and select My Computer from the Look-in pop-up menu. Click the Find Now button. A list appears with all files and folders containing the word Photoshop. Locate the program icon and double-click to launch the program directly from this list.

4. **PC users choose Adobe Photoshop 6.0. (Mac users, double-click on the icon in the Adobe Photoshop window.)**

Adobe Photoshop 6.0 is the item that uses the famous Photoshop eyeball as its icon.

5. Hope it works.

If you see the Photoshop splash screen — a kind of billboard that provides garish graphics and some copyright information — you're in business. If your computer complains that it doesn't have enough memory to open Photoshop, check out the sidebar, "Why does Photoshop give your computer Alzheimer's?" later in this chapter. If you see some equally discouraging message, scream loudly and hope that the resident computer expert is in close proximity. You need help. Check out the Photoshop manual, Adobe's Web site, or phone technical support.

After your computer stops making little shicka-shicka noises and your screen settles down, you see the Photoshop program window, as shown in Figure 2-1. I cover the various elements of the window later in this chapter.

Don't freak out and start running around the room in a frenzy if you're a little fuzzy on what I mean by *menu, dialog box,* and a few other terms. I cover all this stuff in fairly hefty detail, in short order, and in this very same chapter.

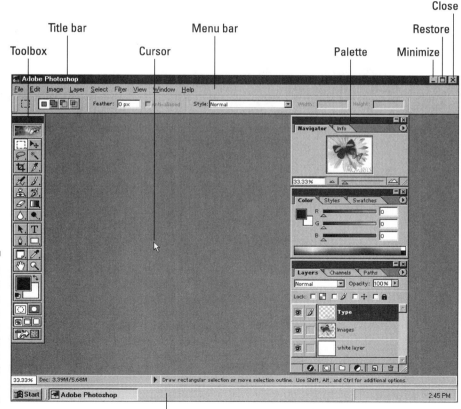

Figure 2-1 (Windows): The Photoshop program window makes its first appearance.

Close

Restore

Minimize

Palette

Menu bar

Title bar

Cursor

Toolbox

Taskbar

Toolbox   Cursor   Menu bar   Application menu   Palette

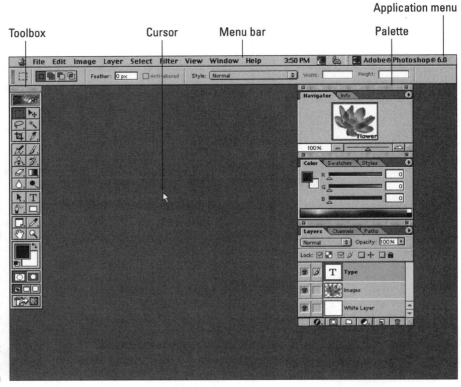

Figure 2-1 (Mac): The Photoshop program window makes its first appearance.

Note: As you read, you'll see that you can also use the keyboard and mouse in tandem. For example, in Photoshop, you can draw a perfectly horizontal line by pressing the Shift key while dragging with the Line tool. Or you can press Alt (Option on a Mac) and click on the Rectangular Marquee tool in the upper-left corner of the Toolbox to switch to the Elliptical Marquee tool. Such actions are so common that you often see key and mouse combinations joined into compound verbs, such as Shift+dragging, Alt+clicking, or Shift+Alt+crushing. (On a Mac, Option+clicking or Shift+Option+crushing.)

Working with Windows

This section is relevant to PC users only. Mac people skip down to the "Switching between Photoshop and the Finder" section below. In Photoshop, as in most other Windows programs, you have two kinds of windows: the program window, which contains the main Photoshop work area, and image windows, which contain any images that you create or edit. To see the program window, refer to Figure 2-1; for a look at image windows, see Chapter 3.

Photoshop windows — both program and image — contain the same basic elements as those in other Windows programs. But just in case you need a refresher or you're new to this whole computing business, here's how the Photoshop program window works with Windows:

- Windows users can click on the Close button in the upper-right corner of the window to shut down Photoshop. If you have open images that haven't been saved, the program prompts you to save them. (For details on saving images, see Chapter 6.) The quickest way to close your program window (and Photoshop) is to press the keyboard shortcut for the Exit command, Ctrl+Q (as in Quit).

- Click on the Minimize button (refer to Figure 2-1) to reduce the program window to a button on the Windows taskbar. To redisplay the program window, just click on the taskbar button.

- You can also use the taskbar buttons to switch between Photoshop and other running programs. In the taskbar, just click on the button of the program you want to use.

- The appearance of the Restore/Maximize button changes depending on the current status of the window. If you see two boxes on the button, as in Figure 2-1, the button is the Restore button. Click on this button to shrink the window so that you can see other open program windows. You can then resize the window by placing your mouse cursor over a corner of the window until you see a double-headed arrow. When you see the arrow, drag the window to resize it. To move the window around, drag its title bar.

- After you click on the Restore button, it changes to the Maximize button, which looks like a single box. Click on the button to zoom the program window so that it consumes your entire screen. After the window zooms, the button changes back to the Restore button. Click on the button to restore your screen to its former size.

Switching between Photoshop and the Finder

In back of the myriad desktop elements of Photoshop, you Mac users can probably see the icons and open windows from the Finder. (I hid these in Figure 2-1 just to make the picture less confusing.) If you click on a Finder element or on the desktop pattern, you're taken back to the Finder, and the Photoshop Toolbox and palettes disappear. If you have an image open, however, the image window remains visible. Here are some tips to help you manage working between the Finder and Photoshop.

✔ If you inadvertently click yourself out of Photoshop, choose Photoshop from the list of running programs in the Applications menu, which is the icon on the far-right side of the menu bar (refer to Figure 2-1). Or just click on the Photoshop image window. The Toolbox and palettes return to the screen to show you that Photoshop is back in the game.

✔ You may be wondering why in the heck this program-switching happens. No, it's not just to irritate you. The Finder is a piece of software, just like Photoshop. The only difference is that the Finder has to be running the entire time you use your Mac. This means that all the time you're using Photoshop, the Finder is working away in the background. When you click on the desktop or some other Finder element, the Finder comes to the foreground, and Photoshop goes to the background. But both programs continue to operate until you quit Photoshop or shut down your computer.

✔ When using Photoshop, if the clutter from the Finder gets too distracting, choose the Hide Others command from the Applications menu to hide every Finder element except the icons.

✔ You can hide the icons by choosing Apple⇨Control Panels⇨General Controls. (If you don't know how to choose things from menus, see the section, "Maneuvering through Menus," later in this chapter.) Inside the General Controls dialog box, click on the Show Desktop When in Background check box to deselect it. Then close the dialog box. Bye-bye go the icons. (Note that you can't click on the background to switch to the Finder if you choose this option; you have to use the Applications menu to switch between programs.)

✔ Remember that you can always tell where you are just by looking at the Applications menu icon in the upper-right corner of your screen. It always shows a miniature version of the foreground program icon. If you're at the Finder, the icon is a little smiley face. If the icon is some variation on an eyeball, you know you're in Photoshop. Other icons vary. A little W means Microsoft Word. A little X means Excel. A little Krusty the Clown means Bart Simpson has been using your computer (you lucky devil, you).

Maneuvering through Menus

As do all Windows and Macintosh programs, Photoshop sports a menu bar (refer to Figure 2-1) at the top of its window desktop. Each word in the menu bar — File, Edit, Image, and so on — represents a menu. A *menu* is simply a list of commands that you can use to open and close images, manipulate selected portions of a photograph, hide and display palettes, and initiate all kinds of mind-boggling, sophisticated procedures.

I explain the most essential Photoshop commands throughout this book. But before I send you off to cope with a single one of them, I feel compelled to provide some background information on how to work with menus:

- To choose a command from a menu, click on the menu name and then click on the command name. Or you can press and hold the menu name, drag down to the command name, and release the mouse button at the desired command.

- Some commands bring up additional menus called *submenus*. For example, if you choose Edit⇨Preferences, you display a submenu offering still more commands. If I ask you to choose Edit⇨Preferences⇨General, you choose the Preferences command under the Edit menu to display the submenu and then choose the General command from the submenu, all in one, beautiful, continuous movement. When you do it just right, it's like something out of Swan Lake.

- Did you notice that I underlined some letters in the commands I discussed in the preceding paragraph? Those letters are called *hot keys*. If you prefer using the keyboard rather than the mouse, and you're using a PC, you can press hot keys in combination with the Alt key to choose a command. For example, to display the Edit menu, press Alt+E. Then to choose the Preferences command from the Edit menu, press N — no Alt key needed this time. You can also use hot keys to access options inside dialog boxes (dialog boxes are explained later in the section, "Talking Back to Dialog Boxes").

In addition to using hot keys, you can access some commands by pressing keyboard shortcuts. For example, to initiate the File⇨Open command, you can press the keyboard shortcut Ctrl+O (⌘+O on a Mac) — that is, press and hold the Ctrl key (⌘ key on a Mac), press the O key, and then release both keys.

- Some keyboard equivalents select tools, and some perform other functions. Either way, I keep you apprised of them throughout this book. If you take the time to memorize a few keyboard shortcuts here and there, you can save yourself a heck of a lot of time and effort. (For the most essential shortcuts, read Chapter 20. Also, tear out the Cheat Sheet at the front of this book, and tape it up somewhere within easy ogling distance.)

- Photoshop offers you yet another way to access some commands. If you right-click (Control-click on a Mac) inside an image window, you display a context-sensitive menu. In nongeek-speak, a context-sensitive menu, also known as a shortcut menu, is a mini-menu that contains commands that are related to the current tool, palette, or image, as shown in Figure 2-2.

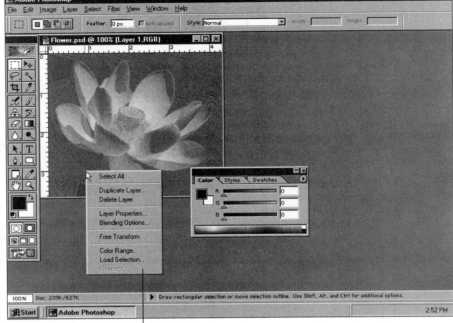

Figure 2-2:
Right-click
(Control-
click on a
Mac) inside
the image
window to
access
context-
sensitive
menus.

Context-sensitive menu

Talking Back to Dialog Boxes

Photoshop reacts immediately to some menu commands. But for other commands, the program requires you to fill out a few forms before it processes your request. If you see an ellipsis (three dots, like so . . .) next to a command name, that's your clue that you're about to see such a form, known in computer clubs everywhere as a *dialog box*.

Figure 2-3 shows a sample dialog box. As the figure demonstrates, a dialog box can contain any or all of six basic kinds of options. The options work as follows:

✔ A box in which you can enter numbers or text is called an *option box*. Double-click in an option box to highlight its contents and then replace the contents by entering new stuff from the keyboard.

✔ Some option boxes come with *slider bars*. Drag the triangular slider to the left or right to lower or raise the associated numerical value. (All without hydraulics, mind you.)

Slider bar · Close button

Title bar | Pop-up menu · Option box · Button

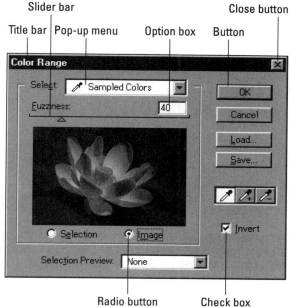

Figure 2-3:
The
anatomy of
a dialog box.

Radio button · Check box

✔ You can select only one circular *radio button* from any gang of radio buttons. To select a radio button, click on the button or on the option name that follows it. The selected radio button is filled with a black dot; all deselected radio buttons are hollow.

✔ Although you can select only one radio button at a time, you can usually select as many *check boxes* as you want. Really, go nuts. To select a check box, click on the box or on the option name that follows it. An X fills the box to show that it's selected. Clicking on a selected check box turns off the option.

✔ To conserve space, some multiple-choice options appear as *pop-up menus*. Click on the ↓ to display a menu of option choices. Then click on the desired option in the menu to choose it, just as if you were choosing a command from a standard menu. As with radio buttons, you can select only one option at a time from a pop-up menu.

✔ Not to be confused with the radio button, the normal, everyday variety of *button* enables you to close the current dialog box or display others. For example, click on the Cancel button to close the dialog box and cancel the command. Click on OK to close the dialog box and execute the command according to the current settings. Clicking on a button with an ellipsis (such as Load . . . and Save . . .) displays yet another dialog box.

As you can with menus, you can select options and perform other feats of magic inside dialog boxes from the keyboard. The following shortcuts work in most dialog boxes:

- ✔ To advance from one option box to the next, press the Tab key. To back up, press Shift+Tab.

- ✔ PC users can also move from option to option by using the hot keys (those underlined letters in the option names). Press Alt plus an option's hot key to move to that option.

- ✔ Press Enter (Return on a Mac) to select the button surrounded by a heavy outline (such as OK in Figure 2-3). Press Esc to select the Cancel button.

- ✔ Press ↑ to raise an option box value by one; press ↓ to decrease the value by one. Pressing Shift+↑ and Shift+↓ raise and lower the value by ten, respectively.

- ✔ If you change your mind about choices you make in a dialog box, you can quickly return things to the settings that were in force when you opened the dialog box. In most dialog boxes, pressing the Alt key (Option key on a Mac) magically changes the Cancel button to a Reset button. Click on the Reset button to bring back the original values.

If a dialog box gets in the way of your view of an image, you can reposition the box by dragging its title bar.

Playing Around with Palettes

Photoshop 6 offers free-floating *palettes* that you can hide or leave on-screen at a whim. The palettes, which are basically dialog boxes that can remain on-screen while you work, provide access to options that affect the performance of tools, change the appearance of images, and otherwise assist you in your editing adventures. I cover the specifics of using the options in the most popular palettes in chapters to come, but here's a brief introductory tour of how palettes work:

- ✔ As illustrated by the palette shown in Figure 2-4, palettes may contain the same kinds of options as dialog boxes — pop-up menus, option boxes, and so on. For information on using these options, see the preceding section.

- ✔ Each of the palettes is actually a collection of palettes sharing the same palette window. For example, the Layers, Channels, and Paths palettes are all housed in the same palette window (refer to Figure 2-4). To switch to a different palette in a palette window, click on its tab.

- ✔ Click on the Close box on the right side of the title bar to — guess what — close the palette. (To make the palette come back, choose the desired palette from the Window menu.)

Palette tab   Title bar   Collapse box

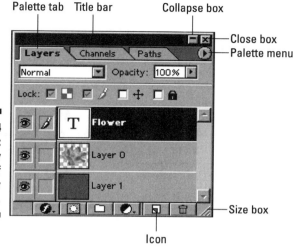

Close box
Palette menu

**Figure 2-4
(Windows):**
The many
elements of
a healthy
palette.

Size box

Icon

Close box   Title bar   Palette tab   Zoom box

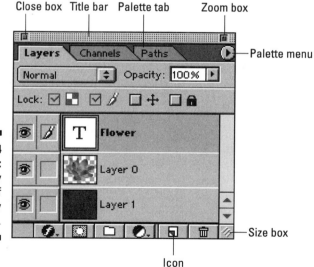

Palette menu

**Figure 2-4
(Mac):**
The many
elements of
a healthy
palette.

Size box

Icon

✔ Press Tab to hide or display the currently open palettes, the Toolbox,
the new Options bar (more on this below) and the status bar (covered
in Chapter 3). Press Shift+Tab if you want to hide or display just the
palettes, but leave the Toolbox, status bar, and the Options bar as is.
Note that this trick doesn't work if an option box inside a palette is
active — that is, if the option box is highlighted or if the cursor is blinking

inside it. In this case, pressing Tab and Shift+Tab moves you from option to option throughout all open palettes. To deactivate the option box, press Enter (Return on a Mac) to make the option box value take effect. You can then use the Tab/Shift+Tab shortcuts to hide and display palettes.

✔ To hide and display individual palettes, press their keyboard shortcuts: F6 for the Color palette, F7 for the Layers palette, and F8 for the Info palette.

✔ Some palettes contain icons, just like the Toolbox does. Click on an icon to perform a function, such as adding a layer or deleting a selected image.

✔ Drag the title bar at the top of the palette to move the palette around on-screen.

✔ Shift+click on a title bar to snap the palette to the nearest edge of the screen. For example, if the palette is near the right side of the screen, Shift+clicking on its title bar moves it all the way over to the right, giving you more space to view your image on-screen.

✔ Some palettes have a size box, as labeled in Figure 2-4. Drag the size box to resize the palette. To return the palette to its default size, click on the collapse box (zoom box on a Mac).

✔ If the palette is already at its default size, clicking on the collapse box (zoom box on a Mac) shrinks the palette so that only the most essential options at the top of the palette are visible, usually only the palette tab. Click on the collapse box (zoom box on a Mac) again to bring all of the palette options into full view.

✔ Alt+click on the collapse box (Option+click on the zoom box on a Mac) to hide all but the title bar and the palette tabs. Or double-click on a palette tab. The advantage is that you free up screen space without closing the palettes altogether.

✔ You can break any palette into its own window by dragging the palette tab out of the current window, as shown in Figure 2-5. You can also combine multiple palettes into a single palette window by dragging a tab from one palette into another.

✔ Want to know my favorite application of this technique? Drag the Swatches palette out of the Color/Swatches/Styles palette window to create a separate Swatches palette. Then close the Swatches palette altogether. See, the Swatches palette isn't very useful, so you may as well get it off the screen. Now, you can drag the History palette into the same palette window as the Color and Styles palette, enabling you to access all three of these very vital palettes quickly while using up a minimum of on-screen space.

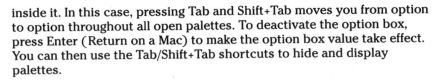

✔ Palettes can now also be docked vertically. Drop the tab at the bottom or top of another palette to stack two palettes.

✔ If you're a veteran Photoshop user, you may have noticed the absence of the Options palette. The trusty Options palette has been reincarnated as a horizontal Options bar. It's located directly under the menu bar and, like the Options palette, enables you to modify the behavior of a tool. And as you use the tools in Photoshop, you may notice the Options bar offers some new tool modifiers as well. The Options bar also offers a cool docking well on the far right side. Drag one or several palette tabs into the well to store them neatly and save valuable screen real estate. And don't worry, you can still access the flyout menu on a palette even when it is docked in the palette well in the Options bar. Simply click on the palette tab and the arrow for the pop-up menu appears.

✔ Press and hold on the right-pointing arrowhead on the right side of the palette, just below the title bar — phew, I need a breather! — to display the palette menu. Here's yet another place to find commands, just in case you manage to master all of the others. Yeah, right.

✔ As you can in a dialog box, you can raise or lower the value in a palette option box by pressing the arrow keys. Press ↑ to raise the value by one; press ↓ to lower the value by one; press Shift+↑ and Shift+↓ to raise or lower the value by ten, respectively.

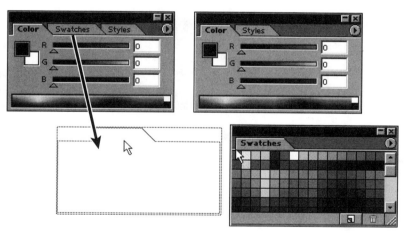

Figure 2-5: Drag the palette tab (left) to break the palette into its own little palette apartment.

Opening Up Your Toolbox

You're ready to move on to the tempestuous world of the Toolbox. As shown in Figure 2-6, the items in the Toolbox fall into three basic categories — tools, color controls, and icons. Future chapters explain in detail how to use the various gizmos in the Toolbox, but here's a basic overview of what's in store:

✔ Photoshop 6 adds ten new tools with this version, which are discussed in detail throughout the book.

✔ The top two-thirds or so of the Toolbox (refer to Figure 2-1) is devoted to an assortment of tools that you can use to edit images, just as you might use an assortment of pencils and paintbrushes to paint a picture. To select one of these tools, click on its icon. Then use the tool by clicking on it or dragging it inside your image.

✔ A tiny, right-pointing triangle in the bottom-right corner of a tool icon indicates that more tools are hidden behind that icon on a flyout menu. To display the flyout menu and reveal the hidden tools, press and hold the mouse button on the icon. Drag over and down the column of tools until your cursor is hovering over the tool you want to use and then release the mouse button.

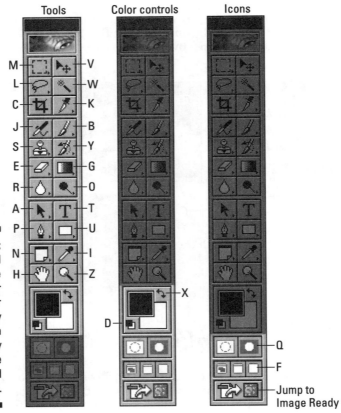

Figure 2-6:
Select a tool
or activate
a color
control or
icon by
clicking on
it or by
pressing the
keys listed
here.

✔ You can also Alt+click (Option+click on a Mac) on a tool icon to cycle through all the tools hidden beneath it, except for the Marquee tool and the Pen tool. Some of the tools on the flyout menu aren't accessible via this method.

✔ The bottom third of the Toolbox contains color selection options and other icons. These icons respond immediately when you click on them.

✔ If you've been clicking away on the Toolbox icons and haven't seen any results, don't panic. Your copy of Photoshop isn't broken; the icons just don't do anything unless you have an image open. To find out how to open images, see Chapter 3.

✔ Actually, one of the icons in the Toolbox does do something with no image on-screen. If you click on the very top icon in the Toolbox — the one with the ghostly looking eyeball — you bring up the Adobe Online dialog window. If you have access to the Internet, you can click on the Refresh button to connect your modem. Download the files from the Adobe servers. After the download, the Adobe Photoshop 6.0 splash screen appears. Clicking on the various buttons gives you access to tons of great info, such as tips, tech support, upgrades, and news on products and events.

✔ You can also access all the tools and icons and two of the color controls from the keyboard. For example, to select the Blur tool, you just press the R key. To select the Sharpen tool, which shares the flyout menu with the Blur tool, you press Shift+R. Other keyboard equivalents are shown in Figure 2-6.

✔ A couple of exceptions to the preceding tip. Press Shift+M to switch between the Rectangular and Elliptical Marquee tools. However, you cannot access the single column and single row marquee tools via a shortcut tool. Press Shift+P to cycle through the Pen and the Magnetic Pen. The remaining tools — Add Anchor Point tool, Delete Anchor Point tool, and Convert Point tool — do not have keyboard equivalents.

✔ If pressing the Shift key with the keyboard letter to access the tools on the flyout menu is just too strenuous, Photoshop gives you the solution. Choose Edit⇨Preferences and uncheck the option Use Shift Key for Tool Switch. You can rotate through the tools by pressing the same letter repeatedly.

✔ If you can't remember the name of a particular tool, pause your cursor over its icon for a second or two. A little label appears telling you the name of the tool and its keyboard equivalent. If this gets annoying, the feature can be turned off in the General panel in the Preferences dialog box under the Edit menu.

✔ The tools residing on the flyout menu also contain the name and keyboard equivalent of the tool in addition to the tool icon — quick and easy identification of all the tools.

One last new tidbit. If you grab a tool and try to use it and all you see is the Cancel (the circle with a diagonal line) icon, simply click on the canvas. Photoshop prompts you with a reason why it can't perform the operation. For example, if you try to apply color on a text layer with the paintbrush, Photoshop displays a message saying you couldn't use the Paintbrush because the pixels in a type layer cannot be edited without first rendering the layer. This talk about type and layers will probably be fuzzy to you because you may not have peeked at Chapters 15 (Layers) and 16 (Type).

Chapter 3

Now the Fun Really Begins

● ●

In This Chapter

▶ Opening and closing images

▶ Creating a new, blank image

▶ Mastering your image windows

▶ Moving around your image

▶ Zooming in and out

▶ Changing views

▶ Turning on grids and guides

● ●

*W*hen you first start Photoshop, you're presented with a plethora of tools, menus, and palettes, as illustrated in Chapter 2. Until you open up an image, those contraptions are intriguing, yet ultimately worthless — it's like having an easel, a full set of brushes, and a whole paintbox full of paints, but no canvas. And with Photoshop, you can't even amuse yourself by creating a political mural on your neighbor's garage door, as you can with traditional paint. No, if you want to become a digital Picasso (or Rembrandt, or Monet, or whatever artistic legend you choose), you need to open an image.

This chapter explains how to open existing images and also how to create a new, blank canvas for an image you want to paint from scratch. Then the chapter explains myriad ways you can display your image on-screen in order to view your masterpiece from just the right perspective.

Don't Just Sit There, Open Something!

If you're a longtime computer buff, you may expect opening an image to be a relatively straightforward process. You just choose File⇨Open or press Ctrl+O (⌘+O on a Mac) and select the image file you want to display, right?

Well, opening files in Photoshop involves a little complication: The steps for opening a Photo CD image are different than the steps for opening images saved in other file formats. The following sections give you the lowdown on opening both types of images.

The term *Photo CD image* can be a bit confusing; it refers to images saved in the Kodak Photo CD file format, not simply to images that come from a CD. A Photo CD image has the letters PCD tagged onto the end of its filename.

For Mac users, Photoshop has added Favorites and Recent documents (second and third icons in the top right) submenus in the Open dialog box enabling you to grab your most popular images. Photoshop also provides a Mounted Volumes submenu. You can find your way around your working environment more easily by clicking on the first icon in the top right. You can find direct routes to your desktop, network, server, hard drives, and external media. You can even eject your external media using this dialog box. Windows users can browse thumbnails of images while in the Open dialog box.

Opening a non-Photo CD image

To open an image that's stored in any format except the Kodak Photo CD format, walk this way:

1. **Choose File⇨Open.**

   If choosing the commands from the menu is too much work — and it is — just press Ctrl+O (⌘+O on a Mac). The Open dialog box rears its useful head, as shown in Figure 3-1. (Your dialog box may not offer all the options in the figure, or the options may have different names, but the basic components work the same.)

2. **PC users, select the disk or folder that contains your image from the Look In pop-up menu.**

   After you select a disk or folder, the contents of that disk or folder appear in the box beneath the pop-up menu. Double-click on a folder in the box to display its contents, if necessary, until you find the file you want to open.

   Mac users, click on the Mounted Volumes button to see the desktop, hard drives, external disks (such as floppies and zips), and networked items currently available to you. Assuming your image isn't lying about on the desktop, select the disk that contains the image you want to open.

   It's also possible that the image is inside a folder on the desktop, in which case you want to select Desktop from the Mounted Volumes button.

The scrolling list in the center of the dialog box shows you all the folders and images that are strewn loose on the disk.

Mac users, open the desired folder in the central list.

Double-click on a folder name to open the folder. The list then displays all folders and images inside that folder. Double-click on another folder if you need to open it, and so on.

3. **Click on the image you want to open.**

   After you locate your image, click on its name in the list to select it. A preview of the image appears in the dialog box so you can see what it looks like. Mac users, make sure the Show Preview button is activated. Be aware that previews may not be available in all circumstances. If you want to open multiple images in one fell swoop, press the Shift key and click on additional images.This applies to both platforms.

   PC users, click on the Details button to display pertinent information about each image, including its size, type, and the date it was last edited.

4. **Click on the Open button.**

   Or, you can press Enter (Return on a Mac) or press Alt+O (⌘+O on a Mac). Alternatively, if you have a single image selected, you can simply double-click on the image to open it.

That's all there is to it. Your image is now open and ready to abuse. But before you have a go at it in earnest, here are a few additional notes on opening images:

- ✔ To close a particular folder and view the contents of the folder that contains that particular folder, PC users click on the Up One Level button at the top of the Open dialog box (or click on the Backspace key).

- ✔ PC users, click on the Look In pop-up menu to display the list of folders that contains the current folder. For example, if the items in the pop-up menu read Elephant, Digestive Systems, and Food-Processing Enzymes, then the Food-Processing Enzymes folder resides inside the Digestive Systems folder, which is on the Elephant disk. Mac users can press ⌘+↑ to advance up a folder. Or you can press the current folder bar to display a pop-up menu of folders that contains the current folder.

- ✔ If you can't find a file in a certain folder, it may be because Photoshop doesn't think it can open the file. To see all files in a folder, whether Photoshop can open them or not, PC users select the All Formats option from the Files of Type pop-up menu. Mac users, select the Show All Readable Documents option. If the file appears, go ahead and try to open it. It may not work, but it's worth a try.

  Mac users, in addition to double-clicking on a folder to open it, you can press ⌘+↓.

Favorites

Create new folder   Details

Current folder   Up one level   List

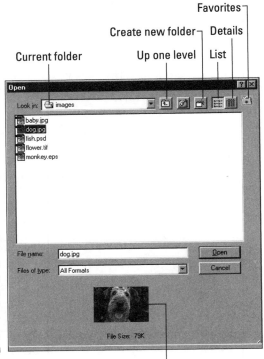

Figure 3-1 (Windows): This dialog box lets you locate and open images on your hard drive or some other disk.

Thumbnail preview

Favorites

Mounted Volumes   Recent documents

Current folder   Thumbnail preview

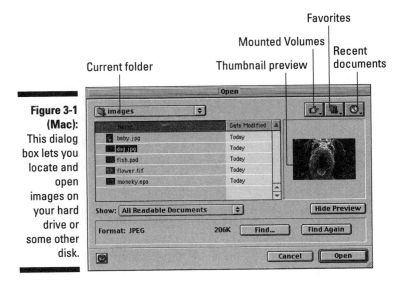

Figure 3-1 (Mac): This dialog box lets you locate and open images on your hard drive or some other disk.

✔ Use the thumbnail preview to help identify images. For example, if you or someone you work with names an image TRX33.Feb24-William (or something equally meaningless), you can click on it and view a small version of the image that may or may not be identifiable. But, hey it's better than nothing.

You can preview an image on a PC even when Photoshop isn't running by right-clicking on the image file in My Computer or Explorer. When you right-click, choose Properties from the menu that appears. Then click on the Photoshop Image tab of the resulting dialog box. Unfortunately, this trick works only for images saved in Versions 4, 5, and 6 and in the native Photoshop format. (Formats are explained in Chapter 6.)

Opening a Kodak Photo CD image

As mentioned earlier, opening a Kodak Photo CD image involves a different process than opening other types of images. Here's the scoop:

1. **Choose File⇨Open or press Ctrl+O (⌘+O on a Mac).**

2. **Select the Photo CD disk from the Look In pop-up menu. On the Mac, select the Photo CD disk from the Mounted Volumes submenu (look for the pointed finger icon).**

   The disk may have some meaningless machine-assigned name, such as PCD0196.

3. **Open the Photo_CD folder.**

   Inside, you find several weirdly-named files.

4. **Open the Images folder.**

   Here's where the real images live. They all have dumb names like IMG0001.PCD;1, and so on. Luckily, every Photo CD disk comes with two or three sheets of tiny thumbnail printouts so that you know which image is associated with each file number.

5. **Double-click on the image you want to open.**

   After what may seem like an interminable amount of time — don't give up and think that your computer has crashed — the dialog box shown in Figure 3-2 appears.

6. **Locate the Source Image section.**

   Here's the tricky part. The Photo CD interpreter built into Photoshop wants more than anything to make sure that the colors in the image are correctly converted from the disc to your screen. Therefore, you have to tell Photoshop a source and destination for the image. It's kind of strange, but just do as I tell you, and you can't go wrong.

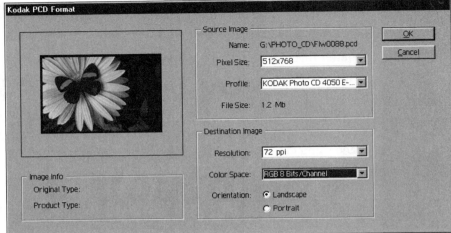

7. Select the pixel size and profile for your image.

Pixel sizes range from a scant 64 x 96 to a whopping 2048 x 3072 pixels.

- If the image you want to open was scanned from a 35mm slide, select the Kodak PhotoCD Universal E-6 V3.2 (Ektachrome) or Kodak PhotoCD Universal K-14 V3.2 (Kodachrome) option, depending on the film used to shoot the photo.

- If the image came from a film negative, select the Kodak PhotoCD Color Negative V3.0 option.

- If you're opening an image from a commercial CD, such as one from Corbis, you can assume that the Source option should be set to Kodak PhotoCD Universal E-6 V3.2 (Ektachrome).

8. Locate the Destination Image section and set the following options.

Select an option from the Resolution pop-up menu. The range is 72 ppi to 550 ppi. Check Chapter 4 for details on appropriate resolutions for specific usages of an image.

Select your desired color space from the pop-up menu. I recommend RGB 8 Bits/Channel. This choice converts the scan to a standard color Photoshop image.

Select the orientation — Landscape or Portrait.

9. Press Enter (Return on a Mac) or click on OK.

Photoshop opens the Photo CD image. If you get an out-of-memory error, try opening the image again and selecting a smaller pixel range, as described in the preceding step.

If an image opens up lying on its side, you can shift it to an upright position by rotating it. If the image is resting on its left side, choose Image⇨Rotate Canvas⇨90° CW (clockwise); if the image is taking a nap on its right side, choose Image⇨Rotate Canvas⇨90° CCW (counter-clockwise). (The latter is more common.) If the image turns upside down, choose Edit⇨Undo and then choose the command that you didn't choose the first time.

After you open an image for the first time, the Source and Destination options remain set. This means that you can skip Steps 6 through 8 when opening future Photo CD images.

Note: To create a new image instead of opening an existing one, choose File⇨New or press Ctrl+N (on a Mac, press ⌘+N). Photoshop displays the New dialog box. There, you can name your file; specify the width, height, and resolution (as discussed in Chapter 4); and set the color mode (as discussed in Chapter 5). However, you'll probably have little reason to create a new image unless you just want to play around with the painting tools. Photoshop is, after all, made primarily for editing existing images.

Behold the Image Window

After you open up an image, Photoshop displays the image on-screen inside a new image window. Several new elements appear when you open an image, as labeled in Figure 3-3.

The following list explains all:

- ✔ The title bar lists the title of your image, hence the name. The added bonus is that you can drag the title bar to move the window to a different location on-screen. Easy stuff.

- ✔ For Mac users, every element labeled in the figure except the page preview box, magnification box, and collapse box (and the odd-looking creature with the goggles, of course) is found in all windows across the board. Click on the zoom box to collapse or expand the window to match the exact size of the image. If the image is too big for the screen, the window expands to include as much of the image as possible.

- ✔ For PC users, just like the main Photoshop program window, each image window has a Close button, Minimize button, and Maximize/Restore button. The buttons work just as they do for the program window (explained in Chapter 2) with one exception: The Minimize button reduces the image window so that only a small title bar is left on-screen. Click on the Restore button to bring the image back into view.

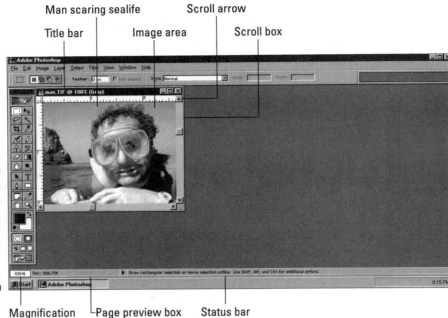

Figure 3-3 (Windows): An image from Corbis' "Active Lifestyles 2" collection.

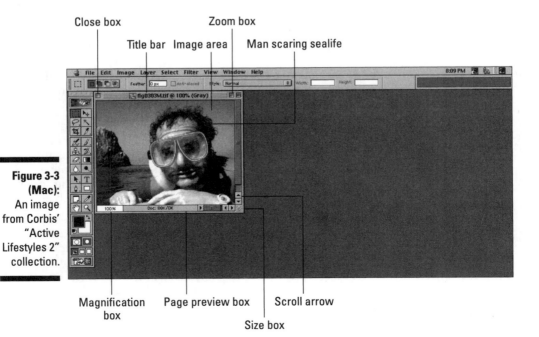

Figure 3-3 (Mac): An image from Corbis' "Active Lifestyles 2" collection.

✔ Alternatively, you can choose File⇨Close or press Ctrl+W (⌘+W on a Mac) to close an image. You know, W as in *hasta la vista, window.* (If you've made some changes to the image, Photoshop asks you whether you want to save the new and improved image, a process explained in great detail in Chapter 6.)

✔ For PC users, to change the size of the image window, place your cursor over a corner of the window. When a double-headed arrow appears, drag the corner. For Mac users, place your cursor over the size box in the lower-right corner of the window and drag. On both platforms, the image remains the same; you're just changing the size of the window that holds the image. Give it a try and see what I mean.

✔ The status bar, on PCs, gives you information about your image and hints about the tool or command you're using.

Don't see the status bar on your screen? Choose Window⇨Show Status Bar to display it. Remember that the status bar disappears when you press Tab to hide the palettes and the Toolbox, as explained in Chapter 2.

✔ In the lower-left corner of the window is the magnification box, which lets you zoom in and out on your image, as explained later in this chapter in the section "Zooming in and out on your work."

✔ Next to the magnification box is the page preview box, which shows how much memory your image is consuming, measured in digital chunks called *bytes.* The first number is the size of the image as the image will be sent to the printer; the second number reflects the size of the image with layer information included. I discuss file size and resolution and all those other thorny issues in Chapter 4, and explain layers in Chapter 15. For the time being, don't worry about the preview box too much. I just didn't want to leave you wondering, "What in the Sam Hill is this thingie here?"

If you click and hold the mouse button down on the page preview box, Photoshop displays a window that shows you where the image will appear on the page when you print the image. The big X indicates the image in the preview.

Hold down Alt (Option on a Mac) as you click on the page preview box, and Photoshop displays a box showing the height, width, resolution, and number of channels in the image. (Channels are discussed in Chapter 5.)

✔ The scroll bars let you navigate around and display hidden portions of the image inside the window. Photoshop offers two scroll bars, one vertical bar along the right side of the image, and one horizontal bar along the bottom.

If you click on a scroll arrow, you nudge your view of the image slightly in that direction. For example, if you click on the right-pointing scroll arrow, an item that was hidden on the right side of the photograph slides into view. Click in the gray area of a scroll bar to scroll the window more dramatically. Drag a scroll box to manually specify the distance scrolled.

Using the scroll arrows isn't the only way to move around your image; in fact, it's probably the least efficient method. For some better options, check out the techniques presented in the section, "The Screen Is Your Digital Oyster," coming up next.

✔ The area inside the title bar and scroll bars is the image area. The image area is where you paint and edit and select details and, otherwise, have at your image. Obviously, you look at the image area a lot throughout the many pages of this book.

You can open as many images on-screen as your computer's memory and screen size allow. But only one image is active at a time. To make a different window active, just click on it or choose its name from the bottom of the Window menu.

The Screen Is Your Digital Oyster

The Photoshop Toolbox includes two navigation tools: the Hand tool, which lets you scroll the image inside the window with much more ease than the silly scroll bars afford, and the Zoom tool, which lets you move closer to or farther away from your image. The Hand tool and the Zoom tool are called navigation tools because they don't change the image; they merely move your view of the image so that you can get a better look-see.

In addition to the above tools, there is another navigation aid, appropriately called the Navigator palette. The palette gives you a super-convenient way to zoom and scroll your image. In fact, after you are familiar with the palette, you may not use the Hand and Zoom tools at all. But in the interest of fair play, I present all your various options for moving around in your image in the upcoming sections.

Using the Hand tool

If you're familiar with other Windows and Macintosh programs, you need to know something about Photoshop: The scroll bars are useless. Keep away from them. I want you to promise me you'll always use the Hand tool or the Navigator palette (explained shortly) instead. Promise? Good. As for you new users, I don't worry about you because I'm going to show you the right way.

Consider the following example: Figure 3-4 shows another Corbis image — this time from the "Children and Teens" collection. The top view in the figure shows a young lad in obvious distress. The problem is that the picture is wider than my screen, so I can't see what's causing him such grief.

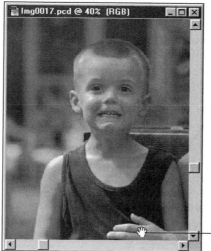

—Hand cursor

Figure 3-4:
Dragging
with the
Hand tool
reveals that
a bad
haircut isn't
the only
thing a kid
has to worry
about.

To view the rest of the scene, I select the Hand tool by clicking on its icon in the Toolbox. Then I position my Photoshop hand over the hand in the picture, as shown in the top example in Figure 3-4, and drag to the left. The image moves with the hand cursor, as shown in the bottom example, and reveals the source of the boy's torment.

Dragging with the Hand tool is like turning your head to view a new part of your surroundings. You can drag at any angle you please — up, down, sideways, or diagonally.

You can also select the Hand tool by pressing the H key. To temporarily access the Hand tool when another tool is selected, press the spacebar. As long as the spacebar is down, the Hand tool is available. Releasing the spacebar returns you to the selected tool.

Using keyboard shortcuts

As in most other programs, you can also use keyboard shortcuts to move about your image. Press Page Up or Page Down to scroll up or down an entire screen. Press Shift+Page Up or Shift+Page Down to scroll in smaller increments. Press Home to go to the upper-left corner of the image, and press End to move to the lower-right corner.

And as if that wasn't enough, Photoshop offers keyboard shortcuts for moving right and left. Press Ctrl+Page Up or Page Down to scroll left or right an entire screen. Press Ctrl+Shift+Page Up or Page Down to scroll left and right in smaller increments.

Zooming in and out on your work

When you first open an image, Photoshop displays the entire image so that it fits on-screen. But you may not be seeing the details in the image as clearly as you want. The first view is sort of like being far away from the image. If you want to inspect it in more detail, you have to step closer.

Photoshop gives you several ways to zoom in and out on your work, as described in these next few sections.

Zooming doesn't change the size at which your image prints. It just affects the size at which you see the image on-screen. Zooming is like looking at some eensey-teensey life form under a microscope. The creature doesn't actually grow and shrink as you vary the degree of magnification, and neither does your image.

The Zoom tool

Using the Zoom tool is one avenue for changing your view of an image. Every time you click on your image with the tool, you magnify the image to a larger size. Here's an example of how it works:

1. **Select the Zoom tool.**

   Click on the Zoom tool in the Toolbox. It's the one that looks like a magnifying glass. You can also press the Z key to grab the Zoom tool.

2. **Click in the image area.**

   Photoshop magnifies the image to the next preset zoom size (the increments are set by Photoshop), as demonstrated in the second example of Figure 3-5. The program centers the magnified view about the point at which you click. In Figure 3-5, for example, I clicked between the girl's eyes.

3. **Repeat.**

   To zoom in farther still, click again with the Zoom tool, as demonstrated in the bottom example of Figure 3-5.

A setting in the Options bar determines whether Photoshop resizes your image window to match the image when you zoom with the Zoom tool. If you want your image windows to be resized when you zoom, select the Resize Windows to Fit option.

The only hitch comes when the window bumps into a palette. When the window hits a palette that's anchored to the side of the screen (as opposed to floating in the middle of the screen), Photoshop thinks that it has hit some sort of wall and stops zooming. To get around the problem, simply select the new Ignore Palettes option located in the Options bar.

Here's some other Zoom-tool stuff to tuck away for future reference:

- ✔ Alt+click (Option+click on a Mac) with the Zoom tool to zoom out on your image.

- ✔ As you zoom, Photoshop displays the *zoom factor* in the title bar. A zoom factor of 100 percent shows you one screen pixel for every pixel in your image. (Pixels are explained thoroughly in Chapter 4.)

  Keep in mind that a 100 percent zoom ratio doesn't necessarily correspond to the printed size of your image, contrary to what you may expect. If you want to view your image at its printed size, use the Print Size command, explained in the next section.

- ✔ To magnify just one section of an image, drag with the Zoom tool to surround the area with a dotted outline. Photoshop fills the image window with the area that you surrounded.

- ✔ To temporarily access the Zoom tool while another tool is selected, press Ctrl+spacebar (⌘+spacebar on a Mac). PressCtrl+Alt+spacebar (⌘+Option+spacebar on a Mac) to get the zoom out cursor. In either case, releasing the keys returns you to the previously selected tool.

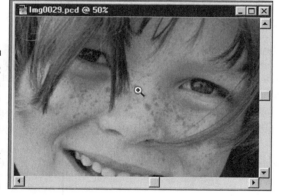

Figure 3-5:
Clicking
with the
Zoom tool
magnifies
your image
in preset
increments.

The View commands

The View menu offers some more ways to change the magnification of your image. The first two zoom commands on the menu, Zoom In and Zoom Out, aren't of much interest; they do the same thing as clicking and Alt+clicking (Option+clicking on a Mac) with the Zoom tool, except that you can't specify the center of the new view as you can with the Zoom tool. But you may find the other View commands helpful at times:

✔ Choose View⇨Actual Pixels or press Ctrl+Alt+0 (zero) (⌘+Option+0 on a Mac) to return to the 100 percent zoom ratio. This view size shows you one pixel on your monitor for every pixel in the image, which is the most accurate way to view your image.

✔ Choose View⇨Fit on Screen or press Ctrl+0 (zero) (⌘+0) to display your image at the largest size that allows the entire image to fit on-screen.

✔ You can also choose the Actual Pixels view by double-clicking on the Zoom tool icon in the Toolbox. Double-click on the Hand tool icon to change to the Fit on Screen view.

✔ Choose View⇨Print Size to display your image on-screen at the same size that it will print. Note that Photoshop provides only an approximation of the print size; your actual printed piece may be slightly smaller or larger.

✔ Or easier yet, select the Actual Pixels, Fit on Screen, or Print Size buttons in the Options bar.

✔ You can choose View⇨New View to create a second view of your image. Don't confuse this with duplicating an image, which creates a new file. New View simply creates a second way of looking at the same file. New View can be useful when you are editing an image in a magnified view, yet want to see the overall results on your entire image without having to continuously zoom in and out.

The Magnification box

The Zoom tool and View commands are great when you want to zoom in or out to one of the preset Photoshop zoom ratios. But what if you want more control over your zooming? The answer awaits in the Magnification box in the lower-left corner of the Photoshop window (labeled earlier in Figure 3-3).

To enter a zoom ratio, just double-click on the magnification box and type the zoom ratio you want to use. If you know exactly what zoom ratio you want, press Enter (Return on a Mac) to make Photoshop do your bidding. But if you want to play around with different zoom ratios, press Shift+Enter (Shift+Return on a Mac) instead. That way, Photoshop zooms your image, but keeps the Magnification box active so that you can quickly enter a new ratio if the first one doesn't work out. When you're satisfied, press Enter (Return on a Mac).

When you use the Magnification box, the image window size doesn't change as you zoom, regardless of whether the Resize Windows to Fit option is selected in the Options bar.

Navigating by palette

The Navigator palette, shown in Figure 3-6, is the best navigational aid because it actually combines the functions of the Zoom and Hand tools in one location. To display the palette, choose Window⇨Show Navigator. Or press F8 to display the Info palette and click on the Navigator palette tab. To make the palette smaller or larger, drag the size box in the palette's lower-right corner.

View box

Figure 3-6:
The
Navigator
palette
provides a
nifty way to
zoom and
scroll your
image.

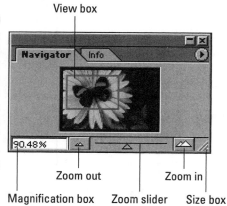

Zoom out   Zoom in

Magnification box   Zoom slider   Size box

The palette provides a handy, all-in-one tool for scrolling and zooming. It's especially useful when you're working on a large image that doesn't fit entirely on-screen when you're zoomed in for detail work. Here are the how-tos for using the palette:

✔ In the center of the palette, you see a thumbnail view of your image, as in Figure 3-6. The palette shows your entire image, even if it's not all visible in the main image window.

✔ See the box that surrounds a portion of the thumbnail? That's called the view box. The area within the box corresponds to the portion of your image that's visible in the main image window. As you drag the box, Photoshop scrolls your image in the main image window to display the area that's surrounded by the box. You can also click on an area in the thumbnail to move the view box over that portion of the image.

✔ Press and hold Ctrl (⌘ on a Mac), and the cursor in the palette changes to a zoom cursor. If you drag with the cursor while pressing Ctrl (⌘ on a Mac), you resize the view box, which, in turn, zooms the image in the image window.

✓ The palette also contains a magnification box, as labeled in Figure 3-6. The box works just like the one in the image window; just enter a zoom factor and press Enter (Return on a Mac).

✓ To zoom in or out in the preset Photoshop increments (as with the Zoom tool), click on the Zoom In or Zoom Out buttons, labeled in Figure 3-6.

✓ You can also zoom by dragging the Zoom slider — drag left to zoom out, and drag right to zoom in.

If you don't like the color of the view box, you can change it. Click on the right-pointing arrow in the upper-right corner of the palette and choose the Palette Options command. Then choose a new color from the Color pop-up menu.

Filling up the screen with your image

The three icons, Standard Screen Mode, Full Screen Mode with Menu Bar, and Full Screen Mode, at the bottom of the Toolbox, let you change the way the window fills the screen. These icons appear as shown in Figure 3-7.

✓ Click on the far-left icon to view the window normally, with scroll bars and title bar and all that stuff. This is the default setting.

✓ Click on the center icon to eliminate the scroll bars and title bar and fill the screen with your image. Any portions of the screen that aren't consumed by the image appear gray. The Toolbox, Options bar, palettes, status bar (for PC users), and menu bar remain visible.

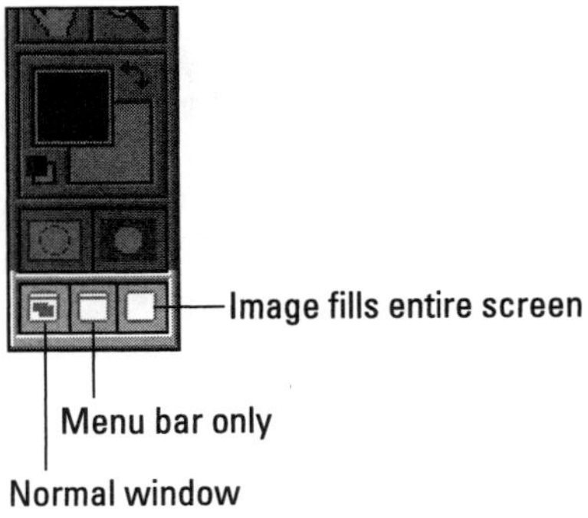

Figure 3-7:
Those weird
little icons
at the
bottom of
the Toolbox
change your
on-screen
landscape.

Image fills entire screen

Menu bar only

Normal window

✓ If you want to take over still more screen real estate, click on the far-right icon to hide the menu bar. Now, portions of the screen that don't contain the image are black. The only desktop elements that remain available are the palettes, Toolbox, Options bar, and status bar (for PC users).

REMEMBER

✔ You can press Tab to hide the Toolbox, Options bar, the palettes, and the status bar; press Tab again to redisplay them (refer to Chapter 2). To hide and redisplay only the palettes, press Shift+Tab.

TIP

You can cycle through the different screen modes by pressing the F key instead of clicking on the Toolbox icons, if you prefer. Press F once to select the second icon, press F again to select the third icon, and press F a third time to return to the first icon.

Tools for the Terribly Precise

If you've ever used a page layout program such as PageMaker or QuarkXPress, you're no doubt familiar with the concept of *grids and guides*. Shown in Figure 3-8, grids and guides are on-screen devices that help you align elements in your image. For example, in the figure I use a horizontal guide to position my text exactly 2 inches from the left edge of the image and 5.5 inches from the top of the image.

Guide   Move guide cursor   Ruler   Grid line

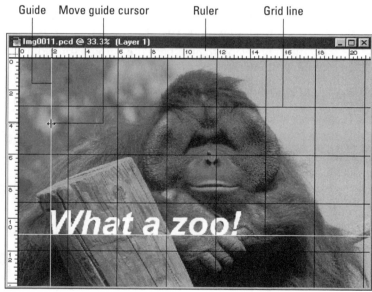

Figure 3-8:
Our furry friend isn't really fenced in; he's just covered with grid lines and guides.

In addition to grids and guides, Photoshop offers rulers that run across the top and left sides of the image window. Grids, guides, and rulers come in handy when you're feeling the urge to be especially precise with your work.

Switching on the rulers

To display rulers, choose <u>V</u>iew⇨Show <u>R</u>ulers or press Ctrl+R (⌘+R on a Mac). To hide the rulers, choose <u>V</u>iew⇨Hide <u>R</u>ulers or press Ctrl+R (⌘+R on a Mac) again.

By default, the rulers use inches as their unit of measurement. But if you want to use some other unit, say picas instead of inches, choose <u>E</u>dit⇨Preferences⇨<u>U</u>nits & Rulers. Or just double-click on a ruler. In the Rulers section of the dialog box that appears, select a new unit of measure from the Units pop-up menu.

Better yet, you can right-click (⌘+click on a Mac) on either ruler to access a shortcut menu where you can select your desired unit of measurement.

Using guides

Guides are horizontal and vertical lines that you create to help you align elements in your image. Guides don't print; they're creatures of the on-screen world only. You can create as many guides as you need.

Before you can create a guide, you have to display the rulers by choosing <u>V</u>iew⇨Show <u>R</u>ulers or pressing Ctrl+R (⌘+R on a Mac). Then drag from one of the rulers to "pull out" a guide. Drag from any point on the horizontal ruler to create a horizontal guide; drag from the vertical ruler to create a vertical guide. Release the mouse button at the spot where you want to place the guide.

Here are some more guides to using guides:

✔ After you create a guide, you can reposition it. First, select the Move tool (it's the upper-right tool in the Toolbox) by clicking on its icon in the Toolbox. Then place the cursor over the guide until you see the double-headed arrow, as in Figure 3-8, and drag the guide to its new home. Alternatively, you can Ctrl+drag (⌘+drag on a Mac) the guide with any other tool except the Hand, Slice, or Slice Select tools.

✔ The New Guide command under the View menu creates a new guide at a specific location on your image. Select horizontal or vertical and specify the destination in pixels.

✔ To remove a guide, drag it out of the image window using the Move tool or Ctrl+drag (⌘+drag on a Mac) with any other tool but the pen or Slice and Slice Select tools. To get rid of all guides, choose <u>V</u>iew⇨Clear Guide<u>s</u>.

✔ To lock a guide in place, choose View⇨Lock Guides or press Ctrl+Alt+; (⌘+Option+; on a Mac). To unlock the guides so that you can move them again, choose View⇨Lock Guides or press Ctrl+Alt+; (⌘+Option+; on a Mac) again.

✔ When you drag an image element near a guide, the element "snaps" into alignment with the guide — as if the guide had some sort of magnetic pull. If you don't want stuff to snap to guides, choose View⇨Snap or Ctrl+; (⌘+; on a Mac). Choose the command again to turn snapping back on. (A check mark next to the command name means that the feature is turned on.)

✔ You can now customize how you want your elements to snap. Select View⇨Snap To and notice the various options available. Grids are explained in detail at the end of the chapter in the "Turning on the grid" section. Slices are used in Web graphics. Document Bounds enable your elements to snap to the edge of your image window. You also have the choice of setting all or none of these options in one fell swoop.

✔ You can also Show and Hide Extras. Extras include the guides and grid mentioned here, as well as selection edges and paths (see Chapter 12), slices, and notes (see Chapter 6). As in the snap options, you can also see and hide all or none of these options.

✔ To change the color of the guides, choose Edit⇨Preferences⇨Guides & Grid, double-click on a guide with the Move tool or Ctrl+double-click (⌘+double-click on a Mac) on the guide with any other tool but the Hand or Slice and Select Slice tools. In the Guides section of the dialog box that appears, you can choose a color and line style for your guides. Press Enter (Return on a Mac) to exit the dialog box and make your changes official.

Holding the Alt key (Option key on a Mac) down while dragging a guide changes the guide from horizontal to vertical or vice versa.

Turning on the grid

Unlike guides, which you can position willy-nilly in the image window, the grid positions lines across your image in preset intervals. You can't move grid lines, but you can change the spacing and color of the lines.

To turn on the grid, choose View⇨Show⇨Grid. To change the spacing and appearance of the grid lines, choose Edit⇨Preferences⇨Guides & Grid. Photoshop presents you with a dialog box in which you can choose a color and line style for the grid lines, specify how far apart you want to space the lines, and choose whether you want to subdivide the grid with secondary grid lines. You can also choose a unit of measurement for the grid.

Like guides, the lines of a grid have "snapping" capabilities — anything you drag near a grid line automatically snaps into alignment with that line. You turn snapping on and off by choosing View➪Snap To➪Grid. A check mark next to the command name in the menu means that snapping is turned on when the Snap command is activated.

Photoshop gives yet another tool for the precision junkies. The Measure tool, which shares a flyout menu with the Eyedropper tool, lets you measure height, width, distance, and angle within your image. All you have to do is drag from one point to another. The numbers are then displayed in your Info palette. The endpoints the Measure tool creates can also be dragged to enable the user to create new measurements.

Part II

The Care and Feeding of Pixels

In this part . . .

I can't tell you how disappointed I was the first time I dissected a frog. We had been looking at all the cool pictures of the animal's colorful innards, and the moment we got the critter open, everything was various shades of pale beige. Where were the blue veins? And the red arteries? And the purple muscles and organs, and the bright yellow fat cells? Was my frog defective?

That's the problem with real life — it's never as interesting as the pictures. But an electronic image is different. An electronic image isn't some natural miracle that tests the minds of our best scientists and absolutely baffles the brains of junior high school students; it's something designed by humans expressly to be understood by other humans. So, you can be sure that the dissection that takes place in Chapters 4 through 7 looks the same on your computer screen as it does in my figures, except more colorful.

The chapters in this part tell you how to manage the colored specks — called *pixels* — that make up the image, how color and black-and-white images work, and how to save and print the image when you're done editing. These chapters aren't obscure experiments; they're straightforward journeys through features that you use every time you open Photoshop. Even better, you don't have to put up with the nauseating smell of formaldehyde.

Oh, and one more thing: The publisher wants me to tell you that no frogs were harmed in the making of this book. One parrot was forced to take notation, but that's it.

Chapter 4

Sizing Up Your Image

· ·

In This Chapter

▶ Taking a close look at the pixels in an image

▶ Using the Image Size dialog box

▶ Understanding resolution

▶ Matching the width of an image to page columns

▶ Changing the number of pixels in an image

▶ Resizing the canvas independent of the image

· ·

*I*mages that you create and edit in Photoshop — or in any other image editor, for that matter — are made up of tiny squares called *pixels.* Understanding how pixels work in an image can be enormously confusing to beginning image editors. Unfortunately, managing your pixel population correctly is essential to turning out professional-looking images, so you really do need to come to grips with how pixels work before you can be successful with Photoshop.

This chapter explains everything you need to know to put pixels in perspective, including how the number of pixels in an image affects its quality, printed size, and size on disk. I also show you how to reduce or enlarge the size of the on-screen canvas on which all your pretty pixels perch. In other words, this chapter offers pages of particularly provocative pixel paragraphs, partner.

Welcome to Pixeltown

Imagine that you're the victim of a terrifying scientific experiment that has left you 1 millimeter tall. After recovering from the initial shock that such terrifying scientific experiments tend to produce on one's equilibrium, you discover that you're sitting on a square tile that's colored with a uniform shade of blue. Beyond your tile are eight other blue tiles, one to your right and one to your left, one in front and one behind, and four others in diagonal directions. In other words, the tiles are aligned in a perfect grid, just like standard floor tiles. You notice upon further inspection that each of the blue tiles differs slightly in shade and tone. As you slowly turn, it becomes evident that you're surrounded by these colored tiles for as far as your infinitesimally tiny, pin-prick eyes can see.

You cry out in anguish and fling your dust-speck body about in the way that folks always do when plagued by these terrifying scientific experiments. As though in answer to your pitiful squeals, you start to grow. In a matter of moments, you increase in size to almost 5 centimeters tall. A bug that was considering devouring you has a change of mind and runs away. You can now see that you sit in the midst of a huge auditorium and that all the tiles on its vast and unending floor are colored differently, gradually changing from shades of blue to shades of green, red, and yellow. You continue to grow: Ten centimeters, 20, 50, a full meter tall. The tiles start to blend together to form some kind of pattern. Two meters, 5, 10. You've now grown several times beyond your normal height, reaching 20 meters tall. Your massive head bursts through the flimsy ceiling of the room.

When you reach the height of a 50-story building, your growth spurt comes to an end. You look down at the ruined auditorium, whose walls have been shredded to rubble by the great edges of your tremendous feet, and you notice a peculiar thing. You stand not on a floor, but on a picture, as rich in color and detail as any you've seen. The tiles, which now appear dot-sized to you, have merged together to create a seamless blend. You had expected the result to have the rough appearance of a mosaic — requiring a heavy dose of imagination to compensate for occasionally choppy transitions — but, in fact, it looks exactly like a continuous photograph.

The vision inspires you to claw at your temples, fling your arms about in circles, and shriek, "What's happening to me?!" The answer, of course, is nothing. Well, okay, your body may be stretched out of shape, but your eyes are working fine. You see, when you get far enough away from a perfect grid of colored tiles — whether via a terrifying scientific experiment or more conventional means — the tiles disappear, and an overall image takes shape.

What does this little trip down sci-fi lane have to do with Photoshop? Well, a lot, actually. Like the image on the auditorium floor, your Photoshop image is made up of a grid of colored squares. In this case, the squares are called *pixels*.

By now, you're probably thinking, "Fine, images are made up of a bunch of itsy-bitsy square pixels. So what? Who cares? Quit wasting my time, darn you." The truth is, these tiniest of image particles are at the heart of what makes Photoshop and your electronic images tick.

Every single painting and image-editing function in Photoshop is devoted to changing either the quantity or the color of pixels. That's all Photoshop does. I know, it sounds so simple that you figure I must be joking, exaggerating, or just plain lying. But with Salvador Dali as my witness, it's the absolute truth. Photoshop is merely an extremely sophisticated pixel counter and colorer, nothing more.

Screen Pixels versus Image Pixels

Like the tiles in the preceding story, each pixel in a computer image is perfectly square, arranged on a perfect grid, and colored uniformly — that is, each pixel is one color and one color only. Put these pixels together, and your brain perceives them to be an everyday, average photograph.

The display on your computer's monitor is also made up of pixels. Like image pixels, screen pixels are square and arranged on a grid. A typical 13-inch monitor measures 640 screen pixels wide by 480 screen pixels tall. These screen pixels are kind of tiny, so you may not be able to make them out. Each one generally measures $\frac{1}{72}$ inch across.

To understand the relationship between screen and image pixels, open an image. After the image comes up on-screen, double-click on the Zoom tool in the Toolbox, or choose View⇨Actual Pixels. The title bar on the image window lists the zoom ratio as 100%, which means that you can see one pixel in your image for every pixel displayed by your monitor.

To view the image pixels more closely, enter a value of **200** percent in the magnification box in the lower-left corner of the Photoshop window (double-click on the box to activate it). A 200% zoom factor magnifies the image pixels to twice their previous size so that one image pixel measures two screen pixels tall and two screen pixels wide. If you change the zoom factor to 400%, Photoshop displays four screen pixels for every image pixel, giving you a total of 16 screen pixels for every image pixel (4 screen pixels tall by 4 screen pixels wide). Figure 4-1 illustrates how different zoom factors affect the appearance of your image pixels on-screen.

Remember that the zoom factor has nothing to do with the size at which your image will print — it only affects how your image looks on-screen. If you want to see your image on-screen at its approximate print size, choose View⇨ Actual Pixels.

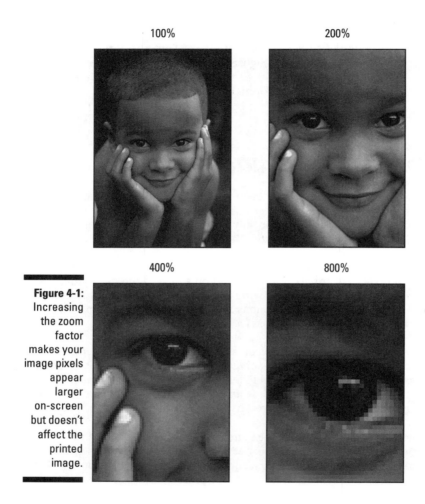

Figure 4-1: Increasing the zoom factor makes your image pixels appear larger on-screen but doesn't affect the printed image.

Image Size, Resolution, and Other Tricky Pixel Stuff

A Photoshop image has three primary attributes related to pixels: *file size, resolution,* and *physical dimensions,* as explained in the following list. You control these attributes through the Image Size dialog box, shown in Figure 4-2. To display the dialog box, choose Image⇨Image Size.

If you just want to get a quick look at the dimensions and resolution of an image, press Alt (Option on a Mac) as you press and hold the mouse button on the page preview box in the lower-left corner of the Photoshop window (next to the magnification box). Photoshop displays a little box listing the dimensions, resolution, and other scary stuff.

- ✔ The *file size* of the image is a measure of how many pixels the image contains. (Photoshop refers to file size as *pixel dimensions*.) The image in Figure 4-1 is 256 pixels wide and 384 pixels tall, for a total of 98,304 pixels. Most of the images you create contain hundreds of thousands or even millions of pixels.

- ✔ The *resolution* of an image refers to the number of pixels that print per inch. For example, the resolution of the first image in Figure 4-1 is 180 pixels per inch *(ppi)*. That may sound like an awful lot of pixels squished into a small space, but it's about average.

- ✔ Not to be confused with file size, the *dimensions* of an image are its physical width and height when printed, as measured in inches, centimeters, or your unit of choice. You can calculate the dimensions by dividing the number of pixels by the resolution. For example, the little boy in Figure 4-1 measures 256 pixels ÷ 180 pixels per inch = 1⅜ inches wide and 384 pixels ÷ 180 ppi = 2⅛ inches tall. Measure him with a ruler, and you see that this is indeed the case.

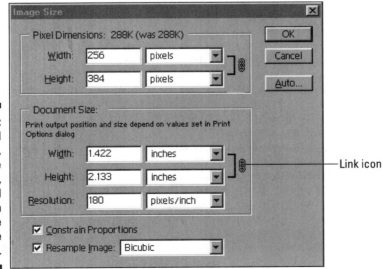

Figure 4-2: You control file size, image dimensions, and resolution through the Image Size dialog box.

No problem, right? I mean, okay, this stuff is a little technical, but it's not like it requires an advanced degree in cold fusion to figure out what's going on. And yet, the Image Size dialog box may well be the most confusing Photoshop dialog box. You can even damage your image if you're not careful. So be extremely careful before you make changes in the Image Size dialog box. (The upcoming sections tell you everything you need to know to stay out of trouble.)

Depending on your printer, on a PC you may be able to simply reduce or enlarge your image for printing via a scaling option in the printer's Properties dialog box, which you access by choosing File➪Page Setup to display the Page Setup dialog box and then clicking on the button and the Graphics button. On a Mac, you may be able to reduce or enlarge your image for printing simply by entering a percentage value into the Reduce or Enlarge options box in the Page Setup dialog box. Choose File➪Page Setup. On both platforms, Photoshop scales your image to the new size during only the print cycle. Your image isn't permanently altered as it is when you use the Image Size dialog box. For more information, see Chapter 7.

Resolving resolution

Although the Resolution option box is positioned unceremoniously toward the bottom of the Image Size dialog box, it's one of the most critical values to consider if you want your images to look good.

The Resolution value determines how tightly the pixels are packed when printed. It's kind of like the population density of one of those ridiculously large urban areas cropping up all over the modern world. Take Lagos, Nigeria, for example, which is a city of nearly 10 million souls — more than London, Paris, or Shanghai. Lagos, in case you're curious, is the fastest-growing major metropolitan area in the world, with an annual population explosion of 5 percent. (If that doesn't sound so bad, consider that it would put Lagos at 33 million people in the year 2020, which would be more than Tokyo, the current topper.) The population density of Lagos is second only to Hong Kong, at roughly 150,000 people packed into each square mile (on average, that's 15 times as crowded as New York City).

In order to increase the population density, you have to either increase the number of people in a city or decrease the physical boundaries of the city and scrunch everyone closer together. The same goes for resolution. If you want a higher resolution (more pixels per inch), you can either decrease the physical dimensions of the image or increase the file size (pixel dimensions) by adding pixels to the image. For example, the two images in Figure 4-3 have the same file size, but the smaller image has twice the resolution of the larger image — 180 pixels per inch versus 90 ppi.

Figure 4-3:
Two images
with the
exact same
number of
pixels but
subject
to two
different
resolutions.

Conversely, population density goes down as people die or as the boundaries of the city grow. For example, if we were to mandate that Lagos spread out evenly over the entire 360,000 square miles of Nigeria, the population density would temporarily drop to 28 people per square mile (assuming, of course, that the other 110 million Nigerian residents happened to be on vacation at the time). Likewise, when you increase the dimensions of an image or delete some of its pixels, the resolution goes down.

Before you get the mistaken idea that this analogy is completely airtight, I should in all fairness mention a few key differences between a typical image and Lagos:

- Although I've never been there, I imagine that Lagos has its crowded spots and its relatively sparse areas. An image, by contrast, is equally dense at all points. Unlike population density, therefore, resolution is constant across the board.

✔ An image is always rectangular. Having misplaced my aerial map of Lagos, I can't swear to its shape, but I imagine that it's rather free-form.

✔ Population density is measured in terms of area — you know, so many folks per square mile. Resolution, on the other hand, is measured in a line — pixels per linear inch. So an image with a resolution of 180 pixels per inch contains 32,400 pixels per square inch. (That's 180 squared, in case you're wondering where I got the number.)

✔ The pixels in an image are absolutely square. The people in Lagos are shaped rather arbitrarily, with undulating arms and legs jutting out at irregular and unpredictable angles.

✔ You have total control over the size and resolution of an image. Like it or not, Lagos is entirely out of your hands.

Changing pixel dimensions

The top two option boxes in the Image Size dialog box enable you to change an image's *pixel dimensions* — the number of pixels wide by the number of pixels tall. (The number of pixels in your image is also known as the *file size*.) Unless you want to risk ruining your image — or you really, really know what you're doing when it comes to pixels — avoid these option boxes like the plague.

Lowering the Pixel Dimensions values can be dangerous because what you're really doing is throwing away pixels. And when you delete pixels, you delete detail. Figure 4-4 shows what I mean. The physical size of all three images is the same, but the detail drops off from one image to the next. The first image contains 64,000 pixels and is printed at a resolution of 140 ppi; the second contains ¼ as many pixels and is printed at 70 ppi. The third contains only 4,000 pixels and has a resolution of 35 ppi. Notice how details such as the shadows from the girl's eyelashes and the distinction between individual hairs in her eyebrows become less pronounced and more generalized as the pixel population decreases.

Increasing the file size (by raising the Pixel Dimensions values) isn't such a hot idea either, because Photoshop can't generate image elements out of thin air. When you raise the Pixel Dimensions values, Photoshop adds pixels by averaging the preexisting pixels (a process computer nerds call *interpolation*) in a way that may result in image softening and never results in the miraculous reconstruction of detail.

If changing the pixel dimensions is so dangerous, you may wonder why Photoshop gives you the option to do so at all. Well, although I don't recommend ever adding pixels to an image, you may need to lower the pixel dimensions on occasion. If your file size is really large — that is, your image contains a ton of pixels — you may want to toss some of the pixels overboard.

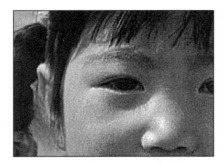

Figure 4-4:
Three images, each containing fewer pixels and printed at a lower resolution than the image above it.

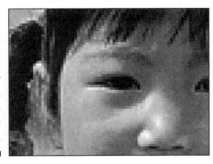

In an ideal world, you'd want as many pixels as possible because more pixels means greater image detail. But the more pixels you have, the more disk space the image consumes, which can be a problem if you're working with limited computing resources. Large file sizes can also slow down Photoshop substantially. Also, if you're publishing your image on the Internet, you may want to reduce your file size so that users can download the image more quickly. Finally, you may need to lower the pixel dimensions in order to make an image print at the size you want.

Even when you dump pixels from an image, however, you shouldn't attack the job from the Pixel Dimensions options boxes; I show you a better way in the steps in the section "Using the Image Size dialog box safely" later in this chapter.

In some particularly nerdy circles, changing the number of pixels in an image is called *resampling*. The idea is that you sample the photograph when you scan it — as if that makes a lick of sense — so any adjustment to the quantity of pixels after scanning is resampling. Photoshop uses the term resampling, but I prefer to call it *resizing*, because this gives folks a fighting chance of understanding what I'm talking about. But just be aware that there are computer aficionados out there who will gladly stick their noses high in the air, trade shocked stares with one another, and mutter pronouncements such as "Don't tell me she has mouse privileges," or "Gad, did you hear what it said?" These things must be endured.

Yeah, okay, but what resolution should I use?

The Auto button in the Image Size dialog box is supposed to generate a perfect Resolution value based on the line screen that your printer will use. The only problem is, no one knows what a line screen setting is. Rather than bother with trying to explain this arcane bit of printing technology to you at this point — what with your head already spinning with Lagos population data — I decided to come up with both ideal and acceptable values for certain kinds of print jobs. See whether these work for you.

Type of Job	Ideal Resolution	Acceptable Setting
Full-color image for magazine or professional publication	300 ppi	225 ppi
Full-color slides	300 ppi	200 ppi
Color ink jet printers	300 ppi	200 ppi
Color image for laser printing or overhead projections	180 ppi	120 ppi
Color images for multimedia productions and World Wide Web pages	72 ppi	72 ppi
Black-and-white images for imageset newsletters, flyers, and so on	180 ppi	120 ppi
Black-and-white images for laser printing	120 ppi	90 ppi

Keep in mind that there are no hard-and-fast rules about resolution settings. You can specify virtually any resolution setting between the ideal and acceptable settings and achieve good results. (If your commercial printer or service bureau tells you that you're getting bad results because your resolution doesn't match some exact ideal, consult a different company; this excuse is an example of a bad carpenter blaming his tools.) Even if you go with a Resolution value that's lower than the suggested acceptable setting, the worst that can happen is that you'll get fuzzy or slightly jagged results. But there is no wrong setting.

Changing the physical dimensions of the image

The Width and Height boxes in the Output Size portion of the Image Size dialog box reflect the actual printed size of your image and the approximate size of your image when distributed over the World Wide Web. (Because monitors may vary from user to user, the actual size of the image may change a little when viewed on different monitors.)

The pop-up menus next to the Width and Height options let you change the unit of measure displayed in the option boxes. For example, if you select picas from the Output Size Width pop-up menu, Photoshop converts the Width value from inches to picas. (A pica is an obscure typesetting measurement equal to ⅙ inch.) The percent option in the pop-up menu enables you to enter new Width and Height values as a percentage of the original values. Enter a value higher than 100% to increase the print size; enter a value lower than 100% to reduce the print size.

When you change the Output size of the image, either the Resolution value or the number of pixels in the image automatically changes, too, which can affect the quality of your image. For more information, read the section "Resolving resolution" earlier in this chapter. And for details on how to change the print size without ruining your image, see the section "Using the Image Size dialog box safely" later in this chapter.

Keeping things proportionate

Both pairs of Width and Height option boxes in the Image Size dialog box list the dimensions of your image in the current unit of measure. If you enter a different value into either option box and click on the OK button (or press Enter), Photoshop resizes your image to the dimensions. Pretty obvious, eh?

But strangely, when you change either the Width or Height value, the other value changes, too. Are these twins that were separated at birth? Is there some new cosmic relationship between Width and Height that's known only to outer-space aliens and the checkout clerk at your local grocery store? No, it's nothing more than a function of the Constrain Proportions check box, which is turned on by default. Photoshop is simply maintaining the original proportions of the image.

If you click on the Constrain Proportions box and turn it off, Photoshop permits you — in a very generous spirit, I might add — to adjust the Width and Height values independently. Notice that the little link icon (labeled back in

Figure 4-2) disappears, showing that the two options are now maverick independents with reckless disregard for one another. You can now create stretchy effects like the ones shown in Figure 4-5. In the first example, I reduced the Width value by a factor of two and left the Height value unchanged. In the second example, I did the opposite, reducing the Height value and leaving the Width value unaltered.

Matching images to columns

What's the meaning of the Columns option in the Print Size Width pop-up menu? Oh, man, you would ask that. All right (sigh), I suppose I'd better tell you.

You see, Photoshop is capable of precisely matching the width of an image to the columns in a printed document. So, for the sake of argument, say that you're working on an image that you eventually want to place into PageMaker. This specific PageMaker document happens to be a three-column newsletter. Each column is 2 inches wide, and the gutter (space) between each column is ¼ inch wide.

To match Photoshop column settings to those in PageMaker, you choose Edit⇨Preferences⇨

Units & Rulers and enter the column specs — in this case, 2 and 0.25 — into the Column Size option boxes, highlighted in the following figure. (Select inches from the pop-up menus if you want to use inches.) From that point on, a column in the Image Size dialog box conforms to your settings. One column, for example, is 2 inches wide; two columns is 4¼ inches wide — 4 inches for the two columns and the extra ¼ inch for the gutter.

Columns is not an option in the Height pop-up menu (inside the Image Size dialog box) because columns run up and down, not left to right. In other words, columns make no sense as a system of measurement for height.

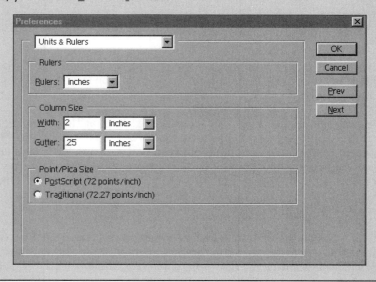

Figure 4-5:
Known to
friends and
family as Kid
Squishums,
this
versatile
little tyke is
the result of
deselecting
the
Constrain
Proportions
check box.

However, in order to deselect the Constrain Proportions check box, you have to select the Resample Image check box. As explained later, in the section "Using the Image Size dialog box safely," when the Resample Image check box is selected, Photoshop either adds or deletes pixels from your image to compensate for the changes to the width and height of the image. Because adding pixels can make your image look like mud, never increase the width or height value with Constrain Proportions deselected. Decreasing the width and height values is okay, as long as the Resolution value stays in the acceptable range (see the sidebar "Yeah, okay, but what resolution should I use?" earlier in this chapter for recommended resolution values).

Using the Image Size dialog box safely

As mentioned earlier in this chapter in the section "Image Size, Resolution, and Other Tricky Pixel Stuff," you have three image attributes — size, resolution, and dimension — all vying for your attention and all affecting each other. These attributes, in fact, are like three points on a triangle. Change any one of the points, and at least one of the others has to change proportionately. If you decrease the file size (number of pixels), for example, either the physical dimensions (printed size) or resolution (number of pixels per inch) must also decrease. If you want to increase the physical dimensions, you have to increase the file size — add pixels, in other words — or decrease the resolution.

Thinking about all the possible permutations can drive you crazy, and besides, they aren't the least bit important. What is important is that you understand what you can accomplish with the Image Size dialog box and that you know how to avoid mistakes. So, now that I've provided all the background you need, it's finally time for me to offer a modicum of fatherly advice:

- Changing the Pixel Dimensions (file size) values can be deadly, as explained in the section "Changing pixel dimensions." To avoid changes to file size, deselect the Resample Image check box at the bottom of the Image Size dialog box. When you deselect the option, the Image Size dialog box changes, and the Width and Height options in the Pixel Dimensions portion of the dialog box become unavailable to you. A link icon also connects the Print Size's Width, Height, and Resolution option boxes, showing that changes to one value affect the other two values as well.

- In order to turn off the Constrain Proportions check box, you have to turn on the Resample Image check box. If you make changes to the image Width and Height values, Photoshop *resamples* (adds pixels by averaging pre-existing pixels) the image. If you lower the Width and Height values, you'll probably be okay. But if you try to raise the Width and Height values, you're likely to muck things up.

- Want a surefire method to tell whether you've changed the file size? Your image looks different on-screen after you change the Resolution or Print Size values and exit the Image Size dialog box. As long as the file size remains unchanged, you won't see any difference — none, zilch, zippo — on-screen. On-screen, Photoshop just shows your image pixels with respect to screen pixels; resolution and dimension enter into the equation only when you print the image. Therefore, you want the image to look the same on-screen after you get done fiddling around with the Image Size command.

✔ If you manage to mess up everything and change one or more settings in the Image Size dialog box to settings that you don't want to apply, you can return to the original settings by Alt+clicking (Option+clicking on a Mac) on the Cancel button. Pressing Alt (Option on a Mac) changes the word Cancel to Reset; clicking resets the options. Now you have your original settings back in place so that you can muck them up again. If you already pressed Enter (Return on a Mac) to exit the Image Size dialog box, choose Edit➪Undo or press Ctrl+Z (⌘+Z on a Mac) right away to undo your changes.

✔ If you performed *another* action after you erroneously resized, you will find, to your dismay, that you can't undo the resize by pressing Ctrl+Z (⌘+Z on a Mac). That command lets you undo only your very last action. Don't dismay. You can undo your mistakes by using the magnificent and powerful History palette (see major details in Chapter 11).

✔ Whatever you do, be sure to use the Bicubic setting in the Resample Image pop-up menu. I'd tell you what *bicubic* means, but you don't want to know. Suffice it to say that it keeps Photoshop running smoothly.

✔ If you want to change the unit of measure that displays by default in the Image Size dialog box pop-up menus, choose Edit➪Preferences➪Units & Rulers and select a different option from the Units pop-up menu.

You may think that changing the image size is something that you never want to do. But you may, in fact, want to reduce the image size on some occasions — to get the image to print at a certain size, to enable your computer to handle the image, or to make the image download faster from the Internet. The following steps show you how to reduce your image size without turning your image into a worthless pile of goo.

Before you follow these steps, choose File➪Save As to save a backup copy of your image. The steps result in Photoshop tossing away pixels, and after you delete pixels, you can't get them back after you close your file. So always make a copy of the original in case things don't work out or you decide you want to use the original again at a later date.

1. **Open the image at the highest resolution possible.**

   For example, if you're opening a Photo CD image, select the 2048 by 3072 option from the Resolution pop-up menu. If that doesn't work — Photoshop may complain that you don't have enough memory to pull it off — try again and select the 1024 by 1536 option. Whatever works, go for it.

2. **Choose Image➪Image Size to open the Image Size dialog box.**

3. **Note the values in the Pixel Dimensions Width and Height option boxes.**

   You may want to write 'em down — they're important.

4. **Enter your desired print width and height in the Output Size option boxes.**

   If you want Photoshop to retain the original proportions of your image, make sure that the Constrain Proportions option box is checked.

5. **Enter your desired resolution in the Resolution option box.**

   Check the sidebar, "Yeah, okay, but what resolution should I use?" earlier in this chapter for some suggestions on acceptable resolution values if you need help.

6. **Check the Pixel Dimensions values.**

   Did either of the values get bigger? If so, you need to reduce your Output Size Width and Height values or lower the resolution. Otherwise, Photoshop adds pixels to your image, and you won't be happy with the results.

   If the Pixel Dimensions values got smaller, on the other hand, proceed to Step 7.

7. **Make sure that the Resample Image check box is selected.**

8. **Make sure that the Bicubic option is selected in the Resample Image pop-up menu.**

9. **Click on the OK button.**

   Photoshop resizes — or, if you prefer, *resamples* — your image in accordance with your perfect settings. If you don't like the results, press Ctrl+Z (⌘+Z on a Mac) or choose Edit⇨Undo *immediately* to put things back to the way they were. And, again, if you perform another action after sizing, the History palette (see Chapter 11) is available for undoing.

Playing It Super-Safe: Using the Resize Image Command

Okay, now that you patiently let yourself be informed of the do's and don'ts of image sizing, I'll tell you about the Resize Image Wizard (Resize Image Assistant on a Mac). (And if you jumped right to this section for the easy way out, definitely read the preceding section first before using this feature.)

Find this feature under Help in the Photoshop menu bar. The Wizard (Assistant on a Mac) presents a dialog box (as shown in Figure 4-6) that asks you questions regarding your wants and intended use for the image and then steps you through the resizing process. If you choose options that it feels are unwise, it warns you that you're lowering your image quality. You can then step back and try another setting. The Wizard (Assistant on a Mac) creates a new file, calling it `Resize Wizard_1`, thereby not disturbing your original. All in all, the Resize Image Wizard (Assistant on a Mac) is pretty smart, but like anything, the more *you* know, the better decisions you can make.

Whereas the Resize Image Wizard (Assistant on a Mac) has some value, the File⇨Automate⇨Fit Image command has very little. Based on numbers that you enter for width and height, Photoshop resizes your file as close to the dimensions as possible, while maintaining the same aspect ratio (proportions). The problem is that Photoshop stretches or shrinks your image while leaving the resolution the same. In other words, it resamples the image. If you're enlarging your image, this process could reduce image quality drastically. I recommend reading this chapter and using the guidelines presented, plus your own brain power, to size images.

Figure 4-6: The Resize Image Wizard (Assistant on a Mac) steps you through the sizing process.

What Does This Canvas Size Command Do?

You should know about one more command related to the topic of image sizing: Image⇨Canvas Size. Unlike the Image Size command, which stretches or shrinks the photograph, the Canvas Size command changes the size of the page — or canvas — on which the image sits. If you increase the size of the canvas, Photoshop fills the new area outside the image with white, the default color (or the background color). If you make the canvas smaller, Photoshop crops the image.

When you choose Image⇨Canvas Size, the dialog box, shown in Figure 4-7, pops up from its virtual hole. You can play with the options found in the dialog box as follows:

- ✔ Enter new values into the Width and Height option boxes as desired. You can also change the unit of measurement by using the pop-up menus, just as in the Image Size dialog box.

- ✔ You can't constrain the proportions of the canvas the way you can in the Image Size dialog box. Therefore, the Width and Height values always operate independently.

- ✔ The Anchor section shows a graphic representation of how the current image sits inside the new canvas. By default, the image is centered in the canvas. But you can click inside any of the other eight squares to move the image to the upper-right corner, center it along the bottom edge, or place it where you like.

- ✔ If you reduce either the Width or Height value and press Enter (Return on a Mac), Photoshop asks you whether you really want to crop the image. If you click on the Proceed button (or press Enter (Return on a Mac)) and decide you don't like the results, you can always choose Edit⇨Undo or press Ctrl+Z (⌘+Z on a Mac) to restore the original canvas size.

Figure 4-7:
Use the
Canvas Size
dialog box
to change
the size of
the page on
which the
image sits.

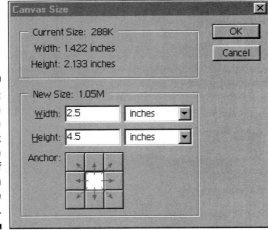

Chapter 5

Auntie Em versus the Munchkins (Death Match)

*I*n case you're wondering what the title of this chapter means, it's all about color — the same kind of color that Dorothy encountered when she passed over the weather-beaten threshold of her old Kansas porch onto a path of lemon-yellow bricks in that beloved classic, *The Wizard of Oz*. As you might imagine, Auntie Em represents the world of black and white, and the Munchkins represent the wonderful world of color.

With that in mind, you might think that Auntie Em is pretty well doomed. I mean, how can one woman cope with an entire Oz full of rowdy Munchkins? And how can drab black and white compete with rich, beautiful color?

Well, I'm rather fond of black and white myself. To me, the absence of color offers its own special attractions. It's the mysterious essence of a torch-lit castle on a stormy night. It's the refreshingly personal vision of a 16mm short-subject film you stumble across one evening on Bravo. It's the powerful chiaroscuro of an Ansel Adams photograph or a Rembrandt oil. In an age when every screen, page, and billboard screams with color that's more vivid than real life, black and white can beckon the eye like an old friend.

But on the off chance you think all that's a pretentious load of hooey, I can tell you one area in which Auntie Em kicks major Munchkin keister, and that's cost. Despite the increasing influence of computers in print houses, color printing remains extremely expensive. Major four-color magazines — including the ones I write for — spend more on ink than they do on their writers. The color medium costs more than the message, and that's a sad fact.

Though by no means free, black-and-white images are substantially less expensive to reproduce. Only one ink is involved — black. Other supplies, such as film and plates for the printing press, are kept to a minimum. Black-and-white printing is also incredibly versatile. You can print black-and-white images with any laser printer, you can photocopy black-and-white images using cheap equipment, and you can fax black-and-white images with relatively little loss in quality. And finally, black-and-white images require one-third of the overhead when you're working in Photoshop, meaning that you can edit black-and-white images that contain three times as many pixels as color images without Photoshop complaining that it's out of memory. I'd say that this is one match in which Auntie Em can be counted on to hold her own. No surprise, really. Farm women are well-known troupers, while the Munchkins — to hear Judy Garland tell it — were a bunch of randy booze hounds.

Whether you choose black and white, color, or — like most folks — vacillate between the two, this chapter tells you how it all works. You find out how to use color, create colors that you can apply with the painting tools, and switch between color modes. Not bad for a chapter based on an old MGM musical, eh?

Looking at Color in a Whole New Light

To understand color in Photoshop, you have to understand a little color theory. To this end, I want you to do me a favor and open some random color image that you have sitting around. Chances are that you'll see the telltale initials RGB inside parentheses in the image title bar. (If you don't, try opening a different image.) These initials mean that all colors inside the image are created by blending red, green, and blue light.

Red, green, and blue? That doesn't sound particularly colorful, does it? But, in fact, these colors are the primary colors of light. The red is a vivid scarlet, the green is so bright and tinged with yellow that you may be tempted to call it chartreuse, and the blue is a brilliant Egyptian lapis. It just so happens that these colors correspond to the three kinds of cones inside your eyeball. So, in theory, your monitor projects color in the same way your eyes see color.

Surfing the color channels

To get a hands-on feel for the inner workings of a color image, follow these
steps:

1. **Open an RGB image.**

    Oh, you already did that. My mistake.

2. **Choose Edit⇨Preferences⇨Display & Cursors.**

    The Preferences dialog box shown in Figure 5-1 appears.

    The Preferences dialog box actually contains several panels of options.
    You switch between the panels via the pop-up menu at the top of the
    dialog box. Another way to display the dialog box is to press Ctrl+K
    (⌘+K on a Mac), which brings up the Preferences dialog box with the
    General preferences panel showing. Then press Ctrl+3 (⌘+3 on a Mac)
    or choose Display & Cursors from the pop-up menu to display the
    options shown in Figure 5-1. After you close the dialog box, you can
    redisplay the last panel you visited by pressing Ctrl+Alt+K (⌘+Option+K
    on a Mac).

3. **Select the Color Channels in Color check box and then press Enter
   (Return on the Mac).**

    Highlighted in the figure, this option makes the individual components
    of red, green, and blue color appear in red, green, and blue. These com-
    ponents of color are called *channels*.

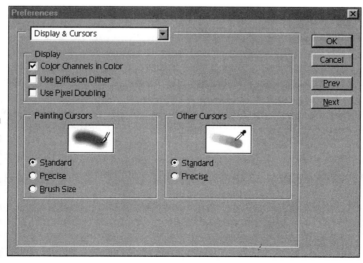

Figure 5-1:
Select the
Color
Channels in
Color option
to see how
the primary
colors work.

4. **Press Ctrl+1 (⌘+1 on a Mac) to view the red channel.**

   You see a black-and-red image. Notice that the RGB in the title bar changes to Red to show that you're viewing the red channel. This image is the one being sent to the red cones in your eyes.

5. **Press Ctrl+2 to view the green channel and then press Ctrl+3 to view the blue channel.**

   (On a Mac, press ⌘+2 to view the green channel and then press ⌘+3 to view the blue channel.)

   These images are the ones being sent to your green and blue cones.

6. **Press Ctrl+~ (tilde) (press ⌘+~ on a Mac) to return to the full-color RGB view.**

   You can find the tilde key in the upper-left corner of the keyboard, next to the 1 key. To type an actual tilde, you have to press the Shift key, but you don't need to press Shift to invoke the full-color view shortcut. The shortcut really is Ctrl+` (grave) (⌘+` on a Mac) because pressing the key without Shift accesses the grave mark. But Photoshop prefers to label this shortcut Ctrl+~ (⌘+~ on a Mac), so I follow suit.

   When you press Ctrl+~ (⌘+~ on a Mac), you can see the red, green, and blue channels all mixed together.

Pretty nifty, huh? Here's another way to think about it: If you were to take the images you saw in the red, green, and blue channels, print them to slides, put each of the slides in a different projector, and shine all three projectors at the same spot on a screen so that the images precisely overlapped, you would see the full-color image in all its splendor. Check out Color Plate 5-1 for the pictorial representation.

Now try something different. Choose Edit⇨Preferences⇨Display & Cursors or press Ctrl+Alt+K (⌘+Option+K on a Mac) to redisplay the Display & Cursors panel of the Preferences dialog box, but this time, turn off the Color Channels in the Color check box. Now look at the color channels again by pressing Ctrl+1, Ctrl+2, and Ctrl+3 (⌘+1, ⌘+2, and ⌘+3 on a Mac). Each channel looks like a standard black-and-white image. Figure 5-2, for example, shows the contents of the red, green, and blue channels as they appear in black and white.

Mixing red, green, and blue to create color

Every channel contains light areas and dark areas, just like a black-and-white image. With the Color Channels in Color check box turned off, you can really see these light and dark areas without a bunch of distracting colors getting in your way (which is why the option is off by default). The light and dark pixels from each channel mix together to form other colors.

Red

Green

Blue

Figure 5-2:
The black-
and-white
channels
combine to
make a
full-color
image.

The following list explains how corresponding pixels from the different channels mix together to form a single full-color pixel.

✔ A light pixel from the one channel mixed with dark pixels from the other two channels produces the color from the first channel. For example, if the red is light, and green and blue are dark, you get a red pixel.

✔ Light pixels from the red and green channels plus a dark pixel from the blue channel form yellow. This description may sound weird — two colors, red and green, mixing to form a lighter color — but that's exactly how things work in the upside-down world of RGB. Because you're mixing colors projected from a monitor, two colors projected together produce a still lighter color.

Are you with me? No? Well, suppose you had a flashlight with a red bulb and your friend had one with a green bulb. I don't know, maybe it's Christmas or something. At any rate, if you were to point your flashlight at a spot on the ground, the spot would turn red. No surprise there. But if you then said, "Look, Nancy, it's the missing key from the old Smithers place," and your friend pointed her green flashlight at the same spot, the spot wouldn't get darker, it would get lighter. In fact, it would turn bright yellow. "Gee wizikers, Ned, do you suppose this means Mrs. Johnson is innocent after all?" I'm afraid we'll never know.

✔ Light pixels from the green and blue channels plus a dark pixel from the red channel make a bright turquoise color called cyan. Light red and blue pixels plus a dark green pixel make magenta.

✔ By a strange coincidence, cyan, magenta, and yellow just happen to be the main ink colors used in the color printing process. Well, actually, it's not coincidence at all. Color printing is the opposite of color screen display, so the two use complementary collections of primary hues to produce full-color images. The difference is that because cyan, magenta, and yellow are pigments, they become darker as you mix them. Yellow plus cyan, for example, make green. This doesn't affect how you edit RGB images, but I thought you might find it interesting.

✔ Light pixels from all three channels mix to form white. Dark pixels form black. Medium pixels make gray.

Although all of this is highly stimulating, I have a feeling that it would make more sense if you could see it. If you're the visual type, take a look at Color Plate 5-2. The left side of the figure shows the RGB combinations I just discussed. The right side shows RGB mixes that result in other colors, including orange, purple, and so on. Give it the once-over and see whether you can't feel your brain grow by leaps and bounds.

Using the Channels palette

Keyboard equivalents, such as Ctrl+1 (⌘+1 on a Mac) and Ctrl+2 (⌘+2 on a Mac), aren't the only way to access different channels. You can also use the Channels palette. Choose Window⇨Show Channels to display the Channels palette, shown in Figure 5-3. Here's how to use the palette:

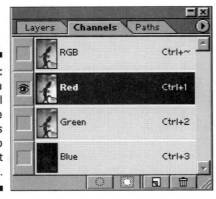

Figure 5-3:
Click on a channel name in the Channels palette to view that channel.

✔ To switch to a different channel in the palette, simply click on its name. Figure 5-3 finds me clicking on the Red channel.

✔ To return to the full-color RGB view, click on the top item in the Channels palette or press Ctrl+~ (tilde) (⌘+~ on a Mac).

✔ The Channels palette includes little thumbnails of the contents of each channel. To change the size of these thumbnails, choose Palette Options from the Palette menu — click on that little right-pointing arrowhead just beneath the title bar — and select a different Thumbnail Size icon.

Photoshop 6 Color Management

Now that you have basic color theory, it's time for basic color management. Color management seems to be the thorn in every Photoshop user's side. To make matters worse (or better, depending on your point of view), Photoshop 6 comes with some complex color management and color conversion capabilities. Even seasoned users may find some of them baffling and mysterious, so I'll boil it down to the essentials, and let you go on to fun stuff.

People want to be able to have a true WYSIWYG (What You See Is What You Get) world. In other words, they want to be able to look at their monitor and get the exact colors they see come out the other end. This "other end" can be in the form of printouts or viewing the image on the Web from another monitor. Getting this exact color is next to impossible. There are devices that can help — expensive hardware and software calibrators that come with high-end monitors — but most of us average Joes have to manage this dilemma on our own. Photoshop 6 does provide some help and it has improved from Version 5.5.

First, you want to calibrate your monitor and identify it to Photoshop. Next, tell Photoshop what color space you want to work in. Then provide Photoshop with directions on how you want your images and the ones you receive from other people to convert from one color space to another. Photoshop embeds *color profiles* that identify the color space of the image and then uses that info to convert colors when it's opened on another computer that uses a different working color space from yours. Finally, you want to define a color profile for your print space before you send your image off to be printed. Luckily, you have to tell Photoshop all this stuff only once. Follow these steps to calibrate your monitor (see Figure 5-4) using the Gamma Wizard:

1. **Choose Start⇨Settings⇨Control Panel and double-click on Adobe Gamma. (On a Mac, choose Apple⇨Control Panels⇨Adobe Gamma.)**

2. **Choose the Control Panel option and click on the Next button.**

   The Control Panel appears, giving you all the necessary setup options in one dialog box.

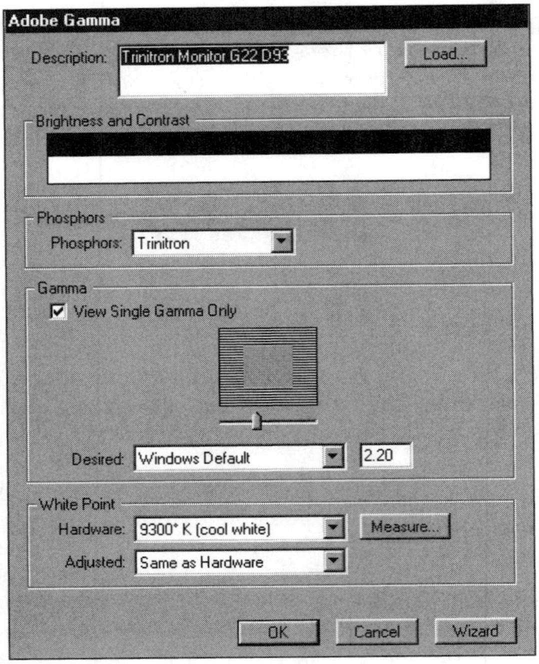

Figure 5-4:
The Adobe
Gamma
Control
Panel helps
you
calibrate
your
monitor.

3. **In the middle of the dialog box, uncheck View Single Gamma Only. Then, using each of the sliders, make the inner colors match the outer colors for the red, green, and blue color swatches. Leave the other settings as they are.**

   If you aren't sure whether a setting is correct, check the documentation that came with your monitor or call the vendor. When you're done, Photoshop knows everything about your monitor.

4. **Click on OK.**

Choosing your color settings

You need to tell Photoshop what color space you want to work in. A working space uses a specific range of colors (depending on which one you select) for all the images you create. Photoshop displays accurate colors by converting the colors from a working space to your monitor. If Photoshop knows your working color space (the source) and your monitor (the destination), the program can do its color conversion intelligently. This entails choosing your color settings. You need to do this same process of choosing settings with CMYK, grayscale, and spot color images. Then you need to tell Photoshop how you want to deal with converting colors in files embedded with color profiles that are different from yours. The Color Settings dialog box, shown in Figure 5-5, is the color "Command Central." Here are the steps for choosing the right color settings:

1. **Choose Edit⇨Color Settings.**

   If you're about to throw this book in the fireplace over this color business, you can hand the reins to Photoshop and let the program recommend the best settings for you.

2. **In the Settings pop-up menu, choose Web Graphics Defaults if you're a Web designer. If you primarily focus on preparing graphics for print, choose U.S. Prepress Defaults, unless you're going to print your images in Europe or Japan.**

   In which case, choose the corresponding default setting. Forget the other options, unless you're a color management guru and know exactly what you're doing.

3. **If you feel independent, you can choose your own settings. Under Working Spaces, choose an RGB color space.**

   If you deal with Web images only, you should try sRGB, which represents the standard PC monitor. Print images work best with Adobe RGB (1998), which is based on a high-definition TV screen. If you work with both kinds of images, I recommend Adobe RGB (1998) as the best overall RGB color space.

4. **Select a CMYK color space.**

   This setting defines a space for CMYK images that will be printed on an offset printing press.

   I recommend talking with your print representative and getting his or her advice on this setting. If that's impossible, stick with U.S. Web Coated (SWOP) for use with coated paper stock or U.S.Web Uncoated for use with uncoated paper.

5. **Select a grayscale color space.**

   Again, if you plan to do a lot of offset printing, talk to your print representative about the dot gain percentage you should use. *Dot gain* occurs when ink is applied to paper and spreads slightly due to the absorbency of the paper stock. If you can't get any advice, stick with Dot Gain 20%. If you're dealing with Web graphics primarily, leave the grayscale color space setting at Gray Gamma 2.2. This setting works well for the standard PC monitor.

6. **Select a spot color space.**

   I'll say it one last time, talk to your print rep about the dot gain percentage you should use. Or you can set it to Dot Gain 20%. (For more information about spot color, see Chapter 7.)

7. **Establish your Color Management Policies:**

   - Set RGB to Convert To Working RGB
   - Set CMYK to Preserve Embedded Profiles
   - Set Grayscale to Off
   - Uncheck the Profile Mismatches and Missing Profiles options

   When you save an image, Photoshop embeds a color profile that tags the image with your working color space. And when you open an image, Photoshop deciphers that embedded color profile. If the file you're opening has a color profile that doesn't match your working color space, Photoshop recognizes this and does any number of things depending on how your Color Management Policies are established. The program ignores the embedded profile if you select Off. It can Preserve Embedded Profiles and use the profile as the working color space for the image. Or it can Convert To Working, which converts the colors in the image from the embedded profile to your working color space.

   I recommend converting RGB images to match your own color space. However, CMYK images are usually set up for specific printers and presses and shouldn't be changed. Grayscale images, however, usually don't need any color management. By unchecking the Profile Mismatches, Photoshop won't prompt you for a response every time it encounters a mismatch. It just gives you a courtesy message, which you can choose to not show again. By unchecking Missing Profiles, you ensure that every time Photoshop opens an image without a profile, it assigns a profile (based on your working color spaces) when you save it.

   By the way, forget about the Advanced options. It offers additional controls and profiles and is way more information than you need to deal with.

8. **Click on Save. Name the file and click on Save again.**

   Save your settings so that you always have access to them just in case someone makes changes to your computer.

9. **Add any comments in the Color Setting Comment dialog box.**

   Your saved settings are now among the list of Settings options. Your comments appear in the Description area at the bottom of the dialog box.

   Just to make sure this stuff about color management is crystal clear, I'm giving you a real-world example. Assume that your RGB working space is Adobe RGB (1998). Suppose that a Web designer friend of yours creates a file in Photoshop on his computer, and his RGB working space is sRGB. Assume that Ask When Opening for our Profile Mismatches option is unchecked. He e-mails you a file. When you open the file, you're confronted by an Embedded Profile Mismatch dialog box, shown in Figure 5-6, that says his embedded profile, sRGB, doesn't match the current

RGB working space, Adobe RGB (1998). You're then asked how you want to proceed — use the embedded profile (sRGB), convert it to your working space Adobe RGB (1998), or discard the embedded file and forget the whole color management thing. Of course, if you read my earlier dissertation, you'll do the right thing and choose convert, and all will be well with the world.

10. Click on OK.

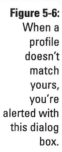

Figure 5-5:
The Color Settings dialog box gives your color conversion directions to Photoshop.

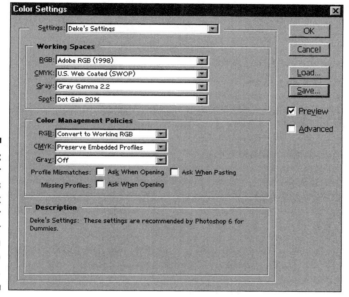

Figure 5-6:
When a profile doesn't match yours, you're alerted with this dialog box.

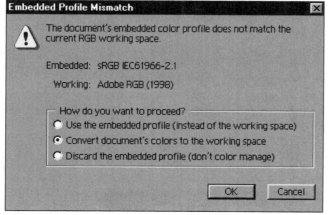

You may have had the experience of getting a color print of your image to see how it will print on another output device, such as an offset press. Now you can view an on-screen preview so that you can see how your image will look when it's printed on a particular printer or viewed on another monitor. Photoshop calls this preview a *soft proof*. But beware that the reliability can be questionable and depends on factors such as the quality of your monitor, lighting in your environment, and the accuracy of your monitor profile (set up in Adobe Gamma). To view a soft proof, choose View⇨Proof Setup. Choose Custom to proof on a specific printer. Choose Working CMYK to view using your current CMYK Working Space. This option is great for seeing how your RGB scan will look when it is printed on an offset press. Or you can choose Macintosh RGB or Windows RGB to see how your image will look on a standard Mac or PC monitor. Then choose View⇨Proof Colors to turn on the option .

Being Your Own L.J. Grand Master Funky Glow

In case you're hip-hop impaired, L.J. stands for Light Jockey, and that's exactly what you have to be to create colors in Photoshop. In other words, to define a color, you have to specify the quantities of red, green, and blue that go into it.

Uh, just so you don't go and make a fool of yourself the next time your kid's friends come over by saying something painfully embarrassing like, "Hey, check me out, I'm L.J. Grand Master Funky Glow!," I thought that I should admit that L.J. isn't a real hip-hop term. I just made it up. I mean, for all I know, L.J. means lemon juice or lantern jaw in today's imaginative middle-school lingo. "You're what, Dad? A lentil jar?"

Juggling foreground and background colors

In Photoshop, you can work with two colors at a time: a *foreground color* and a *background color*. Some tools and commands paint your image with the foreground color; others splash it with the background color.

The two colors are displayed in the lower portion of the Toolbox. As shown in Figure 5-7, the foreground color is on top, and the background color is on the bottom. To get some idea of how these colors work, read the following list. (Skip the following list if you'd like to remain ignorant on the subject of grounds, fore and back.)

Figure 5-7:
The small
collection of
color icons
in the
Toolbox.

✔ The foreground color is applied by the painting tools, such as the Airbrush, Paintbrush, and Pencil.

✔ When you use the Eraser tool, you're actually painting with the background color. (Unless you're on a layer, in which case you would erase to transparency. For more on layers see Chapter 15.)

✔ When you increase the size of the canvas using Image➪Canvas Size (as explained in Chapter 4), Photoshop fills the new empty portion of the canvas with the background color.

✔ The Gradient tool creates a rainbow of colors between the foreground and background colors (assuming that you use the default gradient option, Foreground to Background, as explained in Chapter 14).

The Toolbox includes a few icons that enable you to change the foreground and background colors, swap them around, and so on.

✔ Click on the foreground icon to display the intensely complex Color Picker dialog box, which is filled with about 17,000 options you don't need to know anything about.

✔ Press Esc or click on Cancel to leave that dialog box. Then pick up a Bible or some other holy relic and swear that you'll never go back there again. The next section tells you a better option for defining the foreground and background colors.

✔ Click on the background color to go to that same terrible dialog box. Hey, didn't I specifically instruct you to stay out of there?

✔ Click on the defaults icon (refer to Figure 5-7) to restore the foreground color to black and the background color to white.

✔ Click on that little two-way arrow icon — childishly labeled Swap 'em in the figure — to swap the foreground and background colors with each other.

✔ You can also access the default and swap 'em icons from the keyboard. Press D to restore the default colors, black and white. Press X to swap the foreground and background colors.

Defining colors

You can define the foreground and background colors in Photoshop in four ways:

✔ Click on the foreground or background color icon in the Toolbox and battle your way through the Color Picker. If you read the preceding section, you know that I think that this option is a real stinkeroo and should be avoided at all costs.

✔ Use the handy-dandy Color palette.

✔ Use the Eyedropper tool to lift colors from your image.

✔ Use the Swatches palette.

Using the Color palette

To define colors using the Color palette, shown in Figure 5-8, choose Window⇨ Show Color or press the F6 key. You should see three slider bars labeled R, G, and B (for Reginald, Gertie, and Bert). If you don't see them, choose RGB Sliders from the palette menu. (Click on the → in the upper-right corner of the palette to display the menu.)

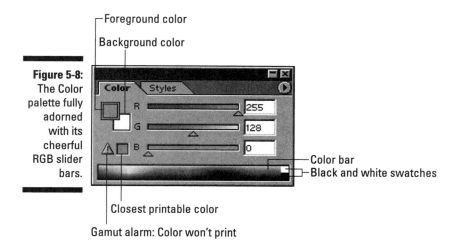

Foreground color

Background color

Figure 5-8:
The Color
palette fully
adorned
with its
cheerful
RGB slider
bars.

Color bar

Black and white swatches

Closest printable color

Gamut alarm: Color won't print

Here's how you go about changing a color using the Color palette:

1. Decide which color you want to change.

The palette offers its own foreground and background color icons, as labeled in Figure 5-8. Click on the icon for the color you want to change. A double outline surrounds the icon to indicate that it's selected.

Clicking on the selected icon again, or double-clicking it initially, takes you back to the dreaded Color Picker dialog box.

2. Drag the little RGB slider bar triangles to change the color.

Think of red, green, and blue as ingredients in baking the perfect color. You can add 256 levels of each of the primary hues, 0 being the darkest amount of the hue, 255 being the lightest, and 128 being smack dab in the middle. For example, if you set the R slider to 255, the G slider to 128, and the B slider to 0, you get a vibrant orange, just like the one shown in the upper-right corner of Color Plate 5-2.

If you've never mixed colors using red, green, and blue, it can be a little perplexing at first. For example, folks often have a hard time initially accepting that all yellows and oranges are produced by mixing red and green. I encourage you to experiment. Better yet, I order you to experiment.

3. Click on the triangular alert icon if desired.

If a little triangle with an exclamation point (referred to as a *gamut alarm*) appears in the lower-left corner of the palette, Photoshop is pointing out that the color you have mixed won't print exactly as you see it on-screen. The color is said to be *out of gamut*. The RGB color spectrum has a large gamut, much larger than the CMYK gamut, and some of the colors cannot be printed, just viewed on-screen. The closest printable color appears inside a little square to the right of the alert icon. Click on either the icon or the square if you want to use the printable color instead.

Isn't the color on-screen the same as a color on the page? No, and the reason is the difference between the principles of colored light and colored pigments. Your monitor creates white by mixing the lightest amounts of red, green, and blue — the opposite of how things work on the printed page. Color printing exploits the fact that sunlight and man-made light (both referred to as "white light") contain the entire spectrum of visible light, including all shades of red, green, and blue. The primary printing inks — cyan, magenta, and yellow — are actually *color filters.* When white light hits cyan ink printed on a page, the cyan ink filters out all traces of red and reflects only green and blue, which mix to form cyan. Similarly, magenta is a green light filter, and yellow is a blue light filter, as illustrated in detail in Color Plate 5-3. This and other factors (such as purity of inks, variation of ink tints, whiteness of paper, and lighting conditions) result in the CMYK world, producing fewer and duller colors. Unfortunately you have to just accept it and go on with life.

Here are just a few other things I want to pass along about the Color palette:

- ✔ If you can't get the knack of using the RGB slider bars, you can select a color by clicking inside the color bar at the bottom of the palette. By default, all the colors in the bar are printable. (To make sure that this is true, right-click (Control+click on a Mac) on the color bar and select CMYK Spectrum from the pop-up menu.)

- ✔ If you look closely, you may notice Photoshop 6 has stuck a little black-and-white square at the end of the color bar to make it quick and easy to select those colors.

- ✔ Alt+click (Option+click on a Mac) on the color bar to change to the opposite color. For example, if the foreground color is active, Alt+click (Option+click on a Mac) to select the background color. If the background color is active, Alt+click (Option+click on a Mac) to select the foreground color.

- ✔ If you want to set the foreground or background color to a shade of gray, you can set all sliders to the same value. Or better yet, choose Grayscale Slider from the palette menu and adjust the single K slider. (K stands for black.)

Lifting colors with the Eyedropper tool

You can also change the foreground or background colors by lifting them from the image. Just select the Eyedropper tool — on the right side of the Toolbox just above the Zoom tool — and click inside the image on the color you want to use. If you have more than one image open, you can even click inside an image different from the one you're working on.

Here's some stuff to know about this incredibly easy-to-use tool:

- ✔ You can press I (for I-dropper) to select the Eyedropper tool instead of clicking on its Toolbox icon.

- ✔ The Eyedropper affects whatever color is selected in the Color palette. So, if the foreground color icon is selected, the Eyedropper tool changes the foreground color, and if the background icon is selected — well, you get the idea.

- ✔ To select the opposite color — in other words, to select the background color when the foreground color icon is active or the foreground color when the background color icon is active — Alt+click (Option+click on a Mac) with the Eyedropper.

- ✔ You can temporarily access the Eyedropper tool when another tool is selected by pressing the Alt key (Option key on a Mac). As long as the key is down, the Eyedropper is available. This trick doesn't always work; in fact, it only works when you're using the Paint Bucket, Gradient, Line, Pencil, Airbrush, or Paintbrush tool. But it can come in handy.

- ✔ If you use the preceding tip, you can change only the active color in the Color palette. You need the Alt key (Option on a Mac) to change the opposite color, so you can't use the key to temporarily access the Eyedropper. You have to select the Eyedropper for real (click on its icon or press I) and then Alt+click (Option+click on a Mac). If your keyboard offers two Alt keys (Option keys on a Mac), it doesn't help to press both of them!

The Color Sampler tool looks like an eyedropper with a small target. The tool shares the flyout menu with the Eyedropper tool but it doesn't lift; it only measures the colors you click on.

Here's how to use this tool:

- ✔ Select the Color Sampler and click on the color you want. Notice the target that's added and labeled #1.

- ✔ Photoshop opens the Info palette and shows you the RGB formula of numbers for that color.

- ✔ You can repeat this procedure three times for a total of four targeted colors.

- ✔ Targets can be moved by dragging with the Color Sampler tool and deleted by holding down the Alt key (Option key on a Mac) and clicking on them.

- ✔ Measure a fifth color by just moving the cursor around the image.

Basically, the big use of the Color Sampler tool is to monitor changes to your image after you apply things like color correction (explained in Chapter 18) and filters (see Chapter 17).

Going Grayscale

Now that I've wasted most of the chapter on the colorful Munchkins, you may be wondering when I'm ever going to get around to discussing the much-lauded Auntie Em. Friends of Kansas, take heart, the heralded hour of black-and-white images has arrived.

The first thing to understand about black-and-white images is that the black-and-white world offers more colors than just black and white. It includes a total of 256 unique shades of gray and is therefore more properly termed *grayscale*. Each one of these shades is a color in its own right, which is why the term "black and white" can inspire fisticuffs among some grayscale devotees.

Second, all the stuff I told you about creating colors in the preceding sections of this chapter holds true for grayscale image editing, as well. You have a foreground and background color. You can define colors in the Color palette. (Be sure to choose Grayscale Slider from the palette menu so that you have to use just one slider bar.) And you can lift or measure colors from a grayscale image using the Eyedropper and Color Sampler tools.

But some aspects of grayscale editing are different than full-color editing, which is what led me to write the next two sections.

The road to grayscale

Most images that you'll come across will be in color. Most commercial images and all Photo CD images are in color. Scans from a commercial quick-printer or service bureau may be in color or in grayscale, but you never know. My point is that working in grayscale generally requires a conversion inside Photoshop.

Unlike a three-channel RGB image, a grayscale image includes only one channel of imagery. That's why the red, green, and blue channels all appear in black and white — each is its own grayscale image. If you plan to print in black and white, you should jettison all the extraneous color information, for two reasons. First, it's easier for Photoshop to keep track of one channel than three. In fact, given the same image size and resolution, Photoshop performs faster and with fewer problems when editing a grayscale image than when editing in color. Second, you can better see what your printed image will look like. When you're designing an image to be printed in black and white, color just gets in the way.

To convert a color image to grayscale, just choose Image⇨Mode⇨Grayscale. Photoshop asks you whether you want it to discard color information. You can click on OK or chicken out and cancel. That's all there is to it. You now have a single-channel grayscale image. No matter what color you choose in the Color palette, the color appears gray in the foreground and background color icons. If you don't like the results of your conversion to grayscale, you can go back to the full-color original by choosing Edit⇨Undo or pressing Ctrl+Z (⌘+Z on a Mac). However, this feature will undo only the last operation. If you perform some other actions and then decide you want to go back to color, you can retrieve the color by using the History palette (explained in detail in Chapter 11).

Before you change a color image to grayscale, you may want to make a backup copy of the original image, just in case you ever want to have the image available in color in the future. For details on saving images, see Chapter 6.

When you choose Image⇨Mode⇨Grayscale, Photoshop merges all three RGB channels together to create the new colorless image. But what if the contents of any one of the RGB channels strikes you as just right, and you want to simply dump the other two? The answer is to just go to that channel by pressing Ctrl+1, Ctrl+2, or Ctrl+3 (⌘+1, ⌘+2, or ⌘+3 on a Mac), and choosing Image⇨Mode⇨Grayscale. This time, Photoshop asks whether you want to discard all the other channels. If the channel you see on-screen is the one you want to keep, press Enter (Return on a Mac) to give Photoshop the go-ahead. Otherwise, click on Cancel and go back to channel surfing.

Figure 5-9 shows an example of the difference between converting all channels in an image and retaining just one. In the first image, I chose Image⇨Mode⇨Grayscale in the RGB view to merge all channels. The result is washed out, with little distinction between lights and darks. I didn't like it, so I chose Edit⇨Undo to restore my RGB image. Then I tiptoed through the channels to find something better, and wouldn't you know, the red channel looked just right. So after pressing Ctrl+1 (⌘+1 on a Mac), I again chose Image⇨Mode⇨Grayscale to toss out the green and blue channels, thus arriving at the second image in Figure 5-9.

Figure 5-9:
The difference between converting a color image to grayscale (left) and throwing away all but the red channel.

More grayscale tips from Auntie Em

Other chapters explain how to edit color and grayscale images, and Chapter 18 explains how to make automated adjustments, such as changing brightness and contrast. Here are my final grayscale tidbits:

- ✔ If you decide to convert a single channel from an RGB image to grayscale, you'll almost always want to use either the red or green channel. The red channel is generally lighter than the other two because skin tones gravitate toward red. The green channel is the detail channel, full of nice edges. Blue is the dark and dank channel. Except for skies and oceans, not much in this world is blue. Also, your eye contains fewer blue cones than red or green ones. Many scanners generate some pretty cruddy detail in the blue channel — knowing that you won't be able to see it.

- ✔ To add color to a grayscale image, convert back to RGB by choosing Image⇨Mode⇨RGB Color. Photoshop won't add a bunch of colors to the image, but it will let you add colors of your own.

- ✔ If you use the Image⇨Mode⇨Grayscale conversion method and your color image contains more than one layer (as explained in Chapter 15), Photoshop asks whether you want to flatten (merge) your image. If you want to keep your layers, click on the Don't Flatten button. If you use the single channel conversion method and your image contains more than one layer, the layers are flattened when you convert to grayscale. So, before you go ahead with the conversion, do all editing that involves layers and also make a backup copy of the layered image.

✔ If you're using an 8-bit monitor — that is, a monitor that can display only 256 colors — you're better off editing grayscale images. When you edit full-color RGB images, Photoshop shows only 256 of the 16 million possible colors at a time, resulting in *dithering,* an effect in which a random pattern of pixels is used to emulate lots more colors. When you edit a grayscale image, however, you can see every shade just right. Don't worry that Photoshop converts your entire screen to grays, including Finder icons and all other background items. This is a normal effect of editing in grayscale on an inexpensive computer system.

Chapter 6

Save Before You Say Good Night

. . . .

In This Chapter

▶ Saving an image to disk

▶ Updating images and making backups

▶ Understanding file formats

▶ Deciding when to use TIFF, EPS, JPEG, PICT, and other formats

▶ Using notes and audio annotations

▶ Quitting Photoshop

. . . .

*I*f you've used a computer before, you may be wondering why I devote an entire chapter to saving files. After all, you just press Ctrl+S (⌘+S on a Mac) and you're done, right? Well, if we were talking about any other program, I'd have to agree with you. If this book were about Microsoft Word, for example, I'd say, "Not to worry, Dear Reader, saving a file is so simple, a newborn lemur could pull it off with the most cursory supervision from a parent or older sibling." If this book were about PageMaker, I'd add, "Saving makes tying your shoes look like a supreme feat of civil engineering," all the while gently smiling and donning a cardigan sweater in a manner not unlike Mr. Rogers.

But this book is about Photoshop. And Photoshop, as you may or may not be aware, enables you to save images in more flavors than Willy Wonka manages to squeeze into an Everlasting Gobstopper. In the software world, these flavors are called *file formats,* and each one has a different purpose.

This chapter offers a thorough explanation of the saving process, including an exhaustive — well, okay, pretty decent review of the various file formats you can use. With this chapter by your side, Ctrl+S (⌘+S on a Mac) can be a pretty easy command, after all.

Save an Image, Save a Life

I don't know you from Adam — or Eve for that matter — but I'm guessing that you're the kind of person who doesn't like to spend hours editing an image only to see your work vanish in a poof of on-screen smoke as the result of some inexplicable and unforeseen computer malfunction. If you are indeed that kind of person, finding out how to save your image is essential. By saving your image early and often, you improve your chances of weathering any digital storm that may come your way.

Saving for the very first time

After applying the first few edits to your image, save it under a new name and — if necessary — specify where you want to store it on disk. If you do this, the original image remains untouched so that you can return to it at a later date for inclusion in a different project. You can also select the Save As a Copy option explained in Step 5 below. Here's how to save your customized image without harming the original:

1. **Choose File⇨Save As.**

   The dialog box shown in Figure 6-1 appears. If you're a veteran Photoshop user, you may notice that the Save As dialog box has grown somewhat. I explain each option as I go along.

   You can also open the dialog box by pressing Ctrl+Shift+S (⌘+Shift+S on a Mac).

2. **Enter a name into the File name option box.**

   PC users: Filenames can include as many as 255 characters (although a 255-character filename is beyond excessive, if you ask me). In both cases, the filename is followed by a three-character file extension (such as TIF) that indicates the file format (explained shortly). Don't use any spaces or special characters, such as ampersands or brackets, in your filenames. Stick with regular letters and numbers to be safe. You don't have to enter the extension because Photoshop does that for you.

   Photoshop lets you save a file with a lowercase extension. Note the check box at the bottom of the Save As dialog box. This option is also located in the Preferences dialog box in the Saving Files panel. Note that the lowercase extension option, whether checked or not, always overrides the Preferences setting.

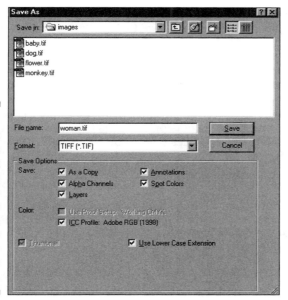

Figure 6-1 (Windows): Use this dialog box to name your image and decide where you want the image to hang out on disk.

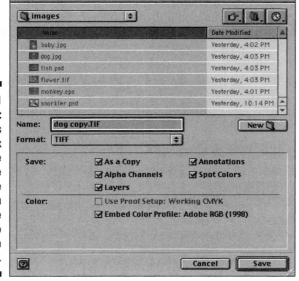

Figure 6-1 (Mac): Use this dialog box to name your image and decide where you want the image to hang out on disk.

Mac users: You can enter any name up to 31 characters long, putting periods and spaces anywhere you want them. Personally, I like to keep my filenames below 20 characters so that I can see them in their entirety at the Finder level. Longer filenames become abbreviated when viewed by name. For example, FamilyReunion.UnpleasantBrawl may appear as FamilyReunionUnpleasan...at the Finder. You also have the option of adding a three-character extension (such as TIF) that indicates the file format (explained shortly in the "Photoshopper's Guide to File Formats" section). The Append File Extension option is located in the Preferences dialog box under the Saving Files panel. You can choose Never, Always, or Ask When Saving. You can also choose to save a file with a lowercase extension. If you select the Ask When Saving option, check boxes for Append and Lower Case Extension appear in the Save dialog box.

For both platforms, I recommend always using the lowercase extension option. This option makes for fewer problems when creating images for the Web and for exchanging files between Macs and PCs.

3. **Select a format from the Format pop-up menu.**

   This is the point at which you have to deal with the image flavors I touch on in the introduction to this chapter. The pop-up menu provides all kinds of options, such as TIFF, JPEG, PICT, and others. I discuss the ramifications of the important formats later in this chapter.

   Some formats are restricted to certain kinds of images. For example, you can save only images that contain layers (as explained in Chapter 15) in the Photoshop, TIFF, or PDF formats. If a format is grayed out in the Format pop-up menu, that format isn't available for the kind of image you're trying to save.

4. **PC users, use the Save in pop-up menu to select the folder in which you want to save the image. Mac users, use the Mounted Volumes button, folder bar, and any other controls to hunt down the folder in which to save the image.**

   All of the controls in these menus are explained in Chapter 3.

5. **Select one or more of the next options. Note that availability is based on the type of image, file format, and whether the image has layers (more on layers in Chapter 15).**

   • **As a Copy:** Instead of giving your image a different name, you can check the As a Copy option. This option automatically adds the word "copy"after your filename, therby ensuring your original remains intact. In addition, this option keeps your current file open on your desktop.

   • **Use Proof Setup:** Checking this option will include a soft proof. A soft proof is an on-screen preview of how your image will look when it's printed on a specific type of printer. For now, leave it unchecked. You can read more on color management in Chapter 5.

- **Alpha Channels:** If you want to retain an alpha channel (a saved selection) in your image, check this option. Some file formats, such as EPS, can't support alpha channels.

- **Layers:** With this option checked, your image preserves all of its layers. If unchecked, your image is flattened into a background. (If this is fuzzy to you, check out Chapter 15.)

- **Annotations:** If you added notes or audio annotations to your file, you may choose to save or discard those notes (see the end of this chapter for more).

- **Spot Colors:** If you created a spot color in your file, you can choose to save the spot color with your file. (See Chapter 7 for details on spot colors.)

- **Embed Color Profile:** Checking this option embeds the color profiles you established in your Color Settings setup (see details in Chapter 5). By default, Photoshop, PDF, JPEG, TIFF, and EPS file formats have this option checked. My recommendation is to leave the defaults as they are, unless you have a very good understanding of color management.

6. **Click the Save button or press Enter (Return on a Mac).**

7. **If another dialog box appears, fill out the options and press Enter (Return on a Mac).**

    Some formats present additional dialog boxes that enable you to modify the way the image is saved. I explain this later in more detail.

Your image is now saved! Come heck or high water, you're protected.

The Thumbnail check box(es) at the bottom of the dialog box are visible (Mac) and accessible (PC) only if you've selected Ask When Saving in your Preferences under Saving. If you don't check the Thumbnail options when you save an image, you don't get a preview when you later try to open that image.

To make sure that Photoshop always saves previews, choose Edit⇨ Preferences⇨Saving Files. When the Preferences dialog box appears, select the Always Save option from the Image Previews pop-up menu. Press Enter to exit the dialog box. Now a thumbnail will be saved by default and the thumbnail options in the Save As dialog box will not be visible. And you don't have to worry about it anymore. The only time not to save a preview is when you're extremely limited on disk space; saving images with previews requires a bit more disk space than saving images without previews. The file-saving process also takes longer if you choose to save images with previews.

Joining the frequent-saver program

After you name your image and save it to disk for the first time, press Ctrl+S (⌘+S on a Mac) or choose File⇨Save every time you think of it. In either case, Photoshop updates your image on disk, without any dialog boxes or options popping up and demanding your attention. Then when something goes wrong — notice that I said when, not if — you won't lose hours of work. A few minutes, maybe, but that comes with the territory.

Creating a backup copy

If creating an image takes longer than a day, you'll want to make backup copies. The reasoning is that if you invest a lot of time in an image, you're that much worse off if you lose it. By creating backup copies — Dog1, Dog2, Dog3, and so on, one for each day that you work on the project — you're that much less likely to lose mass quantities of edits. If some disk error occurs or you accidentally delete one or two of the files, one of the backups will probably survive the disaster, further protecting you from developing an ulcer or having to seek therapy.

At the end of the day, choose File⇨Save As. The Save As dialog box appears, as when you first saved the image. Change the filename slightly and then click the Save button. Want to be doubly protected? More protection, you say? Save to another disk entirely. If the whole disk goes bad, you've got another. Triple protection!

Photoshopper's Guide to File Formats

Selecting a format is a critical decision. So, you need to pay attention to the sections to come, even if the subject is a rather dry one — which it is. Get a double espresso if you need one, but don't skip this information.

What is a file format, anyway?

Glad you asked. A *file format* is a way of saving the electronic bits and pieces that make up a computer file. Different formats structure those bits and pieces differently. In Photoshop, you can choose from about a zillion file formats when you save your image to disk, which makes things a tad bit confusing.

Luckily, you can ignore most of the file format options. The Raw format, for example, sacrifices colors and other image information, so avoid it. The Pixar, Targa, Scitex CT, and the new Alias PIX and Wavefront RLA formats are very sophisticated formats used by very sophisticated (and well-funded) creative types, so you can forget about those formats, too. In fact, you'll probably use only a handful of formats: TIFF, JPEG, EPS, and the native Photoshop format. If you plan on publishing your image on the World Wide Web, you may also want to use the CompuServe GIF format at times, too.

The following sections explain the most important file formats and when to use them.

TIFF: The great communicator

One of the best and most useful formats for saving Photoshop images is TIFF (pronounced *tiff*), which stands for Tagged Image File Format. TIFF was developed to serve as a platform-independent standard so that both Macintosh and Windows programs could take advantage of it. TIFF is an excellent file format to use for printed images. It can be imported into virtually every page layout and most drawing programs.

When you select the TIFF option from the Save As pop-up menu and click on the Save button, Photoshop displays another dialog box, shown in Figure 6-2. In the area labeled Byte Order, you can tell Photoshop whether to save the TIFF image for use on a Macintosh or Windows program. Unless you're going to open your image in a Mac program, select IBM PC. (Why are these options labeled Byte Order? Just to confuse you.)

The TIFF Options dialog box now offers several compression methods. If you select one of the methods, Photoshop compresses your image file so that it takes up less room on disk. The old LZW Compression doesn't sacrifice any data to make your file smaller and is great for compressing images with large sections of a single color. It's known as a *lossless compression scheme.* Zip compression is also a lossless scheme and works well with images containing large areas of a single color. Zip compression is common in the Windows world. The last compression method is JPEG, a lossy compression scheme, meaning that stuff is lost during the compression.

I recommend that you stick with LZW. Most programs that support TIFF also support LZW. For example, you can import a compressed TIFF image into either PageMaker or QuarkXPress. Only obscure programs don't support LZW, so there's really no reason not to select this option, unless your files are very large. In that case, LZW compression makes your files open and save more slowly. It's a trade-off between saving space or saving time — take your pick.

TIFF now supports saving with layers. If you check this option, Photoshop saves a flattened version along with the layered version to ensure compatibility with programs that can't read layers. If the term *layers* is fuzzy to you, check out Chapter 15.

You can use the Save Image Pyramid option to save multiple versions of an image. Each version has a lower resolution. The bottom of the pyramid is the full image. You can choose to open either the full image or one with a lower resolution. Not many programs, including the current version of Photoshop, support pyramid files right now. I'd leave this option unchecked.

And last, you have a Save Transparency option. If you check the Layers option and leave the Save Transparency unchecked, both layers (the flattened version and the layered version) and any transparent areas are preserved. If you leave both Layers and Save Transparency unchecked, your image will be flattened into a Background without any layers or transparency intact. If you leave the Layers option unchecked and the Save Transparency option checked, when you close the file, Photoshop prompts you with a message that says the file hasn't been saved completely because you have chosen not to save certain features in your previous save. In other words, Photoshop can't save transparent areas without also saving layers. Photoshop then asks if you want to save the document. If you choose Save, Photoshop preserves both layers and any transparent areas. If you choose Don't Save, Photoshop merges the layers into one layer without any preservation of transparency. For details on layers, backgrounds, and transparency, see Chapter 15.

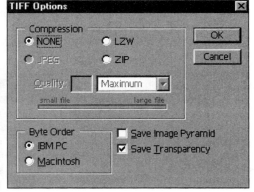

Figure 6-2:
The options that appear when you save a TIFF file.

JPEG: The space saver

Photoshop also supports the JPEG (pronounced *jay peg*) format. JPEG stands for some Joint Photographers convention, but that doesn't really matter. What matters is that the JPEG format uses *lossy compression*. Lossy is the computer nerd's way of saying that stuff is lost during the compression process — namely, some of the data that makes up your image.

The good news, however, is that you probably won't miss what's not around anymore — sort of like when you were a kid and you "lost" your little brother at the park. You may notice a slight difference in your on-screen image after you save the file using JPEG, but when the image is printed, the compression is usually undetectable.

Like LZW compression, JPEG compression saves you lots of disk space. In fact, a JPEG image takes up less space on disk than a compressed TIFF file — half as much space, maybe a tenth as much, depending on your settings. Although JPEG isn't supported by as many programs as TIFF, it's becoming more and more common. JPEG compression works well with continuous tone images, such as photographs.

So should you use JPEG or TIFF? My philosophy is this: Save in TIFF when excellent print quality is vital, for example, in high-resolution printing (see Chapter 4), or when you're editing an image. Then when you think you're finished editing and you want to conserve space, save in JPEG at the Maximum setting. You generally won't see the results of JPEG right away. But editing an image can bring out its weaknesses, and JPEG definitely weakens an image. So, it's best to go to JPEG after you finish editing. This isn't a hard-and-fast rule — I've edited plenty of JPEG images without incident — but it's good to be aware of the risks.

Also, if you want to distribute your image on the World Wide Web, you have to save it in either the JPEG, GIF, or the new and not yet widely supported PNG format. JPEG works well with photographic images, especially people, where there is a wide range of colors. TIFF isn't an option for Web publishing. For a rundown on Web images, refer to the JPEG section of Chapter 19.

When you choose the JPEG option in the Save As dialog box and press Enter (Return on the Mac), the dialog box shown in Figure 6-3 appears. Here's a rundown of the options you need to worry about for images you want to print:

✔ The Quality pop-up menu lets you choose the amount of compression that's applied to your image and therefore the quality of your saved image. The higher the image quality, the less the file is compressed and the more space it takes on disk.

✔ The Quality option box and the slider bar beneath the box give you other ways to choose your compression setting. In this version of Photoshop, the slider bar and option box give you access to 13 settings (0 through 12), whereas the pop-up menu gives you access to only four. But, unless you're a real control freak like me, you can just select one of the pop-up menu options.

✔ Choose the Maximum or High option from the Quality pop-up menu. The Maximum option is best because it preserves the most image data, but the High option is okay if you're really short on disk space.

✔ For Format options, use the default setting of Baseline ("Standard").

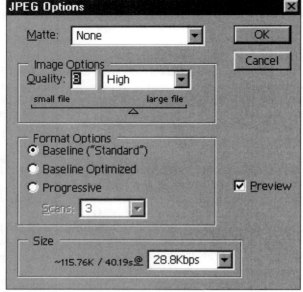

Figure 6-3:
When saving a JPEG file, select the Maximum option or, if space is limited, select the High option.

Photoshop recompresses a JPEG image every time you save it. During a single edit session, this compression won't hurt because JPEG works from the on-screen version. But, if you close, reopen, and resave it in JPEG format, some damage, albeit small, occurs. Repeat this process over and over, however, and the damage increases each time. Some advice — apply all of your necessary edits to the image, save in JPEG format, and leave well enough alone. If you need to edit an image over a longer length of time, it's better to save it as a native Photoshop format. Then save it as a JPEG only after you have completed your editing process.

GIF: For Webbies only

As mentioned above, *GIF* (pronounced *jiff* or *giff*), which was developed for CompuServe specifically for transferring images via modem, is the other option you can consider when you want to distribute your image online, whether on CompuServe, America Online, or the World Wide Web. To get the lowdown on GIFs in all their glory, see Chapter 19.

EPS: The 10 percent solution

EPS (pronounced *E-P-S*) stands for Encapsulated PostScript. PostScript is a page-description language used by many printers such as LaserWriters, Xerox, Linotronic imagesetters, and hundreds of others. Although TIFF and

JPEG can save only images, the EPS format accommodates anything that the printer can print. Unfortunately, an EPS image takes up considerably more disk space than the same image saved in the TIFF format — even more if the TIFF image is compressed.

For the most part, EPS is used by high-end professionals producing high-end projects, for example, if you want to create expert color separations (see Chapter 7) from QuarkXPress or Adobe InDesign. Laymen, however, will want to save in EPS format for images with clipping paths, where a selected portion of the image is transparent (explained in Chapter 12). In addition, EPS is the format of choice for importing to and from drawing programs such as Illustrator, FreeHand, and CorelDraw. By and large, however, you can ignore the EPS format 90 percent of the time and use TIFF instead.

PICT: The generic picture format for Mac users

Apple developed *PICT* as the primary format for Macintosh graphics. Just as EPS is based on the PostScript printer language, PICT is based on the QuickDraw screen language. Although you may think that PICT is the best option for Mac graphics, it can be a rather shaky format. Just about every Macintosh graphics program supports PICT, but support varies. PageMaker, for example, does a terrible job of printing imported PICT images.

Sometimes, I choose PICT if I'm going to be using the image only in Photoshop, however, because it offers JPEG compression. Say that you select the PICT File option from the Format pop-up menu in the Save dialog box and press Return. Assuming that QuickTime is running — Apple's digital video system extension that installs with Photoshop — a dialog box with options appears.

If you're saving a grayscale image, the Resolution options are 2, 4, and 8 bits per pixel. Color images offer Resolutions of 16 and 32 bits per pixel. But regardless of which Resolution options you see in the dialog box, don't change them! Doing so deletes colors from your image and prevents you from accessing the JPEG options.

The JPEG compression options available to PICT files are different than those available to the regular JPEG format. JPEG compression in a PICT file can cause more damage over time — nothing serious, just something to keep in mind. I suggest always selecting the JPEG (Maximum Quality) in the PICT File Options dialog box.

PICT-formatted images are mostly used for graphics to be incorporated into slides, screen presentations (like PowerPoint), multimedia projects, and digital video.

BMP: The wallpaper format for PC users

BMP is a popular format for saving graphics that you want to make part of your computer's systems resources, such as the wallpaper that you see behind your desktop. (Chapter 22 gives you the step-by-step procedure for turning one of your Photoshop images into wallpaper.) Programmers also use BMP to create images that appear in Help files.

When you save a file in the BMP format, the dialog box shown in Figure 6-4 appears. Don't worry about changing the radio button settings; use the defaults that Photoshop picks for you. If you're creating wallpaper, don't select the Compress (RLE) check box; Windows doesn't recognize files saved using this compression scheme. Otherwise, the compression scheme is a lossless (good) one, so select Compress (RLE) if you can.

Figure 6-4:
The BMP format is used mostly to create wallpaper for the Windows desktop.

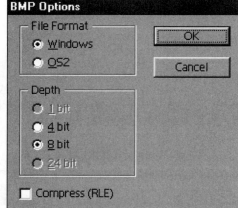

What about the native Photoshop format?

The Format pop-up menu in the Save As dialog box offers one other important format choice: the native Photoshop format.

The Photoshop format, along with TIFF and PDF (see Chapter 19 for more on PDF), are the only formats that save the layers in your image; all the others "flatten" (merge) the layers together.

If you need to open a Photoshop 6 image in earlier versions of the program, you can use the Photoshop format without much worry. Versions 3, 4, 5, and 5.5 can open files saved in the Version 6 native format, although some features may be altered or, in some cases, may disappear altogether.

Like TIFF, the Photoshop format offers a lossless compression scheme. And Photoshop can open and save images faster in its native format than in any other format. But some programs do not support the native format. So, use the native format when you're sure the program you plan to import the image into supports it and you don't need JPEG compression.

Make sure, really sure, absolutely sure, that you do not check the option Maximize Backwards Compatibility in Photoshop Format (bigger files) in the Saving Files panel in the Preferences dialog box. Note that the option is checked on by default, so make sure that you uncheck it.

Why uncheck it, you ask? The Photoshop file format option inserts a flattened (merged) version of the image in your file, which tremendously increases the file size. The option is supposed to ensure compatibility between Photoshop and programs that support the Photoshop file format, but not layers. However, it's not worth the tremendous increase it creates in the file size. If you want to be able to use the image in other applications, save a copy of the image in a TIFF or JPEG format.

What format to use when

Ooh, you cheated, didn't you? You skipped right over the sections on how formats work and why they were invented. Instead of reading all that juicy background information I offered — information that would help you make your own decision about which format to use — you want me to make the decision for you.

Okay, fine. You plunked down good money so that I would make understanding Photoshop 6 easy for you, so I suppose that I can give you a break just this once. Think of the following list as your study guide to File Formats. Just don't blame me when you're standing around at a cocktail party and the discussion turns to JPEG compression versus LZW, and you don't have an intelligent word to offer.

- ✔ If you're just going to use the image in Photoshop, save the image in the Photoshop format. You can open images saved in this format in Versions 3, 4, 5, and 6. And, if you really have to, you can open images in Version 2.5 as well (if you turn on the Maximize Backwards Compatibility in Photoshop Format (bigger files) option in the Preferences dialog box, as discussed in the preceding section), but layers, grids, guides, and other features won't be available to you in Version 2.5.

- ✔ If your image contains layers (as explained in Chapter 15) and you want to preserve those layers, choose the Photoshop format. Also, you can now save layers in the TIFF and PDF formats.

- ✔ If you want to import your image into another program, use TIFF, as long as you have the available disk space.

✔ If you want to import your image into another program and you don't have the available disk space, use JPEG.

✔ If you want to import your image into a program that doesn't support either TIFF or JPEG or you have a clipping path, resort to EPS (see Chapter 12 for information on paths).

✔ If you're creating a photograph for online distribution, use JPEG. For high-contrast graphics or partially transparent images, use GIF (see more on these in Chapter 19).

✔ If you're creating wallpaper to amuse your coworkers or just yourself, use BMP and turn off RLE compression.

Leaving a Friendly Reminder

After a long day of image editing, wouldn't you like to leave yourself or another interested party a digital reminder of what you just did or what is left to do with a particular image? Who wants to keep track of a bunch of notes written furiously on pieces of scrap paper? Well, Photoshop has now given you some tools to keep that clutter off your desk. The new Notes tool enables you to write and save a note on your image. And the new Audio Annotation tool lets you create and save a message in an audio format. Check 'em out in Figure 6-5. Here's the scoop on these two clutter savers:

✔ To use the Notes tool, simply click on the canvas, write the note, and close the box in the top left when you are done. The name at the top of the note defaults to the licensee of the Photoshop software, but you can change the name in the Options bar.

✔ You can change the font, font size, and note color in the Options bar, as well.

✔ To read a note, just double-click on the note icon.

✔ To delete a single note, click on the note once to select it and press the Backspace key (Delete key on the Mac).

✔ To delete all the notes, click on the Clear All button in the Options bar.

✔ To use the Audio Annotation tool, click the canvas. A dialog box with tape recorder-like controls appears. Click on Record, speak into your computer's microphone, and click on Stop when you're done. Click on Save or Cancel if you don't want to keep it.

✔ To play the annotation, simply double-click on the speaker icon and listen to the message.

✔ You can change the annotation color in the Options bar.

✔ To delete an annotation, click on it once to select it and press the Backspace key (Delete key on the Mac).

✔ To delete all the annotations, click on the Clear All button in the Options bar.

These are great tools for tracking progress and approval in a review or exchange process. But be aware that audio annotation can bloat your file size. If file size is a concern, stick to using notes that keep your file size lean and mean.

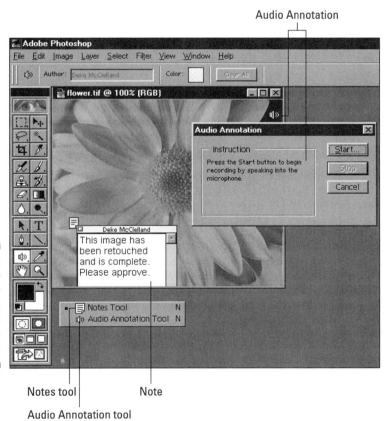

Figure 6-5:
Keep your desk clutter free with image notes and audio annotations.

Good Night, Image — Don't Let the Programming Bugs Bite

To put Photoshop to bed for the night, choose File➪Exit (File➪Quit on a Mac) or press Ctrl+Q (⌘+Q on a Mac). Photoshop may display a message asking you whether you want to save the changes you made to your image. Unless you have some reason for doing otherwise, press Enter (Return on a Mac) to select the Yes button. The program then shuts down.

If you don't want to save your changes, press the N key (Mac users, too), which is the same as clicking on the No button. If you decide that you aren't ready to say good-bye to Photoshop after all, click the Cancel button.

Chapter 7

Going to Hard Copy

. . . .

In This Chapter

▶ Making sure that your printer is ready to go

▶ Previewing the image on the page

▶ Selecting a printer, paper size, and page orientation

▶ Using the Page Setup command

▶ Printing multiple copies

▶ Creating and Printing a contact sheet and a picture package

▶ Making CMYK color separations

▶ Creating spot color separations

. . . .

*I*n case you don't already know, *hard copy* is a term for the printed page. The on-screen image is just a figment of your computer's imagination. The final printed piece is something tangible that you can really sink your teeth into (assuming that you're extremely hungry).

In this chapter, I explain how to go from on-screen, imaginary image to hard copy. But I have to confess that there's a lot I don't know. For example, I don't know what kind of printer you're using, I don't know what kind of cabling is installed, and I don't even know where the printer is located in your home or office. In other words, I'm suffering from a terrific deficit of knowledge. With this in mind, I ask for your sympathy and understanding as I explain — very briefly — how to print from Photoshop using an everyday, generic printer.

For starters, I'm going to be totally rash and assume the following:

✔ You have a printer. If I've said it once, I've said it, I don't know, two or three times: You must have a printer to print.

✔ Your printer is plugged in, it's turned on, and it doesn't have a 16-ton weight sitting on top of it. In other words, your printer works.

✔ The printer is properly connected to your computer. A cable running out of your computer and into your printer is a good sign.

> ✔ The proper printer software is installed on your computer.
>
> ✔ Your printer is stocked with ribbon, ink, toner, paper, film, chew toys, little bits of felt, spring-like gizmos that go "bazoing," or whatever else is required in the way of raw materials.

If you've used your printer before, everything is probably ready to go. But if something goes wrong, I advise that you call your local printer wizard and ask for assistance. Or you can try walking into the boardroom and wringing your hands and weeping in a cloying but professional way. This strategy has been known to produce the desired effects.

This May Be All You Need to Know about Printing

When things are in working order, printing isn't a difficult process. Though it involves slightly more than picking up your mouse and saying "print" into it, printing doesn't require a whole lot of preparation. In fact, a quick perusal of the following steps may be all you need to get up to speed:

1. **Turn on your printer.**

   And don't forget to remove that printer cozy your uncle knitted for you.

2. **Choose File⇨Save or press Ctrl+S (⌘+S on a Mac).**

   Although this step is only a precaution, it's always a good idea to save your image immediately before you print it because the print process is one of those ideal opportunities for your computer to crash. Your computer derives a unique kind of satisfaction by delivering works of art from the printer and then locking up at the last minute, all the while knowing that the image saved on disk is several hours behind the times. If you weren't the brunt of the joke, you'd probably think that it was amusing, too.

3. **Select a printer, paper size, and page orientation.**

   You accomplish all this inside the Page Setup dialog box, which you can display by choosing File⇨Page Setup, pressing Ctrl+Shift+P (⌘+Shift+P on a Mac), or clicking on the Setup button in the Print dialog box. You can display the Print dialog box by choosing File⇨Print or pressing Ctrl+P(⌘+P on a Mac).

   Mac users: If your Mac is on a network, you may have access to more than one printer. If so, select the printer you want to use with the Chooser. (By the way, the following sections in this chapter explain this step and others in more detail, should you need more information.)

4. **Check that the image fits on the page.**

   After you select a printer and set the paper size and orientation, press Enter (Return on a Mac) to close the Page Setup dialog box. Then press and hold on the page preview box in the lower-left corner of the Photoshop window to see a little preview of the printed page. The page preview box is just to the right of the magnification box. (If you can't remember where the preview box is located, see Chapter 3 for a refresher.) Photoshop displays a preview of how your image fits on your chosen paper size. The white area in the page preview represents the size of the page; the rectangle with an X through it represents the image. If the X fits entirely inside the white area, your image fits on the page. If the X exceeds the boundaries of the white area, the image is too big for the page and needs to be reduced. After you know whether the image fits or not, you can release your mouse button.

   If the image doesn't fit on the page, you can reduce the image by using the Image Size command, discussed in Chapter 4. Be sure to deselect the Resample Image check box so that you don't affect the number of pixels in the image. Then increase the Resolution value or decrease the values in the Print Size Width and Height option boxes. (You can find a complete explanation of the Image Size dialog box in Chapter 4.)

   Or, depending on your printer, you may also be able to scale (reduce) your image for printing in the Page Setup or new Print Options dialog boxes. Scaling the image through these dialog boxes changes the image size for printing only; the Image Size command permanently resizes your image.

5. **Choose File➪Print or press Ctrl+P (⌘+P on a Mac).**

   Photoshop displays the Print dialog box, covered in detail later in this chapter. In this dialog box, you can specify how many copies of the image you want to print.

6. **Press Enter (Return on a Mac).**

   Experts say that this is the easiest step. Well, one guy got a blister on the end of his finger, but otherwise the vote was unanimous.

Congratulations! You now have what is commonly known as a brand-new, 1-gram-baby piece of output. But on the off chance that you're unclear on how a couple of the preceding steps work or you're simply interested in excavating every possible nugget of information from this book, I encourage you to probe the depths of the rest of this chapter.

Choosing a Printer in Windows

If you have only one printer hooked up to your computer, you can skip this section entirely. But if you're part of a network or you have more than one printer available to you, you need to tell Photoshop which printer you want to use.

To select a printer, open the Page Setup dialog box. You can do this in several ways: Choose File⇨Page Setup, press Ctrl+Shift+P, or click on the Setup button inside the Print dialog box (choose File⇨Print or press Ctrl+P to open the dialog box). However you go about it, a dialog box similar to the one shown in Figure 7-1 appears. (Your dialog box may look slightly different depending on your printer and which version of the operating system you're using.)

To select a printer, just choose the printer name from the Name pop-up menu. Choose the paper size and printer tray from the two pop-up menus in the middle of the dialog box. (Other options in this dialog box are discussed in other sections in this chapter.) Click on OK or press Enter to exit the dialog box.

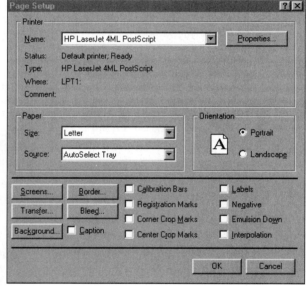

Figure 7-1:
You select a printer, paper size, and page orientation in this dialog box.

Choosing a Printer on a Mac

If you use the same printer day in and day out to produce pages of text and numbers, you probably don't need to worry about the Chooser. Provided with every Mac, this little program is designed to let you confirm the connection to your printer and select a different printer over a network. So, unless you just want to make sure that everything's okay or you want to specify the exact printer you intend to use, skip to the next section.

To access the Chooser dialog box, select the Chooser command from the Apple menu. The left side of the dialog box, as shown in Figure 7-2, contains a bunch of icons that represents the kinds of printer drivers that are available to your system. Not to be confused with the drivers you use to knock golf balls into uncooperative printers, these drivers serve as a liaison between your computer and your printer.

Printer drivers   Networked printers

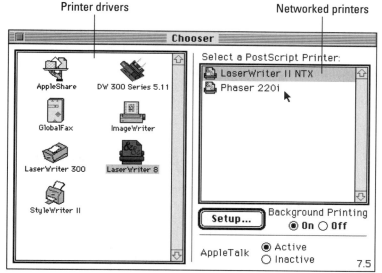

Figure 7-2:
You can
select the
kind of
printer you
want to use
from the
Chooser.

- ✔ If you use a PostScript device — meaning a printer that supports the PostScript printer language — select the LaserWriter Driver icon. Nearly every printer over $1,000 supports PostScript, which is, without a doubt, the professional printing standard.

- ✔ If you see a driver icon that matches your specific model of printer, select it. For example, if you own an Epson 840 and you installed the software that came with it, you should see an icon labeled Epson, which happens to look like your computer. You'd be plum crazy not to select it.

- ✔ Some fax/modems enable you to print to remote fax machines over the phone lines. If you own a fax/modem and it's cabled up correctly, you may be able to select a driver icon for the modem. Be warned, however, that faxing directly from Photoshop can sometimes be unreliable.

After you select a driver from the left-hand list, some additional options appear on the right side of the dialog box.

✔ If you're on a network, you see a list of networked printers. Select the printer you want to use by clicking on it.

✔ If you're not on a network, you are more likely to see two icons labeled Select a Printer Port. The first icon represents the printer port; the second represents the modem port. Select the port in which the printer is hooked up to the printer port, but some people do use the modem port.

After you finish doing all that stuff, click on the close box on the left side of the Chooser title bar. A message may appear telling you to confirm your settings using the Page Setup command. Don't worry, the next section explains how to do exactly that.

If any other message appears — one announcing that the printer is not available or has taken leave of its senses, for example — you very likely have a cabling problem or your printer is not turned on. Otherwise, you're in business.

Getting Image and Paper in Sync

Before you send your image to the printer, you need to make sure that the image you want to print actually fits on a piece of paper. To see whether all is well in this regard, you can utilize the quick and easy method (mentioned in the earlier section "This May Be All You Need to Know to Print") and click and hold on the page preview box in the lower-left corner of the image window. Photoshop displays a preview of how your image fits on your chosen paper size.

However, with this method the image preview isn't particularly accurate when it comes to showing the actual image. Well, Version 6 solves that shortcoming with the new Print Options feature, as shown in Figure 7-3. The huge Print Options dialog box gives you the opportunity to view your actual image as it will appear on the printed page. It also gives you tons of other print choices. Let's take a closer look at these options:

✔ Check the **Center Image** option to position your image. Deselect and enter new position values or simply drag your image preview thumbnail to your desired location on the page.

✔ The **Scaled Print Size** setting enables you to reduce or enlarge the image for printing only. Enter any percentage below 100% to reduce the dimensions of the printed image. The printer still prints all the pixels in the image, but the pixels are just smaller. You can also enter a value in either the height or width boxes. You'll notice that scale, width, and height are linked, meaning that changing any one affects the other two.

Figure 7-3:
You can
preview
how the
image fits
on the page
by using the
new Print
Options
dialog box.

✔ The **Scale to Fit Media** option enables the image to fit exactly on the size of the paper.

✔ **Show Bounding Box** places a box with handles around your image showing the precise image boundaries. This feature is handy if you have a white border around your image and can't quite tell the image boundaries by just the thumbnail.

✔ If you select a portion of your image using one of the tools I don't get around to discussing until Chapter 12, you can print the selected area only by selecting the option that says, surprise, Print Selected Area. If you just want to take a quick look at an isolated area, you can use this option to save time.

✔ **Show More Options** brings up the Color Management and Output options (a pop-up menu below Show More Options lets you toggle between the two). You'll also find these options in the Print and Page Setup dialog boxes. I'll discuss those options in the section "Sending the Image to the Printer." Notice that you can also access the Print and Page Setup dialog boxes by clicking on either button in the top right.

✔ One option that is exclusive to this dialog box is **Include Vector Data.** Checking this option enables Photoshop to send the vector data (mathematically defined objects), shapes, and type to a PostScript printer. Vector graphics are resolution independent so that they can be printed at any resolution without losing quality. However, checking this option increases the size of your file significantly. If you are sending vector data to a non-PostScript printer, you may notice your objects appear jagged. Don't be alarmed, it is just that non-PostScript printers are unable to render smooth edges for vector graphics.

✔ In addition to scaling and positioning your printed image, another possibility is to rotate the image on the page. For example, if the image is wider than it is tall, you can print it horizontally by rotating the page 90 degrees. To rotate the image on the page, choose File⇨Page Setup or press Ctrl+Shift+P (⌘+Shift+P on a Mac) to display the Page Setup dialog box, shown back in Figure 7-1. Or open the Print dialog box by pressing Ctrl+P (⌘+P on a Mac) and then click on the Setup button. Though your dialog box may not look exactly like the one shown in Figure 7-1, you should find two Orientation radio buttons: Portrait and Landscape. If you choose Portrait, your image prints upright on the page; if you choose Landscape, Photoshop rotates the image so that it prints sideways on the paper.

✔ The specific options found inside the Page Setup dialog box vary depending on the kind of printer you're using. Note that the Page Setup dialog box also offers a scaling option. Scaling options that let you reduce or enlarge the image for printing only. Mac users will probably find a Reduce or Enlarge option box somewhere within the Page Setup dialog box. Windows users, to hunt down this option, click on the Properties button. When the Properties dialog box appears, click on the Graphics tab. If you see a Scaling option, you're in business. As you'll notice however, you don't have as much flexibility as you do with the Print Options scaling feature.

✔ The Scaling value remains in effect until you open up the Page Setup dialog box and change it. So, if you don't want to scale future print jobs, be sure to change the setting back to 100% after you print the current image.

Keep in mind that changes made inside the Print Options and Page Setup dialog box have absolutely no effect on anything except how your image prints. You can't do any permanent damage via this particular dialog box, so feel free to change settings recklessly and without regard to personal safety.

Changes made inside the Image Size dialog box are another story. As I explain in Chapter 4, you can easily do permanent damage if you forget to deselect the Resample Image check box.

Sending the Image to the Printer

After you confirm that the image fits inside the page, choose File⇨Print or press Ctrl+P (⌘+P on a Mac) to display the Print dialog box, shown in Figure 7-4. If the image is still too large for the page, Photoshop displays an error message to warn you that a portion of your image will be cut off of the page and asks whether you want to proceed. If you say no, the error message disappears, and you can then resize the image to fit the page, as discussed earlier in this chapter. If you say that you want to go ahead and print anyway, the Print dialog box appears.

If you're absolutely confident that your image should fit on your selected paper size, but Photoshop still barks at you that it won't fit, check the page orientation (portrait or landscape) in your Page Setup dialog box. Even if your image fits on the paper, if it isn't oriented correctly Photoshop sometimes thinks it's too large.

Here's a breakdown of the options inside the Print dialog box:

- ✔ If you want to print more than one copy of the image, enter the number of copies you want into the Copies option box.

- ✔ As mentioned in the "Getting Image and Paper in Sync" section, you can also print just a selected portion of your image by choosing Print Selected Area. If you just want to take a quick look at an isolated area, this option can save time.

Taking a Look at Color Management Print Options

Version 5 gave us the concept of *color spaces.* Different devices operate in different color spaces. Monitors, desktop color printers, and high-end offset printers all have their own unique color space. The Color Management options of Version 6 enable you to convert the color space of your image while printing. For example, if your image color profile is Adobe RGB (1998), you can choose to have your image's color converted to the color space of your Epson printer upon printing. For more on color management, see Chapter 5.

These are the specifics of the Color Management print options:

1. **Select an option under Source Space.**

   Document: Uses the color profile of your image.

Proof Setup: Uses the color profile of your proof (Photoshop uses the profile you selected in the ViewProof Setup menu). For details on proofs, see Chapter 5.

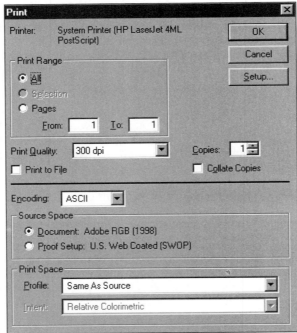

Figure 7-4 (Windows): The Print dialog box.

Figure 7-4 (Mac): The Print dialog box.

2. **Select an option for the Print Space.**

Under Profile, choose Same As Source to print using whatever profile you selected in Step 1, your Source Space. If you want to print using the color profile of another device, for example, an HP or Epson printer, choose that profile from the list.

Choose PostScript Color Management to print to a PostScript printer (PS level 2 or higher). With this option, Photoshop enables the *printer* to manage all the color conversion instead of Photoshop.

Under Intent, I recommend leaving it at the default setting of Relative Colorimetric.

If all you want to do is print color prints on your desktop printer, my recommendation is to first choose Document for your Source Space and choose Same As Source for your Print Space. Then print another copy using your printer's color profile for your Print Space, if you can find the profile in that monstrous list. Compare both copies to see which one looks better. If you have a late model printer, you may also want to check the documentation for the manufacturer's recommendations. If you don't have anything better to do, however, experiment with the different color spaces for both Source and Print Spaces and compare the output results. Before I let you move on, there are a couple of other options under Profile you should be aware of:

- ✔ The working CMYK option doesn't create color separations, incidentally. To accomplish that feat, read the following section. For an explanation on CMYK, check out Chapter 5.

- ✔ If you want to print your color image in grayscale, don't choose the Working Gray color space in the Print dialog box. Instead, convert the image to grayscale as described in Chapter 5. Doing so enables your file to print much faster.

That's it. Just click on the OK button or press Enter (Return on a Mac), and you're off. Depending on the size of the image, you should have a hard copy in a matter of a few minutes.

Creating and Printing a Contact Sheet

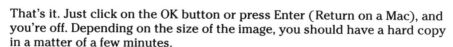

Photoshop has the capability of creating a digital version of a traditional contact sheet. This new feature takes a folder of images, creates thumbnails, and arranges them on a single page. It is good for record-keeping purposes because it enables you to catalog large quantities of files. It is also useful for merely checking out a big batch of images.

Here are the steps for creating and printing a contact sheet:

1. **Choose File⇨Automate⇨Contact Sheet II.**

2. **Click on the Choose button in the Contact Sheet dialog box (see Figure 7-5).**

   Locate the folder containing the images you want to print (refer to Figure 7-4). Count the number of images in your folder.

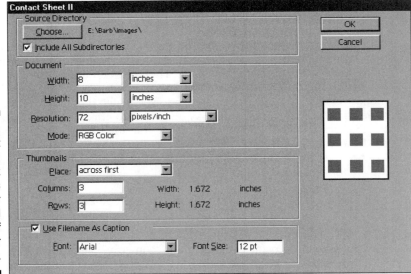

Figure 7-5:
The Contact Sheet dialog box presents options for size and layout of your thumbnails.

3. **Specify the size and resolution of the contact sheet.**

   Make sure to set the width and height large enough to accommodate all your images. If you are unsure about the resolution setting, see Chapter 4 for details.

4. **Specify a color mode — Grayscale, CMYK, RGB, or Lab Color.**

   For information on color modes, see Chapter 5.

5. **Specify the order and the number of columns and rows for your layout.**

   Again, be sure that the number of thumbnails you create can accommodate (or exceeds) the number of images in your folder.

6. **Choose whether you want to use the File Name As A Caption for your Contact Sheet.**

7. **Specify the Font and Font Size.**

   Version 6 now finally lets you set these specs to avoid captions getting cut off.

8. **Press Enter (Return on a Mac) or click on OK.**

   An automated process opens, copies, pastes, and positions each file. Depending on the number of images, this process may take a few minutes. When the process is complete, you should see a file similar to the one in Figure 7-6.

9. **Save the contact sheet and print it by using the guidelines in this chapter.**

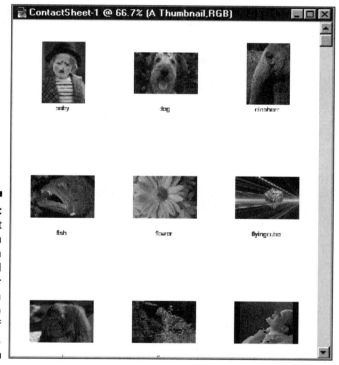

Figure 7-6:
Contact sheets can provide a good method for cataloging a large quantity of images.

Creating and Printing a Picture Package

Another Automate feature that may come in handy is Picture Package. This command fills a page with multiple copies of a single image, scaled to common print sizes, such as 5 x 7, 4 x 5, and wallet snapshots. If you're a photographer or you simply want to print some pictures of the kids for Grandma, this command does it all.

1. **Choose File⇨Automate⇨Picture Package.**

2. **Click on the Choose button in the Picture Package dialog box.**

   Locate your image.

3. **Choose your desired template from the Layout pop-up menu.**

   The preview gives you an idea of what the layout will look like.

4. **Specify a Resolution and color mode.**

   Check out Chapter 4 for more information on Resolution. For information on color modes, see Chapter 5.

5. **Press Enter (Return on a Mac) or click on OK.**

   An automated process opens, copies, pastes, and positions each file. Depending on the number of images, this process may take a few minutes. When the process is complete, you should see a file similar to the one in Figure 7-6.

6. **Save the picture package and print it by using the guidelines in this chapter.**

Printing Color Separations

So far, I've explained how to print *composite* images, in which all colors are combined together on a single page from your desktop printer. Unfortunately, color printing on a desktop printer may not be the best route to go if you intend on having more than 50 copies or so. Although desktop color printers are becoming more economical, they can be very slow, and in some cases, the quality may not be up to par. An increasingly popular intermediate step is short run, on-demand *digital printing,* such as Xeikon or Indigo prints. Digital printing takes your file directly from the disk to print, without the use of *color separations* (see the following section). The quality is very good and the cost can be reasonable.

Creating CMYK separations

After the quantity reaches 500 copies or more, it's wise to look into traditional offset printing. For this, you need to produce color separations. You print four pages, one each for the primary printing colors: cyan, magenta, yellow, and black. Then you let your commercial printer — the person, not the machine — combine the color separations to create mass quantities of colorful pages. This process is the same one used to create magazines, newspapers, and other professional color publications.

To print color separations of a full-color image from Photoshop, you have to go through these steps:

1. **Save your image to disk.**

   Before diving into CMYK, you want to make sure that your RGB image is backed up and safe from harm. If you need help, Chapter 6 provides assistance with the saving process. And if you need a color refresher, see Chapter 5.

2. **Choose Image⇨Mode⇨CMYK Color.**

   Photoshop converts the image from the world of RGB to the world of CMYK. Don't be shocked if your fiery reds and electric blues lose their heat and spark. Converting from RGB to CMYK often causes your image to look muddier and flatter. This is because the gamut (range of color) for CMYK is much smaller than it is for RGB, and colors that are out of the CMYK gamut get converted to their closest match. And that closest match is often not as vivid and bright. Unfortunately, it's the way of the world and there's nothing you can do about it. After the conversion, you have a four-channel image with one channel each for cyan, magenta, yellow, and black. You can even view the channels if you want by pressing Ctrl+1, Ctrl+2, Ctrl+3, and Ctrl+4 (⌘+1, ⌘+2, ⌘+3, and ⌘+4 on a Mac). (This channel thing is explained in Chapter 5.)

3. **Choose File to Print Options and inside the dialog box, check the Show More Options box and select Color Management from the Options pop-up menu.**

4. **Under Source Space select Document (refer to Figure 7-3).**

   It should say U.S. Web Coated (SWOP).

5. **Under the Print Space, select Separations from the Profile pop-up menu.**

   Selecting this option tells Photoshop to print each of the channels from the image to a separate page.

6. **Select Output from the Options pop-up menu. Click on Setup and check Calibration Bars, Registration Marks, Corner Crop Marks, Center Crop Marks, and Labels, as shown in Figure 7-7.**

   These five options print a series of alignment markings that prove very useful to your commercial printer. (If you're printing to a non-PostScript printer, some of these options may not be available; select the ones that are.)

   Version 6 now gives you a preview of all these printer marks around your image.

Be sure to select all these check boxes. If you miss any of them, your commercial printer may have problems lining up the images on the press, and your pages may come out like a page from the Sunday comics.

7. Click on Print.

When printed, each page looks like a standard black-and-white printout, but don't let that worry you. When you take your file to your commercial printer, a technician prints your file on plastic material, referred to as *film*, which is then transferred to sheets of metal called *plates*. Each plate is inked with cyan, magenta, yellow, or black ink. The technician prints all the pages with the cyan plate first. Then he runs the pages by the magenta plate and then the yellow plate and finally the black plate. The inks mix together to form a rainbow of greens, violets, oranges, and other colors.

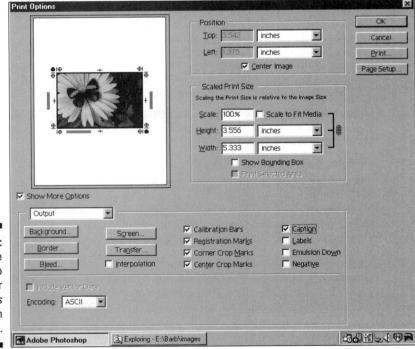

Figure 7-7: Check these options to print color separations from Photoshop.

For example, Figure 7-8 shows four color separations for the full-color photograph that appears in Color Plate 5-1. (Compare these separations to the red, green, and blue channels I included in Chapter 5, Figure 5-2, to get a feel for the dramatic changes that occur when you convert from RGB to CMYK.) Color Plate 7-1 shows the separations as they appear when inked with cyan, magenta, yellow, and black. I also show a few examples of how the inks look when combined.

Cyan   Magenta

Yellow   Black

Figure 7-8:
The black-and-white contents of the cyan, magenta, yellow, and black channels as they appear when printed to separate sheets of paper.

Creating spot color separations

Photoshop allows for *spot color separations*. Spot, or *custom,* colors are predefined colors — that is, premixed inks made by various ink companies, the most popular in the U.S. being Pantone. A spot color is generally used for a logo, type, or small illustration. Spot colors are also used when you need to apply metallic inks or varnishes (a clear, shiny coating). To output the additional separation, Photoshop adds a separate channel for the spot color, as shown in Figure 7-9.

To have Photoshop add a spot color to an Image:

1. **Select the artwork or type to which you want to apply the spot color.**

   Use one of the selection methods described in Chapter 12. If you're applying the spot color to type, press Ctrl+click (⌘+click on a Mac) on the type layer in the Layers palette (for more on layers, see Chapter 15). This action selects the type.

2. **Fill the selection with white.**

   Press the D key to get your default colors. Choose Edit to Fill, and set the Use option to Background and the Opacity option to 100%.

   Or Press Ctrl+Backspace (⌘+Backspace on a Mac). Make sure that you don't deselect.

3. **Select Show Channels under the Window menu. Choose New Spot Channel from the Channels palette pop-up menu or press Ctrl+click (⌘+click on a Mac) on the page icon at the bottom of the Channels palette.**

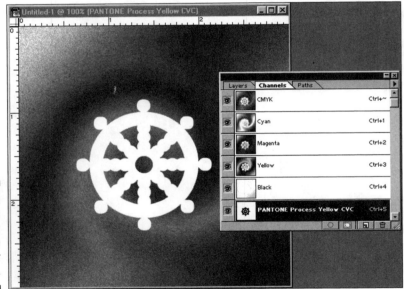

Figure 7-9: Photoshop adds a separate channel for spot colors.

4. **Under the Ink Characteristics option, click on the color swatch in the New Spot Channel dialog box and select your Pantone color from the Custom Colors dialog box.**

   If you get the Color Picker instead, click on the Custom button.

5. **Click on OK twice.**

   Doing so adds a new channel for the spot color and fills your selection.

6. **Save the image as either a native Photoshop or Photoshop DCS 2.0 (Desktop Color Separations) format. Deselecting the Include Halftone Screen and Include Transfer Function options is a good idea.**

   If you want to import the image into a different program, such as PageMaker or QuarkXPress, save in DCS 2.0 format.

Another way to choose spot colors is via the Swatches palette. Click on the palette pop-up menu and select your desired spot color library.

You can also choose Load from the pop-up menu and select multiple spot color libraries (holding the shift key down to select more than one item). And finally, you can also view the libraries by name and swatch by choosing Small List from the pop-up menu.

If you want to use spot colors, I highly recommend that you choose your color from a printed Pantone swatch book. Remember that your screen can only give you its best match to the printed color. For accuracy, the colors must be selected from the printed material.

Part III
Tiptoe through the Toolbox

The 5th Wave   By Rich Tennant

"I'VE GOT SOME IMAGE EDITING SOFTWARE, SO I TOOK THE LIBERTY OF ERASING SOME OF THE SMUDGES THAT KEPT SHOWING UP AROUND THE CLOUDS. NO NEED TO THANK ME."

In this part . . .

In real life, a paintbrush is a fairly static tool. You dip it in
paint and drag it across the canvas; in return, it paints a
line. The line varies depending on how much you dab onto
the brush and how hard you press, but your options are
limited. In Photoshop, on the other hand, a single tool is
capable of literally hundreds of variations. You can change
the size of the brush tip, the angle of the brush, the translucency of the paint, and the way colors mix — all at the drop
of a hat. You can even paint straight lines and change the
brush strokes from hard-edged to soft.

If painting isn't your primary interest, Photoshop provides
an assortment of editing tools for smearing colors, changing their focus, lightening or darkening pixels, and
adjusting the intensity of colors. You'll also find a Rubber
Stamp tool for cleaning up dust and hairs on an image and
an eraser for eliminating mistakes. All these tools go
beyond anything that's available in real life, providing a
degree of flexibility and forgiveness that natural media
simply don't offer.

But my favorite thing about Photoshop is the conve-
nience. No wiping up spills, no soaking brushes, and no
opening windows to clear the fumes. You just paint what
you want and erase what you don't want. Everything you
do on-screen is imaginary — until you print the image,
you haven't changed one scrap of real-life material — so
spills, stains, and fumes are a thing of the past. And when
it comes time to clean up for the day, you just press
Ctrl+Q (⌘+Q on a Mac), and you're finished. Who says
things aren't better now than they used to be?

Chapter 8

Paint Me Young, Beautiful, and Twisted

In This Chapter

▶ Using the Pencil, Paintbrush, and Airbrush tools

▶ Drawing straight lines with the painting tools

▶ Changing the brush size

▶ Creating your own custom brush

▶ Selecting brushes from the keyboard

▶ Creating translucent brush strokes

▶ Painting with strangely named brush modes

▶ Using the new drawing tools

*O*kay, here's a big assumption. As a novice or casual Photoshop user, you fall into one of two camps: artist or nonartist. Some people are so comfortable with a pencil or paintbrush that they feel as though they were born with the device. But a much larger group of Photoshop users falls into a camp that modern sociologists call "artistically challenged."

Take this quick test to determine where you fall:

✔ After doodling in the phone book, are you so horrified by the results that you rip out the page, pour ketchup on it, and feed it to your dog?

✔ When you're asked to draw a map to your house, do you try to lie your way out of the situation by asserting that you have no idea where your house is located and you doubt very seriously that you live anywhere?

✔ Do you have recurring dreams in which you suddenly remember that today is the day your final project is due in the art class you've forgotten to attend all year? And as you attempt to quickly paint a lounging model, you notice that the model is fully clothed and you're the one who's naked?

If you answered "Yes" to any of the preceding questions, you can safely assume that you belong to the nonartists camp. If you answered "Yes" to any two of the questions, you are so firmly entrenched in the nonartistic tradition that completing a dot-to-dot picture seems like an immense and terrifying project. And if you answered "Yes" to two of the questions and "Oh, wow, I had that exact dream just last night!" to the third, I'm obliged by the code of computer ethics to ask you one more question: Are you sure that your analyst isn't overcharging you?

Whatever your level of artistic skill, though, a time will probably come when you'll want to rub a couple of the Photoshop painting tools against an image. Sure, it's scary. But this chapter can help you prepare.

Doodling with the Pencil, Paintbrush, and Airbrush

Photoshop offers just three painting tools — the bare minimum for artists and nonartists alike. Shown in Figure 8-1, they work like so:

- ✔ The Pencil tool draws hard-edged lines of any thickness.

- ✔ The Paintbrush tool draws soft lines with slightly blurry edges to create more natural transitions.

- ✔ The Airbrush tool paints soft lines like the paintbrush. The only difference is that this tool pumps out color continuously — even when you hold it in place — as long as the mouse button is down. By contrast, the Pencil and Paintbrush tools paint only as you drag.

You can select each of the painting tools from the keyboard. Press J to select the Airbrush and press B or Shift+B to select the Paintbrush or the Pencil, which share the same flyout menu.

The Pen tool, by the way, doesn't draw beautiful, flowing lines that look as though they're emanating from a kazillion-dollar status pen. In Photoshop, you use the Pen tool to create *paths*. Paths enable you to select a portion of your image by creating a sort of connect-the-dots outline. The Pen tool and paths are covered in detail in Chapter 12.

By default, Photoshop displays a little paintbrush, airbrush, or pencil cursor when you select the painting tools. If you press the Caps Lock key, however, the cursor changes to a crosshair cursor that makes it easier to see what you're doing. Use the crosshair when the standard cursor gets in your way. Press Caps Lock again to return to the standard cursor.

Airbrush tool

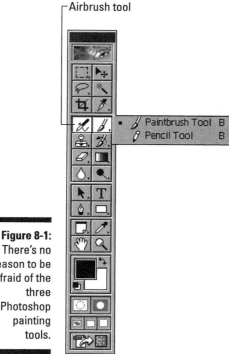

Paintbrush Tool   B
Pencil Tool   B

Figure 8-1:
There's no
reason to be
afraid of the
three
Photoshop
painting
tools.

If you prefer, you can make your cursor match the brush size exactly. (The upcoming section, "Switching the brush size," explains how to change brush sizes.) To make the cursor reflect the brush size, press Ctrl+K (⌘+K on a Mac) to display the Preferences dialog box. Then choose Display & Cursors from the top pop-up menu or press Ctrl+3 (⌘+3 on Mac) to get to the cursor options. Select Brush Size from the Painting Cursors radio buttons and press Enter (Return on a Mac).

The painting tools are small, nonpoisonous, and good with children. So why not take them for a walk and see how you like them? To use the Paintbrush, Pencil, and Airbrush tools to create the friendly Mr. Sun image shown in Figure 8-4 (go ahead, flip forward to take a look), just follow these steps:

1. **Choose File⇨New or Ctrl+N (⌘+N on a Mac) to create a new canvas.**

   Photoshop displays a dialog box that asks what size to make the new canvas. The dialog box offers Width, Height, and Resolution options, as does the Image Size dialog box discussed in Chapter 4.

2. Make the canvas about 400 pixels wide by 400 pixels tall.

That's about 5½ x 5½ inches with a Resolution value of 72 ppi or 4 x 4 inches with a Resolution of 100 ppi. Alternatively, you can select Pixels from the Width and Height pop-up menus, enter **400** into each, and forget about the Resolution value. Also, choose the RGB Color option from the Mode pop-up menu.

3. Press Enter (Return on a Mac).

The new empty canvas appears in a new window.

4. Select the Paintbrush tool.

Click on the Paintbrush icon in the Toolbox or press the B key. That's B for buff, as in, "Boy howdy, Biff, this brush is beaucoup buff!" That's what the programmers told me, anyway.

5. Draw a circle in the middle of your new canvas.

A rude approximation of a circle is fine. Experts agree that a lumpy circle has more personality.

6. Paint some rays coming off the circle.

Figure 8-2 shows more or less how your image should look so far.

Figure 8-2:
The beginnings of a sun, drawn exclusively with the Paintbrush tool.

7. Select the Pencil tool.

To access the Pencil from the keyboard, press Shift+B.

8. Draw a little face inside the sun.

Using the Pencil, you get hard-edged lines, as shown in Figure 8-3.

9. Select the Airbrush tool.

Press J to access the Airbrush from the keyboard.

Figure 8-3:
A face
drawn with
the Pencil
tool.

10. Change the foreground color to orange.

Use the RGB slider bars in the Color palette (press F6 to display the palette). Max out the R slider to 255, set the G slider to 150, and leave the B slider at 0.

11. Click on and hold — without moving your mouse — inside the sun.

Notice that the Airbrush continuously pumps out paint. Neither the Paintbrush nor the Pencil do this.

12. Paint some shading in the lower-right region of the sun.

Figure 8-4 shows what I mean. The Airbrush is useful for shading images. Of course, the real sun can't possibly have a shadow, but it doesn't have a face either, so I think that we can allow room for some personal expression.

That's good enough for now. You may want to save this image, because I come back to it later in this chapter. Then again, if something goes wrong and you don't save the sun, no biggie. You can always re-create it or experiment with a different image.

Remember that at any stage in the previous exercise — or during any other painting mission upon which you may embark — you can eliminate the last brush stroke by choosing Edit➪Undo or pressing Ctrl+Z (⌘+Z on a Mac). Everyone makes mistakes, and the Undo command is there for you to correct those errors. If you need to undo back a few steps, you can use the History palette (see Chapter 11 for details).

Figure 8-4:
Use the Airbrush to paint a highly unrealistic shadow on the sun.

Performing Special Painting-Tool Tricks

Dragging with a tool inside the image window is obviously the most common way to paint in Photoshop. But it's not the only way, as the following list makes clear:

✔ To create a straight line, click at one point in the image with any of the three painting tools, and Shift+click at another. Photoshop automatically creates a straight line between the two points.

✔ To create a straight-sided polygon, continue to Shift+click at various points in the image with any of the three painting tools. This method is great for creating triangles, five-pointed stars, and all sorts of other geometric shapes.

✔ To create a straight line that's exactly vertical or horizontal, click and hold with one of the painting tools, press and hold the Shift key, and then drag with the tool while the Shift key remains down. In other words,

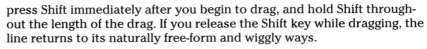

press Shift immediately after you begin to drag, and hold Shift throughout the length of the drag. If you release the Shift key while dragging, the line returns to its naturally free-form and wiggly ways.

✔ You can also use the Line tool to draw straight lines. But using the Shift key in combination with the painting tools is usually a better option because the painting tools give you more flexibility. You can vary the softness of your lines if you use the painting tools, but you can't if you use the Line tool. The only time I use the Line tool is to create lines with arrowheads at the end. To create this kind of line, select the Line tool from the Toolbox. In the Options bar, click on the arrow to the right of the Custom Shape icon. Here you find the Geometry options that enable you to specify the placement of the arrowhead, the shape of the arrowhead, the width of your line, and the concavity (or curvature) of the arrowhead. Then drag with the tool to create the line.

✔ If you can't find the Line tool, it's because Version 6 moved it to the same flyout menu as the New Shapes tool. Press Shift+U to toggle through the shapes until you reach the Line tool. Note that now that the line tool has moved in with the shape tools, it also obtains all the characterisics of a shape, including creating a shape layer.

✔ Alt+click (Option+click on a Mac) to lift a color from the image. Then drag to start painting with that color. Press Alt (Option on a Mac) when you're using the Airbrush, Paintbrush, or Pencil tools to access the Eyedropper tool. Unfortunately, this shortcut no longer works with the Line tool.

Choosing Your Brush

If the preceding two sections covered everything about the painting tools, Photoshop would be a royal dud. But as we all know, Photoshop is not a dud — far from it — so there must be more to the painting tools than I've shown you so far. (This is classic Sherlock Holmes-style deductive reasoning at work here.)

You can modify all three tools to a degree that no mechanical pencil or conventional paintbrush can match. For starters, you can change the size and shape of the tip of the tool, as explained in the next few sections. You can draw thick strokes one moment and then turn around and draw thin strokes the next, all with the same tool.

Switching the brush size

To change one tool tip — called a brush size, or just plain brush — for a different one, click on the Brushes drop-down menu, the arrow to the right of the word Brush in the Options bar, located just below the top menu bar.

Photoshop displays the Brushes palette, shown in Figure 8-5. Here you can find a total of 36 brush sizes (assuming default settings), all free for the taking.

The free-floating Brushes palette in earlier versions of Photoshop is now tucked away as a built-in, drop-down palette in the Options bar.

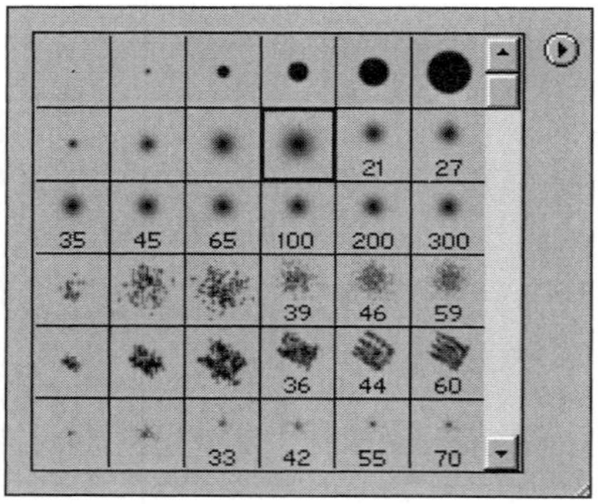

Figure 8-5:
The Brushes
palette lets
you switch
one size
brush for
another.

Most brush size icons are shown at actual size, but the ones labeled 35 to 300 are too large to fit inside their little boxes. The numbers below the icons represent the diameters of the brushes. (In case that year of high school geometry has altogether removed itself from your brain, diameter is merely the width of a circle measured from side to opposite side.) To change the brush size associated with the Pencil, Paintbrush, or Airbrush tool, select the desired tool and then click on the Brushes drop-down palette in the Options bar. The left column of Figure 8-6 shows how each of the predefined brushes affects the performance of the Paintbrush tool. (In each case, an icon from the Brushes palette is shown directly to the left of a stroke created with that brush.) Notice that some of the brushes have soft edges, whereas the others have downright blurry edges. When you begin using the brush, the palette puts itself back in its hiding place. You can also press Enter (Return on a Mac) or Esc to close the palette.

You can now view the Brushes palette in five ways — large and small thumbnails (the default), text only, or a large or small list (a combo of text and thumbnails). Access the Brushes Palette pop-up menu to select any of these viewing options.

Press Shift+Right-click (Control+Shift+click on a Mac) on the canvas to display the Brushes palette underneath your cursor. Select a different brush and continue painting. The palette then disappears.

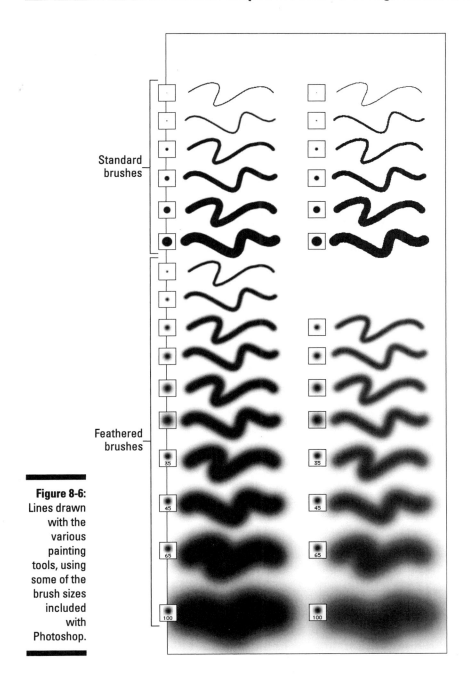

Standard brushes

Feathered brushes

Figure 8-6:
Lines drawn
with the
various
painting
tools, using
some of the
brush sizes
included
with
Photoshop.

In Photoshop, soft edges are said to be *anti-aliased*, whereas blurry edges are *feathered.* Both terms are proof positive that computer professionals actually don't want to be understood by the greater public. They prefer to speak in their own private code.

Figure 8-6 also shows the effect of some of the brushes on the Pencil and Airbrush tools. As you can see, the Pencil tool draws a harsh, jagged line no matter which brush you select. Even the feathered brushes produce jagged lines when used with the pencil. The Airbrush generally produces softer lines than the Paintbrush.

Making your own brush

You may think that 36 brushes are enough to keep you happy well into your declining years. But I assure you, one day you'll want a brush size that's a little thicker than Option A and a little thinner than Option B. So you'll have to modify one or the other to come up with a custom brush of your own.

To edit a brush, just click on a brush icon in the Options bar. In response to your double-click, Photoshop displays the drop-down dialog box, shown in Figure 8-7. Here's how you modify the brush:

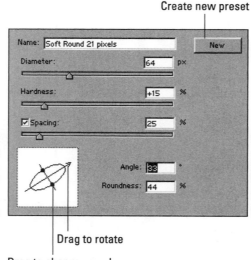

Create new preset

Figure 8-7:
The inner-workings of a brush size.

Drag to rotate

Drag to change roundness

> ✔ Drag the Diameter slider to make the brush bigger or smaller. If you know the exact width value, enter it into the option box on the right side of the slider. This value is measured in pixels.

✔ The Hardness value represents the blurriness of the brush size. A value of 100% is hard, like the first six options in the Brushes palette. Anything else is progressively fuzzier. The twelve feathered options in the Brushes palette have Hardness values of 0%.

✔ Don't change the Spacing value. And don't even think about turning off the Spacing check box. The Spacing option determines how many dollops of paint are applied to your canvas and is better left unmolested.

✔ Before I tell you about the Angle option, which comes next, I need to explain how Roundness works. (You see, the Angle value doesn't have any effect unless you first change the Roundness value.) The Roundness option lets you make the brush oval instead of round. A value of 100% is absolutely circular, as are all the predefined brushes; anything less results in a shape that is shorter than it is wide.

✔ If you want an oval brush to be taller than it is wide or some other variation on its present state, you can rotate it by changing the Angle value. Keep in mind that 360 degrees represents one complete counterclockwise turn, so 90 degrees is a quarter-turn, 180 degrees is a half-turn, -90 degrees is a clockwise quarter-turn, and so on.

✔ I never use the Angle and Roundness option boxes to change the values. Instead, I use that diagram in the lower-left corner of the dialog box. Drag one of the two circular handles on either side of the circle to make the brush oval. To rotate the brush, either drag the gray arrowhead or just click at the position where you want the arrow to point. The labels in Figure 8-7 tell the story.

As you change the settings, the brush icon in the Options bar shows the effect of the modified settings on the brush. If the diameter of the brush is too large for the preview to fit in its box — 74 pixels or larger — Photoshop automatically reduces the preview and displays a zoom ratio above the box. A zoom ratio of 1:2, for example, means that you're seeing the preview at half-size.

After you finish editing the brush, press Enter (Return on a Mac) to accept your changes. Note that this action creates a brush for temporary usage. You can also edit or create a brush and save it for later use. How do you do that? Coming right up.

Photoshop 6 makes creating a new brush easy. Simply click on the brush icon in the Options bar. In the dialog box, name your brush, specify your settings, and click the page icon button. You can also create a new brush by clicking in an empty area in the Brushes palette.

Going nuts with the Brushes palette

Whenever I explain some feature or other associated with Photoshop, I'm tempted to say, "But wait, there's more!" like some daft Ginsu Knife salesman.

But that's because there's always more. Photoshop is never satisfied to supply you with anything short of everything. You have to admire that in a program.

Here's what I mean:

- You don't need to manually click on a brush icon in the Brushes palette to select it. You can change the brush size from the keyboard, even when the Brushes palette is hidden. Press the right bracket key ( ]) to select a larger brush in varying increments. Increments are as follows: 1 pixel in brushes from 1-10 pixels in size; 10 pixels in brushes from 10-100 pixels in size; 25 pixels in brushes from 100 to 200 in size; 50 pixels in brushes from 200 to 300 in size; 100 pixels in brushes from 300 to 900 in size; and finally it jumps to 999 (the max). Press the left bracket key ([ ) to select a smaller brush by the same increments.

- To raise the hardness of a brush in 25 percent increments, press Shift+[. To lower the hardness, press Shift+[.

- To delete a brush size option from the palette, Alt+click (Option+click on a Mac) on it. If you press the Alt key (Option key on a Mac), you get a miniature pair of scissors. That's how Photoshop tells you that you're ready to clip a brush into oblivion.

- You can load additional custom brushes from disk by choosing the Load Brushes command from the palette menu. (Click on the right-pointing arrow in the palette to display the menu.) When you choose the command, you see a dialog box similar to the standard Open dialog box. Go to the Photoshop folder and then to the Presets folder and finally to the Brushes folder, where you find numerous brush libraries. Try Assorted Brushes.abr. That's a fun one. Click on Load to add the custom brushes to the Brushes palette.

  An easier way to load brushes is by selecting them using the Brushes palette menu. They're listed at the bottom of this pop-up menu. After you select a library, Photoshop asks you if you want to replace or append (add to) your current brush set.

- To get rid of any changes made to the brush size options in the Brushes palette, choose Reset Brushes from the palette menu. After the message appears, click on the OK button or press Enter (Return on a Mac).

Photoshop offers presets, which are libraries of different brushes, as well as gradients, color swatches, patterns, shapes, and other goodies. As I explore the various tools, I explain how to load these presets. You load the presets in much the same way that you load the brush libraries. Not too tough.

If you want to check out all the presets Photoshop has to offer, you can always go to Edit➪Preset Manager. All of the various categories of presets are accessible via the Preset Type pop-up menu. To the right of each scrolling list of preset icons is also a pop-up menu that gives you reset and viewing options, as well as accessibility to the various libraries under each preset category. And finally, you can also load, replace, save, rename, and delete libraries using the buttons on the right side of the dialog box.

Exploring More Painting Options

The new Options bar, which replaces the old Options palette, represents the heart and soul of the Photoshop tool modification options. Although the Brushes palette controls only one aspect of a painting tool, the Options bar lets you modify tools in a whole bunch of ways. You can modify nearly every tool in the Toolbox to some extent by using the Options bar.

Ogling the Options bar

The Options bar is especially handy because unlike the other floating palettes, you can always find the Options bar at the top, neatly docked and ready for action. If you don't like it parked there, however, you can undock it by dragging it away from its location. You can have it float anywhere on your screen or even dock it at the bottom.

Figure 8-8 shows the Options bar that appears when the Paintbrush is active. With a few exceptions, these options are the same ones that appear when the Pencil and Airbrush tools are selected. Here's how the options work:

Figure 8-8:
The Paintbrush Options bar is headquarters for modifying the painting tools.

> ✔ The first icon on the far left is the tool identifier, which lets you know which tool is active. I discussed the new Brush and Brushes palette options earlier in the section, "Choosing Your Brush."

✔ The Mode drop-down menu provides access to a bunch of different brush modes that control how the foreground color applied by the tool mixes with the existing colors in the image. The modes have confusing and seemingly meaningless names such as Multiply, Hard Light, and Difference — so beginners tend to avoid them like the plague. I show you some fun tricks you can perform with some of the modes in the next section.

✔ Available when you use the Pencil or Paintbrush, the Opacity slider bar controls the translucency of the foreground color. The Opacity slider bar can be accessed by pressing on the arrow next to the default setting of 100%. A setting of 100% ensures that the paint is opaque so that you can't see the colors underneath. (When you use a feathered brush, the edges are translucent even at 100%, but the center is opaque.) Any Opacity setting lower than 100% makes the brush translucent.

✔ If you're still a little fuzzy on how the Opacity slider works, perhaps that's because you're a visual learner. Figure 8-9 shows four lines drawn with the Paintbrush, two using a standard soft brush and two using a feathered brush. In each case, one line is set to 100% Opacity, and the other line is set to 40%.

✔ When the Airbrush is selected, the Opacity slider bar changes to the Pressure slider bar. Rather than producing translucent lines at lower settings, the Airbrush applies less paint, as though you tightened the nozzle on a real airbrush.

✔ You can change the Opacity or Pressure value in 10% increments by pressing a number key. As long as one of the painting tools is selected, pressing 9 changes the Opacity to 90%, 8 changes it to 80%, and so on. Press the 0 key to change the Opacity back to 100%. If you want a more precise setting — say, 75% — just type in the value.

✔ The Wet Edges check box appears only when the Paintbrush tool is selected. You can select this option to make your lines translucent with dark edges, as though the lines were drawn with a magic marker. Give it a try. For a variation on the effect, choose the Multiply mode from the Brush Modes pop-up menu.

✔ The Auto Erase check box appears when the Pencil tool is selected. You can select this option to draw in the background color whenever you click or drag on a pixel painted in the foreground color (the accepted practice in other painting programs). It's very useful for making touch-ups with the single-pixel brush — click to add the foreground color and click again to change it to the background color. I almost always leave this option on because it lets you add and erase color with a single tool.

✔ Click on the Brush icon at the far right of the Options bar to display the Brush Dynamics options.

As with Version 5.5, you can choose to fade out the stroke or line over the course of several steps (1-9999). One step is equal to one mark of the brush tip. But now you can also specify which options of the brush stroke — size, opacity, and color — you want to fade or change. Size is obvious. Opacity affects the translucency of the stroke. Color makes the color fade in intensity. The Stylus option affects how pressure-sensitive tablets work in Photoshop. But if you've never even seen a pressure-sensitive tablet, let alone have one hooked up to your computer, don't give this option another thought.

✔ At the end of the Options bar, you find the Docking Well, a dark gray rectangular space, as mentioned in Chapter 2. You can drag any palette tabs to this well to store them neatly and out of the way, yet they are still accessible.

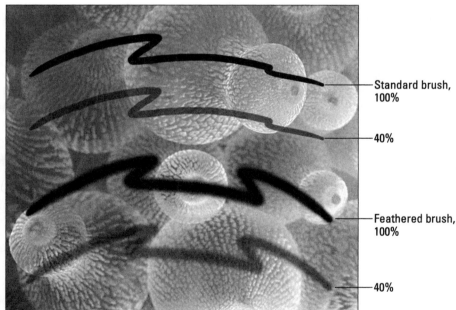

Figure 8-9: Here's what it looks like when you paint over sea anemone at different Opacity settings.

Standard brush, 100%

40%

Feathered brush, 100%

40%

Experimenting with brush modes

Of all the controls in the Options bar, the brush modes in the pop-up menu make the least sense. Don't worry, I'm not going to list every one of them and explain how it works. That would just fry your brain, and you need your brain for other chapters. Instead, I demonstrate a few specific effects you can achieve using brush modes and let you experiment with the others at your own pace.

For example, consider the sun image shown back in Figure 8-4. Suppose that you want to color in the sun with yellow and the sky with blue.

The problem is, if you try to color in the sun and sky with one of the painting tools — even the Airbrush — you end up covering the face inside the sun and the rays outside the sun. You can't fix the problem by lowering the Opacity value, because doing that just results in washed out colors, and you still obscure some of the sun's detail.

The two images in Color Plate 8-1 show what I'm talking about. In the left image, I painted in the sun and sky with the Paintbrush tool at 100% Opacity. Obviously a bad move. In the right image, I changed the Opacity to 40% and tried again. The image looks like I smeared it all over with chalk. Yuk.

The solution is to select a brush mode. Change the Opacity back to 100% by pressing the 0 key. Then select Multiply from the Brush Modes pop-up menu in the Options bar. Miraculously, you can now paint both sky and sun without covering up the rays and the face. This is because the Multiply option darkens colors as though you had painted with watercolors. The Multiply option mixes the colors together to create darker colors. The upper-left example in Color Plate 8-2 shows the result.

Here are some additional brush modes and other information on this subject that you may find interesting:

- The Screen Mode is the exact opposite of Multiply. Rather than mixing colors together to create darker colors, you mix them together to create lighter colors. In the upper-right example of Color Plate 8-2, I was able to apply color exclusively inside the black outlines and orange shadow. When I painted over white areas, nothing happened because any color mixed with white just makes more white.

- Does that make sense? Let me take another stab at it. Multiply mixes colors as though they were pigments, which is why the colors get darker. (You may want to check out my discussion of CMYK and RGB colors in Chapter 5.) By contrast, Screen mixes colors as though they were lights — just like RGB colors — which is why they get lighter.

- The Overlay Mode darkens dark colors and lightens light colors, resulting in a heightening of contrast. In the case of my sun, Overlay creates halos around the black lines because it darkens the inside of the lines and lightens the feathered edges. The lower-left example in Color Plate 8-2 shows what I'm talking about.

✔ The Difference brush mode is the loopiest mode of them all and the most likely to surprise you. It creates a photo-negative effect by mixing colors and finding their opposites. Check out the final example in Color Plate 8-2 to see the resulting plum sun against a tomato sky. Way cool.

✔ You can also have some fun experimenting with Difference's cousin, Exclusion. It sends all blacks to white, all whites to black, and all medium colors to gray.

✔ Use the Color brush mode to colorize grayscale images or change the color of portions of RGB images. Suppose that you want to change the color of the sky in the upper-left example of Color Plate 8-2 from blue to green. You can't use the Normal Mode because that wipes out the rays and the other lines. And you can't use Multiply again because that further darkens the sky. The answer is the Color Mode, which replaces a color with the foreground color without harming underlying detail.

✔ The Color Dodge and Color Burn brush modes offer an interesting new twist on the dodge and burn tools discussed in Chapter 9. In case you haven't discovered the Dodge and Burn tools yet, you drag with the Dodge tool to lighten a portion of your image and drag with the Burn tool to darken a portion of your image. If you use one of the painting tools and the Color Dodge Mode, you can lighten your image and infuse it with color. Using Color Burn, you can darken and infuse with color. For example, to darken your image and give it a greenish tint, you paint with green using the Color Burn brush mode.

✔ To paint normally again, just select the Normal brush mode.

Right-click (Control+click on a Mac) on your canvas with a painting tool to bring up a shortcut menu that provides access to the Edit Brush command and all the brush modes.

I'd rate six of the preceding brush modes — Multiply, Screen, Overlay, Difference, Color, and Normal — as super-useful, the kinds of modes you want to get to know on a first-name basis. Exclusion, Color Dodge, and Color Burn are also worth some attention. The others aren't nearly so useful. In fact, they're mostly boring and obscure. With that in mind, I encourage you to experiment freely with the ones discussed here to the exclusion of all the others.

Isn't Photoshop Just a Paint Program?

Photoshop used to be just a paint program until Version 6 graced us with its presence. Photoshop has now added a whole flyout menu's worth of shape drawing tools. You already met the Line tool that moved in with the other new drawing tools. Now I want to introduce you to the roommates.

Drawing basic shapes

Photoshop 6 has five shape tools — the Rectangle, Rounded Rectangle, Ellipse, Polygon, and Custom Shape tools (six if you include the Line tool). Take a look at the following steps to create a rectangle, ellipse, and polygon (I'll save the Custom Shape tool for later):

1. **Choose the foreground color you want for your shape.**

2. **Select the Rectangle, Ellipse, or Polygon tool from the Toolbox.**

3. **Select an option, as shown in Figure 8-10.**

   From the Options bar, you can choose one of the following settings:

   - **Shape Layer:** Adds a shape on its own separate Shape layer. You can edit it, move it, and transform the shape. A Shape layer acts as a mask. If you take a gander at the Layers palette, you can see that the Shape layer has two thumbnails — one is entirely filled with color, and the other contains the outline of the shape. To state it simply, the color is peeking through the outline of the shape, and the rest of the layer is being hidden or masked.

   A shape layer is a vector path which prints at the full resolution of your printer rather than the resolution of your image. For details on resolution, see Chapter 4.

   - **Work Path:** Adds a shape that acts like a path (see more on paths in Chapter 12). You can use a path as a means of selecting a portion of an image. The path doesn't fill with color as a fill region or shape layer does.

   - **Filled Region:** Adds a shape directly on the layer (for more on layers, see Chapter 15). The Fill Region option is the equivalent of painting directly on your canvas with a painting tool. Note that after you use this option, you can't edit or move the shape.

Figure 8-10:
The Shape Options bars provide all the goodies needed to create and modify various flavors of shapes.

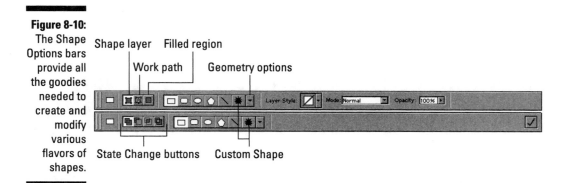

4. **Click on the down-pointing arrow to the right of the Custom Shape icon.**

   The Geometry Options drop-down dialog box appears. In non-geek terms, this enables you to specify the width and height, as well as various options, depending on which shape you choose:

   - **Sides:** Sets the number of sides of a polygon (this option appears in the Options bar).

   - **Unconstrained:** Enables you to draw your shape freely, without restraint.

   - **Fixed Size:** Enables you to draw a shape with a set width and height.

   - **Proportional:** Lets you draw a shape with a proportional ratio of width and height.

   - **From Center:** This option enables you to draw from the center out, rather than from a corner.

   - **Square:** Enables you to draw a square when the Rectangle tool is selected.

   - **Radius:** Sets the width of the polygon.

   - **Smooth Corners:** Makes smooth polygon corners.

   - **Indent Sides By:** Creates the spikes of a star when the Polygon tool is selected. A larger value makes sharper and spikier points.

   - **Smooth Indents:** Curves the sides of a star.

5. **Drag on the canvas to create the shape.**

   If you want to create a perfectly proportional shape, hold down the Shift key as you draw. Press Alt (Option on a Mac) to draw from the center.

You can also apply Layer Styles to your shapes. Choose Layer⇨Layer Style and apply one of the various styles. You can also choose Window⇨Show Styles and select one of the many preset styles that ship with Photoshop. For more on Layer Styles and the Styles palette, see Chapter 15.

Creating custom shapes

Photoshop ships with a bunch of different shapes for you to choose from. You can choose a heart, a moon, a comic strip bubble, and even a cutesy footprint. Can Adobe make it any easier than this? Here's the scoop on how to get custom shapes on your canvas:

1. **Choose the foreground color for your shape.**

   Choose Window⇨Show Color and adjust the sliders until you achieve your desired color.

2. **Select the Custom Shape tool from the Toolbox.**

3. **In the Options bar, select either Shape Layer, Work Path, or Filled Region.**

4. **Click on the Shape drop-down menu in the Options bar to view the various shapes available.**

5. **Select a shape and press Enter (Return on a Mac) to close the palette.**

6. **Select the Geometry Options drop-down menu, the arrow to the right of the Custom shape icon.**

   Select one of the various options. Most are described in the section "Drawing basic shapes." The Defined Propotions option enables you to maintain the original proportions of the shape, regardless of the size of the object. The Defined Size proportions give you a shape of predetermined dimensions. With this option, don't drag, simply click your mouse. Ditto with the Fixed Size option.

7. **Drag your cursor on the canvas to create your shape.**

   Even though you can set the next two options from the Geometry Options drop-down dialog box, you can also implement them "on the fly." If you want to create a perfectly proportional shape, hold down the Shift key as you draw. Press Alt (Option on a Mac) to draw from the center.

Shape shifting

After you create your shape, you may feel the urge to change its appearance. If you select the Filled Region option, you're stuck without any editing capabilities. For those of you who played it safe and chose one of the other two options, read on to find out how to edit your shapes. But before you do, be aware that the Options bar acts a little differently when you're dealing with shapes. As soon as you draw a shape, you notice that the Options bar changes appearance. It gets rid of many of the previously mentioned options and offers a set of four icons, referred to as selection state buttons. If, by chance, all you want to do is draw more shapes and not modify them, you can click on the Dismiss button (the big check mark icon) to return to the previous Options bar.

However, if you want to modify your shapes, you need to stick with the Options bar displaying the selection state buttons. If you want to add to your shapes or subtract from your shapes, just follow these steps:

1. **Select one of the following selection state buttons (refer to Figure 8-10).**

   • **Add to Shape Area:** Adds to your current shape.

   • **Subtract from Shape Area:** Subtracts from your current shape.

- **Intersect Shape Areas:** Retains only the intersection between two shapes.

- **Exclude Overlapping Shape Areas:** Deletes the intersection between two shapes.

See Figure 8-11 for an example each of these state changes in action.

2. **Select a shape drawing tool from the Toolbox.**

3. **Now draw!**

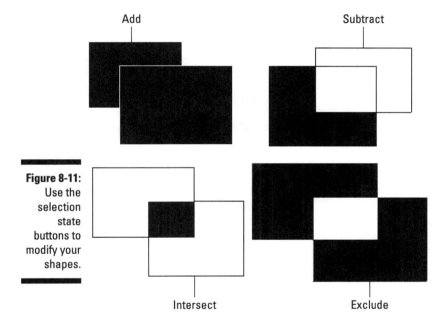

Add   Subtract

Figure 8-11: Use the selection state buttons to modify your shapes.

Intersect   Exclude

Playing with shapes

If you play around a bit, you find that you can't use most of the Photoshop tools on a Shape layer. But here's what you can do:

- ✔ Use the Move tool (the four-headed arrow on the top right of the Toolbox) to move all of the shapes in unison on your canvas.

- ✔ Use the Pen tool to add some free-form shapes (you can find details on the Pen tool in Chapter 12).

- ✔ Use the Eyedropper tool to sample the color of your shape. Unfortunately, you can only use one color per shape layer. If you want additional shapes of different colors, you must create a new shape layer.

✔ Use the Path Component Selection tool to move individual shapes.

✔ Use the Direct Selection tool to manipulate the anchor points, directional handles, lines, and curves of a shape (check out Chapter 12 for information on these elements). Simply select the anchor point, directional handle, line, or curve, and drag to shape. You can also move the entire shape with this tool by pressing Alt (Option on a Mac).

✔ You can transform the shapes in two ways. First, select the shape(s) with the Path Component Selection tool. Then choose Edit➪Transform Path and select one of the transformations. Or check the Show Bounding Box option in the Options bar. The Transform box appears around the shape and the Options bar reflects the various transformation options. For information on transformations, see Chapter 13.

✔ Last but not least, you can align and distribute the shapes. Select the first shape, hold down the Shift key, and select each of the other shapes. Select one of the Alignment (left set of buttons) or Distribute (right set of buttons) options. Voila, your shapes are neat and orderly.

If all this painting and drawing seems a little daunting at first, don't give up. Just keep on plugging away. Remember, everything's daunting at some time. Heck, walking upright on two legs once seemed impossible, and yet look how well you do that today. Sure, not as well as some folks, but you're still getting there. Keep your chin up.

Chapter 9

Making a Mockery of Reality

*B*ack in the old days, retouching a photograph was a formidable task. If you wanted to remove the reflection from someone's glasses, sharpen the focus of a detail, or tidy up a wrinkle or two, you had to paint or airbrush the photo and hope for the best. Anyone short of a trained professional would more often than not make a complete mess of the project and wish to heck it had never been started. Even the pros found it difficult to match flat colors on a palette to the ever-changing landscape of a photograph.

The beauty of Photoshop is that you can paint not only with specific colors (as I explain in Chapter 8) but also with colors and details already found in the image. Using the editing tools — Smudge, Blur, Sharpen, Dodge, Burn, and Sponge — you can subtly adjust the appearance of pixels by shifting them around, boosting contrast between them, or lightening and darkening them. The results are edits that blend in with their surroundings.

With the Photoshop Crop tool and the Image➪Crop and new Image➪Trim commands, you can also snip away unwanted portions of your image. Never before has it been so easy to cut relatives you hate out of your family photos.

Photoshop enables you to retouch images in ways that traditional photographic techniques simply can't and also offers a built-in safety net. You can undo any change you make or simply revert to your original image if you don't like how your retouched image turns out. In other words, Photoshop is a real pleasure for modern retouching enthusiasts. After you finish this chapter, you'll be so inspired to enhance and modify photographic details that you'll welcome problem images with open arms.

Trimming Excess Gunk Off the Edges

In Chapter 4, I explain how to change the size of your image without changing the elements therein — in other words, how to turn that 8 x 10 wedding photograph into a nifty wallet-size snapshot without trimming off anyone's vital body parts. But suppose that your spouse up and runs off to Lagos with your next-door neighbor? What do you do then? Why, you use the Crop tool to cut the cretin out of the picture.

The sharp edges of the Crop tool

Novice photographers have a habit of worrying about getting too much imagery into their pictures. This can be a dangerous concern. In your effort to cut out background flack, you may overcompensate and cut off Grandma's head or the right half of little Joey's body. The fact is, it's better to have too much stuff in your photos than too little, for the simple reason that excess stuff can be cut away, but missing stuff has to be reshot. Since photography was invented, production artists have been taking knives and scissors to just about every image that passes over their light tables in an effort to clip away the extraneous gook around the edges and hone in on the real goods. Called *cropping,* this technique is so pervasive that professional photographers purposely shoot subjects from too far away knowing that someone, somewhere, will slice the image and make it right.

Inside Photoshop, you can cut away the unpalatable parts of an image by using the Crop tool. The Crop tool, which used to share a cramped apartment with the marquee tools, now has its own single-family home in the Toolbox. To select the Crop tool without messing with the toolbox, press C.

Here's how to use the Crop tool:

1. **Drag with the tool around the portion of the image you want to retain.**

   In Figure 9-1, I dragged around the floating spaceman. A dotted rectangle called a *marquee* follows your drag to clearly show the crop boundaries. Don't worry if you don't surround your image elements just right; you get the chance to edit the boundary in the next step.

   Version 6 also covers the area outside the marquee with a translucent *shield* to better frame the image. You can use the shield controls in the Options bar to specify the color and opacity of the shield or to turn it off entirely.

Handle   Resize cursor   ┌Crop boundary

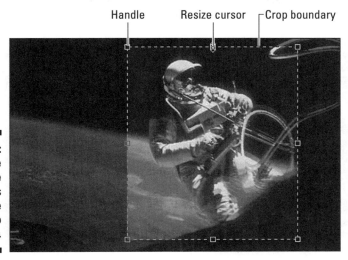

Figure 9-1:
Drag the
square
handles
to change
the crop
boundary.

If you press the spacebar during your drag, Photoshop stops resizing the crop boundary and starts moving the entire boundary. This technique can be helpful when you're trying to position the boundary precisely. (You can also move the boundary after you create it.)

2. **Drag the crop boundaries as desired.**

After you release your mouse button, Photoshop displays square handles around the edges of the marquee (refer to Figure 9-1). If the marquee isn't the right size, drag a handle to change the crop boundary. Your cursor changes to a double-headed arrow when you place it over a handle, indicating that you have the go-ahead to drag the handle. You can drag as many handles as you please — one at a time, of course — before cropping the image.

If you move the cursor outside the crop boundary, the cursor changes to a curved, double-headed arrow. Dragging then rotates the crop boundary.

If you want a non-rectangular crop, check the new Perspective setting in the Options bar to enable the crop handles to move independently.

3. **After you get the crop boundary the way you want it, double-click inside the boundary to crop the image or press Accept in the Options bar.**

Or just press Enter (Return on a Mac). Photoshop throws away all pixels outside the crop boundary, as shown in Figure 9-2. If you rotated the crop boundary in Step 2, Photoshop rights the rectangular area and thus rotates the image, as shown in Figure 9-3.

If you look at the Options bar while the crop marquee is active, you notice Photoshop now gives you the choice of deleting or hiding your cropped area. Delete eliminates the cropped areas. Hide hides the cropped area and only works with layers. The cropped area is still in the image and can be seen if you move the layer with the Move tool. Or you can choose Image⇨Reveal All, and Photoshop expands the canvas to show all the pixels in all layers.

Figure 9-2:
Up close
and
personal
with a
spaceman.

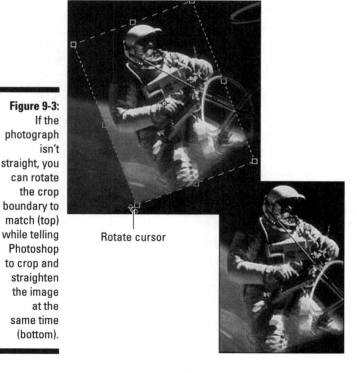

Figure 9-3:
If the
photograph
isn't
straight, you
can rotate
the crop
boundary to
match (top)
while telling
Photoshop
to crop and
straighten
the image
at the
same time
(bottom).

Rotate cursor

When you rotate an image in this way, Photoshop *resamples* your image — that is, it rearranges the pixels to come up with the rotated image. As I discuss in Chapter 4, resampling can damage your image. For best results, don't rotate your image more than once. If you want to rotate your image repeatedly, do so only in 90-degree increments so that Photoshop doesn't resample your image. Also, make sure that the Interpolation option in the General panel of the Preferences dialog box is set to Bicubic. Press Ctrl+K (⌘+K on a Mac) to display the dialog box.

More good news about cropping

Cropping is easy and fun for the whole family. You can do it at home or at work, with friends or by yourself, in the car, or while performing household chores. Find out how you can make cropping an everyday part of your new life.

Sorry, I misplaced the real intro to this section and can't seem to find it. But before I hunt around, I just want to mention briefly that the next few items explain more cropping techniques that you may find useful.

- ✔ If you change your mind about cropping an image, press Esc or Ctrl+period (⌘+period on a Mac) to get rid of the cropping boundary. Or you can also press the Cancel button in the Options bar.

- ✔ If you try to drag with the Crop tool when a portion of the image is selected (as discussed in Chapter 12), Photoshop deselects the image but doesn't respond to your drag. You have to drag a second time to make Photoshop sit up and take notice.

- ✔ To move the cropping boundary in its entirety, just drag inside the boundary.

- ✔ In addition to using the Crop tool, you can crop an area selected with the Rectangular Marquee tool (see Chapter 12) by choosing Image⇨Crop. I take advantage of this alternative often because Photoshop can slow down and react lethargically when you edit the crop marquee. When you press Enter (Return on a Mac), Photoshop asks you whether you want to delete or hide the cropped area.

Not only do you not have to have a perfectly rectangular area to crop anymore, you can even use the Image⇨Crop command with any arbitrary selection — elliptical, polygonal, even feathered. Photoshop really won't crop to that shape, but it gets as close to the boundary as it can.

- ✔ The Width, Height, and Resolution settings in the Options bar are useful for cropping an image to an exact dimension. Another useful setting is the Front Image option. It enables you to crop one image so that it's the exact same size as another image. Suppose that you want to make image B the same size as image A. First, open images A and B. Crop image A to your desired size. Click on the Front Image button. Photoshop loads the

size and resolution settings from image A to the Options bar. Select
Image B. Drag the Crop tool on the canvas and frame your image. When
you press Enter (Return on a Mac) to execute the crop, Photoshop automatically resizes image B to match image A.

✔ You can also crop an image by using the Canvas Size command, as discussed at the end of Chapter 4. You may want to consider this method if
you need to trim your image on one or more sides by a precise number
of pixels to get the image to a certain size. The Canvas Size command
can also come in handy if you want to crop a very small area — say
three pixels worth — along one or more edges of the image and you
have trouble selecting the area with the Crop marquee. You can reduce
the size of the canvas using Image⇨Canvas Size to eliminate the offen-
sive pixels. Version 6, however, gives you an even better way to delete
the little beasts. Read on.

Trimming away the excess

The new Trim command trims away transparent or colored areas around
your image. Choose Image⇨Trim. The Trim dialog box appears requesting
some information. Select either Transparent Pixels (for images with layers),
Top Left Pixel Color, or Bottom Right Pixel Color as a basis for the trim. Then
tell Photoshop to trim away the Top, Bottom, Left, or Right side(s) from the
image.

Touching Base with Retouching Tools

When push comes to shove, the editing tools are more like than unlike the
painting tools. You use an editing tool by dragging with it, just as you do with
a painting tool. You change the size of the tool tip by selecting an option from
the Brushes palette. You modify the performance of an editing tool from the
Options bar. You can even apply Brush modes and Opacity settings. (Brush
modes, the Brushes palette, and the Options bar are all introduced in
Chapter 8, in case your response to these last few sentences was "Huh?")

But the editing tools are sufficiently different from their painting cousins to
confuse and perplex the unsuspecting neophyte. Moreover, unlike the Pencil,
Paintbrush, and Airbrush, the editing tools don't have any common real-
world counterparts. I can't say, "The Photoshop Smudge tool works just like
the conventional Smudge tool that's hanging out in your garage right next to
the leaf rake," because almost no one has a Smudge tool hanging in the
garage (or anywhere else).

What do the editing tools do, exactly?

Editing tools would be extremely useful in real life if only someone would get around to inventing them. Take the task of touching up the walls in your rec room. (Come on, everyone has a rec room!) Using paintbrushes and rollers alone, this job can be a nightmare. The paint on the walls and the paint in the can may no longer exactly match. If you have to scrape away any dry paint, you'll have a heck of a time matching the texture. And knowing you, you may very well trip over something and spill paint all over the carpet.

But scan the walls of the rec room into Photoshop, and your problems are solved. Even if you have to retouch both paint and wallpaper, the editing tools, shown in Figure 9-4, can handle the job without incident:

✔ Use the Smudge tool to smear colors from a pristine area of the wall to the bare spots and the stains. You can smear the paint as far as you want, just as though it were still wet and in infinite supply. This is the editing tool you'll use most often. It's discussed further in the section "Smudging Away Imperfections," later in this chapter.

✔ If the transitions between elements in the wallpaper are a little ragged — for example, if the pixels in the little polka-dot mushrooms don't seem to blend naturally with those in the cute little frogs sitting beneath them — you can smooth the pixels out with the Blur tool, which looks like a water drop. This tool blurs the edges between colors so that the colors blend together.

✔ To rebuild textures, drag with the Sharpen tool — which looks like a pointy cone of some sort. The Sharpen tool increases the amount of contrast between colors and builds up edges.

✔ Together, the Blur and Sharpen tools are known as *focus tools*. The former downplays focus; the latter enhances it. Both tools are eloquently explained later in this chapter in the section, "Focusing from the hip."

✔ To lighten a dark area in the wallpaper, drag with the Dodge tool, which looks like a circle on the end of a stick. This tool lightens up the area evenly.

✔ If an area on the wall has become faded over the years, you can darken it by using the Burn tool, which looks like a hand in the shape of an O.

✔ Are the colors just too darn garish? Or has the color been drained right out? I admit, these aren't common rec room problems, but if they do occur, you can take up the Sponge tool to remedy them.

✔ The Dodge, Burn, and Sponge tools are called *toning tools,* meaning that they change the colors in an image. The last two sections in this chapter are devoted to the toning tools.

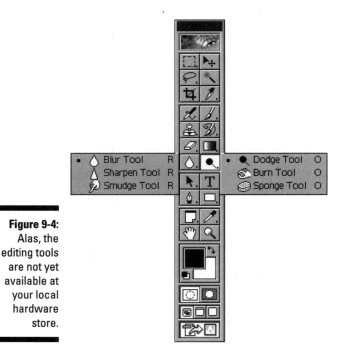

● △ Blur Tool R	▪ ● Dodge Tool O
△ Sharpen Tool R	● Burn Tool O
☞ Smudge Tool R	● Sponge Tool O

Figure 9-4:
Alas, the
editing tools
are not yet
available at
your local
hardware
store.

See, don't you wish you had a crack at using these tools in real life? Seems to me that Bob Vila or that *Home Improvement* guy should get to work on them.

Uncovering hidden editing tools

When you first looked at Figure 9-4, you may have noticed that the Toolbox in the figure doesn't look anything like the one on your screen. In order to show you all the tool icons, I enhanced the screen shot (using Photoshop, of course).

By default, the Blur and Dodge tools appear in the Toolbox. As I discuss in Chapter 2, the little arrow in the lower-right corner of the Blur and Dodge tools means that additional tools lurk behind the icons on a flyout menu. To get to the hidden tools on the flyout menu, press and hold on the icon and then drag across and down to the tool you want to use. Or just Alt+click (Option+click on a Mac) on the icon to cycle through the tools on the menu.

You can also cycle through the tools by using their shortcuts: Press R to select the tool that's currently showing in the blur/sharpen/smudge compartment of the Toolbox; press Shift+R again to switch to the tool that's hidden. Likewise, you can press O (that's the letter O, not zero) and then Shift+O to cycle through the Dodge, Burn, and Sponge tools.

Effects of the edit tools can be a little difficult to predict — especially for beginners. Remember, you can use Ctrl+Z (⌘+Z on a Mac) to undo your last edit, and the History palette (described in detail in Chapter 11) enables you to go back to previous steps. You can use File➪Revert to restore your image to the last-saved version.

Smudging Away Imperfections

The shark image shown in Figure 9-5 provides an ideal subject for demonstrating the powers of the proudest Photoshop editing tool, the Smudge tool. Like so many rough-and-tumble sharks that occupy the inner cities of our oceans, this guy is no stranger to the occasional toothy brawl. Frankly, his face is a mess. If he were old enough to shave, I'd say that he had problems operating a razor. But because he's at that violent age where his friends think it's fun to rumble, I'm guessing that these marks are war wounds.

But whatever caused his scars, I can fix them with the help of the Smudge tool. As you may recall from my earlier rec room analogy, the Smudge tool pushes color from one portion of your image into another. When you drag with this tool, Photoshop "grabs" the color that's underneath your cursor at the start of your drag and smears it in the direction of your drag.

Figure 9-5:
This shark is
on the road
to ruin.

The Smudge tool is a great contraption for smearing away scars, wrinkles, overly large noses, droopy ears, and all the other things that plastic surgeons keep their eyes out for. Figure 9-6 shows a magnified view of the Smudge tool working its magic on the shark. The various sharkish defects are smoothed away to the point that the guy looks like he's made out of porcelain.

Smearing with style

Notice that in Figure 9-6, I rubbed with the grain of the detail. I traced along the shark's gills, rubbed along the length of its fins, and dragged up its snout, all in short, discreet strokes. I was planning on saying something about how you don't want to rub a shark the wrong way, but my editor told me to lay off the puns. So, I'll just point out that you get more natural-looking results if you carefully trace along the details of your subject and don't simply drag haphazardly all over the place.

Retouching with the Smudge tool requires a certain amount of discretion. If you really go nuts and drag over every single surface, you get an oil-painting effect, like the one shown in Figure 9-7. Don't get me wrong, you can create some cool stuff this way, but excessive smudging is not the same as retouching.

Smudge-specific controls

You can modify the performance of the Smudge tool by using the Smudge options (see Figure 9-8):

- ✔ Click and Shift+click to smudge in a straight line. Or Shift+drag to smudge horizontally or vertically. These Shift+click and Shift+drag techniques work for all the edit tools, by the way.

- ✔ Select another brush size in the Brushes palette to enlarge or reduce the size of the smudge brush. You can likewise change the brush size for all the edit tools. To display the Brushes palette, click on the down pointing arrow next to the brush icon in the Options bar. (For more on changing brushes, see Chapter 8.)

- ✔ Access the various smudge options in the Options bar. For example, you can adjust the Pressure slider by clicking on the black arrow to the right of the default setting of 50% to create more subtle retouching effects. Increase the Pressure setting to make the effect more pronounced.

- ✔ Remember that you can change the brush size from the keyboard by pressing the bracket keys and change the Pressure setting by pressing the number keys, as I explain in Chapter 8.

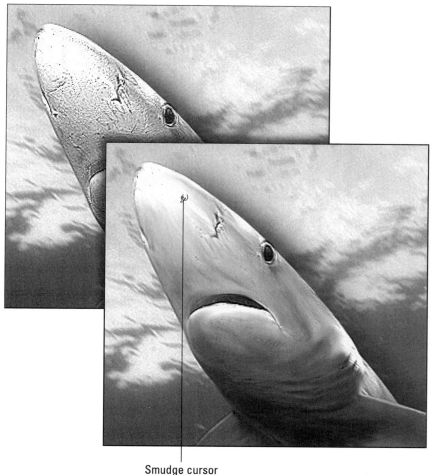

Figure 9-6:
As these before (top) and after (bottom) photos prove, the Smudge tool can take years off a shark's face.

Smudge cursor

✔ The Modes drop-down menu doesn't offer the Multiply, Screen, Overlay, or Difference options, which are discussed at the end of Chapter 8. Instead, you get two options, Darken and Lighten, which let you smear only those colors that are darker or lighter than the original colors in the image.

✔ You also have the Color brush mode, which lets you smear the colors in an RGB image without harming the detail. Pretty nifty.

✔ The other brush modes — Hue, Saturation, and Luminosity — range from nearly useless to completely useless. Don't worry about them.

✔ Change the brush mode back to Normal to make the Smudge tool function, er, normally.

Figure 9-7:
You can convert a photo into an oil painting by dragging the Smudge tool all over the place.

Figure 9-8:
The options that affect the Smudge tool.

✔ As with the painting tools, if you Right-click (Control+click on a Mac) on your canvas, a shortcut menu appears and gives you access to the Edit Brush command and any available brush modes.

✔ Depending on your computer system, Photoshop may slow down dramatically when you increase the Pressure setting above 80% or 90%, select a large brush size, or change the brush mode. And if you do all three at the same time, the program may run so lethargically that you'll think you've crashed. Just go get a cup of coffee, and Photoshop should be finished when you get back.

✔ Select the Finger Painting check box to dip your brush into the foreground color before smudging. Photoshop applies a little dab of foreground color at the beginning of your drag and then begins to smear into the existing colors in the image as usual.

To temporarily turn on Finger Painting when the check box is dese-lected, press Alt (Option on a Mac) as you drag with the Smudge tool. If the Finger Painting check box is selected, Alt+drag (Option on a Mac) to smudge in the normal fashion.

✔ The Use All Layers check box doesn't make any difference unless you're editing an image with layers. It enables you to pierce through and pick up the colors from all of your layers.

Color Plate 9-1 shows before and after shots of a few effects mixed together. I created the second image by selecting the Finger Painting check box, setting the Pressure slider to 90%, and changing the brush mode to Color. I dragged several times with the Smudge tool, about half the time with the foreground color set to red and the other half with it set to yellow.

All Them Other Edit Tools

The remaining edit tools fall into a group that experts call "the other guys." Whereas you may pick up the Smudge tool every third day or so, you'll be lucky if you select one of the other guys once a week. Even so, they can prove fantastically helpful — well, moderately helpful, anyway — if used properly. The upcoming sections contain my choice bits of wisdom for using the other guys.

Focusing from the hip

It's true that the Smudge tool is a wonderful little device. But it's not always the right tool for the job. For example, suppose you have a harsh transition between two colors. Maybe one of the shark's teeth looks a little jagged, or you want to soften the edge of a fin. Which of the following methods would you use to fix this problem?

✔ Smear the colors a bit with the Smudge tool.
✔ Soften the transition between the colors by using the Blur tool.

I prepared you for that question by saying that the Smudge tool isn't always the right tool and using words like "soften," so naturally you chose the second answer. (You did choose the second answer, didn't you?) But believe me, a time will come when you run into this exact situation and your first reflex will be to reach for the Smudge tool.

So let me try to drive home the point a bit with the aid of Figure 9-9. The figure starts off with the harshest of all possible color transitions — that is, between white and its archenemy, black. You want to smear the colors together so that they blend a little more harmoniously, so naturally you reach for the Smudge tool. The problem with this method (as shown in the second example in the figure) is that you can't get a nice, smooth transition between the two colors no matter how hard you try. Even if you Shift+drag with the Smudge tool, you get some inconsistent smudging. You also run the risk of smearing surrounding detail. All this happens because the Smudge tool is designed as a free-form smearing device, not as an edge softener.

Meanwhile, an edge softener is sitting nearby waiting for you to snatch it up. If you drag the Blur tool between the white and black shapes — whether you drag perfectly straight or wobble the cursor back and forth a bit — you get a softened edge like the one shown in the final example of Figure 9-9.

While I've got your attention, let me jot down a few other items about the focus tools:

- ✔ Just as the Blur tool softens transitions, the Sharpen tool firms the transitions back up.

- ✔ At least, that's what the Sharpen tool is supposed to do. In practice, it tends to make an image overly grainy. Use this tool sparingly.

- ✔ You can adjust the impact of the Blur and Sharpen tools by changing the Pressure setting in the Options bar. I like to set the Pressure to about 60% for the Blur tool and 30% for the Sharpen tool.

Harsh transition

Smeared with Smudge tool

Figure 9-9:
The parable of the harsh transition, the Smudge tool, and the Blur tool.

Softened with Blur tool

✔ When you work with the focus tools, you have access to the same brush modes as you do when using the Smudge tool. The important ones are Darken, Lighten, and Color. Any of the three can help downplay the effects of the Sharpen tool and make it more usable.

✔ If you want to adjust the focus of large areas of an image — or an entire image — use the commands under the Filter menu as described in Chapter 17. These commands work much more uniformly than the focus tools.

Dodge? Burn? Those are opposites?

Wondering why the Dodge and Burn tool icons look they way they do? It's because the Dodge and Burn tools have their roots in traditional stat camera techniques in which you shoot a photograph of another photograph to correct exposure problems. The Dodge tool is supposed to look like a little paddle that you wave around to block off light, and the Burn tool is a hand focusing the light. It may seem, therefore, that dodging would make the image darker and burning would make it lighter. But Photoshop is thinking in terms of negative film, where black is white, up is down, right is left, and Tweedle Dee is a Cornish game hen.

I must confess that, although I've been using Photoshop since I was in diapers, I still can't remember which tool lightens and which darkens without looking it up. To help both you and me remember, I offer the following:

✔ The Dodge tool lightens images, just as a dodge ball lightens your body by about ten pounds when it tears off your head.

✔ The Burn tool darkens images, just as a sunburn darkens your body and eventually turns it a kind of charbroiled color.

If those little insights don't help you remember how the Dodge and Burn tools work, nothing can.

Generally, you adjust the performance of the Dodge and Burn tools just like the other edit tools and the paint tools — by changing the brush size, alternating the brush mode, and so on. (Read more about brush sizes and brush modes in Chapter 8.) You can find all the tool options, including brush sizes, in the Options bar, which appears directly under the menu bar when you select a particular tool.

A few of the settings in the Options bar require some explanation:

✔ The Exposure slider bar, accessed by pressing the black arrow to the right of the default setting of 50%, indicates how much an area will be lightened or darkened. As always, lower the value to lessen the impact of the tool and raise the value to increase the impact.

✔ The Range drop-down menu contains just three options: Highlights, Midtones, and Shadows. The default setting is Midtones, which lightens or darkens medium colors in an image and leaves the very light and dark colors alone. Figure 9-10 shows the result of dragging all over the shark with the Dodge tool while Midtones was the active brush mode.

✔ The Shadows brush mode ensures that the darkest colors are affected, while Highlights impacts the lightest colors. In Figure 9-11, I set the brush mode to Shadows and scribbled with the Dodge tool. The payoff is a shark that looks like it ate the world's supply of glowworms. Even the darkest shadows radiate, making the image uniformly light.

✔ To darken an image with similar uniformity, select the Burn tool and set the brush mode to Highlights.

You can use a variation of the Dodge and Burn tools in the form of the Color Dodge and Color Burn brush modes (explained in Chapter 8). When you use the regular Dodge and Burn tools, you simply lighten or darken your image. But if you use one of the painting tools with the Color Dodge or Color Burn brush modes, you can both lighten or darken and infuse the image with color. For example, if you want to lighten an image and give it a yellowish glow, paint with yellow and the Color Dodge brush mode.

Figure 9-10:
By setting the brush mode to Midtones and dragging indiscriminately with the Dodge tool, I lightened the shark without eliminating contrast.

Figure 9-11:
Using the
Dodge
tool in
combination
with the
Shadows
brush mode
makes the
shark's
darkest
shadows
tingle with
light.

Playing with the Color knob

The Sponge tool is designed for use on full-color images. Don't try using it on grayscale images because it doesn't do you any good. It's not that it doesn't work — it does — it just doesn't work correctly. On a grayscale image, the Sponge tool either lightens or darkens pixels like a shoddy version of the Dodge or Burn tool.

When you work on a color image, the Sponge tool increases or decreases saturation. Ever used the Color knob on your television? Turn the knob up, and the color leaps off the screen; turn it down, and the colors look gray. What you're doing is adjusting the TV's saturation. Increasing saturation makes the colors more vibrant; decreasing saturation makes the colors more drab. The Sponge tool works in much the same way.

Here's how you use the Sponge tool:

1. **Select the Sponge tool.**

    Press the O key and Shift+O keys until the sponge icon appears in the Toolbox. Photoshop then displays the appropriate Options bar.

2. **Select the desired Mode option from the drop-down menu in the Options bar.**

    Select Saturate to make the colors vibrant; select Desaturate to make the colors drab.

3. **Press a number key to change the Pressure value.**

   Or drag the slider bar in the Options bar, which you can access by clicking on the black arrow next to the numeric setting. Either way, the setting affects the impact of the Sponge tool.

4. **Drag with the tool inside a color image.**

   Watch those colors change.

The primary reason that the programmers provide the Sponge tool is to desaturate colors that may get lost when you convert from RGB to CMYK. As I mention in Chapter 5, red, green, and blue can mix to form some very bright colors that cyan, magenta, yellow, and black can't express. So you can dab at the colors with the Sponge tool to bring them more in line with the CMYK spectrum.

But I like to use the Sponge tool for the exact opposite purpose — to make colors more saturated. Oh, sure, maybe you won't be able to print the colors correctly, but at least they'll be as bright as they can be. If dragging with the Sponge tool set to Saturate doesn't affect the colors in an image, it's because the colors are already as bright as they can be.

Another good way to use the Sponge tool is to provide a focal point for your image. Suppose that you have a color photo of a group of people and want to have one person stand out among the others. Select your person (see Chapter 12 for methods to select) and then choose Select⇨Inverse. Then carefully take the sponge, set the Mode option to Desaturate in the Options bar, and drag over the other people. You see their colors wash out while your chosen person remains bright and lively and stands out among the crowd. This technique works with any group of objects. You can also set the option to Saturate to make your chosen element brighter than the rest.

Making Taffy with the Liquify Command

I bet you thought Photoshop couldn't possibly give you any more ways to take your image out of the realm of reality, right? Well, hold on to your mouse, because the new Liquify command just came to town.

The Liquify command, among other things, lets you warp, twirl, pucker, and bloat your image. It's enough to make a grown Photoshop user downright queasy! So take a deep breath and prepare to become "liquified."

Select the area of the image that you want to distort and follow these steps:

1. **Open an image and decide whether you want to distort the whole image or just a portion.**

You can use an area selected with one of the tools described in Chapter 12. Or you can select a single layer (see Chapter 15). When you select an area, the unselected areas become *frozen* or protected from distortion. In this example, I use the whole image for now. Figure 9-12 shows a woman who looks like she could use a good warping or two.

2. Choose Image⇨Liquify.

A huge dialog box appears, as shown in Figure 9-12.

3. Select your desired brush size and pressure in the top right portion of the dialog box.

Enter a numeric value or access the slider via the right-pointing arrow.

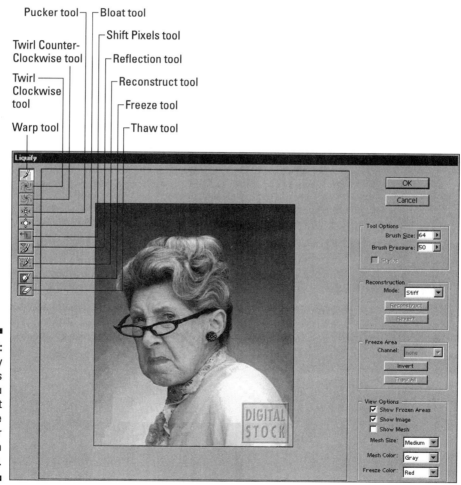

Pucker tool — Bloat tool

Twirl Counter-Clockwise tool — Shift Pixels tool

Reflection tool

Twirl Clockwise tool — Reconstruct tool

Freeze tool

Warp tool — Thaw tool

Figure 9-12: The Liquify dialog box is where you can distort your image into another dimension of reality.

4. If you didn't select an area in Step 1, you can do so now. Define any area in the image that you want frozen. Select the Freeze tool, shown in Figure 9-12, and drag over your desired area.

For our image, I select her body. Notice how the Freeze tool covers the area with a pinkish tint, referred to as a *mask*. The amount of freezing depends on the pressure of the brush. The varying pressure enables you to partially freeze an area so that the effect of the distortion isn't as intense. The tint of the mask gives a good indication of the amount of freezing. Go for the gusto and set the pressure to 100%. If you make an error, press Ctrl+Z (⌘+Z on a Mac) to undo. However, note that if you choose to undo while painting on a freeze mask, you undo all the paint strokes, not just your last stroke.

If you want to distort only a selected portion of your image, I recommend that you select your area with one of Photoshop's wonderful selection tools *before* you select the Liquify command. Your selected area will look much cleaner. The drawback is you will *only* have access to that selected portion. If you want to apply a distortion to a selected area *and* have access to the entire image, save your selection and then load the selection in the Liquify dialog box. The quick and dirty steps to do that are as follows:

1. After you make your selection, choose Select⇨Save Selection.

The Save Selection dialog box appears.

2. In the Save Selection dialog box, make sure the Channel is New.

3. Name your selection and click on OK. If you don't name your selection, Photoshop gives it the default name of Alpha 1. An alpha channel is simply a selection that's been saved.

4. Choose Image⇨Liquify.

The Liquify dialog box appears.

5. Choose your selection from the Channel pop-up menu under Freeze Area.

Your selection appears surrounded by a red mask. As you apply your distortions, the areas covered by the red mask remain unaffected because they're frozen. To apply distortions to the masked (frozen) areas, simply click on Invert under the Freeze Area. Your selection is then masked and the other portions of the image can now be freely distorted.

After you have a frozen area, you can invert it, which then freezes the other portion of your image instead. Or you can Thaw All, which melts, or deletes, all the frozen areas. You can also use the Thaw tool (see Figure 9-12) to drag over any areas you want to unfreeze. Again, brush size and pressure settings affect the amount of thawing.

Check out the various View Options. You can choose to view the frozen area, the image, and the mesh. The *mesh* is a grid of horizontal and vertical lines that hovers over your image. As you distort your image, you can see how the pixels distort based on the twisting and turning of the mesh grid.

And now time for the fun stuff. Use any one of the following tools to wreak havoc on your image. Check out the effects of each in Figure 9-13.

- **Warp tool:** Pushes the pixels forward under your brush as you drag, creating a stretched effect. This tool gives the most "taffy-like" effect.

- **Twirl Clockwise tool:** Rotates the pixels clockwise under your brush as you either drag or hold down the mouse.

- **Twirl Counterclockwise tool:** Ditto the above, only in a counterclockwise direction.

- **Pucker tool:** Moves the pixels toward the center of your brush as you drag or hold down the mouse, giving a kind of pinched look.

- **Bloat tool:** The opposite of Pucker — moves pixels away from the center, creating a kind of spherical effect.

- **Shift Pixels tool:** Shifts pixels perpendicular to the direction you move the brush. (In Figure 9-13 I dragged my brush up, as I also did with the Reflection tool.)

- **Reflection tool:** Copies pixels from the area perpendicular to the direction you drag.

After you use the various tools to pucker, twirl, warp, and generally render your image into something resembling a Salvador Dali painting, you're ready for the next stage. Follow these steps to actually apply the distortion:

1. **Click on OK if you like your crazed masterpiece and want to apply the distortion to the image.**

   See, up until now, Photoshop has just been displaying a proxy of the image, a kind of temporary preview. So if you really want it applied to your image, you have to click on OK and exit the dialog box.

2. **Or click on Cancel to get the heck outta' there. If you need some fine-tuning, read the info below.**

   If you got totally carried away, which is easy to do with these tools, you can tone down the effects on all or part of your image by using the Reconstruct tool and Reconstruction command. Here are some of the finer points of regaining what you just messed up:

   - To get your entire image (all unfrozen areas, that is) back to its pre-liquify, original state, click Revert under Reconstruction.

   - To change a portion of our image (again, any unfrozen areas) back to its original state, choose Revert from the Mode pop-up menu under Reconstruction. Select the reconstruct tool and drag or hold down over an area.

- To slowly reverse the distortion you applied to the image, click on the Reconstruct button. Press Esc and it stops reconstructing at that point.

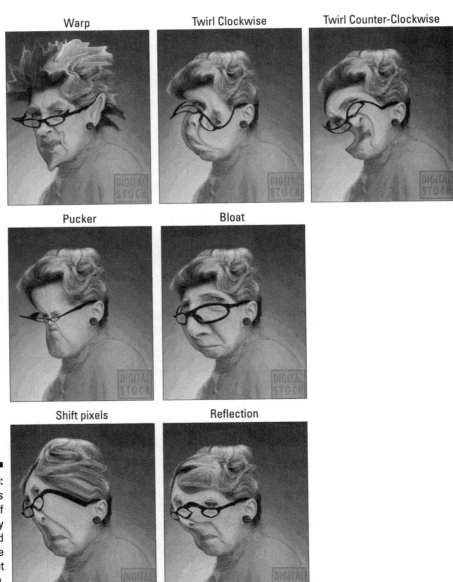

Warp   Twirl Clockwise   Twirl Counter-Clockwise

Pucker   Bloat

Shift pixels   Reflection

Figure 9-13: The various effects of the Liquify command can be downright terrifying.

In addition to refining the effects you applied to your image, you can also extend your distortions in frozen areas into unfrozen areas. This option is great, for example, if you want some transition between your distorted and undistorted areas. Freeze all or part of the areas you have distorted. Or you can select Invert under Freeze Area to flop your frozen and unfrozen areas. Choose one of the following modes of reconstruction and then drag or hold down the mouse over your desired unfrozen area:

- ✔ **Rigid:** Keeps the right angles in the pixel grid at the edge between frozen and unfrozen areas (choose Show Mesh to see this in action). Unfrozen areas begin to appear more like the original.

- ✔ **Stiff:** At the edge between frozen and unfrozen areas, the unfrozen areas continue the distortions in the frozen areas. The closer to the frozen areas, the greater the distortions.

- ✔ **Smooth:** Continues the distortions in frozen areas throughout the unfrozen areas smoothly and continuously.

- ✔ **Loose:** Similar to Smooth, but offers even more continuity.

To reconstruct all unfrozen areas, click the Reconstruct button. Before your very eyes, the image slowly goes back in time and reconstructs itself.

You can also perform reconstruction to match your distorted areas at certain points in the image. Think of it as using a kind of warped Rubber Stamp tool (see Chapter 10 for the rubber stamp lowdown). Choose one of the these remaining options in the Mode menu:

- ✔ **Displace:** Moves pixels in unfrozen areas to match the displacement at the reference point. You can use Displace to move all or part of the image to a different location.

- ✔ **Amplify:** Moves pixels in unfrozen areas to match the displacement, rotation, and scaling applied at a reference point. Use it to duplicate areas in an image.

- ✔ **Affine:** Moves pixels in unfrozen areas to match all distortions at the reference point — displacement, rotation, scaling, and skew.

To apply the above reconstruction modes, first click in the desired distorted area to establish your reference point. Then get the Reconstruct tool and drag or hold down the mouse over the area you want matched. You can always reclick to set a new reference point.

The best advice I can give for understanding the inner-workings of the Liquify command is play, play, play. If you have a few spare moments, open an image and do some reality altering of your own.

Chapter 10
Cleaning Up Goobers

*I*f you've ever had an image scanned to disk or CD, you know the story. You send out a lovely photograph that you've cherished all your life, and the scan comes back looking like someone stuck it inside a dryer lint trap. Big, gnarly hairs wiggle across the image. Little dust flecks seem to have reproduced like rabbits. And if you really hit the jackpot, you may even spy a few fingerprints on your image. It's enough to make you call up the service bureau and ask them whether they recently employed a shedding malamute that hasn't been bathed in six weeks and has a penchant for jelly sandwiches.

Unfortunately, sarcasm doesn't get you anywhere. But the dust-busting tools discussed in this chapter can. With a keen eye and a little bit of elbow grease, you can scrub away those imperfections and make your image appear absolutely spotless.

Photoshop offers two methods for dusting away the specks:

✔ The Dust & Scratches command automates the removal of image imperfections, but it can do more harm than good by getting rid of important detail as well.

✔ The Rubber Stamp tool lets you *clone* (copy) portions of an image to cover up blotches. The rubber stamp takes more time to use than the Dust & Scratches command and requires a considerable amount of clicking and dragging, but it also results in a better-looking picture.

This chapter explains the pros and cons of each method and throws in a few other ideas for spit-shining your images as well.

Using the Dust & Scratches Command

Ever own a really nice sports car, like a Porsche or a Jaguar? Me neither, but I've known folks who have, and they can be amazingly protective of their automobiles. Most Porsche/Jaguar owners would sooner vote for a Socialist than take their cars through one of those drive-through wash joints where big floppy pieces of blue plastic flog your car and take little bits of your paint job along with them. Automobile aficionados know that the only way to clean a car is to tenderly rub its surface with specially treated pieces of felt dipped in no-tears baby shampoo.

Although I might think that those car buffers are off their rockers, I whole-heartedly endorse this policy when it comes to cleaning images. That's why I'm not so fond of the Dust & Scratches filter — it's akin to sending your image through a car wash.

I should mention that the Dust & Scratches command is a *filter,* meaning that it automatically corrects an image by mixing up the pixels in some predefined manner. It works much like filters that change the focus of an image (discussed in Chapter 17).

But just because I may not approve of the Dust & Scratches command, that's no reason not to give you a crack at it. You're an adult. I'm not your keeper. Who knows, maybe the command will be helpful. Maybe you need to clean up an image in a hurry for that last-minute space in the company newsletter, and the car wash solution is the only one you have time to try.

With that enthusiastic endorsement out of the way, it's high time I show you how to use the Dust & Scratches filter. The lab rat for today's outing is Figure 10-1. This figure demonstrates another variety of splatter that can plague images — old photo gunk. The lines, scratches, and dots in this image weren't introduced in the scanning process; they were a part of the original photo. Shot near the beginning of this century, this picture of Halley's comet has held up amazingly well over the years. I hope to look half as good when I'm its age.

Incidentally, if you're a fellow lover of things extraterrestrial, you can't go wrong with Corbis' "Space & Spaceflight" CD, which includes about as many views of the sun, moon, planets, and outlying nebula as a person could hope for.

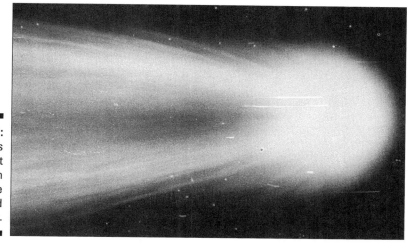

Figure 10-1: Halley's comet as it appeared in 1910, replete with old photo gunk.

To tidy up an image that presents similar symptoms, choose Filter⇨Noise⇨ Dust & Scratches. Photoshop displays the strange and mysterious Dust & Scratches dialog box, shown in all its glory in Figure 10-2 and explained in the next two sections.

If you select a portion of your image before you choose the Dust & Scratches command, the command affects just the selected area.

Preview cursor   Preview box   Zoom buttons

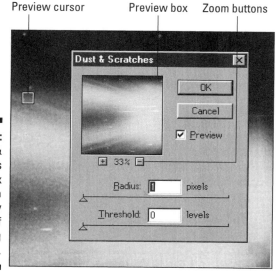

Figure 10-2: The Dust & Scratches dialog box provides a hefty supply of previewing options.

Previewing the filter effects

The makers of the Dust & Scratches dialog box know that it doesn't make a lick of sense, so they thoughtfully provide some preview options (shown in Figure 10-2) to enable you to see what happens when you make some otherwise meaningless adjustment. Here's how these preview options work:

✔ The preview box shows how your modifications look when applied to a tiny portion of the image.

✔ If you move the cursor outside the dialog box, it changes to a hollow square. Click on an area in the image to capture it inside the preview box.

✔ You can also scroll the contents of the preview box by dragging inside the box. Your cursor changes to a little hand.

✔ To magnify or reduce the contents of the preview box, click on the plus or minus zoom button.

✔ You can also access the standard magnifying glass cursor inside the preview box by pressing the Ctrl (⌘ on a Mac) key (to zoom in) or the Alt (Option on a Mac) key (to zoom out).

✔ As long as the Preview check box is selected, Photoshop previews your settings in the image window as well as in the preview box.

✔ You can even use the standard Hand and Zoom cursors inside the image window while the Dust & Scratches dialog box is open. Just press the spacebar to get the hand cursor or Ctrl or Alt (⌘ or Option on a Mac) to get the zoom cursors. This technique is a great way to preview an effect at two different zoom ratios, one inside the dialog box and one outside.

✔ If Photoshop seems to be slowing down too much as it tries to preview an effect in the image window, just click on the Preview check box to turn off the function.

I know, I know, you didn't want to know quite that much about previewing, but it will serve you well in the future. These same options, as well as a couple of others that you may decide to discover on your own (you Vasco da Gama, you), are found in a few dialog boxes that I describe in Chapter 17.

Specifying the size of the speck

The Dust & Scratches dialog box (Filter➪Noise➪Dust & Scratches) offers just two options that affect the performance of the filter: the Radius and Threshold slider bars. The slider bars work as follows:

✔ Change the Radius value to indicate the size of the dust specks and the thickness of the hairs that you want to eliminate. In geometry, radius means half the width of a circle, so the Radius value is half the width of a dust speck. The minimum value is 1, meaning that the filter wipes out all specks and hairs up to 2 pixels thick.

"Ah ha," you may think, "If I just crank up the Radius value as far as it goes (16 pixels), that should be enough to eliminate entire colonies of dust bunnies." Well, no. The Dust & Scratches filter doesn't really know a speck from a tiny bit of detail. So, if you have it rub out 16-pixel radius dust globs, it also rubs out 16-pixel details, such as Uncle Ralph's head. Figure 10-3 shows the effects of setting the Radius value to 1 on the left and 3 on the right. Notice how fuzzy the image became when I applied a 3-pixel radius? If you value my advice, you'll never set the radius value higher than 2.

✔ The Threshold value tells Photoshop how different the color of a dust speck has to be from the color of the surrounding image to be considered a bad seed. The Threshold slider works just like the RGB sliders in the Color palette (discussed in Chapter 5) — that is, it varies from 0 to 255.

The default Threshold value of 0 tells Photoshop that dust and image need only be 0 color levels different from each other. Because all colors are at least 0 levels different, Photoshop ignores the Threshold value and considers only the Radius value. Both images in Figure 10-3 were filtered with a Threshold value of 0.

By raising the Threshold value, you tell Photoshop to be more selective. If you set the value to 10, speck and image colors must vary by at least 10 levels before Photoshop covers up the speck, as in the first example of

Figure 10-3:
The results of applying the Dust & Scratches filter with the Radius slider set to 1 pixel (left) and 3 (right).

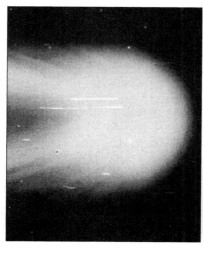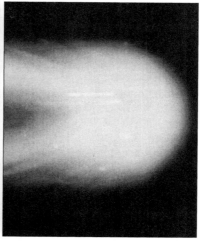

Figure 10-4. If you raise the Threshold to 20 — as in the second example — Photoshop disregards still more potential impurities. Notice that the two horizontal streaks in the second image remain intact, having been ruled out by the Threshold setting. (By the way, I set the Radius value to 3 in Figure 10-4 — something I earlier warned you against doing — in order to make the effects of the Threshold setting more noticeable.)

If you set the Threshold value any higher than 100, the dust specks have to be white and the image black — or vice versa — to receive any attention. I don't recommend using values over 15.

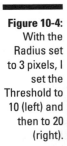

Figure 10-4:
With the Radius set to 3 pixels, I set the Threshold to 10 (left) and then to 20 (right).

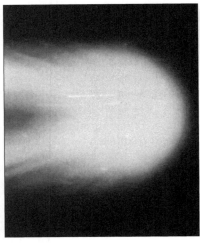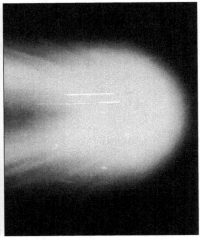

In my long ramblings about the Radius and Threshold values, I neglected to mention one disconcerting fact. Even though the Dust & Scratches filter variously obliterated the detail in Figures 10-3 and 10-4, none of the images are completely free of spots and streaks. Admittedly, this old, moldy picture is a lot worse off than most of your images are likely to be, but the fact remains that the Dust & Scratches filter is an imperfect solution. Just like a cheap car wash, it gets rid of most of the dirt — but not all of it — and it takes away some of the paint and detailing along with it.

Spot Cleaning Your Image with TLC

If you're willing to expend a little extra energy and you can stand up to your friends when they call you compulsive, the tool of choice for cleaning up images is the Rubber Stamp. The fifth tool from the top on the left side of the Toolbox, the Rubber Stamp lets you take a good portion of an image and paint it onto the bad portion. This miraculous process is called *cloning*.

You can also clone part of your image by copying and pasting it, as described near the end of Chapter 13. You should get familiar with both methods of cloning because both have their place in the retouching world. The Rubber Stamp works well for fixing small flaws in images — a scratch in a snapshot; a bruise on a pear; a mole on someone's face; and for cloning images with soft drop shadows. Copying and pasting works well for single, standalone images or images on their own layers.

Stamping out splatters

Want to see how the Rubber Stamp tool works? Try out these steps:

1. **Select the Rubber Stamp tool from the Toolbox.**

   To select the Rubber Stamp from the keyboard, press the S key.

2. **Make sure that the Aligned box is checked in the Rubber Stamp Options bar.**

   This option lets you clone from relative points in your image. You'll see what I mean in a second.

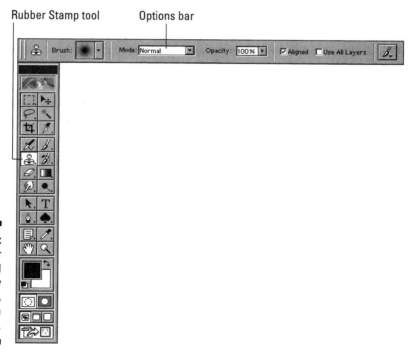

Rubber Stamp tool   Options bar

Figure 10-5:
The Rubber
Stamp and
its trusty
Options bar,
partners in
cloning.

3. **Start dragging randomly inside your image.**

   Whoops, I bet you got an error message, didn't you? If I'm right, the message says something about — I can almost see it; it's becoming clearer — Alt+clicking (Option+clicking on a Mac) to define a source! How do I know these things? Because I'm psychic. Even from here in Boulder, Colorado, months before you'll read this, I can foresee the error messages in your future. Ah, really, it's nothing. Been able to do it since I was a kid.

   Okay, I'm lying, I just got that message myself, and I reckoned that you may get it, too. See, to use the Rubber Stamp tool, you have to tell Photoshop which portion of your image you want to clone before you begin cloning it. Photoshop isn't a mind reader, you know. I may be a mind reader, but Photoshop most certainly is not.

   Now that you've grasped this valuable lesson, grab a pen and put a big X through Step 3 so that you never make the same mistake again.

4. **Alt+click (Option+click on a Mac) on the portion of the image that you want to clone.**

   For example, to fix that big goober near the beginning of the lower tail of Halley's comet, I Alt+clicked (Option+click on a Mac) at a location that appeared to contain similar gray values to the comet stuff that surrounds the goober, as shown in Figure 10-6. The point is to pick a portion of your image that blends in with areas around the blemish you want to eliminate.

   After you Alt+click (Option+click on a Mac), the little upside-down triangle at the bottom of the rubber stamp cursor becomes white. Fascinating, huh?

   According to *Webster's*, the word *goober* is derived from the Bantu word *nguba,* which means peanut. And peanut (wink) is exactly what I mean (nudge, nudge).

5. **Now click or drag on the offending blemish.**

   Actually, that mark on my comet looks more like a pimple than a peanut, doesn't it? To apply the digital zit cream, I clicked directly on the critter and purged it good. No muss, no fuss; the glitch is gone.

When you click or drag with the Rubber Stamp, Photoshop displays a cross cursor along with the stamp cursor, as shown in Figure 10-7. This cross represents the clone source, or the area that you're cloning from. As you move the mouse, the cross cursor also moves, providing a continual reference to the portion of your image that you're cloning. (Things work differently when you have the Aligned option unchecked in the Options bar, however, as I explain in the next section.)

The dreaded cosmic goober

Alt+click with rubber stamp

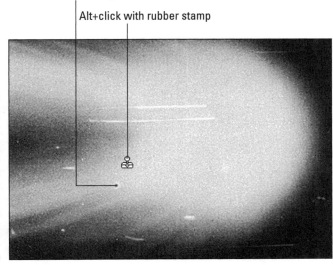

Figure 10-6: Alt+click (Option+ click on a Mac) on a good portion of an image to establish the cloning source.

Clone source   Rubber stamp cursor

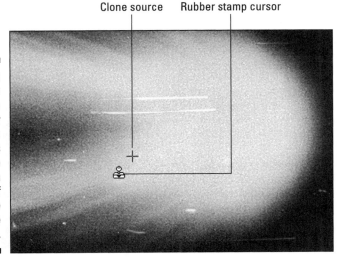

Figure 10-7: When you use the Rubber Stamp, a small cross follows to show you what part of the image you're cloning.

If the cloned area doesn't blend in well, just choose Edit⇨Undo or Ctrl+Z (⌘+Z on Mac) and then Alt+click (Option+click on a Mac) in the image with the Rubber Stamp to specify a better source for your cloning. Click or drag with the tool to test out a different clone. You may have to do this several times to get it just right.

Just for the sheer heck of it, Figure 10-8 shows the comet after I finished using the Rubber Stamp. Now, isn't that way better than anything from Figures 10-3 and 10-4? And it took about 15 minutes.

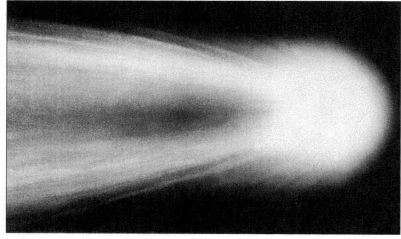

Figure 10-8: Halley's comet, all dressed up and nowhere to go for 74 years.

Performing more magic with the Rubber Stamp

If you never find out another thing about the Rubber Stamp tool, you'll be able to clean images quite easily after reading the preceding section. But the Rubber Stamp is an amazing tool with more facets and capabilities than any other Photoshop tool:

✔ To change the size or shape of the area that's cloned, change the brush size in the Brushes palette, just as you would for other painting or editing tools. For more information about the Brushes palette, see Chapter 8.

✔ To make the clone more translucent or less translucent, use the Opacity slider in the Options bar. Access the slider by pressing the black arrow to the right of the numeric setting. A setting of 100 makes your clone opaque.

✔ To clean up a straight hair or scratch, Alt+click (Option+click on a Mac) with the tool to specify the source for the cloning as you normally would. Then click at one end of the scratch and Shift+click at the other.

✔ If the first clone doesn't look exactly right but is pretty close, you may want to modify the clone slightly rather than redo it. Lower the Opacity setting in the Options bar by pressing a number key and then clone from a different position by again Alt+clicking (Option+click on a Mac) and dragging. This enables you to mix multiple portions of an image together to get a more seamless blend.

✔ The blocky rubber stamp cursor that appears by default makes predicting the outcome of your clone difficult. To get a better idea of the size of your clone before you click, press Ctrl+K (⌘+K on Mac) and then Ctrl+3 (⌘+3 on a Mac) to open up the Display & Cursors panel of the Preferences dialog box. (Or choose Edit➪Preferences➪Display & Cursors.) Select the Brush Size radio button from the Painting Cursors area of the dialog box. Now, your cursor reflects the size of your brush.

✔ Normally, the Rubber Stamp tool clones from a relative location. If you move your cursor to a different location, the clone source moves with you. But what if you want to clone multiple times from a single location? In this case, leave the Aligned box unchecked in the Options bar. Now, you can Alt+click (Option+click on a Mac) once to set the source and click and drag multiple times to duplicate that source.

✔ The Pattern Stamp tool, which shares the same space as the Rubber Stamp tool, clones an area with a repeating pattern. You can define your own pattern by selecting a rectangular area and choosing Edit➪Define Pattern (if you don't define a selection, the entire canvas will be used for the pattern). Select your custom pattern from the Pattern Option drop-down palette in the Options bar. Drag with the Pattern Stamp tool, and you'll see the pattern appear. Cool, but not really useful.

✔ Photoshop now enables you to save multiple custom patterns. In addition, you have a variety of pattern presets availabe for use. Both your custom patterns and the Photoshop presets are accessed via the Pattern Option drop-down palette and its accompanying pop-up menu.

✔ You can clone between images. What am I talking about? If you have two images open, you can Alt+click (Option+click on a Mac) inside one image to specify the source and drag in the other image to clone. It's like painting one image onto another.

✔ Color Plate 10-1 shows an example of cloning between images. Starting with the two images on the left side of the figure (which I scaled to the same file size by using Image➪Image Size, as discussed in Chapter 4), I Alt+clicked (Option+click on a Mac) inside the top image and then dragged with the Rubber Stamp inside the bottom image. I cloned the woman's face and blouse using a large fuzzy brush and then switched to a smaller brush for the touch-ups. To match the skin tones in the forehead and the base of the nose, I cloned from the woman's cheeks at an Opacity setting of 50%. Pretty gruesome, huh?

✔ If your image contains layers (I discuss these in Chapter 15), remember that the Rubber Stamp tool normally clones only from the active layer. If you select the Use All Layers check box in the Options bar, the Rubber Stamp reads the pixels in all visible layers to create the clone. When you then click or drag with the Rubber Stamp, Photoshop paints the clone onto the active layer.

✔ All the brush modes that apply to the painting tools apply to the Rubber Stamp as well. This means that you can achieve interesting special effects by selecting the Multiply, Screen, Overlay, Difference, or Color option from the Mode pop-up menu in the Options bar. For more on brush modes, see Chapter 8.

✔ Try cloning between two different images with a special brush mode in effect. For example, if you clone with the Multiply brush mode, you emblazon the first image onto the second. If you have half an hour to waste, play with the different modes and see what you can do.

Chapter 11

Turning Back the Digital Clock

. . . .

In This Chapter

▶ Undoing operations

▶ Using the Eraser tool

▶ Selecting different kinds of erasers

▶ Choosing the Revert command

▶ Exploring the new History palette

▶ Using the Erase to History option and the History Brush tool

. . . .

*H*ere's how you know that you're a consummate computer nerd: When you snag your favorite sweater, say something highly objectionable to your spouse, or spill a well-known staining agent on your newly installed carpeting, your first reaction is not one of panic or regret. You merely think, "Undo."

Unfortunately, the real world provides no Undo command. After a horrible deed is done, it takes an obscenely disproportionate amount of fussing, explaining, or scrubbing to fix the transgression.

Not so in the magical world of personal computing. Edit⇨Undo is standard equipment with just about every Windows (and Macintosh) program out there. With one press of Ctrl+Z (⌘+Z on a Mac) — the Undo command's keyboard equivalent — your previous operation disappears for good, leaving you one step backward in time.

But Photoshop doesn't stop there. You are also lucky enough to have access to *multiple undos.* Not only can you undo as many as 100 actions, but you can also actually *skip* previous steps. In other words, if you have performed five actions and want to return to the way your image looked after your second action, you aren't required to first undo steps five, four, and three. You merely select step two in the digital undo command headquarters — the History palette. Not only can you turn back the digital clock, you can also truly travel back in time. Adobe definitely deserves an "atta-boy" for this powerful feature.

In this chapter, I explain all the Photoshop methods for regaining the past so that you can edit worry-free, safe in the knowledge that everything you do can be undone. But before you explore the wide and wonderful world of the History palette, look at the Photoshop old-and-trusty ways of undoing what's been done.

Nuking the Last Operation

The more you work with Photoshop, the more reflexive your actions become. Certainly, this means that you can work more quickly, but it also means that you are likely to make more mistakes. Reflexive, after all, is a close cousin to thoughtless. And when you don't think, you can wander into some pretty nasty situations.

Doing the Undo

The Undo command ensures that you aren't punished for working reflexively. To get a sense of just how wonderful this command can be, try out these steps:

1. **Open an image.**

   If you already have an image open, good for you.

2. **Select the Paintbrush tool and drag across the image.**

   Draw a mustache or something. Just make sure to draw a single brush stroke and no more.

3. **Take a break.**

   You've worked hard, you deserve it. Watch TV for your daily allowance of six hours. Take up macramé. Enlist in the armed forces. The point is, no matter how long you're away, Photoshop remembers the last operation you performed (as long as you don't have a power outage or some similar computing disaster).

4. **Choose Edit⇨Undo.**

   Actually, the name of the command should be Undo Paintbrush. The name of the Undo command changes to tell you what action you're about to undo.

   You can also choose the Undo command by pressing Ctrl+Z (⌘+Z on a Mac). Either way, your brush stroke is gone.

After you choose the Undo command, the command changes to the Redo command. For example, if you choose Undo after completing Step 4, the command name is Redo Paintbrush. If you choose the Redo Paintbrush command, your brush stroke comes back, and the Redo Paintbrush command becomes the Undo Paintbrush command again. In other words, you can undo an action, and then redo it, and then undo it, and then redo it, and so on, until you make up your mind or collapse from exhaustion, whichever comes first.

The Undo command works even after you choose File⇨Print. This means that you can adjust an image, print it to see how it looks, and undo the adjustment if you don't like it. Choosing File⇨Page Setup — or any other command except Print — wipes out your chance to undo that adjustment, though.

Undo limitations

Although the Undo command is certainly a good tool, keep in mind that it has some limitations. So, here are a few guidelines to stash away in the back of your brain:

- ✓ You can't undo the Print command. Print involves marking up real pieces of paper, and the Undo command is powerless in the real world. Instead, Undo just ignores Print, as you saw in the preceding steps.

- ✓ File⇨Save, File⇨Save As, and File⇨Save for Web are beyond the reach of the Undo command. After the Save command finishes, the image is saved, and the previous version of the image is gone. (The Save As command leaves the previous version of the image intact, so you need never worry when choosing it.)

- ✓ Not only can you *not* undo Save, Save As, or Save for Web, these commands also render the Undo command null and void. After the Save operation completes, the Undo command appears dimmed, meaning that you can't choose it. The operation you performed before choosing Save is now permanent (doubly so, because the changes are saved to disk).

- ✓ You can't undo the Exit command (Quit command on a Mac). There's a surprise. Also, when you relaunch Photoshop, it has no idea what you did during the previous session, so you can't undo the last changes you made before quitting.

- ✓ You also can't undo changing a foreground or background color, adjusting a setting using one of the commands under the Edit⇨Preferences submenu, hiding or displaying palettes, changing a palette setting, changing a setting in the Options bar, or selecting a tool. Like the Print command, these operations are ignored by Undo, thus enabling you to undo the previous "significant" operation.

- ✓ You may think that Photoshop treats File⇨Page Setup like one of the Edit⇨Preferences commands because you're just adjusting printing preferences. But Photoshop remembers your changes inside the Page Setup dialog box and lets you undo them. So, if you want to undo a brush stroke or other operation after printing the image, don't choose Page Setup before Print.

The Powers of the Eraser

What artist's toolbox would be complete without an eraser? None that I know of. But Photoshop provides not just one eraser, but three — the Eraser tool, the Background Eraser tool, and the Magic Eraser tool. I address the last two in Chapter 12. For now let's check out the regular ol' Eraser tool.

Working with the Eraser

The Eraser tool is directly under the Rubber Stamp tool in the Toolbox and lets you erase in a couple of ways:

- ✔ If you drag with the Eraser in an image that contains only one layer, the tool paints in the background color, which is typically white. I suppose that you can call this process erasing, but it's really just painting in a different color. Who needs it?

- ✔ If your image contains more than one layer (I discuss layers in Chapter 15), the Eraser works a little differently and becomes a lot more useful. If you drag the Eraser on the background layer, the Eraser paints in the background color, as usual. But on any other layer, the pixels you scrub with the Eraser become transparent, revealing pixels on underlying layers. This assumes that the Lock transparent pixels box is unchecked in the Layers palette. If you check the Lock transparent pixels box, the Eraser paints in the background color.

- ✔ Holding down the Alt key (Option key on a Mac) with the Eraser enables you to erase back to a chosen step in the History palette. I explain this feature further in the section on the History palette.

Adjusting your Eraser

The Eraser tool comes in four delicious eraser flavors. To switch erasers, select an option from the Mode drop-down menu in the Options bar, discussed later in this chapter.

Three erasers are named after painting tools — Paintbrush, Airbrush, and Pencil — and work exactly like these tools, down to the inclusion of the Wet Edges check box for the Paintbrush option. This means that you can change the brush size in the Brushes palette and adjust the Opacity setting to partially reveal the image or, in a layered image, make pixels only partially transparent. (For a refresher on changing the brush size and opacity, review Chapter 8.)

The fourth option, Block, changes the eraser to the square, hard-edged, fixed-size eraser. The options in the Brushes palette don't affect the block eraser, nor do the Opacity slider bar or any of the other settings in the Options bar except Erase to History. The Block Eraser can be useful when you want to completely erase general areas, but you probably won't take it up very often.

Abandoning Edits en Masse

Sometimes you make small mistakes, and sometimes you make big ones. If, after several minutes of messing about, you decide that you hate all your edits and want to return the entire image to its last saved appearance so that you can just start over again, you can do one of two things. First, you can select the top step, technically referred to as a *state,* in the History palette (see the next section for details on the History palette). Selecting the top step restores the image back to the way it appeared when you first opened it. Second, and only if all else fails, choose File⇨Revert. Photoshop displays an alert box to make sure that you didn't choose the wrong command; after all, you've been all thumbs today. If you click on the Revert button or press Enter (Return on a Mac), the program reloads the image from disk and throws away all your changes.

You have an advantage in using the History palette rather than the File⇨Revert command. The History palette restores the *original* image regardless of whether you saved along the way, whereas File⇨Revert reloads the last saved version, which may include some undesirable changes.

Just in case you change your mind or your fingers slipped, you can undo File⇨Revert, so breathe easier. And if you've executed another command, don't despair. The Revert command is recorded in the History palette, which I discuss next.

The History Palette

Now I explore this powerful palette in detail. Choose Window⇨Show History to display the History palette (see Figure 11-1). The History palette records all of your operations and creates a running list of the steps — in other words, the condition of your image at that point in history. Okay, so that analogy is a bit dramatic. As you perform each operation, Photoshop names each state and displays a corresponding icon according to the tool or command used. It ignores recording operations such as palette and tool settings and color and preferences changes.

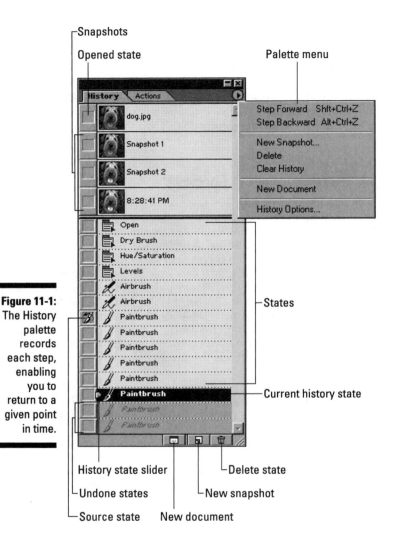

Figure 11-1:
The History
palette
records
each step,
enabling
you to
return to a
given point
in time.

Snapshots

Opened state

Palette menu

States

Current history state

Delete state

History state slider

Undone states

New snapshot

Source state   New document

Here's a list of the History palette's features and functions and how to take advantage of them:

✔ To return to a previous state, click on the desired state. Notice that Photoshop temporarily undoes all steps after that state and that they appear grayed out. Press Ctrl+Z (⌘+Z on a Mac) or choose Edit⇨Undo to return to your last state; you can also simply click on your last state.

✔ The grayed out states are referred to as *undone states.* You can redo an undone state by clicking on it. If you perform a new operation, the undone states disappear. Choose Edit⇨Undo or Ctrl+Z (⌘+Z on a Mac) *immediately* to get the undone states back. After you move on to other commands, they're gone for good.

✔ To step backward through the palette one state at a time, press Ctrl+Alt+Z (⌘+Option+Z on a Mac). To move forward, press Ctrl+Shift+Z (⌘+Shift+Z on a Mac). These commands are also accessible via the History palette pop-up menu.

✔ The keyboard equivalents for stepping backward and forward through the History palette, and also for Edit⇨Undo, can now be customized via the Preferences⇨General menu.

✔ Drag the History state slider (refer to Figure 11-1) forward and backward to scroll through and see each state rapidly disappear and reappear in order.

✔ To set the source state — for painting with the History Brush, erasing to History, or filling with History — click in the column to the left of the state list. The History Brush icon appears.

✔ Select a source state (refer to Figure 11-1) in the palette and paint back to it using the History Brush (see details later in this chapter).

✔ Choose a source state in the palette, select the Eraser tool, check Erase to History in the Options bar, and erase back to that point in time. Alternatively, pressing the Alt key (Option key on a Mac) while erasing can also Erase to History (for more information, see the next section).

✔ Make a selection in your image, and identify a source state in the palette. Choose Edit⇨Fill, and in the Contents pop-up menu, select History. Press Enter (Return on a Mac). The selected area fills with what the image looked like at that point in time while the unselected area remains unchanged. To quickly fill an area with the source state, press Ctrl+Alt+Backspace (⌘+Option+Delete on Mac).

✔ You can save any state in the History palette as a snapshot — a freeze frame, so to speak. Even after you've used up all your 100 steps, you can revert to the way the image looked when you took the snapshot. Choose New Snapshot from the palette pop-up menu or Alt+click (Option+click) on the page icon at the bottom of the palette (refer to Figure 11-1). Snapshots can be taken from the full document (all layers remain separately intact), from merged layers (layers are flattened into a background), or from just the current layer (only the elements on the active layer are retained). For more information on layers, see Chapter 15. You can also click on the new snapshot icon. The dialog box is bypassed, and a snapshot is created by using the default settings (full document). You can create and store as many snapshots as your computer's RAM is capable of storing.

Unfortunately, snapshots are available only as long as your image is open. Snapshots aren't saved with the file. The only way to get a "permanent" snapshot of your image is to create a new file from a chosen state. Select a state in the History palette, and create a new file from that state by choosing New Document from the palette pop-up menu or by clicking on the new document icon at the bottom of the palette (refer to Figure 11-1). You can also drag and drop the state onto the new document icon.

✔ You can establish the number of maximum history states (from 1 through 100) you want to retain in the Preferences⇨General menu. This option no longer resides in the History Options dialog box. If your computer is low on RAM (32MB or less), you may want to set this value to a lower number. Remember that after you exceed your maximum, the oldest step disappears, then the next oldest, and so on.

✔ Always check Automatically Create First Snapshot in the History Options dialog box. You can access the History Options dialog box via the History palette pop-up menu. If this option is unchecked, you don't get a snapshot of the opened state (refer to Figure 11-1). You can always go back to the first state; however, if you exceed your maximum number of history states, this first state disappears. Then, if you have saved any changes along the way, you cannot retrieve your original image.

✔ Automatically Create New Snapshot When Saving is a new option in the History Options dialog box. If this option is checked, every time you save, Photoshop creates a snapshot which it then names based on the time you save the file. If you are a frequent saver, like me, leave this option unchecked, or else you'll end up with a zillion snapshots.

✔ The Allow Non-Linear History option in the History Options dialog box permits undone states to remain when you perform a new operation. Note that you can't undo a state without affecting later states. For example, you paint, airbrush, and pencil on an image. You can go back to the paint state and paint some more without losing your later airbrush and pencil states. However, you can't undo the airbrush state and retain the pencil state. Even if you delete the airbrush state, the strokes you applied remain on the image. Be aware it can be somewhat confusing. Experiment with a test image until you get a good handle on it or leave this option unchecked.

✔ I mentioned earlier that if you click on the new snapshot icon, the New Snapshot dialog box is bypassed and a snapshot is created by using the default settings. If you check the new Show New Snapshot Dialog by Default option in the History Option dialog box, Photoshop *will* display the New Snapshot dialog box every time you click on the New Snapshot icon.

✔ If you're absolutely sure you're happy with your image, and your computer is slowing down or running out of memory, you can delete the history states by choosing the Clear History command from the palette pop-up menu. If you change your mind, immediately press Edit⇨Undo or

Ctrl+Z (⌘+Z on a Mac). If you have multiple files open, you can clear all their histories at once by choosing Edit➪Purge➪Histories. You're prompted with a warning that this *cannot* be undone. Press Enter (Return on a Mac). For either choice, you still retain your opened state and all your snapshots — your original image — but all your other steps are deleted.

✔ You can delete a single state by selecting it and choosing Delete from the palette pop-up menu. You can also simply select the state and click on the trash can icon at the bottom of the palette (refer to Figure 11-1). Alternatively, you can drag and drop the state onto the trash can icon.

✔ Every file has its own history; therefore, you can work on multiple images simultaneously and independently of each other.

✔ After you close your image, its history disappears forever. The states and snapshots in the History palette are not saved with the file. Too bad. New wish list item, anyone? Remember what they say — be careful what you wish for. Imagine the gargantuan file sizes!

Erasing away the present

Although you'll definitely make good use of the all-knowing, all-undoing History palette, the Eraser tool provides a more flexible, fun way to blast to the past. I introduced the capabilities of the regular eraser earlier in this chapter. Now, look at it after it has been further empowered to Erase to History.

The following steps give you an opportunity to try out the Erase to History option for yourself. In these steps, you paint a halo around the central subject of an image without harming the subject. First, you color outside the lines and then you clean it up with the magic eraser:

1. **Open an image.**

   For these steps, open something with a strong central subject, such as a person or an animal. You can't go wrong with a fish like the one in Figure 11-2.

2. **Set the foreground color to white.**

   Press D to get the default colors — black for the foreground and white for the background — and then press X to switch them.

3. **Trace the central subject with the Airbrush tool.**

   Don't worry about getting white all over the central subject. In Figure 11-3, for example, I've made a complete mess of things. There's no way to be careful with the Airbrush — it sprays all over the place.

Figure 11-2:
This lingcod
stands out
proudly
from his
surroun-
dings.

4. **Select the Eraser tool.**

   To select the tool from the keyboard, press the E key.

5. **In the Options bar, select the Paintbrush style from the Mode drop-down menu.**

Figure 11-3:
Using the
Airbrush
tool, I traced
sloppily
around the
lingcod.

6. **Check on Erase to History in the Options bar.**

   Alternatively, you can leave it unchecked and press Alt (Option on a Mac) to Erase to History.

7. **Choose a medium-size, soft brush from the Brushes drop-down palette in the Options bar.**

8. **In the History palette, select the source state you want to erase back to.**

   I chose the Open state.

9. **Drag to erase inside the central subject (in my case, the lingcod).**

   As you drag, you reveal the way the image looked at that point in time.

Getting to the image shown in Figure 11-4 required that I perform Step 9 with some care and effort. I wanted to erase inside the subject only and leave the white airbrush paint intact in the background. Creating similar effects may take many strokes and many undos to get the image just right, but the practice is good for you. Just don't forget to either check on Erase to History in the Options bar or press the Alt key (Option key on a Mac) every time you erase — teaches you patience and all that.

Figure 11-4: The lingcod glows eagerly as he emerges from his nuclear chamber.

Here are some more things to know about erasing to the history of your image:

✔ If you're erasing a multiple-layer image, the Eraser tool erases changes to the active layer only.

✔ You can also select a portion of your image (see Chapter 12) and revert only that portion to a source state by using the Edit⇨Fill command. For details on filling, see Chapter 14.

Brushing back in time

Like the Eraser tool, the History Brush provides a more artistic, free-form way of revealing a previous state of an image.

To brush back to a source state:

1. **Select the History Brush tool.**

   To select the tool from the keyboard, press the Y key. There's no need to press the Alt key (Option key on a Mac).

2. **Select a brush mode from the Mode drop-down menu in the Options bar.**

   Utilizing the brush modes is one advantage the History Brush has over the Erase to History option. You can achieve different effects by using various modes. See Chapter 8 for tips on these modes.

3. **From the Brushes palette in the Options bar, select a brush size and style.**

4. **In the History palette, select the source state you want to brush back to.**

5. **Drag the History Brush on the image.**

   As you drag, you reveal the way the image looked at that point in time.

Why won't the Eraser tool or History Brush work?

A few operations prevent the Eraser tool and the History Brush from reverting back to a source state. These same operations also prevent filling a selection with History. Reverting to a source state by any of these methods works only if the image on-screen and the history states in the History palette share the same file size — that is, they each contain exactly the same number of pixels. Any operation that changes the size of the on-screen image throws a monkeywrench into the works. You'll see the not-allowed cursor (a circle with a slash) when trying to use the History Brush. An on-screen warning appears when you try to use the eraser, and the Erase to History check box is grayed out in the Options bar. The History option in the Contents pop-up menu under Edit⇨Fill is grayed out as well.

The following operations prevent you from erasing or brushing to a source state:

✔ Cropping the image with the Crop tool.

✔ Trimming the image with the Image➪Trim command.

✔ Applying the Image Size command with the Resample Image check box selected. (As long as Resample Image is unchecked, you can change the dimension or resolution without causing problems.)

✔ Using the Canvas Size command.

✔ Applying any of the commands under the Image➪Rotate Canvas submenu (except 180°) to the entire image.

You can still erase or brush to source states that appear *after* the above operations, but not to any source states listed *prior* to that operation. Given all that the History palette, History Brush, Erase to History option, and Fill with History operation can do, these limitations seem insignificant and minor — minuscule.

The Art History Brush

But wait! Before you leave this chapter, I want to introduce to you another History Brush. It made its debut in Photoshop 5.5 and is dubbed the Art History Brush. It lets you create impressionistic effects with the aid of the History palette.

Try this. Open any old file. Then press D to get the default foreground and background colors and press Alt+Backspace (Option+Delete on a Mac) to fill the entire image with black. Press Y to select the History Brush, then Shift+Y to select the Art History Brush — the brush with a curlicue. Now paint inside your black image. Each stroke reveals a bit of your image in painterly detail, as shown in Figure 11-5.

The performance of the Art History Brush depends on three things: the brush size selected in the Brushes palette, the source state specified in the History palette, and any number of settings in the Options bar. You can change the brush size from the keyboard by pressing the [and] keys. That leaves the settings in the Options bar, shown in Figure 11-6. Here are the options:

✔ **Mode:** This drop-down menu assigns a brush mode to the tool. Each mode is covered in Chapter 8.

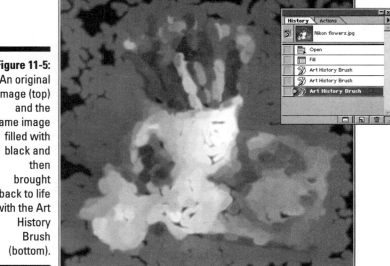

Figure 11-5:
An original image (top) and the same image filled with black and then brought back to life with the Art History Brush (bottom).

✔ **Style:** The Art History Brush paints with randomly generated corkscrews of color. You can decide the basic shapes of the corkscrews by selecting an option from the Style drop-down menu. Combine these

Figure 11-6:
The Options
bar offers
numerous
settings for
the Art
History
Brush.

options with different brush sizes to vary the detail conveyed by the impressionistic image. Tight and short means better detail; Loose and long means more generalized.

- **Area:** This value defines the area covered by a single dollop of paint. Larger pixel values generally mean more strokes are laid down at a time; reduce the value for a more sparse look.

- **Opacity:** Lower this value to create translucent strokes. To lower the Opacity from the keyboard, just press a number key any time the Art History Brush is active.

- **Fidelity:** As it lays down corkscrews, the brush colors each according to a color lifted by the cursor from the original source state. Lowering the Fidelity value enables the corkscrew color to drift away from the source color. This results in random coloring (true to the impressionist tradition), but it also slows down the brush's response.

- **Tolerance:** This value limits where the Art History Brush can paint. A value of 0 lets the brush paint anywhere; higher values let the brush paint only in areas where the current state and source state differ in color.

If impressionism interests you, I encourage you to experiment. If not, give this brush a slip. I happen to think it's pretty nifty (and surprisingly well implemented), but it definitely falls under the heading of Whimsical Creative Tools to Play with When You're Not under Deadline.

Part IV
Select Before
You Correct

In this part . . .

The first time children arm themselves with crayons and coloring books, they all do the same thing: They scribble. Few children have sufficient coordination to color tidily, and, frankly, I doubt that they see much point to it. But there's always one adult who says, "Darling, try to color inside the lines."

It's tough to unlearn a lesson that's ingrained into every one of us at such a trusting age, but the truth is, carefully coloring inside the lines is and always has been a counter-intuitive and nonartistic operation. It defeats expressionism and prevents you from seeing the larger picture.

"This may be so," you might argue, "but what if I'm trying to perform a delicate adjustment to a complex image? I can't just start scribbling all over the place." Ah, but there's where you're wrong. That's exactly what you can do. Any time you want to constrain an effect to a small area of your image, you need to select it first. After you do that, Photoshop automatically ensures that the larger image remains intact, no matter how sloppy your motor skills.

As you might expect, *selecting* is the topic of Chapters 12 through 14. Here, you find out how to select an element in your image, how to modify the selection if you don't get it exactly right the first time, and how to color selections.

So, the next time you see some kids coloring inside the lines, you'll know what to tell them. "Hey you kids, don't you know that tidy people never prosper? Break off the tips of those crayons and start scribbling!"

Chapter 12

The Great Pixel Roundup (Yee Ha)

. . . .

In This Chapter

▶ Picking the right selection tool

▶ Roping pixels with the lasso tools

▶ Drawing straight-sided selections

▶ Selecting with the Magnetic Lasso

▶ Selecting rectangular and oval areas

▶ Using the Magic Wand

▶ Creating paths with the Pen tool

▶ Editing paths

▶ Using the Freeform Pen tool

▶ Exploring the Paths palette

▶ Creating clipping paths

▶ Selecting with the Color Range command

▶ Using the other erasers

▶ Selecting with the Extract command

. . . .

*I*f you're an old ranch hand, you may find it helpful to think of the pixels in your image as a bunch of cows. A pixel may not have any horns and it rarely moos, but it's a cow all the same. Consider these amazing similarities: Both pixels and cows travel in herds. Come on, when's the last time you saw one pixel out on its own? They're both dumb as dirt. And obstinate to boot. And — here's the absolute clincher — you round them both up by using a lasso.

The only difference between pixels and cows is in the vernacular. When you lasso a cow or two on the lone prairie, it's called ropin'. When you lasso a mess of pixels, it's called selectin'. And after you select the desired pixels, you can do things to them. You can move them, duplicate them, and apply all kinds of alterations that I describe in future chapters. Selecting lets you grab hold of some detail or other and edit it independently of other portions of your image. It's a way of isolating pixels to manipulate them.

This chapter and Chapter 13 discuss methods for selecting portions of an image. With a little practice, you can rustle pixels better than most hands rope dogies, and that's no bull.

Learning the Ropes

Photoshop provides several selection tools, all labeled in Figure 12-1. These tools include the Lasso, the Polygon Lasso, the Magnetic Lasso, four so-called marquee tools, and an automatic color-selector known as the Magic Wand. Here's how they work:

- ✓ Drag inside the image with the Lasso tool to select free-form areas. The shape of the selection conforms to the shape of your drag.

- ✓ Use the Polygon Lasso tool, which shares a flyout menu with the regular lasso, to draw polygon selections — that is, selections made up of straight sides. You can still use the old technique of holding down the Alt (Option on a Mac) key and clicking with the regular Lasso, but you also have the option of using the dedicated Polygon Lasso tool.

- ✓ Click the Magnetic Lasso tool, which also shares a flyout menu with the other two lasso tools, on the edge of your object and then move the lasso around that edge. Keep reading this chapter for further details!

- ✓ The Rectangular Marquee tool lets you select a rectangular area. Just drag from one corner of the area you want to select to the other. The outline drawn with the tool looks like a border of moving dots — which is how "marquee" managed its way into the tool name.

- ✓ The Elliptical Marquee draws oval selections. The word *ellipse,* incidentally, is what mathematicians say when they're talking about ovals. In fact, I'd just call it the *ovoid marquee tool,* but I'm afraid that you'd think I was talking about a home pregnancy test.

- ✓ The Single Column and Single Row marquee tools select one solitary column or row of pixels in your image. Both these tools fall under the limited-use category.

- ✓ The Magic Wand selects areas of continuous color. For example, if you want to select the sky without selecting the clouds, you just click in the sky. At least, that's the way it's supposed to work, but you never know. The Magic Wand isn't always as magic as you may think.

Now that you know how the tools work, look at how to get to the tools. The arrow in the lower-right corner of the Marquee and Lasso tool icons in the Toolbox indicates that a flyout menu of hidden tools lurks beneath each icon (see Chapter 2 for more information).

To switch between the tools on the flyout menus, you can Alt+click (Option+click on a Mac) on whichever tool icon happens to be visible in the Toolbox at the time. You can also select tools using these keyboard shortcuts:

 ✔ Press the M key to access the active Marquee tool. If the Rectangular Marquee is active, press Shift+M to toggle through the Elliptical, Single Row, and Single Column Marquee tools.

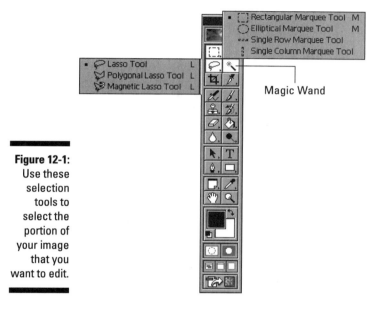

Figure 12-1:
Use these
selection
tools to
select the
portion of
your image
that you
want to edit.

 ✔ Press L to get the lasso tools. As with the marquee tools, the same short-cut switches you between the three lasso tools: If the regular Lasso tool is active, pressing Shift+L brings up the Polygon and the Magnetic Lassos.

 ✔ Press W to get the Magic Wand. The tool is more unpredictable than magic, making W — for Wacky Wand — a logical keyboard equivalent.

Throwing Lassos

Both the regular Lasso tool and the Polygon Lasso tool are so easy to use, your newborn can master them. If you don't have a newborn, I guess you have to muddle through on your own. The Magnetic Lasso is trickier, however, but nothing a toddler couldn't pick up with a little guidance.

Using the regular Lasso tool

I have only one instruction for using the Lasso: Trace around the portion of the image that you want to select with the tool. That's it. In Figure 12-2, for example, I dragged around the mushroom to select it independently of its surroundings. As the figure shows, Photoshop displays a dotted outline around the selected area after you release the mouse button. This outline represents the exact path of your drag. (If you release before completing the shape — that is, before meeting up with the point at which you began dragging — Photoshop simply connects the beginning and ending points with a straight line. So you won't hurt anything if you release too early.)

I was careful to draw the outline just right in Figure 12-2. There's no trick to it; I've just had plenty of practice. If your outlines aren't quite so accurate, however, don't sweat it. There are plenty of ways to modify the outline after you draw it (see Chapter 13).

Drawing straight-sided selections

Suppose that you want to select that cube-with-a-ball thing in the center of the image. You can drag around it with the Lasso tool, but a better option is to use the Polygon Lasso, which makes it easy to create selections with straight sides.

Lasso cursor ⌐ ⌐Selection outline

Figure 12-2:
I selected the mushroom by dragging around it with the Lasso.

To select an object in this manner, click with the polygon lasso to set the beginning of the first line in the selection. Then move the mouse cursor to the point where you want the line to end and click again. Keep clicking to create new line segments. To complete the selection, you have two options. If you double-click, Photoshop draws a segment between the spot you double-click and the first point in your selection. You can also move the cursor over the first point in your selection until you see a little circle next to the Polygon Lasso cursor. Then click to close the selection.

The Polygon Lasso can also be used for images with both curved and straight segments. You can switch to the regular Lasso in midselection to create a curved segment. Just press and hold down the Alt (Option on a Mac) key and drag to draw your curved line. When you release the Alt (Option on a Mac) key, the tool reverts back to the Polygon Lasso.

You can also press Alt (Option on a Mac) while drawing a selection with the regular Lasso to access the Polygon Lasso. Press Alt (Option on a Mac) and click to set the endpoints of your straight-sided segments, as you normally do with the Polygon Lasso. To start another curved segment, just drag. You can keep the Alt key (Option key on a Mac) down or not — it doesn't matter. But be sure that the mouse button is down any time you press or release the Alt (Option on a Mac) key, or Photoshop completes the selection outline.

Selecting with the Magnetic Lasso

This Lasso tool takes a little getting used to and may not produce a great selection in all cases. But it's easy to use, and if you take some time to understand the method behind its madness, it can be a quick remedy to your selection needs.

The Magnetic Lasso works best with high contrast images — that is, the element you want to select is a different color than the background. Using the settings in the Options bar, the Magnetic Lasso analyzes the difference in the color of the pixels between the element you want to select and the background, and snaps to your element's edge. Here's how to use this quirky tool:

1. **Select the Magnetic Lasso tool.**

   Press L and then Shift+L twice to use the keyboard shortcut.

2. **Click on the edge of the element you want to select.**

3. **Move the cursor around the edge of the element.**

   Don't press the mouse and drag — just *move* the mouse. Simple! The Magnetic Lasso creates an outline with square anchor points around the edge of the element. If the line is off the mark, back up your mouse and try again. If you need to delete an anchor point as you are moving around the edge, press the Backspace (Delete on a Mac) key. To create your own anchor points, click with the mouse. Adding your own anchor points can be helpful if the Magnetic Lasso seems reluctant to stick to the edge you select.

4. **Continue around the element and click on your starting anchor point to close the outline.**

   You'll see a small circle next to your cursor indicating closure of the outline.

5. **As soon as the outline is closed and you release the mouse, a selection marquee appears.**

6. **Press Esc or Ctrl+period (⌘+period on a Mac) to cancel the Magnetic Lasso.**

To create a straight segment while using the Magnetic Lasso, press Alt (Option on a Mac) and click with the mouse. You can see that the tool icon of your cursor temporarily changes to the Polygon Lasso. Release the Alt (Option on a Mac) key and drag for a second to reset the tool back to the Magnetic Lasso. From then on, just move the cursor without clicking or dragging.

Exploring your Lasso options

Whether you use the regular Lasso, the Polygon Lasso, or the Magnetic Lasso, you can modify the performance of the tool via the two options common to all three tools in the Options bar (see the next section for options specific to the Magnetic Lasso). Though small in number, the options for the lasso tools are some tough little hombres:

✔ Both options — Feather and Anti-aliased — affect future selection outlines drawn with the lasso tools. In short, Feather makes the outline fuzzy, and Anti-aliased slightly softens the edge of the outline. If you want to modify an outline that you've already drawn, you have to choose a command under the Select menu. Because these commands affect outlines drawn with any tool, I describe them in Chapter 13.

✔ Normally, selections drawn with the lasso tools have soft, natural-looking edges. This softening is called *anti-aliasing* (see Chapter 8). To turn off the softening, click on the Anti-aliased check box in the bar to get rid of the check mark. From now on, outlines drawn with the tool will have sharply defined and sometimes jagged edges.

✔ Figure 12-3 shows two lassoed selections moved to reveal the white background in the image. In the left example, the Anti-aliased check box was turned off; in the right example, the option was turned on. The edges of the left example are jagged; the edges of the right example are soft. (Chapter 13 explains all the ways to move selections. But if you want to try moving a selection now, just drag it with the Move tool, which is the top-right tool in the Toolbox.)

Anti-aliasing off   Anti-aliasing on

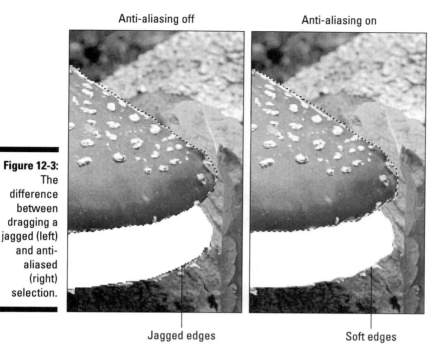

Figure 12-3:
The difference between dragging a jagged (left) and anti-aliased (right) selection.

Jagged edges   Soft edges

✔ Most of the time, you want to leave the Anti-aliased check box turned on. Just turn it off when you want to select precise, hard-edged areas. (Which may be never. Who knows?)

✔ Enter a value into the Feather option box to make the outline fuzzy. The value determines the radius of the fuzziness in pixels. If you enter a value of 3, for example, Photoshop extends the fuzzy region 3 pixels up, 3 pixels to the left, 3 pixels down, and 3 pixels to the right. As shown in the first example of Figure 12-4, that's a lot of fuzz. A higher value results in a more fuzzy selection outline, as witnessed in the right example, which sports a Feather value of 10.

Looking at the unique Magnetic Lasso options

The Magnetic Lasso has unique options in the bar that are related to the sensitivity of the tool's operation. They are the following:

✔ **Width:** This option determines how close to an edge you have to move the mouse for Photoshop to "see" the element. You can set it to a higher number for smooth, high contrast elements, and it will still hug the edge of the element. Set it to a lower value if the image has a lot of nooks and crannies or the contrast isn't that high. The range of the width option is 1 to 40 pixels. To change it while you are actually using the tool, press the [key to lower the number and the] key to raise the number.

Feather 3 pixels   Feather 10 pixels

Figure 12-4:
A bigger
Feather
value means
fuzzier
fungus.

✔ **Edge Contrast:** This option tells the Magnetic Lasso how much contrast is required between the element and the background before the lasso can be "attracted" or can hug that edge. The range for the Edge Contrast option is 1% to 100%. If you find a good deal of contrast between the element and the background, put in a higher value in order to get a cleaner selection. If the image is low contrast, lower the value for this option.

✔ **Frequency:** The number in the Frequency option tells the Magnetic Lasso when to automatically insert anchor points. The range for Frequency is from 0% to 100%. If you want more points, insert a higher number; for less points, use a lower value. High values are better for rough, jagged edges, and low values are better for smooth edges. As you move around the edge of your element and create the outline, Photoshop pins it down with an anchor point.

 Start with default settings for the preceding Magnetic Lasso options, carefully make your selection, and see how it works. If your image is low contrast, you may want to lower the Edge Contrast to 5% or so. If edges are jagged or rough, try raising the Frequency to around 70% and lowering lasso Width to 5 pixels.

If all else fails, and the Magnetic Lasso just isn't behaving, you can always go back to the regular Lasso and the Polygon Lasso. They may not be as high-tech, but they're reliable.

Selecting Rectangles, Squares, Ellipses, and Circles

If you want to create a selection that's rectangular or elliptical, you use — guess what — the Rectangular and Elliptical Marquee tools. The Rectangular and Elliptical Marquee tools are so easy to use that they make the lasso look complicated. You just drag from one corner to the opposite corner and release the mouse button. (Okay, ovals don't have corners, so you have to use your imagination a little bit.) The dotted marquee follows the movements of your cursor on-screen, keeping you apprised of the selection outline in progress.

But Photoshop has never been one to provide you with only one way to use a tool — or, in this case, two tools. For example, you can also use these tools to select perfect squares or circles. The program's cup of flexibility forever run-neth over, and the marquee tools are no exception.

Grabbing a square or circle

Every so often, you may feel the urge to apply some puritanical constraints to your selection outlines. Enough of this random width and height business — you want perfect squares and circles. Lucky for you, Photoshop obliges these fussbudget impulses by letting you constrain shapes drawn with the Marquee tool:

✔ To draw a perfect square, press the Shift key after you begin dragging with the Rectangular Marquee tool. To draw a perfect circle, press Shift after you begin dragging with the Elliptical Marquee tool.

✔ Drawing squares and circles is a little trickier than you might expect. For the best results, you should first begin dragging, press and hold Shift, drag to the desired location and release the mouse button, and finally release Shift. In other words, press Shift after you start the drag and hold it until after you complete the drag.

✔ If you press Shift before dragging, you run the risk of adding to the previously selected area, as I describe in lucky Chapter 13. Here's the deal: If a portion of your image was selected before you started Shift+dragging, Photoshop sees to it that the area remains selected and selects the marqueed area as well. Meanwhile, the shape of the marquee is not constrained to a square or a circle. Befuddling, huh? If this happens to you, press Ctrl+Z (⌘+Z on a Mac) to undo the selection and try again, taking care to press Shift during — not before — your drag.

The marquee tools can come in handy not only for selecting part of your image, but for creating geometric shapes as well. For example, if you want to draw a rectangle, create a marquee with the Rectangular Marquee tool. Then choose Edit⇨Stroke to *stroke* the marquee with the foreground color — in other words, to paint a line along the marquee. For more on the Stroke command, see Chapter 14.

Getting even more control over selections

Are you crazed for control? Do your tyrannical desires know no bounds? If so, you probably aren't appeased by drawing a square or a circle. What you want is to apply even more stringent constraints.

For example, suppose that you're the sort of pixel-oppressor who wants to select a rectangular or oval area that's exactly twice as wide as it is tall. With your Marquee tool selected, choose Constrained Aspect Ratio from the Style pop-up menu in the Options bar. The Width and Height option boxes come to life, letting you specify an aspect ratio, which is a precise proportion between the width and height of a marquee. To make the marquee twice as wide as it is tall, enter **2** as the Width value. Then press Tab to highlight the Height value and enter **1**. The deed is done.

But that's not all. You can also set up the marquee to select a row or column of pixels that is a single pixel tall or wide. To do this, select the Single Row or Single Column icon from the Marquee flyout menu in the Toolbox. Then click to create the marquee. If you select Single Row, the marquee is 1 pixel tall and extends across the entire width of your image; if you select Single Column, the marquee is 1 pixel wide and as tall as your image. After you click to create the marquee, you can drag it to reposition it if necessary.

Finally, to constrain the marquee to an exact size, select Fixed Size from the Style pop-up menu. Then enter the exact dimensions of your desired marquee into the Width and Height option boxes. The values are always measured in pixels. It's very unlikely that you'll ever want to do this — even if you live to be 103 — but I didn't want you to think that I neglected to explain one of these silly options for no good reason.

One last item submitted for your approval: Like the Lasso options discussed earlier in this chapter, the Marquee options sport Anti-aliased and Feather options, which respectively soften the selection outline and make it blurry. However, the Anti-aliased check box is dimmed when you use the Rectangular, Single Column, and Single Row Marquee tools. Perpendicular edges never need softening because perpendicular edges can't be jagged. Anti-aliasing, therefore, would be a waste of time.

Drawing from the center out

As I mentioned earlier, you draw a rectangle or oval from corner to opposite corner. But you can also draw a marquee from the center outward. To do this, begin dragging with either Marquee tool and then press Alt (Option on a Mac).

If you decide midway into your drag that you don't want to draw the shape from the center outward, just release the Alt (Option on a Mac) key and continue dragging. What was once the center of the marquee now becomes a corner.

To draw a square or circle from the center outward, press both Shift and Alt (Option on a Mac) after you begin dragging with the appropriate Marquee tool. (If you press Shift and Alt (Option on a Mac) before you begin dragging, you select the intersection of two selections, as explained in Chapter 13.)

Wielding the Wand

The Magic Wand is even easier to use than the Marquee tools. (Pretty soon, things get so easy you won't need me at all.) But it's also the most difficult selection tool to understand and predict. To use the tool, you just click inside an image. Photoshop then selects the area of continuous color that surrounds the cursor.

'Scuze me while I click the sky

Figure 12-5 shows how the Magic Wand works. In the first image, I clicked with the Magic Wand tool in the sky above the fake dinosaur. Photoshop automatically selected the entire continuous area of sky. In the second example, I made the selection more apparent by pressing Ctrl+Backspace (⌘+Delete on a Mac), which filled the selection with the white background color. I also got rid of the selection outline by deselecting the area. (Don't worry, I explain deselecting in full, rich detail in Chapter 13.)

Notice that the wand selects only uninterrupted areas of color. The patch of sky below the creature's tail, for example, remains intact. Also, the selection bit slightly into the edges of the dinosaur. Very small pieces along the top of the plastic behemoth were removed when I pressed Ctrl+Backspace (⌘+Delete on a Mac).

Figure 12-5: Look what happens when I click in the sky above the T-Rex with the Magic Wand (top) and fill the selection with white.

Teaching the wand tolerance

You can modify the performance of the Magic Wand by accessing the ever popular Options bar which offers four options — Anti-aliased, Contiguous, Use All Layers, and Tolerance.

I covered Anti-aliased earlier in this chapter, in the section "Exploring your Lasso options," so I'm not going to beat that poor horse anymore. The Use All Layers option comes into play only when your image contains more than one layer (see Chapter 15). When Use All Layers is turned off, the Magic Wand selects colors only on the active layer. If you want the Magic Wand to select colors from all visible layers, turn the option on.

When Contiguous is checked on, the Magic Wand selects only pixels that are adjacent to each other. If it is checked off, the Magic Wand looks throughout the image for any pixels that fall within the Tolerance range.

Which brings me to Tolerance, which has the most sway over the performance of the Magic Wand. It tells Photoshop which colors to select and which not to select. A lower Tolerance value instructs the wand to select fewer colors; a higher value instructs it to select more colors.

Color Plate 12-1 shows what I mean. Each row of images demonstrates the effect of a different Tolerance value, starting with the default value of 32 at the top and working up to 180 at the bottom. In each case, I clicked at the same location, just to the right of the big giraffe's schnoz. The left image in each row shows the selection outline created when I clicked; the right image shows what happened when I filled the selection with white and then deselected the selection.

In the color plate, a Tolerance value of 32 selected too little sky; a value of 180 selected all the sky but also got some huge chunks of giraffe face and rolling foothill. A value of 90 appears to be just right.

The problem is that finding the best Tolerance setting is a completely random exercise in the futile art of trial and error. Like changes to any tool setting, changes to the Tolerance value have no effect on the current selection. You have to click with the Magic Wand to try out each and every new value. In fact, here's the typical approach:

1. **Click with the Magic Wand tool.**

   The point at which you click marks the base color — the one Photoshop uses to judge which other colors it should select.

2. **Express displeasure with the results.**

   Gnash your teeth for good measure.

3. **Enter a new Tolerance value in the Options bar.**

   Enter a higher value to select more colors next time around; enter a lower value to select fewer colors.

4. **Choose Select⇨Deselect or press Ctrl+D (⌘+D on a Mac).**

   Photoshop deselects the previous selection.

5. **Repeat Steps 1 through 4 until you get it right.**

Believe me, even longtime Photoshop hacks like me who've been using the software since Copernicus discovered that the Earth orbits the sun go through this ritual every time they use the Magic Wand tool. What can I say? It's a useful little tool, but it requires some experimenting.

The Best Tool for the Job: The Pen Tool

The variety of selection tools and methods we've just explored have an advantage and a disadvantage — the advantage is that they are easy to use, the disadvantage is that sometimes they aren't that precise and require some additional cleanup. Fortunately, you have another option. The last remaining selection tool is the Pen tool. Of course, as you know, there's a catch. Although the Pen tool yields the most precise selection, it's also a difficult tool for novices to master. Many new Photoshop users try it, can't get it to do what they want, and vow never to touch it again, while reaching for the friendly Magic Wand or Lasso.

Before you're totally dissuaded from using the Pen tool, let me mention that Photoshop also offers two more amicable versions of the Pen tool — the Freeform Pen tool and the Freeform Pen tool with a magnetic option. This section tells you what you need to know about pens and paths.

The path to a better selection

Before you move on to how to use the pen tools, consider the product they make — paths. Unlike the other selection tools, using the Pen tool doesn't produce a selection marquee right away. As you click and drag around your chosen element, you create the three components of a path — anchor points (like those you saw with the Magnetic Lasso), straight segments or lines, and curve segments or curves. These paths are referred to as *Bezier paths,* which means that the paths are based on a mathematical model where a path is controlled by direction lines and handles (explained in detail soon).

After the path is drawn, you can then fine-tune the appearance by moving, adding, deleting, or converting anchor points. The path hovers over the image in its own unique space. You can't see a separate layer in the layer palette (for more on layers, see Chapter 15), but you can see the path "layer," for lack of a better word, in the Paths palette. After you create the path, you can fine-tune the path through editing and then turn the path into a selection. The pen tools and Paths palette, as shown in Figure 12-6, work together to handle the world of paths and their selections.

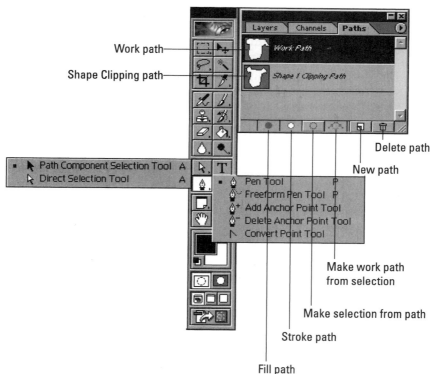

Work path

Shape Clipping path

Delete path

New path

Path Component Selection Tool   A

Direct Selection Tool   A

Figure 12-6:
The pen tools and the Paths palette work together to create and edit paths.

Pen Tool   P

Freeform Pen Tool   P

Add Anchor Point Tool

Delete Anchor Point Tool

Convert Point Tool

Make work path from selection

Make selection from path

Stroke path

Fill path

Creating paths with the Pen tool

Now that you know what a path is, look at how to create a path with the Pen tool. You can start with straight lines and then graduate to curves. Remember that this isn't easy the first few times, so hang in there:

1. **Select the Pen tool.**

   The keyboard equivalent is the P key.

2. **In the Options bar, select one of two options (look for the two icons just to the left of the pen):**

Create Shape Layer enables you to create a shape on its own separate shape layer. The path you create will possess all the attributes of a shape on a shape layer. For details on shapes and shape layers, see Chapter 8.

Create Work Path lets you make the old, traditional path that hovers over the image. If your end goal is to create a path in order to achieve an awesome selection, you want to select this option.

3. **To draw a straight line, click the mouse where you want the line to begin and then to end, leaving anchor points at those positions.**

   A straight segment, or line, connects the two anchor points. Drawing straight lines requires just a click and release of the mouse, no dragging. To draw a constrained line — horizontal, vertical, or a 45° — hold the Shift key down as you click. To create connecting straight lines, repeat the process. To end the path, click on the Pen tool. Better yet, hold down the Ctrl key (⌘ key on a Mac), which gives you the Direct Selection tool (white arrow), and click away from the curve. Release the Ctrl key (⌘ key on a Mac), and the Pen tool reappears.

4. **To draw a curve, you position the cursor where the curve is to begin, press the mouse, drag toward the bump of the curve, and release the mouse.**

   You create an anchor point along with two direction lines, and at the end of those, direction points. These direction lines and points control the appearance of the curve — in other words, its angle and how steep or flat it is.

5. **Move the cursor to the end of the curve, press the mouse, and drag in the opposite direction, away from the bump.**

   You now see another anchor point, a set of direction lines and points, and the actual curve. See the finished curve in Figure 12-7.

In the Options bar, which you may notice has changed in appearance, check the Rubber Band option. Photoshop then draws a segment between the last anchor point you create and wherever your cursor is located, thereby giving you a kind of preview of how the path will appear.

To return to the previous Options bar, which contained the Create Shape Layer and Create Work Path options, simply click the Dismiss button (the check icon) at the end of the Options bar.

6. **To create multiple, alternating curves, just continue Steps 4 and 5, dragging your mouse in an opposite direction each time.**

   Try to keep anchor points on either side of the bump, not on top. Also, try to use the fewest anchor points possible to create your path. Remember, a path is a mathematical formula, and the less complex it is, the fewer problems you'll have.

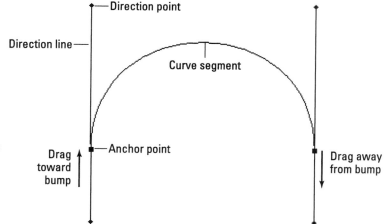

Direction point

Direction line

Curve segment

Anchor point

Drag toward bump

Drag away from bump

Figure 12-7: The anatomy of a curve.

How far should you drag? Imagine that your curve is a piece of string and you stretch it into a straight line. Divide that line into thirds. The distance you drag your mouse is one-third the length of that line.

At what angle should you drag? You should drag straight from the anchor point for a steeper curve and at an angle from the anchor point for a flatter curve.

7. **Creating curves that all go in the same direction is a little more involved. After you create your first curve, position your cursor over the second anchor point.**

   You see a *caret* (a fancy name for an upside down V symbol) next to your cursor. This caret tells you that you are converting this anchor point, which is smooth (curvy), to a corner (pointy).

8. **Hold down the Alt key (Option key on a Mac), press the mouse, and drag toward the bump of the next curve.**

   You now see another direction line appear.

9. **Release the mouse and release the Alt key (Option key on a Mac).**

10. **Move your cursor to where you want the curve to end and drag away from the bump to create your second curve.**

11. **Repeat Steps 7 through 10 to create similar, connecting curves.**

12. **To create a straight line from a curve or vice versa, you also need to convert points where the path changes from one to the other.**

    After drawing your curve, position your cursor over the second anchor point and click your mouse. Doing this creates the corner point by deleting one of the direction lines. Move your cursor to where your line will end and then click. You then see your straight line segment. To return to a curve, position your cursor on the last anchor point you drew and drag your mouse toward the bump of your next curve, adding a direction line in the process. Finish the curve by positioning your cursor where you want your curve to end and drag away from the bump.

13. **Return to your first anchor point and click if you want to close the path.**

    You see a small circle next to your cursor, which indicates that the path will be closed upon clicking.

14. **If you choose to leave the path open, end the path by clicking on the Pen tool.**

    Alternatively, you can hold down the Ctrl key (⌘ key on a Mac), which gives you the Direct Selection tool (white arrow), and click away from the curve. And you can also click the Dismiss button in the Options bar, or just press Enter (Return on Mac) to deactivate the path and hide it from view.

Editing paths to perfection

When first working with the Pen tool, you may find it difficult to draw a perfect path. Fortunately, you can easily fine-tune your path by using the melange of edit tools (refer to Figure 12-6) that share space with the Pen tool. The arrow tools, officially known as the Path Component Selection tool and the Direct Selection tool, are also lifesavers when it comes to tweaking your path. The following are tips to getting your paths exactly the way you want them.

✔ To select or move an entire path, use the Path Component Selection tool, the black arrow. To select multiple paths, just shift-click on each path. When the Path Component Selection tool is active, you may notice the Show Bounding Box option in the Options bar. Checking this option places a box around the path, enabling you to scale it by dragging the handles and rotating it by dragging outside the box. You can also press Ctrl (⌘ on a Mac) and drag a handle or side to distort or skew the path. Other options available are the Simplify and Align and Distribute settings. Simplify combines all visible paths according to the path state buttons (add, subtract, and intersect exclude). These buttons work like the selection state buttons described earlier in this chapter. Align and Distribute aligns two or more paths and distributes three or more paths.

✔ To move an anchor point, select the Direct Selection tool, the white arrow. The Direct Selection tool used to share a space on the flyout menu with the Pen tool, but Photoshop 6 has moved it in with the Path Component Selection tool. Fortunately, its keyboard shortcut is still the A key. With the Direct Selection tool, click on the anchor point you want to move. (Notice that the point becomes solid, whereas the unselected anchor points are hollow.) Press the mouse and drag to move the anchor point. You can also click on the curve or straight line to move those.

✔ To change the shape of the curve, you can move the direction points. Click on the anchor point of the curve you want to alter. Move the cursor to the upper direction point (the one going the same direction as the bump), press the mouse, and lengthen or shorten the direction line. Notice how the curve steepens or flattens, respectively. By rotating the direction line (moving left or right), the slope of the curve changes.

✔ Two tools enable you to delete or add an anchor point in your path: the Add Anchor Point and the Delete Anchor Point tools. The Add Anchor Point tool looks like the Pen tool with a small plus sign next to it. The Delete Anchor Point tool looks like the Pen tool with a small minus sign next to it. To add an anchor point, simply click on the tool in the path where you need an anchor point. Note that it always adds a smooth point. To delete an anchor point, position the cursor over the anchor point you no longer need and click on it. It disappears while keeping your path intact.

✔ The AutoAdd/Delete check box in the Options bar enables you to add or delete an anchor point with the regular Pen tool. This is a great time saver and works exactly like the tools mentioned above.

✔ To convert an anchor point from smooth to corner or vice versa, you need to select the Convert Point tool. This is the last tool in the flyout menu of the Pen tool and looks like a caret (the same symbol you saw when holding down the Alt key (Option key on a Mac) with the pen). Position your cursor on the anchor point you wish to convert. If the anchor point is a corner point, press the mouse and drag away from the anchor point to create the direction line that will create a smooth point. If the point is a smooth point, simply click (don't drag) over the anchor point, and the point becomes a corner.

✔ To copy a path, select it, hold down the Alt key (Option key on a Mac), and drag the path away from the original with the Path Component Selection tool.

✔ If the path is open, and you want to continue the path, click or drag on the endpoint with the Pen tool and continue drawing. Your addition to the path is then connected.

✔ If the path is open, and you want to close the path, click or drag on the endpoint with the Pen tool and go back to the first anchor point in your path. You'll see a circle appear next to your cursor to assure you the path is closing.

✔ To delete a path, select the entire path with the Path Component Selection tool and press the Backspace key (Delete key on a Mac) or select a point on the path with the Direct Selection tool and press Backspace (Delete on a Mac) twice.

    ✔ Photoshop gives you another option in editing your paths by letting you apply transformations to a path, such as scale, rotate, and skew, without affecting the underlying image. See the section on transforming selections and paths in Chapter 13.

The friendlier Pen tool

Hopefully you survived the tedious and technical explanation of paths and the various pen tools, because now I want to introduce you to a kinder and gentler version of the pen — the Freeform Pen (refer to Figure 12-6).

The Freeform Pen acts much like the Lasso tool. Simply drag around the element you want to select, and the tool creates an outline that follows your cursor. After you release your mouse, Photoshop provides the anchor points, lines, and curves for that path. None of that Bezier curve drawing business! To create straight lines with this tool, press the Alt key (Option key on a Mac) while the mouse button is pressed and click to create the anchor point. When you want to return to drawing curves, release the Alt key (Option key on a Mac), keeping the mouse button pressed. If you release the key while the mouse button is not pressed, Photoshop ends your path.

You find an option called Curve Fit in the Options bar. The Curve Fit option is the amount of error Photoshop permits when trying to fit your cursor movement to a path. You can enter a value from .5 to 10 pixels, the default setting being 2 pixels. This means that Photoshop does not register any movement of your cursor that is 2 pixels or less. Setting the value to .5 pixel makes the Freeform Pen very sensitive to your movement; setting it to 10 pixels makes it less sensitive. To get a better idea of the Curve Fit setting, try using the Freeform Pen at each of these settings and then compare the path it makes. Remember that after your path is created, using the editing methods described can always clean it up.

If you used previous versions of Photoshop, you notice that the Magnetic Pen has disappeared from the Toolbox. That's because Photoshop 6 has made the Magnetic Pen part of the options of the Freeform Pen. If you check the Magnetic option in the Options bar, the Freeform pen acts much like the Magnetic Lasso. Begin by clicking on the edge of the element you want to select. Move, don't drag, the cursor around the edge. Notice how it hugs the edge of your element, creating anchor points and segments. To create an anchor point yourself, click your mouse. To create straight segments, you can press the Alt key (Option key on a Mac) and click. To return to the Regular Magnetic pen, release the Alt key (Option key on a Mac), click again, and continue moving the cursor.

The Curve Fit option in the Options bar affects the sensitivity of the tool. The lower the Curve Fit value, the more sensitive the tool behaves, and the closer it follows the edge. The disadvantage is that this lower value creates an over-abundance of anchor points. The other options — Width, Contrast, and Frequency, found in the drop-down menu under the magnetic option icon, — operate exactly like the Magnetic Lasso options. For details, see the section, "Looking at the unique Magnetic Lasso options," earlier in this chapter.

The Paths palette

As stated earlier in this section, the pen tools work in concert with the Paths palette. Here are some tips on how to understand and use this palette. Refer to Figure 12-6 to see the Paths palette.

✔ When you create a path, it automatically appears in the Paths palette as a Work Path in its own space, a kind of path layer. You can create a new space for a path prior to drawing it by selecting the page icon at the bottom of the Paths palette.

✔ You can delete a path by dragging it to the trash can icon at the bottom of the palette.

✔ Paths can be filled. To fill a path, select the path in the Paths palette, choose the Fill Path command from the pop-up menu, or press the Alt key (Option key on a Mac) and click on the fill path icon (a solid circle) at the bottom of the palette. The dialog box gives options for Contents, Opacity, and Rendering (feathering and anti-aliasing options). For details on Contents and Opacity options, see the section on fills in Chapter 14. The feathering option gradually dissolves the edges of the fill into the background. The anti-aliased option just slightly softens or blurs the edge of the fill so that the edge doesn't appear as jagged. If you select one or more paths with the Direct Selection tool, the Fill Path command changes to Fill Subpath(s), enabling you to fill only the selected paths.

✔ Paths can also be stroked with color. To stroke a path, select the path in the Paths palette, choose the Stroke Path command from the pop-up menu, or press the Alt key (Option key on a Mac) and click on the stroke path icon (an outlined circle) at the bottom of the palette. In the dialog box, choose the paint or edit tool you want to use to apply color to the stroke. If you select one or more paths with the Direct Selection tool, the Stroke Path command changes to Stroke Subpath(s), enabling you to stroke only the selected paths.

✔ Photoshop uses the current tool options and the brush size when it strokes your path. Be sure and check the particular tool's options and the active brush size in the Brushes palette prior to stroking the path.

- If your end goal in all this pen and paths business is to simply make a nice, clean selection, now is the time. Choose Make Selection from the Paths palette menu. You can choose to feather your selection by adding pixels to the radius or leave the feather radius at 0 for a harder-edged selection. You can also anti-alias the selection to slightly blur the edges so it doesn't appear as jagged. If you have another selection active at the time you go to make your path into a selection, you can have Photoshop add, subtract, or intersect with that other selection. You can also reach the dialog box by pressing the Alt key (Option key on a Mac) and clicking on the Make Selection icon in the Paths palette. After the path is made into a selection, it acts like any other selection, as described in the beginning of this chapter and also in Chapter 13.

- To make your selection quickly, press Ctrl+Enter (⌘+Return on a Mac) while your path is selected in the Paths palette. You can also Ctrl+click (⌘+click on a Mac) on the path in the Paths palette.

- Photoshop can also work in reverse and take a selection and create a path. With your selection active, choose Make Work Path from the Paths palette pop-up menu. A dialog box appears asking you for a Tolerance value. This number controls how sensitive Photoshop is to the nooks and crannies in the selection marquee when it creates the path. The lower the value, the more sensitive it is, and the better it approximates your selection. But the lower value may create too many anchor points. The default of 2.0 is a good starting point. Remember, the path can always be edited and cleaned up. To quickly create a path from a selection, click on the Makes Work Path from Selection icon in the Paths palette.

- To hide the path after the selection is made, choose Turn Off Path from the Paths palette pop-up menu or simply click your mouse in the gray area below the path names in the Paths palette. Note that if you want to create a new work path, which resides on its own path layer, you have to hide all other paths.

- And last, but not least, you want to save your paths. After going to all that trouble to make the path, be sure to save it so that it can be used again with your image. Unlike layers, paths are mathematical formulas and take up very little storage space. To save a path, choose the Save Path command from the Paths palette pop-up menu or double-click on the Work Path in the Paths palette. Name the path and click on OK.

Cutting away with clipping paths

One of the more common uses for creating a path, outside making a nice clean selection, is to make a clipping path. A clipping path lets areas that fall outside your path be transparent, while displaying the area inside the clipping path. Suppose that you want to import a flower into PageMaker, or another page layout or illustration program, and place it against a colored background. Without a clipping path, the flower appears against a rectangular white background, regardless of whether the background was transparent in Photoshop (as shown in Figure 12-8). Read on to find out how to create these unique paths.

1. **Using one of the selection tools, make your path around the part of the image you want to display.**

    A Work Path appears in the Paths palette.

2. **Save the path by double-clicking on the Work Path in the Paths palette.**

    Enter a name and click on OK.

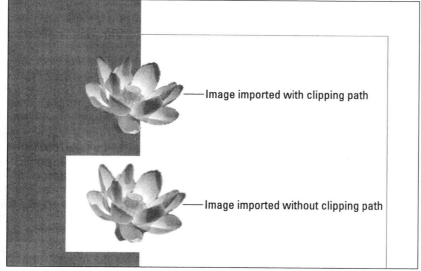

Figure 12-8:
Note the difference between importing an image with and without a clipping path.

Image imported with clipping path

Image imported without clipping path

3. **Choose Clipping Path from the Paths palette pop-up menu.**

    In the dialog box, choose your path name from the Path pop-up menu. Choose a flatness of 3. Simply put, *flatness* represents how closely your curves approximate a true mathematical curve. A higher number leads to more of a polygon shape, but easier printing.

4. **Choose File⇨Save As and choose Photoshop EPS from the Format pop-up menu (for other Save As options, see Chapter 6).**

5. **Windows users, leave Preview at Tiff (8 bits/pixel) and encoding as ASCII. Mac users, leave Preview at Macintosh (8 bits/pixel). Leave encoding as Binary and then click on OK.**

The file is now ready to be imported into your page layout or drawing program.

Be aware that sometimes when you import the clipped image into certain Windows page layout programs, the screen preview may not display the clipped image correctly. The clipped regions (the portion of the image outside the path which you are hiding) may appear opaque (solid white or black) on-screen. It should, however, print correctly to a PostScript printer. In addition, you may notice that images with clipping paths (and EPS files in general) may not always print correctly on a non PostScript printer.

If you created a shape using either the Pen tool or one of the shape tools, you'll notice that a shape clipping path is created in the Paths palette. This clipping path acts a little differently than the one I described above. Rather than clipping away (or hiding) everything outside the path for the entire image, a shape clipping path only clips away the color of that particular shape layer. You can delete this shape clipping path by choosing Layer⇨Delete Layer Clipping Path. You're left with just a layer of solid color. In addition you can also disable the clipping path, which hides it from view but won't eliminate it.

Clipping paths are notorious for causing printing problems, especially if too many are used or if the paths are too complex (many anchor points). Use clipping paths only when you have no other option. For example, if you want to silhouette an element against a background, composite the element and background in Photoshop and then import the composited image into your page layout or drawing program. Not only does this process ensure that the file prints, but it also ensures that the file prints much faster.

Photoshop helps you create images with transparency via the Export Transparent Image Assistant, located under the Help menu. The Assistant steps you through exporting an image with transparency. It helps you prepare the image for print or the Web. To use the Export Transparent Image Assistant, you must have an active selection marquee or your element must be on a transparent layer (see Chapter 15). With either of these two scenarios, go to Help⇨Export Transparent Image, and answer the questions.

Automated Masking Tools

Selecting images has long been one of Photoshop's core strengths. You can make general selections quickly and with little effort, draw precise outlines with the Pen tool, and brush exclusively inside a selection with any of the paint or edit tools. In addition to devoting an entire menu to selections,

Photoshop even goes so far as to track selection modifications in the History palette so that you can quickly undo wonky drags, clicks, and feathers. Unlike many other programs, Photoshop treats selections as first-class citizens, which is only fitting given that they are every bit as elemental and essential as pixels themselves.

But the satisfying glow of selections grows a bit dim as you submerge yourself into the complex underworld of masking. Clearly, Photoshop's masking tools are powerful, but they are also exceedingly difficult to use. Previously, Adobe has devoted almost no effort to making masks accessible to novices and intermediate users. But that changed with Photoshop 5.5 and has been improved further in Photoshop 6.0.

In case you're not sure what I'm talking about, a *mask* is a way of creating highly precise selections, so exact that they accurately account for elusive details such as leaves, reflections, and hair. I explore masks in detail in the *Photoshop Bible* (published by IDG Books Worldwide, Inc.). Because of their advanced nature, I don't cover masks much in this book.

Fortunately, you don't have to know a thing about masking to use Photoshop automated masking tools. The Color Range command, Magic Eraser, Background Eraser, and Extract command employ masking theory, but they do it in such a way as to hide the unpleasant details from you, the user. None of these tools is a miracle worker — for many complex images, full-blown masking is still the better way to go — but each may be helpful when time is of the essence.

Selecting with the Color Range command

The Color Range command is the veteran of the four automated masking tools. You can think of it as a magic wand on steroids. It is found under the Select menu. This command lets you select multiple areas of color at a time, even if they aren't continuous. Also, you can adjust the equivalent of the Tolerance setting and see its effect on the selection before you apply the command. The Color Range command is a little complex but it makes the Magic Wand look like dog meat.

If you were to investigate the Color Range command and its accompanying dialog box on your own, you might mistake it for one of the most complicated Photoshop functions. But deep down inside, it's a pussycat. You just have to know which options to use and which to ignore.

Strolling through the Color Range

Because we're venturing into some pretty unfriendly territory, I'm going to step you through the Color Range command. Just look where I tell you to look and avert your eyes from the scary stuff, and you won't go wrong.

1. **Select the Eyedropper tool.**

   You select the Eyedropper by pressing the I key.

2. **Click on a spot inside the area you want to select.**

   Use the Eyedropper as though it were the Magic Wand tool. Nothing becomes selected, of course, but you change the foreground color. The Color Range command uses the foreground color as the base color, just as the Magic Wand uses the color on which you click as the base color.

3. **Choose Select⇨Color Range.**

   The Color Range dialog box shown in Figure 12-9 appears. I've taken the liberty of dimming all the options that aren't important.

   The Selection Preview box shows your selection in black and white. The white areas are selected, the black areas are not selected, and the gray areas are blurred selection edges (just as though you had feathered them).

   In case you're wondering what that big black blob is in the middle of Figure 12-9, it represents the giraffe image shown in Color Plate 12-2. Before choosing the Color Range command, I clicked to the right of the big giraffe's snout.

4. **Change the Fuzziness value from 1 to 200 to adjust the tolerance.**

   As with the Magic Wand's Tolerance setting, higher Fuzziness values select more colors, and lower values select fewer colors. As you change the value, the Selection Preview box shows you how the new Fuzziness setting affects the selection. In Figure 12-10, you can see how the selected area — in white — grows as I increase the Fuzziness value.

5. **Click on the OK button after you finish.**

   Or press Enter (Return on a Mac). Photoshop selects the area displayed as white in the selection preview.

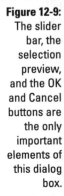

Figure 12-9: The slider bar, the selection preview, and the OK and Cancel buttons are the only important elements of this dialog box.

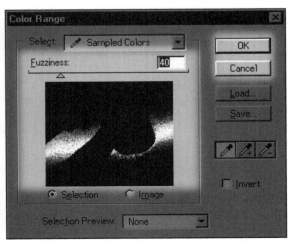

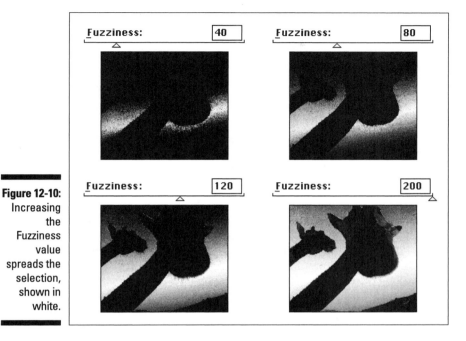

Figure 12-10: Increasing the Fuzziness value spreads the selection, shown in white.

The left example in Color Plate 12-2 shows the result of applying the Color Range command with a maximum Fuzziness value of 200 to the giraffe image. I then pressed Ctrl+Backspace (⌘+Delete on a Mac) to fill the selection with white and deselected the image to arrive at the right example. The Color Range command selected colors on both sides of the giraffe, even though I lifted the base color from the right half of the sky.

The Color Range dialog box offers an Invert check box, which does the same thing as the Select⇨Inverse command. Invert selects everything that's currently not selected and deselects everything that's selected. In other words, it selects the exact opposite of what's currently selected. (For more on the Select⇨Inverse command, see Chapter 13.)

If you choose the Color Range command when a portion of your image is selected, the command selects colors only if they fall inside the current selection. Colors outside the selection are ignored. Therefore, unless you specifically want to isolate part of your image to create a precise selection, be sure to press Ctrl+D (⌘+D on a Mac) to deselect the image before choosing Select⇨Color Range. Doing so makes the entire image accessible to the command.

Broadening your color base

Despite the Color Range command's prowess, I wouldn't call Color Plate 12-2 an unqualified success. A lot of blue remains in the second example that the Magic Wand managed to pick up in Color Plate 12-1.

The fact is, the Magic Wand and Color Range commands evaluate colors differently (which is why their color-sensing options — Tolerance and Fuzziness — have different names). The wand uses the Tolerance value to decide whether colors are similar to the base color and then selects them. The Color Range command selects all occurrences of the base color in an image and then feathers the selection according to the Fuzziness value. So the Magic Wand creates definite selection outlines with anti-aliased edges; the Color Range command creates more nebulous ones with blurry edges.

But there's more to the Color Range command, Horatio, than is dreamt of in your philosophy. Unlike the Magic Wand, the Color Range command lets you specify more than one base color. After choosing Select⇨Color Range, move the cursor outside the Color Range dialog box and over the image. The cursor changes to the Eyedropper tool, enabling you to change the base color if you want to. Press and hold the Shift key, and you see a small plus sign appear next to the Eyedropper. Click with this cursor to add a second base color. Continue to Shift+click to add a third base color, fourth, fifth, and so on. Add as many as you like.

In Color Plate 12-3, I specified three base colors. I set the first one before choosing Select⇨Color Range by clicking to the right of the giraffe's nose with the Eyedropper tool, just as in Color Plate 12-2. I set the other two by Shift+clicking in the image while inside the Color Range dialog box, once above the giraffe's ear and once below its neck (as the cursors in the Color plate indicate).

Adding base colors increases the size of the selected area. To make the selection outline less blurry, I lowered the Fuzziness value to 60. The first image in Color Plate 12-3 shows the resulting selection outline; the second image shows what happened when I filled the selection with white and then deselected the selection. Even though the background is now completely white, the giraffes still blend in naturally, an effect that you can't easily achieve with the Magic Wand.

It's possible to add too many base colors. As a result, you may select portions of your image that you don't want to select. If this happens, you can delete base colors from inside the Color Range dialog box by Alt+clicking (Option+clicking on a Mac) on the image. When the Alt key (Option key on a Mac) is pressed, a little minus sign appears next to the Eyedropper cursor.

If adding and deleting base colors starts to get confusing, you can reset the selection in the Color Range dialog box by clicking on the image without pressing Shift or Alt (Option on a Mac). Resetting returns you to a single base color.

The other erasers

Next in the automated masking tool lineup are two other eraser tools — the *Background Eraser* and the *Magic Eraser*. To select one of these erasers, click and hold on the Eraser tool icon in the Toolbox and then select the desired tool from the pop-up menu.

- **Background Eraser:** Used properly, this tool erases away the background from an image and leaves the foreground intact. Used incorrectly, it just erases everything. I'll explain the difference in a moment.

- **Magic Eraser:** This tool deletes a range of similarly colored pixels each time you click in the image window.

To switch between the three eraser tools from the keyboard, press Shift+E. Select the Mode — Paintbrush, Airbrush, Pencil, or Block — manually from the Options bar.

The somewhat Magic Eraser

Of the two erasers, the Magic Eraser is the easier to use and the less capable, so I'll explain it first. If you're familiar with the Magic Wand (see the earlier section on "Wielding the Wand"), then the magic eraser is a cinch. The two tools operate virtually identically, except that the Wand selects and the Eraser erases.

When you click on a pixel with the Magic Eraser, Photoshop identifies a range of similarly colored pixels, just as it does with the Magic Wand. But instead of selecting the pixels, the Magic Eraser makes them transparent, as demonstrated in Figure 12-11. Bear in mind that in Photoshop, transparency requires a separate layer. So if the image is flat (without layers), Photoshop automatically floats the image to a separate layer with nothing underneath. Hence the checkerboard pattern shown in the second example in the figure — transparency with nothing underneath.

Notice in Figure 12-11 that the Magic Eraser deleted some of the blue sky, but not all of it. This is a function of the Tolerance value in the Options bar. Just like the Magic Wand's Tolerance value, the Magic Eraser's Tolerance value determines how similar a neighboring color has to be to the clicked color to be made transparent. A higher value affects more colors; a lower value affects fewer colors. Therefore, if I want to erase a larger section of the sky in Figure 12-11, I can raise the Tolerance value and click again. (Remember, any change to the Tolerance value affects the *next* click you make; it does not affect the existing transparent area.)

Figure 12-11:
To delete a homogeneously colored background, like the sky at top, click inside it with the Magic Eraser (bottom).

The other options work as follows:

   ✔ **Anti-aliased:** To create a soft fringe around the outline of your transparent area, leave this option turned on. If you prefer a hard edge — as when using a very low Tolerance value, for example — turn this check box off.

   ✔ **Contiguous:** This final check box is both inside the Magic Eraser Options bar and the Magic Wand Options bar. When turned on, the Magic Eraser deletes *contiguous* colors only — that is, similar colors that touch each other. If you prefer to delete *all* pixels of a certain color, turn the Contiguous check box off.

✔ **Use All Layers:** When turned on, this check box tells Photoshop to factor in all visible layers when erasing pixels. The tool continues to erase pixels on the active layer only, but it erases them according to colors found across all layers.

✔ **Opacity:** Lower this value to make the erased pixels translucent instead of transparent. Low values result in more subtle effects than high ones.

For a more detailed description of these options as they affect the Magic Wand tool, read the "Wielding the Wand" section in this chapter.

The more magical Background Eraser

The Magic Eraser is as simple to use as a hammer and every bit as indelicate. It pounds away pixels but it leaves lots of color fringes and shredded edges in its wake. You may as well select an area with the Magic Wand and press the Backspace key (Delete key on a Mac). The effect is the same.

The more capable, more scrupulous tool is the Background Eraser. As demonstrated in Figure 12-12, the Background Eraser deletes background pixels as you drag over them. (Again, if the image is flat, Photoshop floats the image to a new layer to accommodate the transparency.) The tool is intelligent enough to erase background pixels and retain foreground pixels provided — and here's the clincher — that you keep the cross in the center of the eraser cursor squarely centered on a background-color pixel. Move the cross over a foreground pixel, and the background eraser deletes foreground pixels as well. As Figure 12-13 demonstrates, it's the position of the cross that counts.

Figure 12-12: Drag around the edge of an image with the Background Eraser to erase the background but leave the foreground intact.

Figure 12-13:
Keep the
cross of the
background
eraser
cursor over
the
background
you want to
erase (top).
If you
inadver-
tently move
the cross
over the
foreground,
the
foreground
gets erased
(bottom).

Like the standard Eraser tool, the Background Eraser responds to the brush size specified in the Brushes palette. Use the bracket keys [and] to make the brush size larger or smaller.

You can also modify the performance of the Background Eraser using the options in the Options bar. These options are a bit intimidating at first but they're actually pretty easy to use:

✔ **Limits:** By default, the Background Eraser deletes colors inside the cursor as long as they are contiguous with the color immediately under the cross. To erase all similarly colored pixels, whether contiguous or not, set the pop-up menu to Discontiguous. One additional option, Find Edges, searches for edges as you brush and emphasizes them. While interesting, Find Edges has a habit of producing halos and is rarely useful.

✔ **Tolerance:** Raise the Tolerance value to erase more colors at a time; lower the value to erase fewer colors. Low Tolerance values are useful for erasing around tight and delicate details, such as hair.

✔ **Protect Foreground Color:** Select this check box to prevent the current foreground color (by default, black) from ever being erased. Stupid, really, but there it is.

✔ **Sampling:** This pop-up menu determines how the Background Eraser decides what it should and should not erase. The default Continuous setting tells the erasers to continuously reappraise which colors should be erased as you drag. If the background is pretty homogenous, you may prefer to use the Once option, which samples the background color when you first click and erases only that color throughout the drag. Select the Background Swatch option to erase only the current background color (by default, white).

✔ **Brush Dynamics:** Indicated by a paintbrush icon at the right end of the Options bar, this pop-up menu lets you specify the rate at which a brush stroke fades based on tolerance and/or size. If you own a pressure-sensitive tablet, such as the Pen Partner or Intuos from Wacom, you can use the Stylus setting to specify whether pen pressure affects the size and tolerance of the eraser.

The still more magical Extract command

If you can't quite get the results you want out of the Background Eraser, you may want to dig deeper and investigate the Extract command. But I feel compelled to offer a few words of warning: In my estimation, Extract is only slightly more powerful than the Background Eraser and several times more complex. Some images respond very well to the command, others do not.

That said, I have to give credit where credit is due. Adobe has made some improvements to the Extract command. Most notably, you can now access the Undo function from within the Extract dialog box. Version 6 also offers new tools — the Cleanup tool and Edge Touchup tool — and options such as Smart Highlighting to aid in the extraction and cleanup of your image. In addition, there are lots of good keyboard shortcuts.

With these improvements, Extract can generally be counted on to produce reasonably good results if you get the steps down right. Here's how it works:

1. **Choose Image⇨Extract. Or use the keyboard shortcut Ctrl+Alt+X (⌘+Option+X on a Mac).**

   Either way, Photoshop displays the large Extract window shown in Figure 12-14 .

2. **Select the Edge Highlighter tool.**

   Most likely, this tool is already active, but if not, press the B key to select it.

   Photoshop now offers a Smart Highlighting option. If your image has a well defined edge, but the foreground and background colors are similar or the image has a lot of texture, the Smart Highlighting option helps to hug the edge as you are highlighting. For now, keep it unchecked.

   To toggle Smart Highlighting on and off, press Ctrl (⌘ on a Mac) while you drag.

3. **Outline the subject of the image that you want to retain.**

   In my case, I want to delete the background, so I traced around the lion, as shown in Figure 12-15. Be sure to either completely encircle the subject or, if the subject is partially cropped, trace all the way up against the outer boundaries of the photograph.

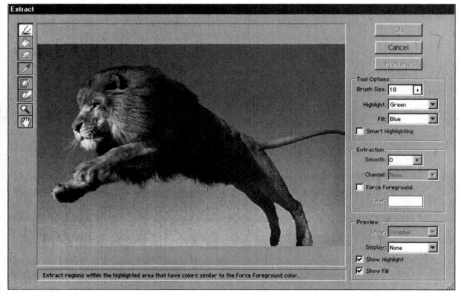

Figure 12-14:
The Extract window serves as a miniature masking laboratory, complete with a Toolbox and options.

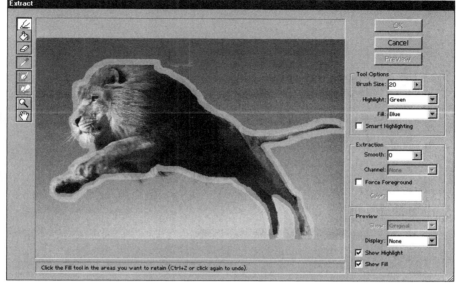

Figure 12-15:
Trace around the portion of the image you want to keep with the Edge Highlighter tool.

Often it's easier to Shift-click around the perimeter of an image than drag manually. Shift-clicking creates a straight highlight from one click point to the next. As long as you do a reasonably careful job, the performance of the Extract command won't be impaired.

4. **As you trace, use the bracket keys [and] to make the brush larger or smaller.**

Each press of [or] changes the brush size. To expand or reduce the brush size more dramatically, press and hold a bracket key. (Uh, pardon me, why don't we have this kind of control when working with brushes outside the Extract window?)

Small brush sizes result in sharper edges. Larger brush sizes are better for fragile, intricate detailing such as hair, foliage, wispy fabric, bits of steel wool, very thin pasta — you get the idea.

5. **If you make a mistake, press Ctrl+Z (⌘+Z on a Mac).**

The Extract window now sports an Undo function. So if you draw a bad outline, you can choose to Undo. Another option is to erase it. Select the Eraser by pressing the E key.

To completely erase the highlight, press Alt+Backspace (Option+Delete on a Mac).

To toggle between the Edge Highlighter and Eraser tools while you drag, press Alt (Option on a Mac).

6. Navigate as needed.

If you can't see all of your image, you can access the Hand tool by pressing the spacebar. You can also zoom by pressing Ctrl+plus (⌘+plus on a Mac) or Ctrl+minus (⌘+minus on a Mac) or by using the Zoom tool.

7. Select the Fill tool (the paint bucket).

To select it from the keyboard, press G.

8. Click inside the subject of the image.

The highlighted outline should fill with color, as in Figure 12-16. If the fill color spills outside the outline, you probably have a break in your outline someplace. Scroll the image with the Hand tool to find the break and patch it with the Edge Highlighter. Then click with the Fill tool again. (If you should need to unfill an image, just click in the filled area with the Fill tool. I know it's bizarre, but that's how the tool works.)

9. Click on the Preview button.

10. Preview your extraction so that you can gauge the finished effect, as in Figure 12-17.

You can now exit the Extract window without previewing by clicking OK, but I think it is a good idea to check out extraction first.

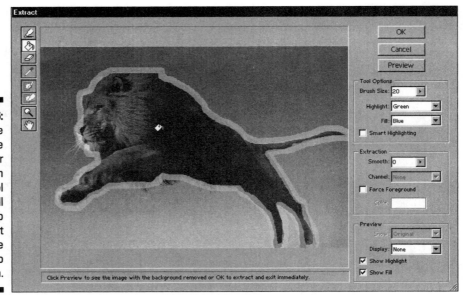

Figure 12-16: Click inside the highlighter outline with the Fill tool to tell Photoshop which part of the image you want to retain.

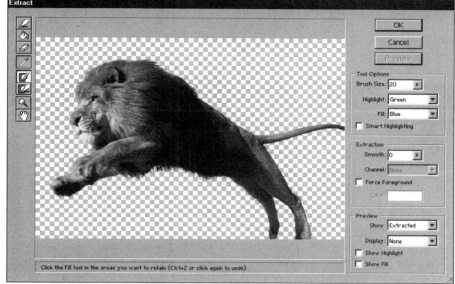

Figure 12-17:
Click on the
Preview
button to
gauge the
appearance
of the final
masked
image.

Press X to toggle between the original image and the extraction.

11. **If you like what you see, click on the OK button.**

    The Extract command deletes the masked portion of the image. If the
    image was flat, Photoshop floats it to a separate layer. Then use the
    Move tool to drag the masked image against a different background. In
    Figure 12-18, I set my lion against an Italian landscape. The composite
    isn't perfect but it's not half bad for five to ten minutes of work.

12. **If, on the other hand, you don't like the mask that the Preview button
    delivers, feel free to tweak it.**

    Choose the Original option from the Show pop-up menu. Then select the
    Show Highlight and Show Fill check boxes. Now you're ready to erase,
    highlight, and fill until you get it right.

    Photoshop gives us a couple of new edit tools that become available
    after you show your extraction: the Cleanup tool and Edge Touchup tool.
    The new Cleanup tool (press C on the keyboard) can help you edit your
    extracted image. Drag it over an area to gradually erase to transparency.
    Alt-drag (Option-drag) to bring the opacity back. You can create soft or
    feathered areas with this tool. The other newcomer, the Edge Touchup
    tool (press T on the keyboard), essentially does the opposite of the
    Cleanup tool. It helps to sharpen the edges of the extraction. This tool
    adds opacity to your extraction or subtracts opacity from the back-
    ground in order to better define the edge.

Figure 12-18:
I believe this
particular
lion is
stuffed, but
even a dead
creature
may enjoy a
change in its
diorama.

Press the 1 to 0 keys to change the pressure for the Cleanup and Edge Touchup tools. One is for minimum pressure and 0 is for maximum pressure.

13. **After you exit the Extract window, fix any problems you find using the Background Eraser and History Brush.**

    Use the Background Eraser to erase stray pixels that you wish the Extract command had deleted. Use the History Brush to restore details that you wish the Extract command hadn't deleted (for more on the History Brush, check out Chapter 11).

That's 99 percent of what you need to know about the Extract command. For those of you who care to learn the other 1 percent, here's a quick rundown of the options that appear along the right side of the Extract window:

✔ **Brush Size:** This option controls the diameter of the Edge Highlighter and Eraser brushes. Enter a value or drag the slider to specify a size. You can change this value as you paint by pressing the bracket keys: [reduces the brush size and] enlarges it.

✔ **Highlight, Fill:** Use these pop-up menus to change the highlighter and fill colors. You can use whatever color you want, so long as it shows up well against the image.

✔ **Smooth:** This option is designed to remove stray pixels from the mask. A high Smooth value smoothes out the edges around the image and fills in holes. Basically, if the edges are a big mess, give this option a try.

✔ **Channel:** Advanced users may prefer to prepare the highlighter work by tracing around the image inside an independent mask channel, which you can create in the Channels palette prior to choosing the Extract command. Then load the mask by selecting it from the Channel pop-up menu. You can further modify the highlight using the Edge Highlighter and Eraser tools. One weirdness: When loading a mask, black in the mask channel represents the highlighted area, white represents the non-highlighted area. Strikes me as upside down, but that's how it goes.

✔ **Force Foreground:** If the subject of your image is predominantly a single color, you can select Force Foreground and use the Eyedropper to sample the color in the image you want to preserve. (Alternatively, you can define the color using the Color swatch, but it's a lot more work.) Then use the Edge Highlighter tool to paint over all occurrences of the foreground color. (Note that this check box is an alternative to the Fill tool. When you select Force Foreground, the Fill tool is dimmed.)

✔ **Show:** After previewing an extraction, the Show pop-up menu lets you switch between the Original image and the Extracted view.

✔ **Display:** You don't have to preview the image against the transparent checkerboard background. Instead, you can view it against white (White Matte) or some other color. Or you can view it as a mask, where white represents the opaque area and black the transparent area. (Ironically, you can't export the extraction as a mask — go figure.)

✔ **Show Highlight, Show Fill:** Use these check boxes to hide and show the highlight and fill colors.

One final tip: Before using any of the new masking tools — Magic Eraser, Background Eraser, or Extract command — you may want to copy the image to a separate layer or take a snapshot of the image in the History palette. Either way, you have a backup in case things don't go exactly according to plan.

Chapter 13

More Fun with Selections

*I*n the old days, image-editing programs expected perfection from their users. If you didn't get a selection outline right the first time, too bad. You had to start over and try again.

Photoshop broke this heartless trend by expanding its range of selection options. In other words, it got smarter so that you and I can be dumber. Like all the world's best computer programs, Photoshop knows that human beings are a pretty fallible lot and need all the help they can get.

So Photoshop lets you modify a selection outline after you draw it. You can select additional pixels or trim the selection down to a smaller area. You can even smooth out sharp corners, expand a selection to include all similar colors, or swap the selected and deselected portions of the image. All things considered, Photoshop is about the most flexible selector there ever was.

This chapter explains how to modify an existing selection and also touches on more techniques that you can use with the selection tools discussed in Chapter 12. It also tells you how to move and clone selections and explores a wealth of commands under the Select menu that you probably haven't even looked at yet. By the end of this chapter, you'll have a clearer understanding of selection outlines than any other kid on the playground (unless he or she reads this chapter, too).

The Wonders of Deselection

Before I plow into all that whiz-bang, awesome stuff that Photoshop lets you do to a selection outline, I need to touch on selection's exact opposite, deselection. Though this may seem at face value to be a ridiculously boneheaded topic — one that hardly merits space in a scholarly tome like *Photoshop 6 For Dummies* — deselecting is actually an integral step in the selection process.

Suppose, for example, that you select one part of your image. Then you change your mind and decide to select a different portion instead. Before you can select that new area, you have to deselect the old one. You can deselect an existing selection outline in several ways:

- ✔ Click anywhere in the image with one of the lasso or marquee tools.

- ✔ To get rid of an existing selection and create a new one at the same time, just drag or click to create the new selection as you normally would. Photoshop automatically deselects the old selection when you create a new one.

- ✔ Click inside the selection with the magic wand. (If you click outside the selection, you not only deselect the selection, you create a new selection.)

- ✔ Choose Select⇨Deselect or press Ctrl+D (⌘+D on a Mac).

- ✔ Choose Select⇨Reselect or Ctrl+Shift+D (⌘+Shift+D on a Mac) to regain your most recent selection. You can do this even after you have performed numerous actions.

Selecting Everything

When no part of an image is selected, the entire image is up for grabs. You can edit any part of it by using the paint or edit tools or any of about a billion commands. But you can also make the entire image available for edits by choosing Select⇨All or Ctrl+A (⌘+A on a Mac) to select everything.

Beginning to see the mystery here? If you can edit any part of the image by deselecting it, why choose Select⇨All, which also lets you edit everything? Because some operations require a selection, that's why. In fact, if you want to apply any of the following operations to your image in its entirety, you must first press Ctrl+A (⌘+A on a Mac):

- ✔ Clone an image by Alt+dragging (Option+dragging on a Mac) it with the Move tool, as discussed later in the section "Moving and Cloning Selections." You can also clone an image without having a selection, but doing so creates another layer (see Chapter 15 for more on layers).

✔ Cut, copy, or paste an image using any of the commands under the Edit menu (discussed in Chapter 15).

✔ Apply Edit➪Stroke (explored in Chapter 14) on the Background layer of an image (as explained in Chapter 15).

✔ Apply the Edit➪Free Transform command or any of the commands under the Edit➪Transform submenu on the Background layer of an image. (The Transform commands are explored later in this chapter and in Chapter 20.)

Unless you're doing one of these things, you need never worry about Select➪All. A deselected image usually serves just as well.

Selective Arithmetic

I almost never like the first selection outline I create. Whether I draw it with a Lasso or Marquee tool, the Magic Wand, the Color Range command, or some-times even with the Pen, I usually have some problem with the selection. I didn't quite get the hair selected right, or that finger is still clipped off. Whatever the problem, I can remedy it by adding to the selection outline or subtracting from it. And so can you.

Chapter 12 explains how you can Shift+click on an image while inside the Color Range dialog box to add base colors and Alt+click (Option+click on a Mac) to delete base colors. These two keys — Shift and Alt (Option on a Mac) — are the universal add and subtract selection modifiers throughout Photoshop.

Adding and subtracting from a selection

To add an area to the current selection, Shift+drag with a Lasso or Marquee tool. Or Shift+click with the Magic Wand. It doesn't matter which tool you used to select the image previously, nor does it matter whether you Shift+click inside or outside the selection.

For example, in the obligatory person-holding-up-the-Tower-of-Pisa photo in Figure 13-1, I first selected the tower by dragging around it with the Lasso tool, as shown in the left example. To add the woman to the selection, I pressed Shift and dragged around her perimeter, creating the selection out-line shown in the right example.

To remove an area from a selection, Alt+drag (Option+drag on a Mac) with a Lasso or Marquee tool or Alt+click (Option+click on a Mac) with the Magic Wand. To deselect the gap between the woman's legs in Figure 13-1, for example, I could Alt+drag (Option+drag on a Mac) with the Lasso tool. To deselect the area under the right arm (her left arm), I could Alt+click (Option+click on a Mac) with the Magic Wand.

Photoshop has now given you another way to add and subtract to your selections. The four state change buttons in the Options bar enable you to make a new selection, add to a selection, subtract from a selection, or intersect a selection. Simply click on your desired state change button and then drag. Notice that if you do choose to use the keyboard method, the buttons automatically become selected when you press Shift or Alt (Option on a Mac) or both keys together.

Here are a few more addition and subtraction items to keep in mind:

✔ When you're adding to a selection, a little plus sign appears next to your cursor. When you're subtracting from the selection, a little minus sign appears. And when you're selecting the intersection of two existing selections (as explained next), a little multiply sign appears. See, your math teacher was right — knowing arithmetic comes in handy in all kinds of situations.

✔ You can also use the Shift and Alt (Option on a Mac) keys in conjunction with the Color Range command. Press Shift and choose Select➪Color Range to add to the selected area; Press Alt (Option on a Mac) and choose the command to subtract from the selection.

Figure 13-1:
First, I selected the tower (left), and then I pressed Shift and dragged around the woman to select her, too (right).

Intersecting a selection with a selection

If you press the Shift and Alt (Option on a Mac) keys together while clicking with the Magic Wand or dragging with a Lasso or Marquee tool, you select the intersection of the previous selection and the newest one. (Like that made any sense, right?) Take a look at Figure 13-2. I first dragged around the black rectangle. Then I Shift+Alt+dragged (Shift+Option+dragged on a Mac) the gray rectangle. Photoshop then selected all portions of the second marquee that fell inside the first marquee and deselected everything else, leaving me with the selection shown in the right half of the figure. That's an *intersection*.

You can also use the Intersect Selection state change button in the Options bar to obtain an intersection.

Figure 13-2:
I marqueed the black rectangle and then Shift+Alt+marqueed (Shift+Option+marqueed on a Mac) the gray rectangle (left). Photoshop then selected the intersection of the two marquees (right).

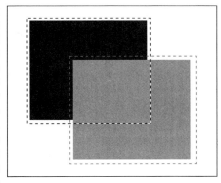
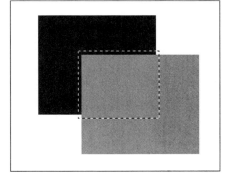

Try selecting an area with the lasso or one of the marquee tools and then Shift+Alt+clicking (Shift+Option+clicking on a Mac) inside the selection with the Magic Wand. Or click with the magic wand and then Shift+Alt+drag (Shift+Option+drag on a Mac) with one of the other selection tools. Either technique lets you limit the area of colors selected with the Magic Wand tool.

As I mentioned in the section "Adding and subtracting from a selection," if a portion of your image was selected using the Color Range command, you can Shift+choose or Alt+choose (Option+choose on a Mac) the command again to add to or subtract from the selection. If you don't press a key when choosing Select⇨Color Range, Photoshop selects an area inside the current selection. In other words, Photoshop already creates an intersection, so you don't gain anything by pressing both Alt (Option on a Mac) and Shift when choosing this command.

Avoiding keyboard collisions

In Chapter 12, I discuss a variety of ways to use the lasso and marquee tools while pressing keys. Pressing Alt (Option on a Mac) while using one of the lasso tools, you may recall, temporarily accesses one of the other lasso tools. Pressing Shift while using a marquee tool results in perfect squares and circles.

But what happens when you start combining all these add, subtract, and intersect shortcut keys with the ones discussed in Chapter 12? The following list answers your most burning questions:

✔ To add a square or circular area to an existing selection, start by Shift+dragging with the appropriate marquee tool. You get an unconstrained rectangle or oval, just as though the Shift key weren't down. Then midway into the drag — here's the catch — release the Shift key and then press it again, all the while keeping the mouse button down. The shape snaps to a square or circle with the second press of Shift. Keep the Shift key down until after you release the mouse button. Bet you didn't see that one coming.

✔ Pressing Alt (Option on a Mac) to temporarily access the Polygon Lasso when the regular Lasso is active causes trouble when you have an existing selection because pressing Alt (Option on a Mac) in that scenario sets you up to subtract from the selection. So, if you want to add or subtract a straight-sided selection, use the Polygon Lasso — don't try to Alt+click (Option+click on a Mac) with the regular lasso.

✔ The same advice goes if you want to find the intersection of a selection and a straight-sided shape.

Automatic Selection Discombobulators

Shift+dragging, Alt+dragging (Option+dragging on a Mac), and all those other wondrous techniques that I just finished describing — and, possibly, you just finished reading about — are wildly helpful when it comes to selecting complex details. But they aren't the only selection modifications you can make. Photoshop offers a handful of automatic functions that reshape selection outlines, blur them, and otherwise mess them up.

All the commands discussed in the next few sections — Grow, Similar, Inverse, Feather, and so on — reside under the Select menu. I don't discuss every command under the Select menu, just the ones you need to know. But you can take it from me, the commands I don't mention are just so much wasted space.

Extending the Magic Wand

Two commands, Grow and Similar, are extensions of the Magic Wand tool (for details on the Magic Wand see "Wielding the Wand" in Chapter 12). The Grow command expands the size of the selection to include still more continuous colors. For example, if clicking with the Magic Wand doesn't select all the colors you want it to, you can either increase the Tolerance value inside the Options bar and reclick with the tool or just choose Select⇨Grow to incorporate even more colors. It's kind of a clunky method, especially because the Grow command doesn't have a keyboard shortcut. I prefer to Shift+click with the Wand tool, but every once in a while, the Grow command works like you'd expect. (You can use the Grow command with selections made with tools other than the Magic Wand, by the way.)

The Similar command selects all colors that are similar to the selected colors regardless of whether they're interrupted by other colors. In other words, Similar selects all the continuous colors that Grow selects, as well as all similarly colored pixels throughout the image.

Both Grow and Similar judge color similarity exactly like the Magic Wand tool does — that is, according to the Tolerance value in the Options bar. So, if you increase the Tolerance value, the commands select more colors; if you decrease the value, the commands select fewer colors. For example, if you want to select all colors throughout the image that are exactly identical to the ones you've selected so far, enter **0** into the Tolerance option box, and choose Select⇨Similar.

Swapping what's selected for what's not

Sometimes it's easier to select the stuff you don't want to select and then tell Photoshop to select the deselected stuff and deselect what's selected. This technique is called *inversing a selection,* and you do it by choosing Select⇨Inverse or pressing Ctrl+Shift+I (⌘+Shift+I on a Mac).

For example, suppose that you want to select the clock tower shown on the left side of Figure 13-3. A typical work of baroque madness, this building has more spikes and little twisty bits than a porcupine. Therefore, selecting it would prove a nightmare.

Figure 13-3:
This building (left) is too darn ornate to select easily, but it's a snap to select the sky and then inverse the selection. Filling the selection with white shows how accurate the selection is (right).

Selecting the sky, on the other hand, is quite easy. By clicking and Shift+clicking a couple of times with the Magic Wand tool (set to the default Tolerance of 32), I was able to select the entire sky in a matter of two or three seconds. Then, when I chose Select⇨Inverse, I "inversed" the selection so that the building was selected and the sky was deselected. To better show off the selection, I filled it with white, as shown in the example on the right.

Making the selection fuzzy around the edges

Chapter 12 explains how you can blur the edges of a selection created with the lasso or marquee tools by increasing the Feather value in the corresponding Options bar. But more often than not, you want to leave the Feather value set to 0 and apply your feathering after you finish drawing the outline.

To feather an existing selection, choose Select⇨Feather or press Ctrl+Alt+D (⌘+Option+D on a Mac). A dinky dialog box with a single option box appears on-screen. Enter the amount of fuzziness, in pixels, that you want to apply to the selection, and press Enter (Return on a Mac). The selection outline probably won't change very much, but you see a distinct blurring effect when you edit the selection.

You can use feathering to make an image appear to fade into view. For example, take a look at the kid-in-a-basket image shown on the left side of Figure 13-4. I selected the Elliptical Marquee tool and encircled the little duffer. Then I chose Select⇨Inverse to select the background instead. Next, I chose Select⇨Feather, entered a value of 8 pixels, and pressed Enter (Return on a Mac). Finally, I pressed Ctrl+Backspace (⌘+Delete on a Mac) to fill the selection with white. The result is the locket with fuzzy edges, as shown on the right side of Figure 13-4. Isn't he just adorable?

Figure 13-4:
A tiny tot trapped in a basket (left) receives a classic feathering treatment (right).

Using Border, Smooth, and the rest

The remaining selection outline modifiers, found in the Select⇨Modify submenu, aren't quite as useful, but they come in handy every now and then:

✔ The Border command selects an area around the edge of the selection. You tell Photoshop the width, in pixels, of the border you want to select. This command is probably the least useful command of the bunch. If you want to color the outline of a selection, it's easier to use , as described in Chapter 14.

✔ Select⇨Modify⇨Smooth rounds off the corners of a selection outline. If the selection is very irregular and you want to straighten the twists and turns, use the Smooth command. Photoshop asks you to enter a value from 1 to 100 to tell it how far it can move any point in the outline. Enter 2 or 3 to be safe.

✔ If you want to increase the size of a selection a few pixels outward, choose Select➪Modify➪Expand and enter the number of pixels. The maximum value is 100 pixels; if you want to expand the outline farther, you have to choose Expand a second time.

✔ Select➪Modify➪Contract is the opposite of the Expand command. This command shrinks the selected area by 1 to 100 pixels all the way around.

The maximum value for these modifiers in previous versions is 16, which sometimes forces you to choose the command a second time. Photoshop 6 generously increases these values to 100.

Transforming Selections and Paths

Photoshop gives you the choice of being able to transform actual pixels or just selection marquees and paths without affecting the underlying pixels. Check out the fifth exercise in Chapter 21 to see how to transform actual pixels. For now, take a look at transforming selection marquees and paths.

Transforming selections

To transform a selection marquee or outline, choose Select➪Transform Selection. You see a box with handles and a *centerpoint* (also referred to as an *origin point*) framing your selection marquee, as shown in Figure 13-5. Using this box you can apply the following transformations:

✔ **Scale:** Drag any handle to scale your selection. Press Shift+drag to maintain proportions. Press Alt+drag (Option+drag on a Mac) to scale from the center point outward. Note that the centerpoint can be moved by dragging.

✔ **Rotate:** Position the centerpoint where you want the axis for the rotation to be. Drag outside the transform box to rotate the selection. Your cursor appears as a double-headed curved arrow.

✔ **Skew:** To skew a selection marquee, Ctrl+Alt+drag (⌘+Option+drag on a Mac) a side or a top or bottom handle. Skew permits distortion on a given axis.

✔ **Distort:** Ctrl+drag (⌘+drag on a Mac) a corner handle. Distort enables handles to move independently with no axis restrictions.

✔ **Perspective:** Ctrl+Shift+Alt+drag (⌘+Shift+Option+drag on a Mac) a corner handle. The opposite corner handle on the same side moves, as well.

Color Plate 5-1:
The red, green, and blue color channels in Photoshop act like slides in separate projectors pointed at the same spot on a screen. You may find it hard to believe that three primary hues could mix together to produce so many colors, but it's true.

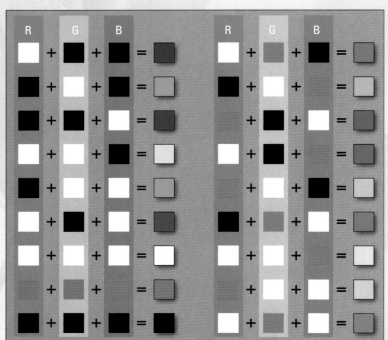

Color Plate 5-2:
This figure shows the way light, dark, and medium pixels in the red, green, and blue channels mix to form various sample colors. Altogether, you can create more than 16 million color variations.

Color Plate 5-3:
Pure white light from the sun (or a man-made light source) is made up of red, green, and blue light. When light passes through the cyan, magenta, or yellow printing ink, the ink filters out the red, green, or blue light and lets the other two pass through.

Color Plate 7-1:
The cyan, magenta, and yellow channels as they appear when inked in their proper colors (top row). Each color channel takes on new depth and detail when combined with black (middle row). During the commercial printing process, the cyan image is first combined with magenta (bottom left), and then yellow (bottom center), and then black (bottom right).

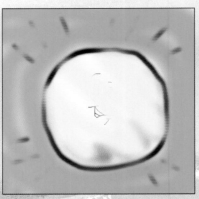

Color Plate 8-1:
When I used the Paintbrush tool to paint in the sun with yellow and the sky with blue, the paint obscured the sun's face and rays. When I started over again and lowered the Opacity setting to 40%, I just got weaker color (right).

Multiply

Screen

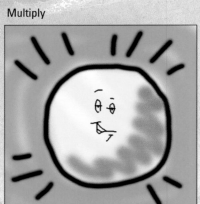

Overlay

Difference

Color Plate 8-2:
The results of applying yellow and blue with the Paintbrush using each of four brush modes.

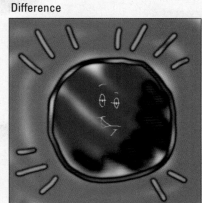

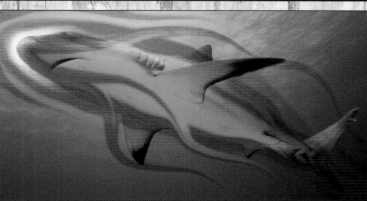

Color Plate 9-1: Using the Smudge tool, I turned a common, household-variety shark into a red-hot shark torpedo. In the Options bar, I turned on the Finger Painting check box, set the Mode to Color, and set the Pressure slider bar to 90%.

Color Plate 10-1: By cloning from the top left image onto the bottom left image with the Rubber Stamp tool, I was able to merge the two images to create the strange but nonetheless believable specimen on the right.

Tolerance: 32

Tolerance: 90

Tolerance: 180

Color Plate 12-1:
By raising the Tolerance value in the Options bar, I instructed Photoshop to select a wider range of colors around the point at which I clicked (just to the right of the forward giraffe). In this case, 90 seems to be the best setting.

One base color, Fuzziness: 200

Color Plate 12-2:
The result of clicking just to the right of the monster's nose and applying the Color Range command with a Fuzziness setting of 200. In the right image, I filled the selection with white and then deselected it.

Three base colors, Fuzziness: 60

Color Plate 12-3:
By Shift-clicking in the image while inside the Color Range dialog box and lowering the Fuzziness value, I selected more of the blue sky and made the selection outline less blurry.

Color Plate 14-1:
I filled the area behind the jar with custom gradients created by using the Gradient Editor.

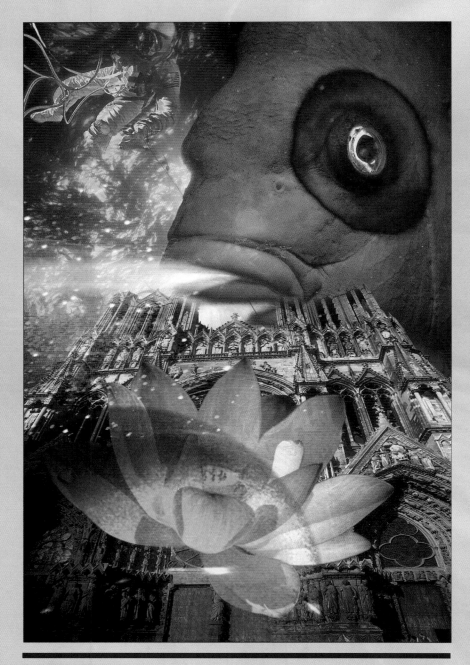

Color Plate 15-1:
To create this composition, I combined eight images and blended them together by using various modes and Opacity settings from the Layers palette. I selected all the images using the Color Range command, tinted the astronaut by using the Variations command, and erased, scaled, and rotated a few others.

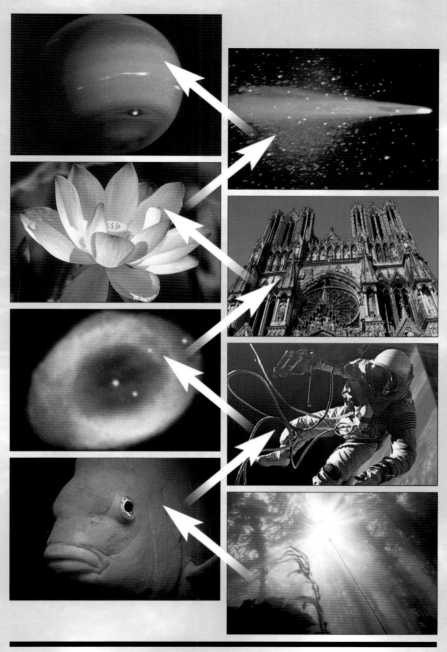

Color Plate 15-2:
The eight images I used to create Color Plate 15-1. The arrows show the layering order of the images, from the kelp (lower right) at the bottom of the heap to the planet Neptune (upper left) at the top.

Normal, 100% Opacity

50% Opacity

Fish: Multiply; Cathedral: Screen

Difference

Color Plate 15-3:
After positioning the cathedral on one layer, the fish on a layer beneath it, and the kelp
in the Background layer (top left), I experimented with various Opacity settings and
modes. First, I changed the Opacity of both layers to 50% (top right). Then I returned the
Opacity to 100% and applied the Multiply mode to the fish and the Screen mode to the
cathedral (bottom left). Finally, I applied the Difference mode to both layers (bottom right).

Overlay

Fish: Soft Light; Cathedral: Hard Light

Color

Luminosity

Color Plate 15-4:
Continuing from Color Plate 15-3, I applied the Overlay mode to both fish and cathedral (top left). Then I applied Soft Light to the fish and Hard Light to the cathedral (top right). Finally, I tried out the Color (bottom left) and Luminosity (bottom right) modes on both layers.

Color Plate 16-1:
Photoshop lets you create some wild type effects that are either difficult or impossible to produce in other programs. Some examples include double outline type (top), text with soft drop shadows (middle), and translucent text (bottom).

Color Plate 17-1:
Starting with the original inset image, I selected the dark portions of the image with Select⇨Color Range, applied the Add Noise filter with an Amount value of 25% and the Gaussian option selected, and then followed things up with the Motion Blur filter. The only difference between the top and bottom images was the setting of the Monochromatic check box in the Add Noise dialog box. In the top image, it was turned off; in the bottom image, it was on.

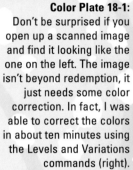

Color Plate 18-1:
Don't be surprised if you open up a scanned image and find it looking like the one on the left. The image isn't beyond redemption, it just needs some color correction. In fact, I was able to correct the colors in about ten minutes using the Levels and Variations commands (right).

Color Plate 18-2:
The results of adding blue (left) and yellow (right) to the image by using Image⇨Adjust⇨Variations. Colors that have little or no blue or yellow in them — such as the reds in the bows and the greens in the packages and apples — remain virtually unaffected.

Color Plate 18-3:
Here, I used the Levels command to correct the colors in a muted image. For reference, the histogram and Input Levels options from the Levels dialog box are inset with each step. Starting with the uncorrected Photo CD scan (top left), I adjusted the black slider triangle (top right), the white triangle (bottom left), and the gamma point (bottom right) to create a sound image with excellent color depth.

Original

More Blue

More Blue

More Magenta

More Magenta

More Blue

Color Plate 18-5:
I fixed an image that had a preponderance of yellow and green (top left) by clicking on the labeled previews in the Variations dialog box. For example, to produce the top middle image, I clicked on the More Blue preview; to get the top right image, I clicked on the same preview again.

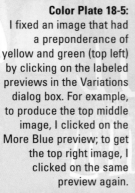

✔ **Flip Horizontal or Vertical:** Right mouse click (Control+click on a Mac) on your image to access the shortcut menu (described and shown in Chapter 2) and choose Flip Horizontal or Flip Vertical.

✔ **Rotate 180 degrees, 90 degrees CW, and 90 degrees CCW:** To rotate in these predetermined amounts, right mouse click (Control+click on a Mac) on your image to access the shortcut menu, and choose the rotation value.

✔ **Numeric:** You can no longer bring up the numeric Transformation dialog box by accessing the shortcut menu. Now if you want to make a transformation by entering a numeric value, you need to use the settings in the Options bar. You can move, scale, rotate, or skew via the Options bar. Entering the values applies the transformation. Click on the OK button only after you've finished transforming and want to apply it to the outline and exit the transform box.

After you finish transforming, press Enter (Return on a Mac) or double-click inside the transform box or click the Commit button (the check icon) in the Options bar. To cancel, press Esc or Ctrl+period (⌘+period on a Mac).

Figure 13-5:
You can apply transformations to selection marquees without affecting pixels.

Handle   Selection marquee

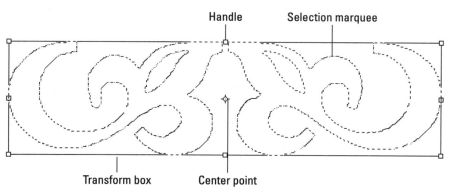

Transform box   Center point

Transforming paths

After the transform box is around the path, the transformation methods for paths are exactly the same as for selection marquees, except that distort and perspective can be applied only to whole paths. The big difference between transforming paths and selections is in how you first select the path.

To transform all paths:

1. **Choose Window➪Show Paths.**

2. **Click on the path name in the Paths Palette.**

   3. **Choose Edit⇨Free Transform Path.**

      The keyboard shortcut is Ctrl+T (⌘+T on a Mac).

To transform a single path:

   1. **Choose Window⇨Show Paths.**
   2. **Click on the path name in the Paths Palette.**
   3. **Choose the Path Component Selection tool.**
   4. **Click on the path with the Path Component Selection tool.**
   5. **Choose Edit⇨Free Transform Path.**

      The keyboard shortcut is Ctrl+T (⌘+T on a Mac).

To transform a part of a path:

   1. **Choose Window⇨Show Paths.**
   2. **Click on the path name in the Paths Palette.**
   3. **Choose the Direct Selection tool.**

      Or press A (or Shift+A) for the keyboard shortcut.
   4. **Select the points you want with the Direct Selection tool.**
   5. **Choose Edit⇨Free Transform Points.**

Photoshop lets you repeat your last transformation on another path by pressing Ctrl+Shift+T (⌘+Shift+T on a Mac) or choosing Edit⇨Transform⇨Again. This repeat transformation command also works with selections and layers (see Chapter 15) but not with selection marquees (outlines) alone.

Moving and Cloning Selections

Before bidding a fond farewell to Chapter 13, I want to quickly touch on the two most common things you can do with a selection: Move it and clone it.

Here's the lowdown:

   ✔ To move a selection, grab the Move tool, the four-headed arrow, (press V to select the tool from the keyboard), and drag the selection. A little pair of scissors appears by your cursor to show that you're about to remove the selection from its current home. When you move the selection, the area where the selection used to be is filled with the background color, as illustrated in Figure 13-6.

✔ You can temporarily access the move tool by pressing Ctrl (⌘ on a Mac) when any tool but the following is selected: Hand tool, pen tools, slice tools, Path Component Selection tool, Direct Selection tool, and shape tools.

✔ To nudge a selection 1 pixel, press one of the arrow keys while the Move tool is selected. Or press Ctrl (⌘ on a Mac) and an arrow key when any tool but the ones mentioned above is selected. The up arrow nudges the selection 1 pixel up; the right pixel nudges it to the right, and so on, just like you'd think. To nudge a selection 10 pixels, press Shift along with an arrow key while the Move tool is selected.

✔ To clone and move a selection, Alt+drag (Option+drag on a Mac) with the Move tool or Ctrl+Alt+drag (⌘+Option+drag on a Mac) with any other tool than the tools listed above. Your cursor changes into two arrow-heads — your reminder that you're creating a clone of your selection.

✔ To clone and nudge, select the Move tool and then press Alt (Option on a Mac) and one of the arrow keys. Or, when any tool other than the tools mentioned above is selected, press Ctrl and Alt (⌘ and Option on a Mac) as you press the arrow keys. Press Shift and Alt (Shift and Option on a Mac) with an arrow key to clone the selection and move it 10 pixels.

✔ To move a selection outline without moving the image inside it, select a lasso, marquee, or Magic Wand tool (see Chapter 12 for more on these tools). Then just drag the selection outline or nudge it with the arrow keys. This is a great way to reposition a selection outline without disturbing so much as a single pixel in the image.

✔ You can move and clone selections and selection outlines between images just as you would within a single image. Just drag the selection or selection outline from its current window into the other image window. For more on this topic, see Chapter 15.

✔ Yet another way to move a selection is to use the Edit⇨Free Transform command, discussed in Chapter 21. Free Transform enables you to move, resize, rotate, and distort your image by manipulating a special transform box. To move the selection, just drag inside the box. To discover how to perform other Free Transform tricks, also see Chapter 21.

✔ When you're moving or cloning a selection, those animated dots that parade around the outline — called *marching ants* in some quarters — can be downright distracting. Sure, the ants permit you to see the boundaries of your selection, but sometimes you need to see how the edges of the selection blend in with their new surroundings. To do this, choose View⇨Hide Extras or press Ctrl+H (⌘+H on a Mac).

✔ To bring back the marching ants, press Ctrl+H (⌘+H on a Mac).

Figure 13-6:
After
selecting
the
Washington
Monument
(top), I
dragged it to
a more
convenient
location
(bottom),
leaving a
gaping hole
in the
Capitol
skyline.

Chapter 14

Coloring inside the Lines

. . . .

. . . .

*H*ave you ever spray painted using a stencil? In case you've never engaged in this riveting pastime, let me explain how it works:

1. **Hold the stencil up to the surface you want to paint.**

2. **Spray recklessly.**

When you take the stencil away, you discover a painted image that matches the shape of the stencil. It's the epitome of a no-brainer.

In Photoshop, a selection outline works the same way. Just as a stencil isolates the area affected by the spray paint, a selection outline isolates the area affected by a paint or edit tool. You can also fill a selection outline with color or trace around the selection outline.

Sounds easy, doesn't it? Like an unremarkable bit of information that virtually flings itself at the attention of the most casual observer. Like something you could have figured out on your own, for example, and saved $19.99. Well, whatever it sounds like, I intend to walk you through every nuance of painting, filling, and tracing selections. Chapters 12 and 13 explain how to create and manipulate selection outlines. This chapter shows you what to do with them. (The selection outlines, that is, not the chapters. You already know what to do with the chapters — tear them out and use them to line the parrot cage.)

Put Down Newspaper Before You Paint

If some portion of an image is selected, Photoshop treats all deselected areas as protected. You can use any paint or edit tool inside the selection without worrying about harming areas outside the selection.

In this chapter, I took a jar-in-a-nook, which has a certain austere beauty about it — it's just the sort of prop that would feel right at home in a hoity-toity kitchen of the idle rich — and, overcome with desire, I mucked it up. Specifically, I painted inside the jar without harming the background. And you can, too. To this end, do the following:

1. **Select the jar.**

   This is the only step that takes any work. You can start out by selecting the body of the jar with the Elliptical Marquee tool. If you have problems getting the marquee exactly on the jar — it's hard to know where to start dragging so that it comes out right — just make sure that the marquee is approximately the right size, select one of the marquee or lasso tools, and then use the arrow keys to nudge the outline into position. After you select the body to your satisfaction, you can Shift+drag with the Lasso tool to incorporate the neck of the jar into the selection as well.

2. **Make any modifications you deem necessary.**

   In this case, you may want to blur the selection outline a tad using Select➪Feather, as explained in Chapter 13. If your selection outline isn't dead on, the Feather command helps to fudge the difference a little.

3. **Choose View➪Hide Extras or press Ctrl+H (⌘+H on the Mac).**

   This step is extremely important. By hiding the selection outline, you can see how your edits affect the image without those distracting animated dots, referred to as *marching ants,* getting in your way.

4. **Paint and edit away.**

   Feel free to use any tool you want. You can paint with the Paintbrush, Airbrush, or Pencil; edit with the Smudge, focus, or toning tools; clone with the Rubber Stamp; use the Eraser and erase to a previous version of the image — all with the assurance that the area outside the selection will remain as safeguarded from your changes as the driven snow (or whatever the saying is).

While editing away, try not to press Ctrl+D (⌘+D on a Mac) or click with one of the selection tools. Because the selection outline is hidden, you won't notice any difference when you deselect the image. If you do inadvertently deselect, press Ctrl+Z (⌘+Z on a Mac) right away. If you wait until after you apply a brush stroke, Ctrl+Z (⌘+Z on a Mac) undoes the stroke but not the selection outline.

But don't fret. Even after performing several actions, you can retrieve your last selection by choosing Select⇨Reselect or pressing Ctrl+Shift+D (⌘+Shift+D on a Mac).

In Figure 14-1, I painted inside my selected jar using a single tool — the Airbrush — with a single brush size and only two colors, black and white. As a result, I was able to transform the jar into a kind of marble. Looks mighty keen, and there's not so much as a drop of paint outside the lines.

This stenciling feature is so all-fired handy that I almost always select an area before applying a paint or edit tool. The fact is, the selection tools are easier to control than the painting or editing tools, so you may as well take advantage of them.

Figure 14-1: Using the Airbrush, I painted inside the selected jar. (You can't see the selection outline because it's hidden.)

Dribbling Paint from a Bucket

Photoshop enables you to fill a selection with the foreground color, the background color, a pattern, or a gradual blend of colors called a *gradient*. You can even fill a selection with a previous version of the image — referred to as the *history source state* (see Chapter 11 for details).

But before I explain any of these eye-popping options, I want to cover the Paint Bucket tool, which is part selection tool and part fill tool. The Paint Bucket tool (looks like a tilted bucket of paint) shares a flyout menu with the Gradient tool and lets you fill an area of continuous color by clicking on the area.

In Figure 14-2, for example, I set the foreground to white and clicked with the Paint Bucket tool on the row of broccoli in the jar. Photoshop filled the broccoli with white, turning it into the rough facsimile of cauliflower.

To adjust the performance of the Paint Bucket, access the Options bar, also shown in Figure 14-2. As with the Magic Wand tool, the Tolerance value determines how many pixels in your image the Paint Bucket affects. The only difference is that the Paint Bucket applies color instead of selecting pixels. You can also select the Anti-aliased check box to soften the edges of the filled area. (In Figure 14-2, the Tolerance value is 32, and Anti-aliased is turned on, as it is by default.)

Paint Bucket tool

Figure 14-2:
The Paint
Bucket
fills a
continuous
area of
color with a
different
color.

The problem with the Paint Bucket tool is that it's hard to get the Tolerance value just right. You usually end up choosing Undo several times and resetting the Tolerance value until you find the value that colors only the pixels that you want to color. Overall, I consider the Paint Bucket a poor tool for filling areas in Photoshop. If you select an area in your image by using the Magic Wand tool, which chooses pixels of similar color surrounding the cursor (discussed in Chapter 12) and then fills the area with a color (described in the next sections), you produce the same effect as with the Paint Bucket, *and* you have more alternatives at your disposal.

If you decide to ignore my advice and take up the Paint Bucket at your earliest opportunity, you can select the tool quickly by pressing G and then Shift+G.

Applying Color to Selection Innards

Now that I've expressed my opinion regarding the Paint Bucket — ick, yuk, stay away — it's time to move on to the essential methods for filling a selection outline in Photoshop:

- ✔ To fill a selection with the foreground color, press Alt+Backspace (Option+Delete on a Mac).

- ✔ To fill a selection with the background color, press Ctrl+Backspace (⌘+Delete on a Mac).

- ✔ When you're working on a layer and want to fill the opaque part of a selection with the foreground color while leaving the rest of the selection transparent, press Shift+Alt+Backspace (Shift+Option+Delete on a Mac). Press Ctrl+Shift+ Backspace (⌘+Shift+Delete on a Mac) to fill the opaque area with the background color. (And if all this makes no sense at all, you may want to turn to Chapter 15, which explains layers and transparency.)

- ✔ Choose Edit⇨Fill to display the Fill dialog box, which lets you fill the selection with translucent color, a pattern, or history (see Chapter 11).

- ✔ Drag with the Gradient tool to create a gradient (a gradual blend) between two or more colors.

Two of these options — Edit⇨Fill and the Gradient tool — require more discussion than I have devoted to them so far, which is why the rest of this chapter is so filled to the gills with text.

Fill, I Command You!

Choose Edit⇨Fill to display the Fill dialog box, shown in Figure 14-3. The Use pop-up menu lets you specify the color or stored image with which you want to fill the selection; the Blending options let you mix the filled colors with the colors already inside the selection. All these options are discussed in more detail in this section.

You can also display the Fill dialog box by pressing Shift+Backspace (Shift+Delete on a Mac).

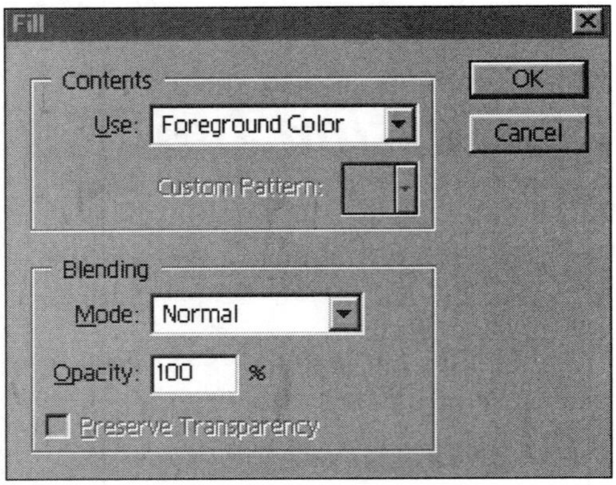

Figure 14-3:
Specify how
you want to
fill a
selection by
using the
options in
the Fill
dialog box.

Select your stuffing

The most important part of the Fill dialog box is the Use pop-up menu. Here you select the stuff you want to use to fill the selection. The options are as follows:

- ✔ The Foreground Color option fills the selection with the foreground color, and the Background Color option fills the selection with the back-ground color. I can see by your expression that you're not surprised by this news.

- ✔ The next option, Pattern, fills a selection with a repeating pattern. You can define a pattern by selecting a rectangular area and choosing Edit⇨Define Pattern. If you don't define a selection, Photoshop creates the pattern from the entire canvas. Photoshop now lets you store more than one pattern at a time. You can access the patterns you've created, along with a variety of preset patterns, via the Custom Pattern drop-down menu.

✔ Choose the History option to fill the selection with a previously saved step of that portion of the image. In short, the History palette remembers all your previous steps, which are called *source states.* You select a previous source state in the palette, and the selection fills with the image as it appeared at that point in time. If this is totally confusing, be sure and check out Chapter 11.

✔ The last three options — Black, 50% Gray, and White — fill the selection with black, medium gray, and white, respectively. What's the point? Not much. If the foreground and background colors are set to blue and orange and you don't want to change them, I suppose that you may find these options useful. And pigs may fly. You just never know.

How not to mix colors

You can enter a value into the Opacity option box of the Fill dialog box to mix the fill color or history source state with the present colors in the selection. You can also mix the fill and the selected color using the options in the Mode pop-up menu, which include Multiply, Screen, Difference, and other wacky brush modes (see Chapter 8 and Color Plate 8-2).

Notice that I said you can do these things, not that you should. The truth is, you don't want to use the Fill dialog box's Blending options to mix fills with selections. Why? Because the Fill dialog box doesn't let you preview the effects of the Blending options. Even seasoned professionals have trouble predicting the exact repercussions of Opacity settings and brush modes, and it's likely that you will, too. And, if you don't like what you get, you have to undo the operation and choose Edit⇨Fill all over again.

The better way to mix fills with selections is to copy the selection to a new layer, fill it, and experiment with the Opacity slider and mode options in the Layers palette. Naturally, you have no idea what I'm talking about if you haven't read the supremely insightful Chapter 15. Until then, take my valuable advice and be content to ignore the Opacity and Mode options in the Blending area at the bottom of the Fill dialog box.

The Preserve Transparency check box comes into play when you're working on a layer other than the background layer, as discussed in Chapter 15. If the check box is turned on, only the opaque pixels in a selection are filled when you apply the Fill command — the transparent areas remain transparent. If the check box is turned off, the entire selection is filled. The option is dimmed if the Preserve Transparency option in the Layers palette is turned on.

The Ever-Changing Color Sea

The Gradient tool lets you fill a selection with a fountain of colors that starts with one color and ends with another. By default, the two colors are the foreground color and background color.

But Photoshop can do more than create simple two-color blends. You can create custom gradients that blend a multitude of colors and vary from opaque to transparent throughout the blend. Photoshop has five gradient types: Linear, Radial, Angle, Reflected, and Diamond. And the Options bar offers settings that enable you to play with blend modes, opacity, and reversing colors.

Press Shift+Right-click (Shift+Control+click on a Mac) to bring up the gradient palette right under your cursor for quick and easy selections.

Checking out the Gradient tool

The following steps provide one of those in-depth introductions to the Gradient tool that folks find so helpful nowadays:

1. **Select some portion of your image.**

   In Figure 14-4, I selected the jar again. I love that jar. It's so pristine; it just begs for me to mess it up.

   If you don't select a portion of your image before using the Gradient tool, Photoshop fills the entire image with the gradient. (Or, if you're working on a layer, as discussed in Chapter 15, the gradient fills the entire layer.)

2. **Select the Gradient tool.**

   To do it quickly, just press the G key.

3. **From the Options bar, select your desired gradient type.**

4. **Select the Foreground to Background option, the first swatch, from the Gradient Picker drop-down palette in your Options bar.**

   It creates a gradient that begins with the foreground color and ends with the background color.

5. **Set the foreground and background colors the way you want them.**

   This step is up to you. You can stick with black and white or select new colors with the Eyedropper tool or Color palette. For the purposes of Figure 14-4, I just set my colors to the defaults, black and white.

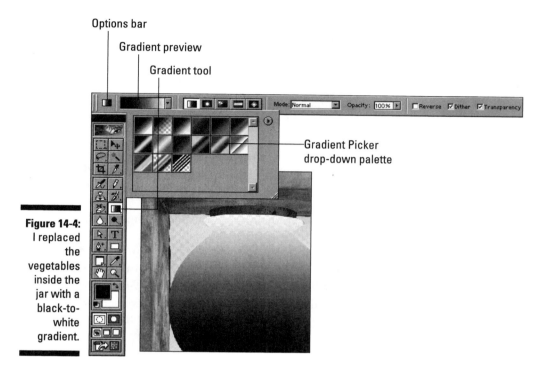

Options bar

Gradient preview

Gradient tool

Gradient Picker
drop-down palette

Figure 14-4:
I replaced
the
vegetables
inside the
jar with a
black-to-
white
gradient.

6. **Begin dragging at the point where you want to set the foreground color.**

   In Figure 14-4, I began my drag at the bottom of the jar.

7. **Release where you want to position the background color.**

   I released at the top of the jar. The result is a black-to-white gradation.

If you Shift+drag with the Gradient tool, Photoshop constrains the direction of your drag to a horizontal, vertical, or 45° diagonal angle.

Changing the way of the gradient

You can mess around with the performance of the Gradient tool by accessing the settings in the Options bar (refer to Figure 14-4).

Like the Opacity settings and Modes available inside the Fill dialog box, the Opacity and Mode options inside the Options bar for each of the gradients are best ignored. If you want to mix a gradation with the existing colors in a selection, create the gradation on a layer and select options inside the Layers palette, as discussed in Chapter 15.

Choosing between the five gradient tools

As stated at the beginning of this section, Photoshop gives you five gradient tools, which are described below and illustrated in Figure 14-5.

- ✔ **Linear:** Creates a gradient in which colors blend in a straight line.
- ✔ **Radial:** The colors blend in concentric circles, from the center outward.

    Note: In every example in Figure 14-5, the foreground color is black and the background color is white. You almost always want to set the lighter color to the foreground color when using the Radial option because doing that creates a glowing effect. If the foreground color is darker than its background compatriot, the gradation looks like a bottomless pit as you can see from the radial gradient shown in Figure 14-5.

- ✔ **Angle:** Creates a conical gradation with the colors appearing counterclockwise.
- ✔ **Reflected:** If dragged from edge to edge of your selection, a reflected gradient acts like a linear gradient. However, if dragged from the interior to an edge of the selection, the gradient reflects back on itself.
- ✔ **Diamond:** Like the radial gradient, this tool creates concentric shapes — in this case, diamonds or squares, depending on the angle you drag.

Linear   Radial

Figure 14-5:
Jar filled with five different gradient types — Linear, Radial, Angle, Reflected, and Diamond.

Angle   Reflected   Diamond

Choosing gradient options

You find three check boxes in the Options bar: Dither, Transparency, and Reverse.

- ✔ The Dither check box is easy. When turned on, it helps eliminate banding. Banding is a problem in which you can see distinct bands of color in a printed gradient — that's a bad thing in 9 out of 10 households. Leave the check box turned on unless you're feeling especially contrary and want to create a banding effect.

- ✔ The Transparency check box is a little more complicated. Here's the scoop: Gradients can include areas that are partially or fully transparent. In other words, they fade from a solid color to a more transparent color. When the Transparency check box is turned off, Photoshop creates the gradient by using all opaque colors, ignoring the transparency information.

  The best way to get a grip on what the Transparency check box does is to try a little experiment. First, turn on the check box and press D to get the default foreground and background colors. Then, choose the Transparent Rainbow option, the next to last swatch, from the Gradient Picker drop-down palette and draw a gradient. You get a fill pattern that consists of a multicolored rainbow with your background peeking out at the beginning and end of the gradient. Next, draw the gradient with the Transparency check box turned off. You now get a fill of a multicolored rainbow with no background peeking out because Photoshop is ignoring the transparency at either end of the gradient. In most cases, you don't need to bother with the check box — just leave it turned on.

- ✔ When the Reverse check box is checked, the gradient will start with the background color and end with the foreground color. This option is useful for creating radial gradients while keeping the default colors intact.

Selecting your colors

The Gradient Picker drop-down palette lets you change the way colors blend inside the gradation and select from a variety of prefab gradients. Here's a description of those gradients:

- ✔ Normally, Foreground to Background is selected. This option does just what it sounds like it does: It blends between the foreground and background colors, as in the examples in Figure 14-5.

- ✔ If you select one of the Transparent options, the gradient tool blends the foreground color into the original colors in the selection. The examples in Figure 14-6 were created with the Foreground to Transparent option selected.

Linear   Radial

Figure 14-6:
Here's the jar filled with a linear and radial gradient and with the Foreground to Transparent option selected.

Foreground to Transparent

✔ The remaining options in the gradient picker drop-down palette create a variety of factory-made gradients, some involving just a few colors and others blending a whole rainbow of colors.

 ✔ Photoshop now offers a vast array of gradient libraries. These gradient libraries have preset gradients that you can easily load for your painting pleasure. Simply click on the Gradient Picker arrow to access the drop-down palette. Click on the palette pop-up menu and scroll down to the bottom where you find the various gradient libraries. Select one and either replace or append your current gradient set.

 ✔ To access the various viewing options, click on the Gradient Picker Palette pop-up menu.

 When you select a gradient from the drop-down palette, Photoshop displays the gradient in the Gradient Preview in the Options bar, as labeled earlier in Figure 14-4.

If none of the existing gradients suits your taste, you can create your own custom gradient, as I did in Color Plate 14-1. The next section explains the ins and outs of building your own gradients.

 Like with the Color Swatches menu, you can view your gradients by thumbnails, text only, or a combination of both text and thumbnails.

Becoming a gradient wizard

It's pretty easy to design your own custom gradient if you just spend a few moments to dissect and understand the elements of the Gradient Editor dialog box. Start out by clicking on the Gradient Preview in the Options bar, as annotated in Figure 14-4. The Gradient Editor dialog box, shown in Figure 14-7, appears. Uh-oh. Looks like you've ventured too far into geek space, doesn't it?

The Gradient Editor dialog box is a bit complex, and chances are you won't use it much. But I don't want you to feel as though you didn't get the full value for your $19.99, so the following list gives you a brief introduction to the dialog box and starts you off on creating your own gradient:

✔ The palette at the top of the dialog box lists all the preset gradients — the same ones in the Gradient Picker drop-down palette in the Options bar. Select the gradient you want to use as a starting point for your custom gradient from this palette. It doesn't much matter which you choose, you can change it to your heart's content.

✔ **Gradient Type:** You can choose between gradients made with Solid colors or those created with Noise. Noise gradients add noise that randomizes the colors of selected pixels and produces some interesting, yet unpredictable results.

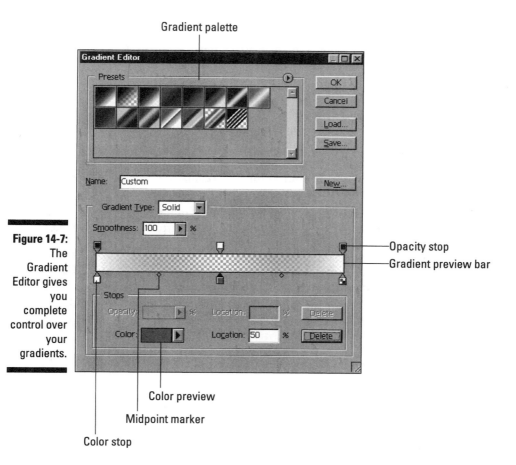

Gradient palette

Opacity stop

Gradient preview bar

Figure 14-7:
The
Gradient
Editor gives
you
complete
control over
your
gradients.

Color preview

Midpoint marker

Color stop

- **Smoothness:** Drag the slider or enter a value to determine how smoothly you blend one color into another color. The Smoothness slider changes to a Roughness slider when a Noise gradient type is selected.

- **Roughness:** This option is only available if you choose a Noise gradient. Roughness affects how smooth or sharp one color transitions into another.

The following options are only available when the Noise gradient type is selected:

- **Color Model and Color Sliders:** Enable you to change the color model and or limit the color range by moving the sliders.

- **Restrict Colors:** Limits the colors to printable CMYK colors (see more on CMYK in Chapter 5).

- **Add Transparency:** Enables you to incorporate transparency in your noise gradient.

- **Randomize:** Changes the colors in a noise gradient. Remember, it is *random* and every time you click, you get a new set of colors. Better than watching reruns on T.V.

- The little house-shaped boxes beneath the fade bar are called *stops*. There are color stops on the bottom and opacity stops on the top. You use these stops to change the colors, opacity, and location of the gradient, as explained in the upcoming two sections.

- The Gradient Preview bar in the dialog box displays both the colors and transparent areas of your gradient. Transparent areas are represented by a gray-and-white checkerboard pattern.

- The Save button saves your gradient to a different location on disk. You don't need to save the gradient using this button unless you want to store your gradient in some spot other than where the rest of the gradients are located. After you edit and name a gradient, click on New, and then OK; the gradient is automatically added to the Gradient Picker palette in the Options bar for the gradient tools.

- To remove a gradient from the list, press Alt+Shift (Option+Shift on a Mac) and click on the gradient. Note that the scissors icon signifies "delete".

Changing, adding, and deleting colors

To change one of the colors in the gradient, first check to see whether the roof on that color's color stop is black. The black *roof* indicates the active color stop — the color that is to be affected by your changes. If the roof isn't black, click on the color stop to make it active.

After you activate the color stop, you have one of three choices. You can click on the Color Preview, which also brings up the Color Picker. Or you can access the Foreground or Background color from the Color pop-up menu. To change the color in the Color Preview, you can click on a color in your image, a color in the color bar of the Color palette, or a color in the Swatches palette.

If you select the color via the Foreground or Background color options, you change the color marked by the color stop to the foreground or background color, respectively. Keep in mind that if you change the foreground or background color, the color in the gradient changes automatically. The change doesn't affect gradients that you've already drawn, but it does affect any future gradients you create. But you can always select the color stop and choose User Color from the Color pop-up menu which leaves the Foreground or Background color, but untags it as such so no changes can occur.

Here's some more stuff you need to know about playing with the colors in your gradient:

✔ To add a color to the gradient, click just below the Gradient Preview bar at the point where you want the color to appear. You get a new color stop icon representing the color.

✔ To remove a color from the gradient, drag its color stop down and away from the Gradient Preview bar.

✔ If you drag a color stop to the right or left, you can change the position of the color in the gradient. Suppose that you have a gradient that fades from black to white. If you want more black and less white, drag the black color stop toward the white stop.

✔ The little diamonds on top or underneath the Gradient Preview bar represent the midpoint between two colors or two opacity settings. Using the example of a black-to-white gradient again, the midpoint marks the spot at which the gradient contains equal amounts of black and white. To move a midpoint, just drag the diamond.

✔ The Location option box shows the placement of the active color stop or midpoint marker. If you want to be terribly precise, you can enter a value into the Location box to position a color stop or midpoint marker instead of dragging the icons.

When a color stop is active, a value of 0% (zero) represents the very beginning of the gradient; 100% represents the very end. Midpoint values are always relative to the two color stops on either side of the midpoint. A value of 50% places the midpoint an equal distance from both color stops. For reasons unknown, the minimum and maximum Midpoint values are 5% and 95%. Just thought you might like to store that useless bit of information in your memory bank.

Changing the transparency

Hold on to your stomach — now we're really veering into the land of the propeller heads. Photoshop lets you adjust the amount of opacity in a gradient. You can make a portion of the gradient fully opaque, completely transparent, or somewhere in between the two.

Suppose that you want to create a gradient that starts out white, gradually fades to completely transparent, and then becomes completely white again. In other words, you want to create a variation of the effect shown back in Figure 14-6. Here's how to create such a gradient:

1. **Make the foreground color white.**

2. **Click on the Gradient Preview in the Options bar to bring up the Gradient Editor dialog box.**

3. **Inside the Gradient Editor dialog box, choose the Foreground to Transparent (the second swatch) gradient from the Gradient palette.**

4. **Take the opacity stop on the right and move it to the center of the Gradient Preview bar. Leave the Opacity setting at 0% (completely transparent).**

5. **Add another opacity stop at the far right. Change the Opacity setting to 100% (completely opaque).**

   The Gradient Preview bar now shows your gradient in terms of transparent and opaque areas. Black stops represent opaque areas; white stops represent transparent areas; gray areas represent everything in between. The Gradient Preview bar also shows you the opaque areas in their actual colors and transparent areas in a gray and white checkerboard pattern.

6. **Name your gradient.**

7. **Click on New.**

   Your gradient, with its new name, is added to the palette of gradients above. You now have a gradient that fades from fully opaque white to . . . fully opaque white. Apply the gradient to an image to get a better idea of what you just created. Wow, that's exciting, huh?

It's tempting to press Enter (Return on a Mac) after you change the Opacity value, but don't — pressing Enter (Return on a Mac) closes the dialog box. The value you enter into the opacity setting takes effect without a press of the Enter (Return on a Mac) key. To switch to another option, press Tab.

You can also add as many opacity stops as you want and set different Opacity values for each. To move an opacity stop, just drag it right or left; to delete a stop, drag it off the bar. To move a midpoint, drag it right or left.

The Transparency check box in the Options bar determines whether transparency settings are ignored when you apply a gradient. If the check box is turned off, your gradient is completely opaque. For example, if you turn off the check box when applying the gradient created by the preceding steps, you get a completely white gradient instead of one that fades from white to transparent and back again.

Your Image Needs Strokes, Too

The last item on today's agenda is Edit⇨Stroke, a command that traces borders around a selection. When you choose this command, Photoshop displays the Stroke dialog box, shown in Figure 14-8. Enter the thickness of the border you want into the Width option box. This value is measured in pixels and the range is 1–250 pixels.

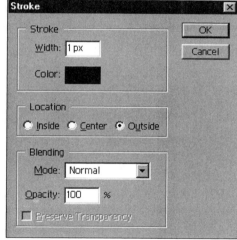

Figure 14-8:
Use the Stroke dialog box to draw a border around a selection.

You can, however, enter units other than pixels. For example, if you type in "2 inches," Photoshop accepts it and converts the value to an equivalent number of pixels.

In Figure 14-9, for example, I traced a 16-pixel wide black border around the jar (which is the maximum Width value, incidentally). Then I swapped the foreground and background colors, chose Edit⇨Stroke again, and entered 8 into the Width option box. The result is a white border inside a black border. Slick, huh? (Oh, come on, say it is, even if it's just to make me feel better.)

Photoshop now lets you pick a color from within the stroke dialog box. Simply click on the color swatch and you are transported to the Color Picker. No more slapping yourself on the head for not picking the right color before hand.

How the border rides the track

The Location options in the Stroke dialog box determine how the border rides the selection outline. The border can cruise around fully inside or fully outside the selection, or it can sit astride (centered on) the selection. Why might you want to change this setting? Well, take another look at Figure 14-9. Suppose that instead of the white border being flanked on either side by black (which I created using the Center option), I want the borders to sit beside each other. If I select the Inside option, the white border appears inside the selection, and the black border inside the white border. If I select Outside, the white border traces the outside of the jar, and the black border extends even farther.

Actually, I don't recommend selecting the Outside option. It has a nasty habit of flattening the edges of curves. For the best results, stick with Inside or Center.

Figure 14-9:
The classic double-border effect, so in demand at today's finer jar emporiums.

Mix your stroke after you press Enter (Return)

Like the Blending and Opacity options in other dialog boxes, the ones in the Stroke dialog box don't provide you with a preview of how the effect will look when applied to your image. So, if you want to play with the blend modes or opacity of your stroke, ignore the options in the dialog box. Instead, create a new layer (as explained in Chapter 15) and do your selecting and stroking on that layer. You can then adjust the blend mode and opacity via the Layers option palette (also discussed in Chapter 15).

On the off chance that you're curious about the Preserve Transparency check box, it affects only images with layers. If you don't have any layers going, don't worry about it. (Again, layers are explained in Chapter 15.) Even if your image does contain layers, don't worry about this option. It just ensures that the transparent portions of layers remain transparent.

Part V

So, You Say You're Serious about Image Editing

The 5th Wave   By Rich Tennant

©RICHTENNANT

"...and here's me with Cindy Crawford. And this is me with Madonna and Celine Dion..."

In this part . . .

*O*ne of the great legacies of Walt Disney — the man, not the company — was his insistence that animation take full advantage of its unreal medium. He and his staff perfected techniques, camera angles, and character movements that would have proven impossible had the studio been working with live actors and sets. Ironically, these very unreal techniques produced the effect of heightened realism, in which backgrounds shifted on multiple planes, cameras swooped and glided without regard for terrain, and characters moved more gracefully and far more expressively than their human counterparts.

Simply put, Walt figured that there was no point in creating cartoons if all you intended to do was slavishly adhere to the dictates of real life. The same argument can be made for digital image editing. What's the point of going to all the trouble of scanning an image to disk and opening it up in Photoshop if you're not going to take it beyond the boundaries of real life in the process? In a word, none. In a few more words, if you're going to use Photoshop, there's no reason not to make every image you create more real than reality.

Chapters 15 through 19 show you how. Here, you discover how to mix images to create breathtaking visual collages, add type to your images, automatically correct the focus of images, stamp images in metal and create other special effects, and bring out brilliant colors that you never knew were there. In other words, you discover how to turn your images into something much better than they were. And because everyone is in the midst of Internet frenzy, I've thrown in a small chapter (Chapter 19) on preparing images for the wide and wonderful World Wide Web.

Chapter 15

Layers upon Layers upon Layers

• •

In This Chapter

▶ Working with layers

▶ Combining images

▶ Pasting an image inside a selection outline

▶ Dragging and dropping selections

▶ Scaling an image to fit the composition

▶ Moving and merging layers

▶ Aligning and distributing layers

▶ Adjusting the Opacity setting

▶ Locking and color coding layers

▶ Using Layer sets

▶ Applying blend modes

▶ Erasing holes in layers

▶ Using the Layer Styles feature

▶ Using the Styles palette

• •

*I*nsofar as "high art" is concerned, the heyday for surrealism was 60 to 70 years ago. But the problem with guys like Max Ernst, René Magritte, and even Salvador Dalí was that they never got around to learning how to use Photoshop. Oh, sure, Ernst and Magritte were long dead by the time Photoshop debuted, and Dalí may have had better things to do in his final days than learn a new piece of software. But still, think of what they could have done. A paintbrush is great, but it pales when compared to Photoshop as a means for merging photo-realistic images to create flat-out impossible visual scenarios.

Color Plate 15-1 shows what I mean. No matter how hard you work at it, you can never assemble these elements in a photo shoot. It's just so darn difficult to squeeze a giant fish, the Reims Cathedral in France, and the planet Neptune into the same room. If you had talent streaming like fire-hydrant jets out your ears, you might be able to paint the image, but most of us would have thrown in the towel at the prospect of re-creating a High Gothic cathedral facade that took a team of thirteenth-century masters 65 years to carve.

But we live in a sparkling modern age, filled with more dazzling masterworks of automation than we know what to do with. Thanks to one such masterwork — I speak here of Photoshop, naturally — I was able to throw together Color Plate 15-1 in a couple of hours. Altogether, the composition comprises eight separate images; however, it required not so much as a single stroke of a painting or editing tool. I simply selected the images, combined them, blended them together, and erased a few stray pixels that weren't doing the final study in surrealism a lick of good.

Because it can be difficult to distinguish every one of the eight images, Color Plate 15-2 shows each one on its own. The arrows indicate the order in which the images are stacked on top of each other. For example, the underwater kelp jungle in the lower-right corner of Color Plate 15-2 lies at the bottom of the composition in Color Plate 15-1; the photo of Neptune in the upper-left corner of the second color plate rests at the top of the composition. The image appears as if I cut out a picture of the kelp and pasted it onto a page, cut out the fish and pasted it on the kelp, cut out the astronaut and pasted him in front of the fish, and so on.

Some images are blended together using the same brush modes I discuss in Chapter 8 — for example:

✔ The Multiply mode darkens colors as though they were painted on top of each other with watercolors (see Chapter 8 for more details). I used Multiply to blend the nebula — the image just below the flower in Color Plate 15-2 — with the fish to create the black eye effect in Color Plate 15-1.

✔ The spray coming out of the fish's mouth is the comet from the upper-right corner of Color Plate 15-2. I blended the two using the Screen mode.

✔ I blended the Reims Cathedral and Neptune with the images behind them using modes I haven't discussed yet. Respectively, these modes are Luminosity and Hard Light. I explain more about them in the section "Playing around with blend modes," near the end of this chapter.

This is the point at which you ask, "Yeah, yeah, yeah, but how in the world do I pull off something like this?" Well, wouldn't you know it — that's what this chapter is all about. I tell you how to get different images into the same document, how to assign them to separate layers, and how to mix them together using modes and the Eraser tool. And, remarkably, it's all a lot easier than you may think.

Pasting Images Together

Suppose that you want to paste the fish image from the bottom of Color Plate 15-2 into the neighboring kelp image. How do you go about it? Here's one approach:

1. **Open the fish image and select the fish.**

2. **Press Ctrl+C (⌘+C on a Mac).**

   Ctrl+C (⌘+C on a Mac) is the time-honored keyboard shortcut for the Edit⇨Copy command, which places a copy of your selection onto the Clipboard. The *Clipboard* is a temporary storage area for image data. Any previous occupant of the Clipboard (sent there via Edit⇨Copy or its close cousin, Edit⇨Cut) is displaced by the fish.

3. **Open the kelp image.**

4. **Press Ctrl+V (⌘+V on a Mac).**

   That's the shortcut for the Edit⇨Paste command, which dumps the current contents of the Clipboard into your image. Consider fish and kelp combined into one. The original fish image remains intact because the fish you pasted into the kelp was merely a copy.

But these steps aren't the only way to combine images. You also have these options at your disposal:

✔ To cut a selection from one image and paste it into another, choose Edit⇨Cut and then Edit⇨Paste. The selection is removed entirely from the first image and planted in the second.

✔ You can clone a selection between images by dragging it with the Move tool or Ctrl+dragging (⌘+dragging on a Mac) it with any tool except the following: the pen tools (all the various flavors), the Hand tool, the Slice and Slice Select tools, the Path Component Selection tool, the Direct Selection tool, and any of the shape tools.

   This method of cloning between images is known in the computer world as *dragging and dropping,* by the way.

✔ To transfer an entire image to another image window, choose Select⇨All or Ctrl+A (⌘+A on a Mac) before dragging or using the Cut or Copy commands.

✔ For a weird but occasionally useful trick, use Edit⇨Paste Into to paste an image inside an existing selection, as described in the upcoming section "Filling a selection with a selection."

When you use the Paste command, Photoshop places the pasted image on a new layer. When you drag and drop a selection from one image to another, Photoshop places the selection on a new layer as well. For more on working with layers, start reading at the section "Excuse Me, but What's a Layer?" and keep going to the end of the chapter.

Filling a selection with a selection

The Edit⇨Paste Into command lets you insert an image into an existing selection outline. For example, I wanted to paste the fish behind some of the vegetation in the neighboring kelp image so that the fish would appear to be intertwined with his environment. In the first example of Figure 15-1, I selected an area inside the kelp stalks and feathered the selection by choosing Select⇨Feather, as discussed in Chapter 13. Then I chose Paste Into or Ctrl+Shift+V (⌘+Shift+V on a Mac) to create the fish-inside-the-kelp shown in the second example. (Note that I've hidden the selection outlines in the second example so that you can better see the transitions between fish and stalks.)

Photoshop pastes the selection to a new layer. You can then move and blend the pasted image just as though it were a floating selection. It's just that the pasted image is invisible outside the boundaries of the previous selection outline.

You can also paste into the unselected area of an image by pressing the Alt key (Option key on a Mac) as you choose Edit⇨Paste Into. If I had done this with the image in Figure 15-1, for example, the fish would show through the exact opposite area of the kelp bed that he does now.

Figure 15-1: After selecting an area of kelp (left), I chose the Paste Into command to introduce the fish to his new kelpy home (right).

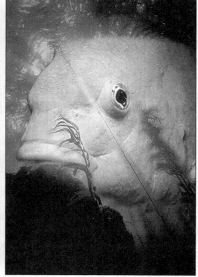

Resizing an image to match its new home

When you bring two images together, you always have to deal with the issue of relative size. For example, the fish that I've been having so much fun with is too large for its surroundings. Here's how to ensure that the two images you want to combine are sized correctly:

1. **Magnify the two images to exactly the same zoom factor.**

   To see them side by side, a zoom ratio of 50% or smaller is necessary.

2. **If either of the two images appears disproportionately large, scale it down (bad pun, I know) by using Image⇨Image Size.**

   In this case, you don't care at all about the dimensions or resolution of the image; all you care about is the file size — that is, the number of pixels comprising the image. If the image you want to copy or drag (fish) is too large, scale it down just enough to fit inside the destination image. If the destination image (kelp) is too large, reduce it as desired. Keep Ctrl+Z (⌘+Z on a Mac) ready in case you accidentally go too far. (See Chapter 4 for more information about the Image Size command.)

   Be careful not to over-reduce! Remember that you're throwing away pixels and, therefore, sacrificing detail. And you definitely don't want to enlarge the image after you've reduced it. Your image will turn to mush. (For more info on how to size your images safely, see Chapter 4.) If you go too far, you can always restore the original by choosing File⇨Revert, or undoing your steps using the History palette, as discussed in Chapter 11.

3. **Combine the two images.**

   Copy and paste, drag and drop, or punt on fourth down.

4. **Position the image more or less where you want it.**

   For my part, I stuck the fish in the upper-right corner.

5. **Choose Edit⇨Transform⇨Scale.**

   This command lets you fine-tune the relative size of the imported image with respect to its new home. A marquee with four corner handles surrounds the image.

6. **Drag a corner handle to scale the image.**

   Shift+drag a handle to scale the image proportionally. The first example in Figure 15-2 catches me in the act. After you release the handle, Photoshop previews how the resized image will look. Don't worry that the preview is a little choppy; the scaled image will be smooth.

Don't scale the image up; only scale it down. Otherwise, Photoshop has to make up pixels, which is most assuredly not one of the program's better capabilities.

7. **Move your cursor inside the transform box and double-click.**

After you resize the image as desired — you can drag the corner handles all you want — move your cursor inside the box. Double-click or press Enter (Return on a Mac) to accept the image's new size and tell Photoshop to work its magic. The resized image will appear perfectly smooth.

If the scaled image looks choppy after you double-click, you probably have a preference set wrong. Choose Edit➪Preferences➪General, or press Ctrl+K (⌘+K on a Mac) and then select the Bicubic (better) option from the Interpolation pop-up menu.

If you decide that you don't want to scale the image before you double-click or press Enter (Return on Mac), press Esc or Ctrl+.(period) (⌘+.(period) on a Mac) to get rid of the box. You can also click the Cancel button (the X icon) in the Options bar. If you've already double-clicked or pressed Enter (Return on Mac), you can restore the image to its original size by pressing Ctrl+Z (⌘+Z on a Mac).

Figure 15-2:
Use the Scale command to refine the image size.

Excuse Me, but What's a Layer?

Here's a little analogy to get things rolling. Imagine that you have three sheets of acetate — you know, like folks used to slide into overhead projectors to bore audiences before the days of multimedia presentations. Anyway, on one sheet you draw a picture of a fish. On a second sheet, you draw a fishbowl. And on a third sheet, you draw the table on which the fishbowl sits. When you stack all the sheets on top of each other, the images blend together to create a seamless view of a fish in his happy home.

Layers in Photoshop work just like that. You can keep different elements of your image on separate layers and then combine the layers to create a composite image. You can rearrange layers, add and delete layers, blend them together using different opacity values and blend modes, and do all sorts of other impressive things.

Another advantage of using layers is that you can edit or paint on one layer without affecting the other layers. That means you can safely apply commands or painting tools to one portion of your image without worrying about messing up the rest of the image — and without bothering to select the element you want to edit.

Layers debuted in Photoshop 3. They played bigger roles in Versions 4 and 5. Now, in Version 6, layers are even bigger stars.

You aren't restricted to the layers that Photoshop creates automatically, however. You can create as many new layers as your computer's memory allows. (In fact, the 99-layer limit from Version 5 has been eliminated.) In the case of the image shown in Color Plate 15-1, I kept kelp, fish, astronaut, nebula, cathedral, flower, comet, and Neptune on separate layers. Though they may appear to blend together along the edges, they are, in fact, as distinct as peas in a pod.

Photoshop also lets you create a couple of other special kinds of layers called adjustment layers and fill layers. An *adjustment layer* enables you to play with the color-correction commands without permanently affecting any of your image layers. A fill layer lets you add a layer of solid color, a gradient, or a pattern and includes a layer mask. For more on these juicy kinds of layers, see Chapter 18.

Finding your way around the Layers palette

The Layers palette, shown in Figure 15-3, is the Grand Central Station for managing layers. To display the palette, choose Window⇨Show Layers or just press F7.

Link

Display layer

Blend layer   Active layer

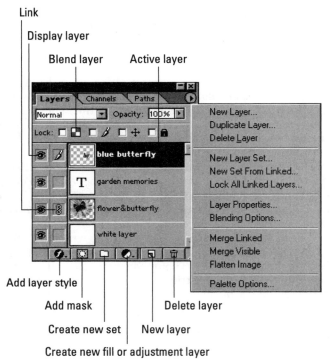

Figure 15-3:
The Layers
palette is
key to
managing
your layers.

Add layer style

Add mask

Create new set   New layer

Delete layer

Create new fill or adjustment layer

Here's what you need to know to navigate the Layers palette:

- ✔ The Background is the bottom layer in the image. Every image has a Background (unless the Background has been turned into a layer — read on to see how).

- ✔ The order of the layers in the Layers palette represents their order in the image. The top layer in the palette is the top layer in your image, and so on.

- ✔ You can edit only one layer at a time — the *active layer*. The active layer is the one that's highlighted in the Layers palette and that has a little paintbrush icon to the left of its layer name. To make another layer active, just click on its name.

- ✔ Press Alt+] (right bracket) (Option+] on a Mac) to move up one layer; press Alt+[(left bracket) (Option+[on a Mac) to activate the next layer down. Press Shift+Alt+] (Shift+Option+] on a Mac) to move to the top layer; press Shift+Alt+[(Shift+Option+[on a Mac) to move to the Background or bottom layer.

- ✔ An eyeball icon next to a layer name means that the layer is visible. To hide the layer, click on the eyeball. To display the layer, click on the eyeball column to bring the eyeball back.

✔ To hide all layers but one, Alt+click (Option+click on a Mac) on the eyeball in front of the name of the layer you want to see. Alt+click (Option+click on a Mac) again to redisplay all the layers.

✔ If you hide the Background layer, you see a checkerboard pattern surrounding your images. The checkerboard represents the transparent areas of the visible layers.

✔ To find out how to use the blend Mode pop-up menu and the Opacity setting at the top of the palette, read the upcoming section, "Tending Your Many Splendid Blends."

✔ To create a new, blank layer, click on the new layer icon at the bottom of the palette (refer to Figure 15-3). To create a duplicate of an existing layer, drag the layer to the new layer icon.

When you create a layer in the manner mentioned in the preceding paragraph, Photoshop gives the layer a name like Layer 1 or Layer 2, and so on. If you want to name the layer, Alt+double-click (Option+double-click on a Mac) on the layer name in the Layers palette and enter a name in the Layer Properties dialog box that appears. You can also select the layer and choose Layer Properties from the Layers palette or Layer menu.

✔ Alternatively, you can create the layer by choosing the New Layer or Duplicate Layer command from the Layers palette menu (click on the right-pointing arrow at the top of the palette), or choose Layer⇨New⇨ Layer or Layer⇨Duplicate Layer. If you use this method to create a layer, Photoshop prompts you to give the layer a name.

✔ To delete a layer, drag it to the Trash icon. Keep in mind that you're throwing away the layer along with the image on it. Layers can also be deleted via Layer⇨Delete Layer or by choosing Delete Layer from the Layers palette pop-up menu.

✔ Just in case you ever want to re-create that selection outline around the elements on a layer, though, Photoshop gives you an easy way to do it. Just Ctrl+click (⌘+click on a Mac) on the layer name in the Layers palette.

Moving and manipulating layers

Layers are flexible things — you can move them, group them together, shuffle their order, and otherwise rearrange them as though they were a deck of playing cards. Here's a look at some of the more common layer-manipulation moves you may need to make:

✔ To move an image on a layer, drag it with the Move tool or Ctrl+drag (⌘+drag on a Mac) with any other tool except the pen tools (all the various flavors), the Hand tool, the Slice and Slice Select tools, the Path Component Selection tool, the Direct Selection tool, and any of the shape tools. To move the layer in 1-pixel increments, press an arrow key with the move tool selected or press Ctrl (⌘ on a Mac) plus an arrow key with any tool but the Hand or Pen. To move the layer in 10-pixel increments, press Shift as you press the arrow key

✔ Check the Auto Select Layer in Options bar to switch to a layer when you click with the Move tool on any part of that layer.

I recommend keeping this option unchecked. You run the risk of switching layers when you don't want to.

✔ The Show Bounding Box option, which also appears in the Options bar when the Move tool is active, surrounds the contents of the layer (or the selection) with a box with handles. This box lets you transform a layer without choosing a command. (For more on transformations, see Chapters 13 and 20.)

✔ To link an active layer to another layer, click on the second column of the Layers palette — just to the left of the layer name — next to the layer that's not active. A Link icon appears in the column. Now, you can move, scale, and rotate both layers at once. To remove the link, click on the Link icon.

✔ To delete linked layers in one fell swoop, select one of the layers in the group, and Ctrl+click (⌘+click on a Mac) the Trash icon in the Layers palette.

✔ Can't figure out what layer holds the element you want to edit? With the Move tool selected, press Alt+right-click (Control+Option on a Mac) on the element. Or Ctrl+Alt+right-click (⌘+Control+Option on a Mac) with any tool but the ones mentioned above. Photoshop automatically activates the appropriate layer. Or right-click (Control+click on a Mac) on the element. Photoshop tells you what layer the element resides on and enables you to *select* the layer, but doesn't automatically activate the layer upon clicking.

✔ After you get a few layers going, you can move one in front of or behind another by dragging it up or down in the list of layers in the Layers palette. A black line shows where the layer will be inserted. You can't reorder the Background or move any layer below the Background until you convert it to a layer. To convert, double-click on the Background in the Layers palette, enter a name for the layer, and press Enter (Return on a Mac). Or you can leave the default name of Layer 0 and press Enter (Return on a Mac).

✔ To add a new Background, choose Layer⇨New⇨Background From Layer.

✓ Another way to rearrange layers is to use the commands in the Layer➪ Arrange submenu. Click on the layer that you want to move in the Layers palette. Then:

1. Choose Layer➪Arrange➪Bring to Front (Shift+Ctrl+]/Shift+⌘+]) to make the layer the topmost layer.

2. Select Bring Forward (Ctrl+]/⌘+]) to move the layer one level up.

3. Select Send Backward (Ctrl+[/⌘+[) to move the layer one level down.

4. Select Send to Back (Shift+Ctrl+[/Shift+⌘+[) to move the layer to just above the Background layer.

✓ You can copy an entire layer to a new image by selecting the layer in the Layers palette and dragging and dropping the layer to the new image. The layer is dropped at the spot where you release the mouse button and resides one layer above the active layer in the new image.

Flattening and merging layers

Sadly, layers aren't all fun and games. To put it bluntly, they come at a steep price and require some concerted management skills. First, if an image contains layers, saving it in any other format other than the Photoshop or TIFF formats (refer to Chapter 6) merges all the layers into one. The Photoshop, TIFF, and PDF formats are the only formats that preserve layers. The ability to preserve layers in TIFF and PDF formats is a new feature in Photoshop 6. Second, every layer you add also makes your file size grow. And third, layers can really slow down Photoshop. To keep running at peak efficiency, it's best to juggle as few layers at a time as possible.

If you want to save your image for use in a different program that cannot utilize either Photoshop or TIFF formats, but you're not willing to sacrifice your layers just yet, you can save the composition to a different file and flatten it — that is, smush all the layers together. To do this, choose File➪Save As. The Save As dialog box appears on-screen. Check the As a Copy option. And then select EPS, JPEG, or some other option from the Format pop-up menu. Notice that the Layers option is grayed out, meaning that Photoshop will flatten the image for you upon saving.

To get the scoop on the other Save options, see Chapter 6. Name the image and press Enter (Return on a Mac). Photoshop saves the flattened image to a different file; the layers in the on-screen image remain intact. Even the name on the title bar remains unaffected, meaning that the next time you press Ctrl+S (⌘+S on a Mac), Photoshop saves to the original file in the Photoshop format, not the Save As file in the new format.

But useful as that is, you're still going to want to merge layers every so often to keep your image manageable. Otherwise, operations slow to a snail's pace, and that's an insult to the snail. Slow is hardly the word. So here are your merging options:

✔ To merge several layers into one, hide all layers except the ones you want to merge. In other words, eyeball icons should appear in front of the layers you want to merge. Hide the eyeball if you don't want to merge the layer. Then choose Merge Visible from the Layers palette menu (by dragging from that right-pointing arrowhead in the upper-right corner of the palette) or from the regular Layer menu at the top of the Photoshop window. Or, even simpler, press Shift+Ctrl+ E (Shift+⌘+E on a Mac).

You can merge one layer with other layers to which it has been linked. Choose Merge Linked from the Layers palette menu or from the top Layer menu. Easier yet, press Ctrl+E (⌘+E on a Mac). Note that the Merge Linked command changes to the Merge Down command if you have no linked layers selected. Merge Down will merge your selected layer with all layers residing below it.

✔ If you want to flatten the entire image and get rid of all the layers, choose the Flatten Image command from the palette menu or from the Layer menu. You can undo the command right after you choose it by pressing Ctrl+Z (⌘+Z on a Mac). If you performed other operations after flattening, you can undo by using the History palette (see Chapter 11 for details).

Aligning layers

Photoshop also gives you a nifty feature — aligning and distributing layers. Here are the steps you take to make sure your layers are neat and orderly:

To align:

1. **In the Layers palette, select the anchor layer that all of the other layers will align to.**

   The selected anchor layer will remain stationary, and the other layers will align to the anchor.

2. **Link the layers you want to align. Click in the second column next to the layer thumbnail to display the link icon.**

3. **Choose Layer⇨Align Linked and then select one of the alignment commands.**

To distribute:

1. **In the Layers palette, link three or more layers that you want to distribute.**

   The distribute feature evenly spaces the layers between the first and last elements.

2. **Choose Layer➪Distribute Linked and select one of the distribute commands.**

Locking and Color Coding Layers

In Chapter 14, I mention that you can paint inside a selection outline to paint just the selection and leave the surrounding areas untouched. But when you send a selection to a layer, the selection outline disappears. So how do you paint only inside the image on a layer? For example, maybe I want to paint stripes on my fish without going outside the lines. The solution is to select the Lock Transparent Pixels check box near the top of the Layers palette, as shown in Figure 15-4. The transparent areas around the fish stay transparent, letting you paint only inside the opaque and translucent fishy bits. For a quick way to turn the Lock Transparent Pixels check box on and off, press the forward slash key (/).

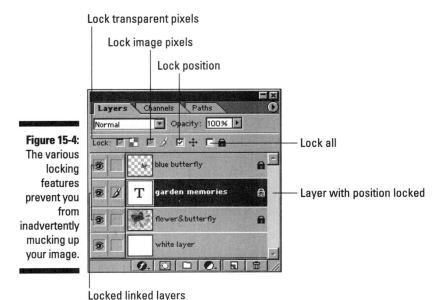

Lock transparent pixels

Lock image pixels

Lock position

Lock all

Layer with position locked

Locked linked layers

Figure 15-4: The various locking features prevent you from inadvertently mucking up your image.

Photoshop 6 adds a few other locking mechanisms to prevent you from mucking up your layers:

- ✔ The Lock Image Pixels option prevents you from painting or editing your layer. You can, however, still select, move, or transform items on the layer. This option was called Preserve Transparency in previous versions.

- ✔ The Lock Position option prevents you from moving and transforming the layer, but gives you free rein on everything else.

- ✔ And finally, Lock All prevents you from painting, editing, moving, or transforming your layer. (But you can still make selections.)

- ✔ You can also lock your linked layers. Choose Lock All Linked Layers from the Layers palette or Layer menu. In the dialog box, check which attributes you want to lock.

To even further manage and organize your layers, Photoshop now lets you color code your layers. Simply choose Layer⇨Layer Properties or choose Layer Properties from the Layers palette menu. Choose a color from the pop-menu and press Enter (Return on a Mac). You can also Alt+double-click (Option+double-click on a Mac) on the layer to bring up the Layer Properties dialog box. You can change a color at any time. In addition, Layer sets can be color coded in a similar fashion.

Managing Your Layers Using Sets

With the introduction of Layer sets, Photoshop 6 provides a new tool for managing layers. Basically, you can now group your layers into sets that can be expanded or collapsed in the Layers palette, which goes a long way in reducing both palette clutter and the endless scrolling trying to locate layers.

To create a Layer set, simply click on the New Set icon (the little folder at the bottom of the Layers palette), as shown in Figure 15-5. You can also choose New Layer Set from the Layers palette menu. And if that isn't enough, you can also choose Layer⇨New⇨Layer Set. If you use the last two methods, the New Layer Set dialog box appears, asking you for a name. And as mentioned in the section "Locking and Color Coding Layers," you can also color your set. In addition, you can specify blend Mode and Opacity settings if desired. Note that the default mode is new. Pass Through lets the blend modes applied to the individual layers remain intact. If you choose any other mode, it overrides all the layers in the set. From there, simply drag your desired layers into the set folder in the Layers palette. If the set is collapsed when you drag, the layer is placed at the bottom of the layer set. If the set is expanded, you can drag the layer to your desired spot within the set. By the way, to collapse or expand the set, simply click on the Triangle icon to the left of the Folder icon.

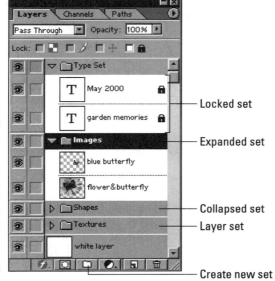

Figure 15-5:
The Layer
set feature
helps
manage
your layers
and reduces
palette
clutter.

Locked set

Expanded set

Collapsed set

Layer set

Create new set

Here are a few things you need to know about Layer sets:

✔ You can select, duplicate, move, rearrange, display, and hide Layer sets, just as you can with regular layers. To review these operations, check out "Finding your way around the Layers palette" and "Moving and manipulating layers," earlier in this chapter.

✔ You can't move one set into another, nor can you create a new set within an existing set.

✔ You can, however, merge layer sets. Select the set and choose Merge Layer Set from the Layers palette menu or from the top Layer menu.

✔ You can lock all the layers in a set. Choose Lock All Layers In Set from either the Layers palette menu or Layer menu. You have the option of locking transparency, image, position, or all, just as you can with regular layers. To see more details on these options, check out the preceding section, "Locking and Color Coding Layers."

✔ You can rename your set by choosing Layer Set Properties from the Layers menu or Layers palette menu. More easily, Alt+double-click (Option+double-click on a Mac) on the set in the Layers palette.

✔ You can create a layer set from linked layers. Link the layers you want in a set and choose New Set From Linked from the Layers palette menu or choose Layer➪New➪Layer Set From Linked.

Tending Your Many Splendid Blends

Segregating different portions of your image onto separate layers is a great help for editing one part of your image without harming another. But as image editing goes, this aspect of layers isn't terribly exciting. The real fun begins when you start playing around with different options that Photoshop gives you for blending all your various image layers together.

Fooling with layer opacity

One neat trick to try with a layer is to make it partially translucent by using the Opacity slider in the Layers palette. In Figure 15-6, for example, I made the fish partially translucent by setting the Opacity to 70%. In the second example, I made him even more ghostly by lowering the Opacity to 30%. Whether the image is on its own layer or temporarily floating, you can use the Opacity slider bar in the Layers palette to achieve this effect. To access the slider bar, click on the right-pointing arrow to the right of the Opacity numeric setting.

To change the Opacity setting for a layer from the keyboard, make sure that any tool, except a painting or editing tool, is selected and press a number key. Press 9 for 90%, 8 for 80%, and so on, down to 1 for 10%. To return to 100%, press 0. You can also enter more specific Opacity values — such as 72 — from the keyboard.

Opacity: 70%   Opacity: 30%

Figure 15-6:
Hey, kids, it's Phantom Phish, the exciting translucent character whose merchandising will clutter markdown shelves any day now.

To see Phantom Phish in color, turn to Color Plate 15-3. In the upper-left image, both the fish and the cathedral are positioned on their own layers, and both layers are fully opaque. In the upper-right image, I changed the Opacity for both layers to 50%. Sends a chill down your spine, doesn't it?

Keep in mind that the Opacity setting applies only to layers. You can't change the Opacity of the Background layer, kelp, because nothing lies behind it. You'd be looking through the kelp into the empty void of digital space, a truly scary prospect. The same is true for the blend modes discussed in the next section.

Playing around with blend modes

The options in the blend mode pop-up menu in the upper-left corner of the Layers palette correspond exactly to the Modes in the Options bar (see Chapter 8). You have Multiply, Screen, Overlay, and the rest of the gang. These options aren't called brush modes when they're applied to layers because no brush is involved. You can call them overlay modes or blend modes; some folks call them *calculations*. But just plain modes is fine, too.

✔ Multiply burns the floating image into the images behind it, darkening all colors where they mix. Screen does just the opposite, lightening the colors where they mix.

I love descriptions like that because they make no sense. Pure wonderful computer gibberish. If you want sense, take a look at the lower-left example in Color Plate 15-3. I applied Multiply to the fish and Screen to the cathedral. Imagine this: The kelp background is a poster on a wall. The fish is printed on a piece of transparent film and tacked in front of the kelp. The cathedral is a slide loaded in a projector and shined onto the poster. This is precisely how Multiply and Screen work.

✔ The Difference mode has no real-world analogy. It creates a photo negative — or inversion — of the blended images according to their colors. Where one of the images is black, no inversion takes place. Where the images are light, you find lots of inversion. In the lower-right example of Color Plate 15-3, for example, the cathedral looks normal at its base because the kelp beneath it is black. The center of the kelp is white, however; so the fish's face changes from yellow to its opposite — that is, blue — and the top of the cathedral changes from light brown to deep violet.

✔ Overlay, Soft Light, and Hard Light are similar options. Overlay multiplies the dark colors and screens the light ones, as witnessed by the fish and cathedral in the upper-left example of Color Plate 15-4. Soft Light — applied to the fish in the upper-right example in the color plate — produces a more subtle effect. Hard Light is more dramatic than Soft Light or Overlay. You can still see the base of the cathedral in the upper-right image in Color

Plate 15-4, even though it overlaps the black area of the kelp. Meanwhile, the base of the Overlay cathedral is swallowed up in the murk.

✔ Like Multiply and Screen, the Color and Luminosity modes produce exactly opposite effects. The Color mode blends the color of the layer with the detail from the underlying images. Luminosity keeps the detail from the layer and mixes it with the colors of the underlying images.

In the lower-left image in Color Plate 15-4, for example, Color is applied to both fish and cathedral. The colors from the fish are bright; those of the cathedral are muted. But you can see each stalk of kelp clearly because Color doesn't obscure detail.

In the lower-right image, I applied the Luminosity mode to fish and facade. Now, you can clearly see the fish pores and the cathedral carvings, but the color comes from the kelp.

✔ For some other interesting effects, experiment with the Color Dodge, Color Burn, and Exclusion modes. Suppose that you have two layers, a Background layer and Layer 1. Color Dodge lightens the pixels in the Background layer and infuses them with colors from Layer 1. Color Burn darkens the pixels and infuses them with color. Exclusion works similarly to Difference; it turns all black pixels white, all white pixels black, and all medium colors gray.

✔ Darken is another mode that can be useful. Say that you want to composite something like a scanned handwritten letter or sheet of music over an image. Obviously, you want only the handwriting or music notes to appear and not the white paper, which would obscure the underlying pixels. By choosing Darken, only the dark pixels appear, the light area appears transparent. Lighten does just the opposite — displays the light pixels and makes the dark pixels transparent.

✔ You can skip the other blend modes — Dissolve, Hue, and Saturation. They range from boring to duller than dull, and they rarely come in handy.

Just so you know, you can mix a translucent Opacity setting with a blend mode. But you can't select more than one blend mode at a time. It would be fun to combine Luminosity with Multiply, for example — you know, to apply detail that only darkens — but you just can't do it. Oh well.

Erasing holes in layers

If a layer has a lot of weird little flecks in it or some other distracting gook, you can erase it away with the Eraser tool. When you work on a layer, the Eraser tool erases transparent holes in the layer, assuming the Erase to History check box in the Options bar isn't turned on (see Chapter 11 for more on Erase to History). If Erase to History is turned on, you can Alt+drag

(Option+drag on a Mac) with the eraser to make holes in the layer. Also, the Lock Transparent Pixels check box must be deselected in the Layers palette. If the check box is turned on, the eraser paints over pixels in the background color.

Figure 15-7 shows examples of erasing parts of the fish layer. In the first example, I erased around the outside of the fish; in the second example, I erased inside the fish. In both cases, the eraser was set to the Airbrush mode, ensuring soft, subtle transitions between the opaque pixels in the layer and the transparent ones.

Figure 15-7:
Two ways to erase a fish layer, around the outside (left) and inside (right).

Using Layer Styles to Shine and Shadow

Photoshop makes the application of effects like drop shadows, glows, and bevels mere child's play with the Layer Styles feature. These effects used to be called — no big surprise — Layer Effects. But Photoshop 6 adds five more effects, includes some additional options for those effects, and throws in a new blending feature, calling the whole works Layer Styles. (Technically, Adobe says that after these effects have been *applied* to a layer they then become a layer style, but you can use the monikers somewhat synonymously.)

Layer Styles can be applied to regular layers and type layers (see Chapter 16), but not to a Background. Layer Styles are also linked to the contents of a layer. If you edit the contents, the effects are updated dynamically, which means less work for you.

Here is a step-by-step guide to applying a layer style:

1. **Make a selection using one of the selection methods described in Chapter 12.**

2. **Press Ctrl+J (⌘+J on a Mac).**

   This command quickly copies and pastes the selection to a new layer. Alternatively, you can take the long road and choose Edit⇨Copy and then choose Edit⇨Paste.

3. **Choose Layer⇨Layer Style.**

4. **Select one of the ten effects (described later in this section) from the Style submenu.**

   A huge dialog box with numerous settings appears. For all of the styles, make sure that the Preview box is checked on. Play with the settings while viewing the effect on your image. Note that numeric settings can be entered or you can use the sliders for each.

5. **Press Enter (Return on a Mac) or click OK.**

The various effects and their settings are described in the following list, yet a picture is worth a thousand words. See Figures 15-8 and 15-9 for some examples.

✔ **Drop Shadow:** Applies a soft shadow behind the element. In the dialog box, you specify settings for blend modes and opacity. Color can be specified by clicking on the color swatch, which takes you to the Color Picker (see Chapter 5 for more on color). The Angle value sets the angle of the light source. Distance determines how far the shadow is offset from the object. The Spread and Size settings determine the softness, intensity, and size of the shadow. You can choose to apply anti-aliasing, which slightly softens the effect.

You can now also choose to apply various contours to your shadow, which changes the distribution of the colors in the shadow. The default contour is linear. You can now also apply Noise to your effect. As discussed in Chapter 14, Noise randomizes the colors of selected pixels, producing a textured, gritty appearance. And finally, check the Layer Knocks Out Drop Shadow option when you have a transparent object on top of the shadow. This prevents the shadow from showing through the object. Toggle this option on and off and look at the thumbnail preview to note the difference.

✔ **Inner Shadow:** Applies a shadow on the element itself. The effect is one of a shadow being cast onto the image. The settings are basically the same as for Drop Shadow.

✔ **Outer Glow:** Creates a glow or halo effect. You can control the Blend Mode, Opacity, Color, Noise, Spread, Size, and Contour settings. Additional settings include the ability to apply different gradients for the outer glow. The same Gradient drop-down palette is accessible as is the Gradient Editor for editing any gradients. (You can check out Chapter 14 for the lowdown on gradients.) Technique gives you the choice between Softer and Precise. Precise gives you a larger glow effect. And finally there are Range and Jitter options for the Contour. Reduce the range to get a less feathered, tighter, and larger glow. Jitter does nothing to the appearance of the default glow but on other gradients moves the pixels to give a roughened effect.

Figure 15-8:
The Layer Style feature makes it easy to apply shadows, glows, and other effects to images and type.

Drop Shadow

Inner Shadow

Outer Glow

Inner Glow

Stroke

Outer Bevel

Inner Bevel

Emboss

Pillow Emboss

Figure 15-9:
The Bevel
and Emboss
effects
provide five
styles to
choose
from.

Stroke Emboss

> ✔ **Inner Glow:** Makes a glow on the element itself. The settings are the
> same as Outer Glow, with the addition of the Source option (Center or
> Edge) and Choke instead of Spread. Center applies the glow over the
> whole image except the edge, whereas Edge applies only to the ele-
> ment's edge. Choke acts similar to spread, described above.

✔ **Bevel and Emboss:** There are five Bevel and Emboss styles. Because there are so many options, the dialog box is spilt into two parts — one for texture and one for contour. Outer Bevel creates a 3D raised edge around the outside of the element. Inner Bevel makes an edge on the element itself. Emboss combines inner and outer bevels to give the effect that the element is raised off the page. Pillow Emboss reverses an inner bevel to give the impression that the element is punched in along the edges and raised in the center. And the new Stroke Emboss enables you to emboss a stroke that has been applied via the Stroke command under Layer Styles menu. The Bevel and Emboss effect has some unique settings. Because this effect is more 3D in nature, there are settings for Highlight and Shadow (each with separate Blend modes and Opacity options) and Depth. Depth affects how raised or sunken the edge appears. You can choose between Smooth, Chisel Hard, or Chisel Soft for the Technique. This option determines how soft or hard the edge of the bevel is. Smooth also results in a smaller effect. The Up radio button positions the highlight along the edge, closest to the light source and the shadow on the opposite edge. The Down radio button does the opposite and positions the shadow near the light source. The Gloss Contour option l changes the distribution of color in the effect *over* the layer, while the regular Contour option does the same for the areas around the perimeter of the layer.

Photoshop has added some additional styles, however, you probably won't use them nearly as much as the ones described above. Here is the 10-cent explanation of each:

✔ **Satin** creates what Photoshop calls a "satin finish" over your layer. Try using this effect with different contour options.

✔ The **Color Overlay, Gradient Overlay,** and **Pattern Overlay** affect overlay color, a gradient, or a pattern over your layer. To see these effects in action, check out the various presets in the Styles libraries. A lot of them utilize color, gradients, and patterns.

✔ **Stroke** creates a stroke around the layer using a color, gradient, or pattern.

Now that you have an understanding of what Layer Styles are and what they look like, here are some things to remember when working with Layer Styles:

✔ Styles can be combined on a single layer and applied all at once. When you're in a styles's dialog box, you can select the various effects from the menu on the left. To remove the application of an effect, simply uncheck the box.

✔ Photoshop has added a great new feature that lets you easily identify and manage your styles. Styles are now listed in a submenu under the layer. If the styles aren't visible, click on the triangle to the left of the layer style icon (a cursive *f* called a florin) to expand the submenu.

✔ You have the choice of having the style combined with the image on the same layer (great for moving and transforming the layer as a unit) or putting the effect on a separate layer. To put the style on a separate layer, apply the style first, then select the "styled" layer, and choose Layer⇨ Layer Style⇨Create Layer. You will notice a new layer in the Layers palette with a name such as "Layer 1's Drop Shadow."

Putting the style on a separate layer gives you greater manual editing capability; however, you won't be able to edit the styles via the Layer⇨ Layer Style menu described in the next bullet. Notice that the Styles icon disappears from the layer in the Layers palette.

✔ Styles can be edited. If you decide you want to change the style, double-click on the Style name or icon on the layer in the Layers palette. The Layer Style dialog box appears, so that you can make adjustments. Uncheck the Style box in the menu on the left to remove the style entirely. To apply a new style, select the style in the menu, adjust your
✔ settings, and click Enter (Return on a Mac).

For shortcut access to the Layer Style submenu, click on the Layer Style icon in the Layers palette to bring up the Layer Style submenu.

✔ Effects can be copied and pasted onto other layers. Select the layer containing the effect. Choose Layer⇨Layer Style⇨Copy Layer Style and select the layer on which you want to apply the effect. Then choose Layer⇨Layer Style⇨Paste Layer Style. To copy an effect onto multiple layers in one fell swoop, link the layers together (described earlier in this chapter) and choose Layer⇨Layer Style⇨Paste Layer Style to Linked.

✔ You can make it even easier on yourself. Effects now support the coveted drag and drop method. Just select the effect in the Layers palette and drag it onto your target layer.

✔ Effects can be hidden. Choose Layer⇨Layer Style⇨Hide All Effects. To have them reappear, choose Layer⇨Layer Style⇨Show All Effects. You can also Alt+double-click (Option+double-click on a Mac) on the style in the Layers palette.

✔ A Global Light can be specified, thereby ensuring that all the shadows and highlights of all your elements look consistent. In other words, all your effects have the same light source. You wouldn't want one of the elements in your image to look like it was photographed at 9 a.m. and the other to look like it was shot at 2 a.m. — would you? To set a Global Light, choose Layer⇨Layer Style⇨Global Light and enter the angle and altitude you want. Then make sure that the Use Global Light check box is on in the Global Light dialog box. The great thing is that if you change the angle on a single Layer Style, *all* the styles that have been applied to your layers adjust to that new angle automatically. No fuss, no muss.

✔ To remove all the effects on a layer, choose Layer⇨Layer Style⇨ Clear Layer Style. You can also drag the Effects bar to the trash in the Layers palette. To remove only one of the multiple effects on a layer, double-click the effect in the Layers palette and then uncheck it in the menu in the Layer Style dialog box. Or you can just drag and drop the effect into the trash in the Layers palette.

✔ You can now size your effect by choosing Layer⇨Layer Style⇨Scale Effects. Enter a value between 1% and 1000%. Make sure to check the Preview option.

✔ The other component of the Layer Styles is Blending Options. Part of this dialog box consists of the usual Blend Modes and Opacity options. The Advanced Blending options are much more complex and are beyond the scope of this book. If you have a burning desire to know more about them, check out the layers chapters in the Photoshop Bible (published by IDG Books Worldwide, Inc.).

Creating your own style

If you create a whiz-bang drop shadow or some other cool effect that you want to be able to use again and again, you can create a new style and save it to the new Styles palette. Here's all you need to know about creating custom styles and about the Styles palette in general:

✔ You can create a new style from a single effect or a group of effects.

✔ After you complete your style, just click on the New Style button, name your style, check include Layer Effects, and click on OK. You can also drag and drop your style from the Layers palette right into the Styles palette or onto the New Style icon at the bottom of the palette. When the New Style dialog box appears, name your style, keep Layer Effects checked, and press Enter (Return on a Mac).

Alternatively, you can select a layer and choose New Style from the Styles palette menu or click on the New Style button in the Styles palette. All the effects on that layer are included in the new style.

✔ Choose Window⇨Show Styles. Your custom style should be included among the preset styles in the Styles palette.

✔ You can also access more preset libraries via the Styles palette menu. Simply choose your desired library and tell Photoshop whether to replace or append (add) your current styles. There are a lot of neat presets, so be sure to check them out during a spare minute.

(continued)

(continued)

- You can also delete and clear styles via the icons at the bottom of the Styles palette, as shown in the following figure.

- You can save styles to a location on your hard drive or disk if you want to trade them with your friends or load them for later use. Both the save and load commands are accessible via the Styles palette menu.

- You can reset your Styles palette back to the default set or replace your current set with another. Again both commands, reset and replace, are found under the Styles palette menu.

- Like other Photoshop palettes, various View options are available via the Styles palette menu.

- To apply any style to a layer, you simply drag the style from the Styles palette onto the layer in the Layers palette. Press Shift while dragging to preserve any styles already present on the layer. Or simply select the layer and click on the desired style thumbnail in the Styles palette. You can also drag the style directly from the Styles palette onto your document window. It's then applied to the top layer where the style is dropped. Again, press Shift to preserve the existing effects on the destination layer, otherwise they will be replaced with the new effect.

- Note that the Styles palette also resides in the Options bar when a shape tool is active. Click on the Layer Style arrow in the bar to access the Styles drop-down palette. Choose your desired style and draw your shape. The style is automatically applied to the shape. Quick, clean, and effortless.

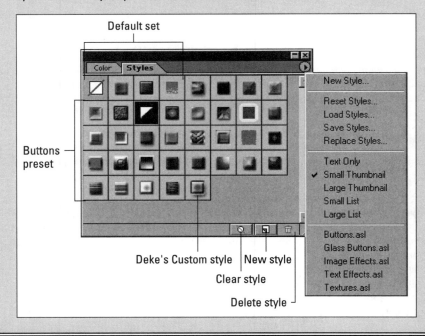

Default set

Buttons preset

Deke's Custom style | New style

Clear style

Delete style

Chapter 16

Digital Graffiti

● ●

In This Chapter

▶ Using the new and improved Type tool

▶ Working with a text layer

▶ Working with Character and Paragraph palettes

▶ Using the Options bar

▶ Warping text

▶ Entering and editing text

▶ Creating outline type

▶ Adding drop shadows

▶ Making your text translucent

● ●

C hapters 12, 13, and 14 lead you on a merry tour of the various tools and commands for selecting a part of your image. But those chapters skip one other type of selection outline that you can create in Photoshop, and you'll never guess what it is. Not in a million years. Give up? The answer is *text*. That's right, Photoshop lets you build a selection outline out of numbers, vowels, consonants, and any other character you can tap in from your keyboard.

The Photoshop approach to text makes it an ideal program for subjecting large letters to special effects. The bigger your text, the better it looks. On the other hand, you shouldn't mistake Photoshop for a word processor. Even though treatment of type has improved tremendously in Photoshop, don't attempt to use Photoshop to create large chunks of text; instead, use a desktop publishing program like PageMaker, InDesign, or QuarkXPress.

The New and Improved Type Tool

Once again, Type got a major revamping with this latest version of Photoshop. Version 5 gave the Type feature added respect, and this version makes us want to get on our knees and shout, "We're not worthy!"

The biggest new feature is actual on-canvas text entry and editing. That's right. No more typing your message in a cheesy dialog box first. Other cool features include a choice between point and box text, word wrapping, increased typographic controls, being able to convert text to shapes (outlines) and paths, and the ability to warp text to create various special effects. So hang on for the ride — I cover the whole enchilada right here in this chapter.

Photoshop 6 changes the configuration of the type tools. What used to be four separate tools residing in the Toolbox now consists of one tool in the Toolbox with four options in the Options bar, as displayed in Figure 16-1. The regular Type tool icon looks like a big letter T, and the keyboard shortcut is the letter T as well. The four options in the Options bar consist of creating a text layer, creating a mask or selection, and horizontal and vertical orientation settings.

Create text layer

Create mask or selection

Horizontally orient text

Vertically orient text

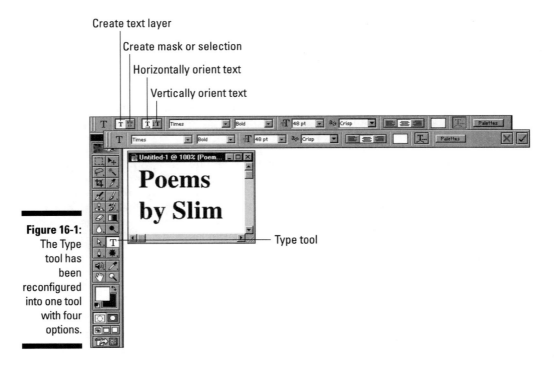

Figure 16-1: The Type tool has been reconfigured into one tool with four options.

Type tool

Here's a briefing on the Type tool and its options:

✔ The regular Type tool creates text on a new text layer (layers, in general, are explained in excruciating detail in Chapter 15), which enables you to work with the text without worrying about touching the underlying image. You can now edit the text contents and attributes by simply highlighting the text with the Type tool. Although you cannot use painting or editing tools on a text layer, you can make the text more or less translucent by adjusting the Opacity percentage in the Layers palette, and you can blend the text with the underlying layers using the Blend Modes pop-up menu.

When you select the Type tool, the text layer option automatically becomes selected, enabling you to create type on a text layer.

✔ The mask or selection option enables you to create your text as a selection outline. You can manipulate, edit, paint, and otherwise play with the selection outline as you can with any other selection outline. And because the Type tool with the mask option works like any other selection tool, you can use it to add to or subtract from an existing selection outline (see Chapter 13). Note that you can't edit the type created with the Type Mask tool like the type created with the Type tool.

✔ The Vertical Orientation option enables you to enter type or type masks along a vertical axis. Great for Asian fonts but not quite as useful for Roman letters. And of course the Horizontal Orientation option enables you to enter text along a horizontal axis.

So, which option do you use when? If you want to retain true editability, obviously, use the regular Type tool with the Text Layer option. Otherwise, it depends on what sort of effect you're trying to create. If you want opaque type, again use the regular Type tool with the Text Layer option. If, on the other hand, you want to create character outlines, such as those shown in the top example in Color Plate 16-1, use the Type tool with the Mask option and then stroke the selection outline using Edit➪Stroke. If you want to soften the edges of your letters — for example, to create a fuzzy shadow behind your letters, as in the middle example in Color Plate 16-1 — you can use the Type tool with the Text Layer option in combination with the new Layer Styles feature. (I give the how-tos for creating both these examples later in this chapter.) You can also use the Type tool with the Mask option to create the shadow effect. It just involves more steps and a different approach.

Just remember that the basic difference between the two options is that one creates editable type on a new text layer and the other gives you a selection outline in the shape of your characters. Pick the option that gives you the quickest route to the effect you're trying to achieve.

The biggest disadvantage of the Type tool with the Mask option is that when you deselect the text selection, the text becomes permanently fused to the underlying image. But you can get around this problem by creating a new layer in the Layers palette before you click with the Type tool with the Mask option. Now, any text you create exists on its own layer so that you can easily move, rotate, paint, and so on. Remember, however, that a regular layer is not the same as a *text* layer. A text layer provides for editability of contents and attributes. Read on!

Putting Your Words On-Screen

To type a few letters in Photoshop, select the Type tool and click inside the image. It doesn't really matter where you click, by the way. Photoshop positions your text at the spot you click, but you can always move the text after you create it.

Now instead of responding with the old type dialog box, you get a little blinking cursor (called an *insertion marker*) that you may be familiar with from working in other programs. Yes folks, type in real time has finally arrived in Photoshop. After the insertion marker appears you are free to enter your text. This "click and type" method results in *Point Text*. Photoshop now gives the option of creating either Point Text or *Box Text* (also referred to as paragraph text). This correlates with how text is treated in Illustrator, Adobe's drawing program. Basically Point Text is type created from a single point and is free-floating with each line being independent from one another. It's great for short bursts of text — a word or short line. Box Text is text created in a bounding box that flows according to the dimensions of the box. It's useful for larger quantities of type. Box Text is also useful if you want your text to automatically word wrap with the boundary, or you want to justify your text. Here are the mechanics of creating both kinds of text:

To create point text:

1. **Select the Type tool from the Toolbox.**

2. **Click on the canvas to set an insertion marker.**

3. **Type your text.**

4. **Press Enter on the numeric keypad or click the Commit button (the check icon) in the Options bar.**

To create box text:

1. **Select the Type tool from the Toolbox.**

2. **Drag the tool diagonally on the canvas to define a text box.**

   A dotted box with handles and an insertion maker within the box appear. Text automatically wraps within the boundaries of the box.

3. **Type your text.**

4. **Adjust the text box if necessary.**

   Grab a handle to scale the size of the box. Move the cursor outside the box until a curved arrow appears. Drag with the curved arrow to rotate the box. Press Ctrl (⌘ on a Mac) and grab a side or side handle to skew the box. Press Ctrl (⌘ on a Mac) and drag a corner handle to scale both the text and the box together. (You can drag a side handle as well but you run the risk of skewing it as well.)

5. **Press Enter on the numeric keypad or click the Commit button in the Options bar.**

   To convert between Point and Box Text, select the text layer in the Layers palette and choose Layer⇨Type⇨Convert to Point Text or Convert to Paragraph Text.

Typing what must be typed

After you "commit" your text by pressing Enter (Return on a Mac) or the Commit button, you've created a text layer. In the Layers palette (Window⇨Show Layers) you'll notice a layer with a capital letter T icon indicating that it is indeed a text layer. The name of the text layer corresponds to the text you typed. I want to cover a few more things you may need to know while inputting text on your canvas. I cover formatting a little later in the section "Changing how the type looks."

✔ After entering your text, you may find that you've made a mistake or two. To delete a letter, click after it and press the Backspace key (Delete key on a Mac). To add text, click at the point where you want to insert it and enter the new text from the keyboard.

✔ To replace text, drag over it with the cursor to highlight it and then start whacking those keys. To delete more than one letter, highlight the letters and press the Backspace key (Delete key on a Mac).

✔ If you're typing point text, Photoshop places all words on a single line in the image unless you insert a paragraph by pressing the Enter key (Return key on a Mac). In Figure 16-1, for example, I typed "Poems," pressed Enter (Return on a Mac), and then typed "by Slim."

While typing your text, you can use the Cut, Copy, Paste, and Undo commands under the Edit menu. These commands enable you to move text around and undo mistakes. For example, to move some letters from one place to another, follow these steps:

1. **Highlight the text you want to move.**

   Drag over the text with the I-beam cursor.

2. **Press Ctrl+X (⌘+X on a Mac).**

   Photoshop removes the text and puts it in a special location in your computer's memory called the *Clipboard*. Ctrl+X (⌘+X on a Mac), by the way, is the shortcut for the Edit⇨Cut command.

3. **Click at the point where you want to move the text.**

   Your click repositions the insertion marker.

4. **Press Ctrl+V (⌘ +V on a Mac).**

   Ctrl+V(⌘ +V) is the shortcut for the Edit⇨Paste command. Photoshop retrieves the text from the Clipboard and inserts it at the desired spot.

If you want to duplicate a word, you can highlight it, choose Edit⇨Copy or Ctrl+C (⌘+C on a Mac), reposition the insertion marker, and choose Paste. You can also undo the last edit by choosing Edit⇨Undo or by pressing Ctrl+Z (⌘+Z).

Changing how the type looks

The cumbersome Type tool dialog box has been replaced with the new sleek Character and Paragraph palettes. Check them out in all their streamlined glory in Figure 16-2. These palettes provide all the typographic options needed to format your text. These options control the typeface, the type size, the type color, the amount of space between lines and letters, alignment, and all that other rigmarole. When all these characteristics get together in the same room, they're usually called *formatting attributes*. You can, of course, make additional enhancements to the appearance of your text after you return to the image window, but the formatting options let you set up the fundamental stuff.

Many of the major options are also found in the Options bar. You can use these options interchangeably with the options in the palette. But note that the formatting attributes in the Options bar are only available when the Type tool is active, whereas you can utilize the palettes no matter what tool is active. The Options bar, however, contains a couple exclusive options. We'll cover these exclusive options a little later. Here's how to assign the main formatting attributes to your text using the palettes:

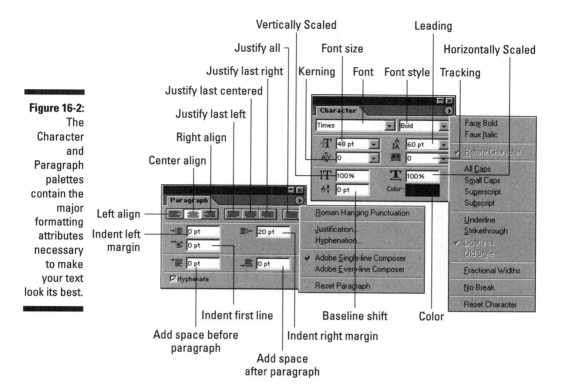

Figure 16-2:
The Character and Paragraph palettes contain the major formatting attributes necessary to make your text look its best.

Vertically Scaled

Justify all

Justify last right

Justify last centered

Justify last left

Right align

Center align

Font size

Leading

Horizontally Scaled

Kerning   Font   Font style   Tracking

Left align

Indent left margin

Indent first line

Add space before paragraph

Add space after paragraph

Baseline shift

Indent right margin

Color

The Character palette

The Character palette controls options that affect the formatting of the characters of your type. Read on to find out the specific formatting attributes of this palette:

✔ In order to change the attributes of your text, you must tell Photoshop what text you want to edit. If you only want a portion of your text, highlight it with your Text tool. If you want to select all the text, either highlight it all or simply have that particular text layer selected in the Layers palette. Any tool can be active.

✔ If you know what you want, you can always establish your formatting attributes *before* you create your type. Who knows, you may get it exactly right the first time around with no need for further editing.

✔ Select a typeface from the Font pop-up menu. Select a style from the Font style pop-up menu. Assuming that you installed Photoshop correctly, type styles such as bold and italic appear in their own submenus.

✔ In order to successfully use PostScript fonts in Photoshop, you must be using ATM (that's Adobe Type Manager, not Automatic Teller Machine or Arbitrary Toaster Molester). If your text comes up smooth and beautiful, not to worry. If your text is so jagged that it looks like you drew it on an Etch A Sketch — as in the case of "Bad type" in Figure 16-3 — something's wrong. Either use a different font or consult with your local computer know-it-all to figure out the problem. You may also see jagged type if your image is of low Resolution (details on Resolution in Chapter 4) and you have your Anti-aliasing option turned off. Fortunately, you can remedy this by increasing the Resolution of your image (again consult Chapter 4 on how to do this correctly) and by turning on Anti-aliasing in the Options bar.

✔ Enter the size of the text into the Font size option box. The Size value is measured in either points (one point equals $\frac{1}{72}$ inch), pixels, or millimeters, depending on the setting in your Preferences dialog box (Edit⇨Preferences⇨Units & Rulers).

✔ The Leading value controls the amount of space between lines of type. If you don't enter a Leading value, Photoshop assigns spacing equal to 120% of the Size value. If you do enter a value, I recommend that it be equal to at least 90% of the Size value to keep the lines from overlapping. In Figure 16-4, for example, the Size value was 144 pixels and the Leading value was 130 pixels.

✔ Kerning controls the spacing between two letters. Positive values move letters apart, negative values move letters closer together. Kerning values are measured in units that are $\frac{1}{1000}$ of an em space. The width of an em space depends on your font size. For example, in a 10-point font, 1 em equals 10 points; in a 100 point font, 1 em equals 100 points. To manually kern, click your I-beam to set an insertion point between two letters and then enter a kerning value or choose a value from the Kerning pop-up menu. Selecting Metrics from the pop-up menu utilizes the kerning built into the font by its manufacturer.

Figure 16-3: If your text looks smooth (top), super. If not (bottom), try a different font or ask your local computer guru for help.

Good type

Bad type

Figure 16-4:
Here's how the Size (dark gray) and Leading (light gray) values are measured.

Leading

Size

✔ The Tracking value controls the spacing between more than two letters. If you want to adjust the spacing of a word or sentence, enter a positive or negative value to move letters apart or together, respectively. You can also choose a setting from the Tracking pop-up menu. Tracking is also measured in units of $\frac{1}{1000}$ of an em space.

✔ Photoshop has added character Height and Width options as available formatting attributes. To vertically or horizontally scale your type, select the entire text layer or highlight specific characters and enter a value in the Character palette. Values over 100% heighten or widen the type, and any value under 100% does the opposite. My advice, however, is to use these options sparingly or else you run the risk of totally destroying the appealing proportions of a typeface. I mean, these type-faces have been designed by trained artists who spend their lives per-fecting the shape and form of each letter.

✔ Baseline shift refers to the distance the type sits from its baseline. Type can be raised or lowered to create superscripts and subscripts for items such as fractions and trademark and copyright symbols. To adjust the baseline shift, highlight the character and enter a baseline value. Or if you want to adjust the whole layer, just make sure that you select the layer. Positive values move horizontal type above and vertical type to the right of the baseline. Negative values move type below or to the left of the baseline. The range of values is from −85 to 85.

✔ Like the Size value, Leading, Kerning, Tracking, and Baseline Shift values are all measured in points, pixels, or millimeters depending on the units chosen in your Preferences.

✔ You can find other formatting attributes, such as Small Caps, Superscript, and Underline, among others, under the Character pop-up menu. Highlight the character(s) to be formatted and select the attribute from the pop-up menu. The uses for Faux Bold and Faux Italic are for online type. See Chapter 19 for more information.

✔ Fractional Widths enables the space between letters to vary by using fractions of pixels between some characters. For the most part, keep Fractional Widths checked on. It provides the best spacing for type, except for small type that is to be viewed online, in which case you may not want to use this option.

✔ To rotate vertical type by 90 degrees, select the Rotate Character option from the Character pop-up menu. The type rotates so that it flows parallel to the text line. Roman characters are much easier to read with this orientation.

✔ By default, the color that first appears in the Character palette is the current foreground color. To change the color before you create the text, you can use the Color palette or the Color Picker, which can be accessed by clicking on either the Foreground swatch in the Toolbox or the color swatch in the Character palette or Options bar. (If you need a basic color refresher, see Chapter 5.)

✔ To change the color of subsequent text you create, be sure to deselect a text layer (for example, select the Background or a regular layer). If you don't and you change the color via the Color palette or Options bar, you inadvertently change the color of the active text layer. And if you have an active text layer and try to change the color via the Foreground swatch in the Toolbox, it flat won't take. You have to deselect the text layer first.

The Paragraph palette

The Character palette's partner in crime for formatting is the Paragraph palette. Here's the skinny on what this palette can do for you:

✔ Select an Alignment option to determine whether multiple lines of text are aligned by their left edges, right edges, or centers.

✔ You can now also justify text in various flavors, as indicated by the icons in the palette. To customize justification settings, select Justification from the Paragraph palette pop-up menu.

✔ Check on the Hyphenate option to have Photoshop automatically hyphenate your text. To customize hyphenation settings, select Hyphenation from the Paragraph palette pop-up menu.

✔ Enter values in the various indentation options to add space to the left, right, or before and after a paragraph. You can also indent just the first line of a paragraph.

✔ Roman Hanging Punctuation, found under the Paragraph pop-up menu, controls whether punctuation marks such as quotations, apostrophes, colons, commas, and the like appear outside or inside the bounding box for box text. Turn it on to have the marks "hang" outside the box.

✔ The Adobe Single-line and Every-line Composer affects the way Photoshop handles composition. Composition entails using a variety of parameters such as word and letter spacing and hyphenation to evaluate where a line should break. Leave this option at the default of the Every-line Composer.

✔ You can mix most formatting attributes within the same text layer. Alignment is one attribute that cannot be mixed. And although you can mix leading, the entire line of text conforms to the largest leading value.

Now I get to a couple of the options found exclusively in the Options bar and not in the Character or Paragraph palettes. (But they aren't totally exclusive even to the Options bar. You can also find them under the Type submenu under the Layer menu.)

✔ **Anti-aliasing.** You always want to select some kind of anti-aliasing because if you select None, your text has tiny jagged edges, and you usually don't want that. I say usually, because in some cases, if you are creating type for a Web page, you may want to avoid anti-aliasing. (Check out Chapter 19 for more on type for the Web.)

As far as anti-aliasing goes, you have three flavors. **Crisp** makes the type look sharper. **Strong** makes the type look heavier. And finally, **Smooth** makes the type look, as you can guess, smoother.

✔ **Warp Text.** This feature is so neat it deserves its own section, so read on.

Warping type into strange and unusual shapes

Warping text in Photoshop is its way of simulating the feature of path text found in drawing programs, such as Illustrator, Freehand, and CorelDraw. You can now twist, push, and pull to create a variety of cool and crazy effects. Take a glance at Figure 16-5 to see a small sampling of these effects.

Follow these easy steps to warp your very own text:

1. **Select the text layer in the Layers palette.**

2. **Select the Type tool in the Toolbox and click on the Warp Text icon in the Options bar. Or choose Layer⇨Type⇨Warp Text (any tool can be active to choose this).**

3. **In the Warp Text dialog box, select a Style from the pop-up menu.**

4. **Play with the options.**

   Choose either Horizontal or Vertical orientation. Adjust the Bend to apply more or less warping. Use the Distortion sliders to apply perspective to the warp.

5. **If you're happy with your warp, click on OK.**

Arch   Flag

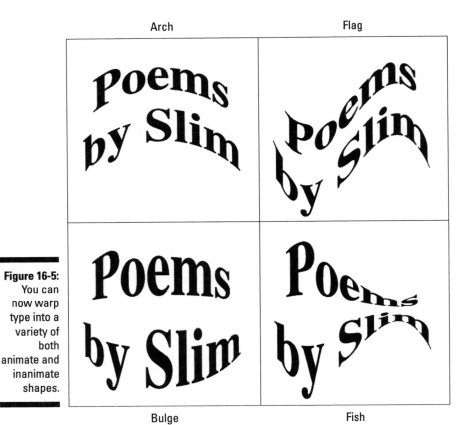

Figure 16-5:
You can
now warp
type into a
variety of
both
animate and
inanimate
shapes.

Bulge   Fish

Editing the Text Layer

If you notice a misspelled word or some other typographical gaffe, select the offending text layer and drag over the text with a Type tool to edit it. You can then edit the contents or any of the attributes. Press Enter (Return on a Mac) on the keypad or click on the Commit button in the Options bar. The great thing is that text layers save with the image, so you can revise the text at any time, as long as you don't rasterize (see section "Rastering a text layer" for more info) or outline the text or flatten the layers, that is (see Chapter 15 for more on layers).

Here are some things you can do to a text layer and still be able to edit the text:

✔ You can reorder or duplicate the Type layer, just as you can with a regular layer. To move the layer in front of or behind another one, drag it up or down in the list of layers in the Layers palette. A black line shows where the layer will be inserted. To duplicate, drag the layer onto the new layer icon at the bottom of the Layers palette.

✔ You can lock and color code text layers (see Chapter 15 for more on these features).

✔ Move or clone the text. Drag with the Move tool to position the text. Alt+drag (Option+drag on a Mac) to clone the text. Note that Alt+drag (Option+drag on a Mac) creates another text layer.

✔ Change the orientation of a layer. Choose Layer➪Type➪Horizontal or Vertical to change the orientation.

✔ You can now apply any of the blend modes and adjust the opacity of the Text layer.

✔ Perform transformation commands, such as Rotate, Skew, and Scale. Perspective and Distort transformation are not available to text layers.

✔ Apply Layer Styles (see details in Chapter 15) to the Text layer. Even after you apply the effect, if the type changes in any way (such as a different font or even a different word), the effect magically updates to the changes!

✔ Fill the type with the foreground or background color by using the Fill command keyboard shortcuts. Press Alt+Backspace (Option+Delete on a Mac) to fill with the foreground color. Press Ctrl+Backspace (⌘+Delete on a Mac) to fill with the background color. Note that the Edit➪Fill menu command is grayed out — you can only utilize the keyboard shortcuts.

Here are the two things you can't do to a text layer, unless you render the Text layer and convert it to a regular layer (see more about this in the next section):

1. You can't use any of the painting and editing tools. When you hold the painting and editing tools over the Type layer, you see a slashed circle symbol indicating "No can do!"

2. You can't apply filters under the Filter menu.

A text layer can't be created for images in indexed color, bitmap, or multi-channel modes because these modes don't support layers of any kind — Type or otherwise. Type created in these modes is treated like type created with the Mask option and gets applied to the Background and cannot be edited. If you want type included in images you're preparing for the Web, for example, be sure and wait until you finish compositing your layers and editing your type to convert the image to indexed color. (For more on color modes, see Chapter 6.)

If you decide you don't want the Type layer any longer, delete it by dragging the layer to the Trash icon at the bottom of the Layers palette (for help, see Chapter 15). Or just click on the layer name and then click on the Trash can icon.

Rasterizing a Text Layer

In order to apply a filter or paint on a type layer, you must first do what Adobe calls *rasterizing* the layer. To rasterize a type layer, choose Layer⇨ Rasterize⇨Type. Rasterizing basically converts the text layer to a regular layer. The type then acts as though it was created with the Type Mask option. After rasterizing, the type looks the same; however, you can no longer edit the type. Notice that the T icon isn't there anymore! So a word of advice — be sure the text is exactly like you want it before you render the Text layer because editing capabilities go down the drain.

Making Shapes and Paths from Text

By default, Photoshop creates type that is bitmap. Makes sense. Photoshop is basically a bitmap editing program and only recently acquired some vector capabilities, like creating objects on special vector-based shape layers. Short and sweet, *bitmap* programs are based on a grid of square colored pixels that can vary in density. *Vector* programs are based on mathematical equations, which are used to define points and paths.

But just because type is bitmap by default, Photoshop 6 isn't about to let it stop there. You can easily convert a text layer in this version. Going hand in hand with the ability to create vector objects is Photoshop's new feature of letting you convert your type to outlines, which it refers to, like it does for objects, as a shape. Outlined type is now vector based, which means it can be scaled without losing image quality — it retains its crisp, clean edges and doesn't get jaggier as bitmap type would. Note that the text remains as vector outlines unless you rasterize the layer, merge the layer, or flatten the image.

To create outlined type, select the text layer and choose Layer⇨Type⇨ Convert to Shape. The text layer then converts to a shape layer, as shown in Figure 16-6, and obtains all the characteristics of a shape layer. It, in turn, loses all text editing capabilities. You see the appearance of a path around the letters, which can be manipulated with the Path Component Selection tool or the Direct Selection tool. For details on working with shapes, see Chapter 8.

The command above Convert to Shape is Create Work Path. This command creates a path that traces the characters on your text layer to create a work path (for more on paths see Chapter 12). The work path then appears in the Paths palette and can be manipulated just like your average path. The text layer, however, isn't converted — it remains editable and also remains as bitmap type. If you edit the text layer, the path doesn't change accordingly. To get a new path, delete the old path from the Paths palette and choose the Create A Work Path command again.

Text layer converted to shape layer

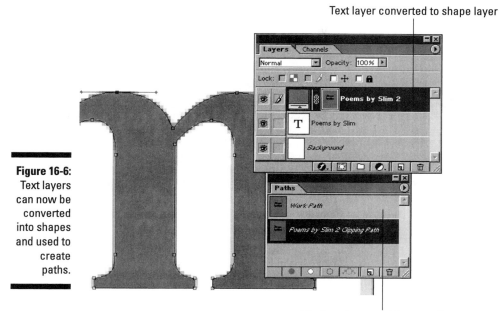

Figure 16-6:
Text layers can now be converted into shapes and used to create paths.

Work path created from text layer

Declaring Open Season on Type Selection Outlines

If you have used previous versions of Photoshop, the first thing you may notice when you click with the Type tool with the Mask option is the appearance of a funky pink overlay. And as you type your letters will appear white. This is Photoshop's way of telling you that you are creating a mask. It's similar to editing using the Quick Mask mode in the Toolbox. When you press Enter on the numeric keypad or click Commit in the Options bar, the overlay disappears and the familiar marching ants of the Selection marquee appear. (See Chapter 12 for more on selection marquees.) Now that your newly-created type is there selected inside your image, you can do all kinds of things with it, including the following:

✔ To move a text selection outline, drag with the one of the selection tools. Or press the arrow keys to nudge the selection outline this way or that. You can no longer drag with the Type tool but you can still use the arrows while the Type tool is active.

✔ To move or clone the text selection, use the same techniques you use to move or clone any other selection (refer to Chapter 13). Drag with the Move tool to move the text; Alt+drag (Option+drag on a Mac) to clone the text.

In other words, selections that you create with the type Mask option work just like any other selection.

✔ You can paint inside the text. After you paint inside the letters, you can use the edit tools to smear the colors, blur them, lighten them, and so on.

✔ You can fill the text with the foreground color by pressing Alt+Backspace (Option+Delete on a Mac). To fill the text with the background color, press Ctrl+Backspace (⌘+Delete on a Mac). To fill the text with a blend of colors, just drag across the text with the Gradient tool. It just couldn't be easier.

✔ You can apply a border around your type by choosing Edit⇨Stroke.

✔ Before you fill or stroke a selection outline, be sure that your text is positioned where you want it. You can't move the stroked text after you create it without leaving a hole on your layer. Ditto with any other painting or editing commands you apply to a text selection outline. That's why it is a good idea to create a new layer before you create your text selection outline. It enables you to move the text without affecting the underlying image.

✔ If you want to delete text that was created with the type Mask option — and you didn't take my advice to create that text on its own layer — you need to undo your steps by using the History palette (see Chapter 11), to bring your image back to its pretext appearance.

Every one of these techniques can achieve some truly remarkable effects. Just to show you what I mean, in the following section, I show you how to create outline type and text with shadows. I also show you how to create translucent type. For full-color demonstrations of these techniques, see Color Plate 16-1.

Tracing outlines around your letters

The following steps tell you how to create genuine outline type, like the stuff shown in the top example in Color Plate 16-1. You can see through the interiors of the letters, and you can make the borders as thick as you please. What more could you ask from life?

1. **Create a new layer.**

   You don't have to put your text on its own layer, but doing so makes it simpler to edit the text later on if necessary. To create a layer, click on the new layer icon in the Layers palette, as discussed in Chapter 15.

2. **Select the Type tool in the Toolbox and the Mask option in the Options bar.**

3. **Set the formatting attributes in the Character and Paragraph palette or in the Options bar.**

4. **Click with the Type tool on your canvas.**

   Type away and then press Enter on the numeric keypad or click on the Commit button in the Options bar. Then move the text selection outline into the desired position by dragging it or nudging it with the arrow keys.

5. **Set the foreground color to white.**

   You can do this quickly by pressing D to get default colors and then X to swap them.

6. **Make sure that the Lock transparent pixels check box in the Layers palette is deselected.**

   In the next step, you apply a stroke to the center of your selection outline (that is, with half the stroke appearing on the inside of the outline and half appearing on the outside). If you don't deselect the Lock Transparent Pixels check box, Photoshop doesn't let you paint on the layer.

7. **Choose Edit⇨Stroke, select the Center radio button, and enter 12 as the Width value.**

   After making your selections in the Stroke dialog box, press Enter (Return on a Mac). You now have a 12-pixel thick, white outline around your type.

8. **Make black or some other dark color the foreground color.**

   To create the top example in Color Plate 16-1, I changed the foreground color to red.

9. **Choose Edit⇨Stroke and enter 4 as the Width value. Leave the Location at Center.**

   Then press Enter (Return on a Mac). Congratulations! You get the effect shown in Figure 16-7 and the top of Color Plate 16-1. If you created your text on a layer, as I heartily recommended back in Step 1, you can use the Move tool to reposition the text if needed. You can also play with the blend modes and Opacity slider in the Layers palette to change how the text blends with the underlying image.

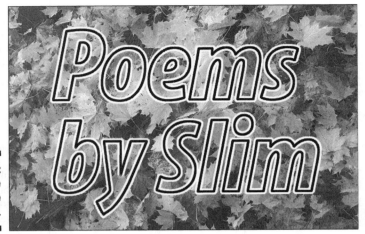

Figure 16-7:
Outline type
created the
correct way.

Adding shadows behind your letters

In these steps, you create letters with shadows, as shown in Figure 16-8 and the second example in Color Plate 16-1. These kinds of shadows are commonly called *drop shadows* because they don't extend away from the letters; instead, they merely rest behind the letters. The new automated Layer Styles feature makes applying shadows quick and easy. See Chapter 15 for the comprehensive lowdown on Layer Styles (which can all be applied to text layers and regular layers).

1. **Set the foreground color to white. To do it quickly, type** D **and then** X.

2. **Format and create your text using the regular Type tool with the Text Layer option and the appropriate palettes or Options bar.**

   Blah de blah de blah. (In other words, do what needs to be done, Bucko.)

3. **Position the text with the Move tool if necessary.**

4. **Choose Layer⇔Layer Style⇔Drop Shadow.**

   A dialog box appears with various settings. Make sure that the Preview check box is on. Play with settings while previewing the effect on your type. I recommend leaving the Blend Mode on the default of Multiply. For type, a 65% to 75% opacity is usually good.

   Angle lets you determine where your light source is coming from to create the shadow. Move the line on the dial or type a value to set yur desired angle. Distance determines how far the shadow offsets from your type. Keeping the shadow fairly close to the type usually results in a better effect. Spread and Size affect the softness, intensity, and size of the shadow. For this exercise keep Angle, Distance, Blur, and Intensity at the default settings.

5. **Press Enter (Return on a Mac) when you are satisfied with the shadow's appearance.**

6. **Change the foreground color to medium gray or some other medium color.**

   In Color Plate 16-1, I used purple. This color is for the soft shading inside the letters.

7. **Choose Layer⇨Rasterize⇨Type.**

   This step enables you to paint on the type.

8. **Check on Lock transparent pixels in the Layers palette.**

   This step protects the transparent areas and enables only the paint to be applied to the type.

9. **Select the Airbrush tool and choose a large, soft brush from the Brushes palette in the Options bar (click on the arrow next to the brush icon to access the Brushes drop-down palette).**

10. **Paint a couple of streaks across the letters with the Airbrush tool.**

    You now have something resembling the image shown in Figure 16-5 and in the middle of Color Plate 16-1.

Turning your letters into ghosts of their former selves

This last set of steps explains how to create translucent letters, which are just the ticket for creating *ghosted* or tinted text (see the third example in Color Plate 16-1). You may think that this effect would be rather difficult, but in truth, it's way easier than the previous techniques.

1. **Start with a light background.**

   I explain how to adjust the colors in your image in Chapter 18.

2. **Change your foreground color to something dark.**

   Note that in Color Plate 16-1, I opted for dark orange.

3. **Select the regular Type tool and create your text.**

   Photoshop creates type in the background color and places it on a new text layer.

4. **Drag or nudge the text into position by using the Move tool.**

5. **Press a number key.**

   When you're working with a layer, pressing a number key changes the opacity of the layer. Higher numbers make the selection more opaque; lower numbers make it more transparent. Chapter 15 explains all of this in more detail, but for now, just press the number keys until you get the effect you want. (You can also drag the Opacity slider in the Layers palette, if you prefer.)

6. **Select the Airbrush tool.**

   Press A to get the airbrush.

7. **Choose a large, soft brush from the Brushes palette in the Options bar.**

8. **Click on the Background layer.**

9. **Set the foreground color to white and take a couple of swipes at the background with the airbrush.**

   Ooh, isn't that pretty. I can't decide whether it looks more like the title for a wedding invitation, a soap opera, or a wake, but it sure is pretty.

Chapter 17

Forays into Filters

● ●

In This Chapter

▶ Applying, reapplying, and fading filter effects

▶ Sharpening an image

▶ Using the Unsharp Mask command

▶ Blurring a background with Gaussian Blur

▶ Applying the Motion Blur command

▶ Randomizing pixels with Add Noise

▶ Creating images in relief by using Emboss

▶ Filling areas with flat colors by using Facet

▶ Averaging colors with Median

● ●

*I*f you're a photographer or you've taken a photography course or two, you know how photographic filters work. They refine or refract light to modify the image as it comes into the camera. A daylight filter strains some of the blue out of the image; a polarization lens eliminates reflected light; a fish-eye lens refracts peripheral imagery into the photo.

But real-life filters present some problems. They take up a ton of room in your camera bag, they generally bang around and get scratched, and you never know when you're going to contract a sudden case of butterfingers and drop a lens on a marble floor. Also, you have to decide which filter you want to use while shooting the photo. Not only is it difficult to experiment through a viewfinder, but also whatever decision you ultimately make is permanent. If you go with a fish-eye lens, you can't go back and "undistort" the image later.

The Photoshop filters are another story:

✔ All filters reside under a single menu (surprisingly called Filter).

✔ You can undo a filter if you don't like the results.

✔ You can preview the outcome of the most common filters.

✔ You can apply several filters in a row and even go back and revisit a single filter multiple times.

✔ Most Photoshop filters have no real-world counterparts, which means that you can modify images in ways that aren't possible inside a camera.

If you're a photographer, you may want to forgo a few of your camera's filters and take up Photoshop filters instead. Granted, you may still want to use corrective lenses to adjust color and keep out reflected light, but avoid a special-effects filter that makes the image look like more than what your eyes can see. Such filters merely limit the range of effects you can apply later inside Photoshop.

If you aren't a photographer, filters open up a whole new range of opportunities that no other Photoshop function quite matches. Filters apply changes automatically, so there's no need to be an artist (although an artistic vision certainly comes in handy). Filters can make poor images look better and good images look fantastic. And you can use them to introduce special effects, such as camera movement and relief textures. Frankly, filters turn Photoshop into a lean, mean (though good) photo-munching machine.

Photoshop 6 doesn't bring you any new filters. But, hey, you have almost 100 filters to play with. This chapter doesn't even start to cover all the Photoshop filters, just those that you're likely to use on a regular basis. To see some of the others in action, check out Chapter 21.

A Few Fast Filter Facts

Before launching into explanations of Photoshop filters, check these facts:

✔ If some portion of your image is selected, the filter affects the selection and leaves the rest of the image unmodified. If no portion of the image is selected, the filter affects the entire image.

✔ To create smooth transitions between filtered and unfiltered areas in an image, blur the selection outline by choosing Select⇨Feather (see Chapter 13).

✔ After you apply a filter, you can reapply it in the same manner by choosing the first command in the Filter menu or by pressing Ctrl+F (⌘+F on a Mac).

✔ Some filters display a dialog box so that you can control how the filter is applied. If the last filter was one of these, press Ctrl+Alt+F (⌘+Option+F on a Mac) to redisplay the dialog box and apply the filter again using different settings. (Chapter 10 explains how to use the preview options and other controls inside filter dialog boxes.)

✔ To undo the last filter, press Ctrl+Z (⌘+Z on a Mac). Unlike a canceled filter, the undone filter remains at the top of the Filter menu, so you can later apply it by pressing Ctrl+F (⌘+F on a Mac).

✔ Some filters take a few seconds or even minutes to apply. You can cancel such a filter in progress by pressing Esc. The name of the previous filter remains at the top of the Filter menu, so you can't press Ctrl+F (⌘+F on a Mac) to apply a canceled filter.

✔ If you don't like the results of the filter or filters you've applied and you can't undo by pressing Ctrl+Z (⌘+Z on a Mac), use the History palette to return to a source state — Photoshop's term for a previous saved step — that you're happy with (see Chapter 11 for details on the History palette).

✔ The Fade command is designed for blending a filtered image with its unmolested twin. *Note:* If you're a veteran Photoshop user, you may be confused when you try to find the Fade command under the Filter menu. It has been relocated under the Edit menu. If you choose Edit⇨Fade or press Ctrl+Shift+F (⌘+Shift+F on a Mac) immediately after applying a filter, the Fade dialog box appears, enabling you to play with the Opacity and Blend mode of the filtered image. This command enables you to create all sorts of variations on a filter, as shown in Figure 17-1. In this example, I applied the Fresco filter once, then used the Fade command with a 60% opacity setting, and finally applied the Darken blend mode.

✔ You can also apply the Fade command after you've painted, focused, or toned an image. So in other words, you can fade the effect created with any of the following tools: Paintbrush, Airbrush, Pencil, Rubber Stamp, History Brush, Art History Brush, Gradient, Blur, Sharpen, Smudge, Dodge, Burn, Sponge, and all of the eraser tools. Whew! And if that wasn't enough, you can also apply the Fade command to an area you have filled or stroked or even liquified. Check the index for the chapters that explain these tools and techniques.

✔ Remember, you have to apply the Fade command *immediately* after you apply the filter. If you choose another command or apply a painting or editing tool to the image, you can't use the Fade command. The only alternative is to use the History palette and revert to the source state prior to applying the filter. You can reapply the filter and then choose the Fade command. (Again, for more on the History palette, see Chapter 11.)

Original Fresco

Opacity 60% Opacity 60%, darken

Figure 17-1: A dapper gentleman takes on a new look.

How to Fortify Wishy-Washy Details

No matter how good an image looked before you scanned it, chances are that it appears a little out of focus on-screen. The image in Figure 17-2 is an exaggerated example. Snapped around the time Stonehenge was built, this photo has suffered the cruel scourges of time. It probably wasn't that sharply focused in the first place, but all these many years later, it looks so soft you'd swear that it was sculpted out of gelatin.

The solutions to softness are the four commands under the Filter⇨Sharpen submenu. The following sections explain how these filters work and when — if ever — to apply them.

The single-shot sharpeners

The first three sharpening filters — Sharpen, Sharpen Edges, and Sharpen More — are what I call *single-shot filters*. You choose them, and they do their work without complex dialog boxes or other means of digital interrogation. These filters, with their straightforward names, are a breeze to use.

Figure 17-2:
Antique
images such
as this
one are
notoriously
soft on
focus.

Unfortunately, when it comes to Photoshop, you get back what you put in —
mentally, that is. In other words, if you don't have to work at it, it's liable to
deliver rather mediocre results. As demonstrated in Figure 17-3, all three of
these Sharpen filters sharpen, but none satisfactorily remedies the image's
focus problems.

Figure 17-3 shows the results of applying each of the three single-shot sharpeners to a detail from the image. In each case, I applied the filter once (as
shown in the middle row) and then a second time (as shown in the last row).
For the record, here's what each of the filters does:

✔ Filter➪Sharpen➪Sharpen enhances the focus of the image very slightly.
  If the photo is already well focused but needs a little extra fortification
  to make it perfect, the Sharpen filter does the trick. Otherwise, forget it.

✔ The Sharpen More filter enhances focus more dramatically. Although it's
  easily the most useful of the three single-shooters, it's still fairly crude.
  For example, the center image in Figure 17-3 isn't sharp enough, whereas
  the bottom image is so sharp that little flecks — called *artifacts* — are
  starting to form in the woman's dress. Boo, hiss.

Figure 17-3:
The effects
of applying
each of the
single-shot
sharpeners
are
shockingly
shabby.

✔ The Sharpen Edges filter is a complete waste of time. It sharpens the so-called edges of an image without sharpening any of the neutral areas in between. In the figure, for example, the filter sharpens the outline of the guy's face but ignores the interior of his jacket. The result is an inconsistent effect that eventually frays the edges and leaves nonedges looking goopy by comparison.

As you may have gathered by now, I'm not a big fan of these filters. Still, you may want to go ahead and apply Sharpen or Sharpen More to an image to see whether it does the trick. If a single-shot sharpener turns out to be all you need, great. If not, undo the effect (press Ctrl+Z (⌘+Z on a Mac)) and try out the Unsharp Mask command, explained next. It's a little scarier, but it works like a dream.

Unsharp Mask: The filter with a weird name

If the Photoshop programmers had been in charge of naming Superman, they would have called him "Average Guy from Krypton." Rather than describing what the guy does, the programmers describe his origins. I say this because that's exactly what they did with Filter⊅Sharpen⊅Unsharp Mask. Rather than calling the filter "Supersharpen," which would have made a modicum of sense and may have even encouraged a few novices to give it a try, they named it after a 40-year-old stat camera technique that a few professionals in lab coats pretend to understand in order to impress members of the opposite sex.

So forget Unsharp Mask and just think "Supersharpen." To use the "Supersharpen" command, choose Filter⇨Sharpen⇨Unsharp Mask. The "Supersharpen" dialog box appears, as shown in Figure 17-4.

Inside the "Supersharpen" dialog box

Like the Dust & Scratches dialog box (see Chapter 10), the Unsharp Mask dialog box, shown in Figure 17-4, enables you to preview what happens when you change the values in the three option boxes. You can preview the filter inside the dialog box and in the main image window. If you can't quite remember how these previewing functions work, check out Chapter 10. To sharpen an image, use the three slider bars like so:

✔ Change the Amount value from 1% to 500% to change the amount of sharpening. This may strike you as obvious, but just to be sure, higher Amount values produce more sharpening.

Figure 17-4: Experts agree that the Unsharp Mask dialog box really should be called the *Super-sharpen* dialog box.

✔ Adjust the Radius value to specify the width of the edges you want to sharpen. If the image is generally in good shape, use a Radius of 0.5. If the edges are soft and syrupy, like the ones in Figure 17-2, use a Radius of 1.0. And if the edges are almost nonexistent, go with 2.0. Generally, you don't want to go any lower than 0.5 or any higher than 2.0 (though 250.0 is the maximum).

✔ You don't have to enter 1.0 or 2.0 into the Radius option box. A simple 1 or 2 will suffice. It's just that you can enter $\frac{1}{10}$ values — such as 1.1 and 1.9 — if you're in a particularly precise mood.

✔ As with the Threshold option in the Dust & Scratches dialog box, the Unsharp Mask Threshold option determines how different two neighboring pixels must be to be considered an edge. (See Chapter 10 for a review of this concept.) The default value of 0 tells Photoshop to sharpen everything. By raising the value, you tell Photoshop not to sharpen low-contrast pixels.

✔ This idea is great, but the implementation by Photoshop leaves something to be desired. The filter creates an abrupt transition between sharpened and ignored pixels, resulting in an unrealistic effect. Therefore, I recommend that you leave Threshold set to 0.

Some sharpening scenarios

Figure 17-5 demonstrates the effects of several different Amount and Radius values on the same detail to which I applied the piddly little Sharpen More command in Figure 17-3. Throughout Figure 17-5, the Threshold value is 0.

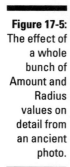

Figure 17-5: The effect of a whole bunch of Amount and Radius values on detail from an ancient photo.

200%, 0.5   100%, 1.0   50%, 2.0

500%, 0.5   250%, 1.0   125%, 2.0

Figure 17-5 is organized into two rows. To create the images in the top row, I started with an Amount value of 200% and a Radius of 0.5. Then I halved the Amount value and doubled the Radius in each of the next two images. Though the effect is similar from one image to the next, you can see that the right image has thicker edges than the left image. (The differences are subtle; you may have to look closely.)

The bottom row of the figure features more pronounced sharpening effects. Again, I started with one set of Amount and Radius values — 500% and 0.5 — and progressively halved the Amount and doubled the Radius. Notice that the edges in the right image are thicker and the left image contains more artifacts (those little flecks in the jacket and hat).

After experimenting with a few different settings, I decided that my favorite setting was an Amount of 250% and a Radius of 1.0. The final image sharpened with these settings as shown in Figure 17-6.

Myopia Adds Depth

If you want to make a portion of your image blurry instead of sharp, you can apply one of the commands under the Filter⇨Blur menu. Right off the bat, you quick thinkers are thinking, "Blurry? Why would I want my image to be blurry?" This is a classic problem. You're thinking of blurry as the opposite of sharp. But blurry and sharp can go hand in hand inside the same image. The sharp details are in the foreground, and the blurry stuff goes in the background.

Take Figure 17-7, for example. In this image, I selected and blurred the background. The scene becomes a little more intimate, as though the background were far, far away. It also has the effect of making the foreground characters seem more in focus than ever.

To make the effect complete, I selected the lower-right corner of the image, which represents the ground coming toward us. I feathered the selection (using Select⇨Feather set to a value of 30) and then blurred it. The result is a gradual blurring effect, as though the ground were becoming progressively out of focus as it extends beyond our field of vision.

For the most part, then, blurring is a special effect. Unlike sharpening, which has the effect of correcting the focus, blurring heightens reality by exaggerating the depth of an image. In other words, you never have to blur an image — and you probably won't do it nearly as frequently as you sharpen — but it's a lot of fun.

Figure 17-6:
The image from Figure 17-2 sharpened with an Amount value of 250% and a Radius value of 1.0.

Choosing your blur

The first two commands under the Filter⇨Blur submenu — Blur and Blur More — are the Dumb and Dumber of the blur filters. Like their Sharpen and Sharpen More counterparts, they produce predefined effects that never seem to be quite what you're looking for.

The "Superblur" command — the filter that offers the powers you need to get the job done right — is Filter⇨Blur⇨Gaussian Blur. The filter is named after Karl Friedrich Gauss, a dusty old German mathematician who's even older than the photograph from Figure 17-2. But just think "Superblur" — or, as Mr. Gauss would have put it, *Ueberblur*.

When you choose Filter⇨Blur⇨Gaussian Blur, Photoshop displays the dialog box shown in Figure 17-8. The Radius value determines the number of pixels that get mixed together at a time. You can go as high as 250.0, but any value over 10.0 enters the realm of the legally blind. In Figure 17-7, I blurred the background with a Radius value of 4.0 and the lower-right patch of ground with a Radius of 2.0.

Figure 17-7:
Blurring the
background
as well as a
small tip
of the
foreground
(bottom
right) brings
the family
up close
and
personal.

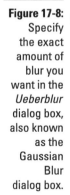

Figure 17-8:
Specify
the exact
amount of
blur you
want in the
Ueberblur
dialog box,
also known
as the
Gaussian
Blur
dialog box.

Creating motion and puzzle pieces

The Filter⇨Blur submenu contains three additional filters — Motion Blur, Radial Blur, and Smart Blur — all of which are exclusively special-effects filters. The Motion Blur filter makes an image appear to move in a straight line; the Radial Blur filter can be used to move the selection in a circle or to zoom it outward toward the viewer. The Smart Blur option finds the edges in your image and then blurs only between the edges — it's as though Photoshop is carving your image up into puzzle pieces and then blurring each piece. If you apply the effect in heavy doses, the result is an image that resembles a watercolor painting and isn't too far removed from the effect created by the Filter⇨Artistic⇨Watercolor filter.

Of the three filters, Motion Blur is the filter you're most likely to use. First, the dialog box offers the standard previewing options, making this filter accessible and predictable. Second, it's much easier to use. Finally, when compared with Radial Blur, it takes a lot less time to use; Radial Blur is one of the slowest Photoshop filters.

When you choose Filter⇨Blur⇨Motion Blur, Photoshop displays the Motion Blur dialog box. The filter smears pixels at a specified angle and over a specified distance. Enter the angle and distance into the appropriately named option boxes. You can also drag the spoke inside the circle on the right side of the dialog box to change the Angle value.

For example, Figure 17-9 shows a couple of discrete applications of the Motion Blur filter. To blur the boy, I selected him, feathered the selection, and applied the Motion Blur filter with an Angle value of 90° — straight up and down — and a Distance of 30 pixels. To blur his sister's arm — the one nearest her beaming brother — I used an Angle of 45° and a Distance of 6 pixels. As you can see, Distance values over 20 smear the image into oblivion; smaller Distance values create subtle movement effects.

Figure 17-9:
Two unlikely applications of the Motion Blur filter.

Filter Potpourri

The Filter➪Sharpen and Filter➪Blur submenus contain the filters you use most often. In fact, if you like, you can blow off the rest of the chapter without being much the poorer for it. But if you have five minutes or so to spare, I'd like to show you a few other interesting commands scattered throughout the Filter menu.

Giving your images that gritty, streetwise look

For starters, you have the Add Noise command. Not to be confused with the as-yet-uncompleted Adenoids filter, Add Noise randomizes the colors of selected pixels. The result is a layer of grit that gives smooth images a textured appearance.

Choose Filter➪Noise➪Add Noise to display the Add Noise dialog box shown in Figure 17-10. Here's how to use the options found therein:

Figure 17-10: This filter adds "noise" to your image to give it a gritty texture.

✔ Drag the Amount slider triangle or enter a value between .10% and 400% to control how noisy the image gets. Photoshop 6 uses noise values based on percentages rather than pixels as in previous versions. Low values — such as the default value of 12.5% or lower — permit a small amount of noise; high values permit more. Anything over 50% pretty much wipes out the original image.

- ✔ Select a Distribution radio button to control the color of noise. The Uniform option colors pixels with random variations on the shades it finds in the original image; the Gaussian option — which should be labeled High Contrast — colors pixels with more exaggerated light and dark shades. Therefore, Gaussian produces a noisier effect, about twice as noisy as Uniform. For example, an Amount value of 12.5% combined with Gaussian produces a similar visual effect to an Amount value of 25% combined with Uniform.

- ✔ The Monochromatic check box adds grayscale noise to full-color images. When the option is turned off, Photoshop adds all colors of noise. (The option has no effect on grayscale images except to shift the pixels around a little.)

To rough up the dark areas in the mother and son detail shown on the left side of Figure 17-11, I used Select⇨Color Range to select the dark areas in the image and then applied the Add Noise filter. By changing the Amount value to 25% and selecting Gaussian, I arrived at the effect shown in the middle example in the figure. To achieve the far-right image, I applied Filter⇨Blur⇨Motion Blur with an Angle value of 45° and a Distance of 6 pixels. Photoshop creates an etched metal effect that suits these two characters to a T.

Original	Add Noise	Motion Blur

Figure 17-11: I selected the dark portions of the image on the left and applied the Add Noise filter (middle) followed by Motion Blur (right).

Color Plate 17-1 shows the same Add Noise and Motion Blur effect applied to the dark portions of a full-color image. But there's a slight twist. In the top image, I applied the Add Noise filter with the Monochromatic check box turned off; in the bottom image, the check box is turned on. As a result, the top image contains color streaks, and the bottom image contains black-and-white streaks. I prefer the black-and-white streaks for this particular image — they give it a more rustic look — but you, of course, are free to do as you see fit.

Stamping your image in metal

Another intriguing and sometimes useful filter is Emboss. This filter makes your image appear as though it were stamped in metal. The edges in the image appear in relief, and the other areas turn gray.

When you choose Filter⇨Stylize⇨Emboss, Photoshop displays the dialog box shown in Figure 17-12. You enter the angle of the light shining on the metal into the Angle option box. The Height value determines the height of the edges, and the Amount value determines the amount of contrast between blacks and whites.

I'm breezing over these options because they aren't the most useful gang in the world. In fact, they can be big time wasters. From personal experience, I can tell you the following:

✔ How you set the Angle value doesn't matter. Feel free to drag the spoke on the circle until you get what you want, but don't expect big differences between one angle and another.

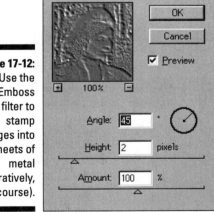

Figure 17-12: Use the Emboss filter to stamp images into sheets of metal (figuratively, of course).

✔ Set the Height value to 1 or 2. Any value over 2 can impair detail.

✔ Okay, the Amount value is useful. Enter 50% for a very subtle effect, 100% for a medium Emboss effect, and 200% for added drama. You can go as high as 500%, but higher values make the contrast between blacks and whites too abrupt (in my humble opinion).

Like Add Noise, Emboss isn't the kind of filter you go around applying to an entire image. I mean, after you've done it once or twice, it gets a little old. Rather, you want to apply it to selected areas.

In the first example of Figure 17-13, I selected the dark areas in the mother and son image and applied the Emboss filter with an Angle of 45°, a Height of 2, and an Amount of 200%. In the middle example, I blurred the selection using the Gaussian Blur filter set to a Radius of 2 pixels. Then I applied Unsharp Mask with an Amount of 500% and a Radius of 2 pixels, arriving at the thrilling mottled metal effect on the far right.

Your reaction may be one of, "Whoa, hold up a minute here. First you blur and then you sharpen? What kind of crazy logic is that?" Well, pretty sound logic, actually. After I applied Gaussian Blur, the image turned overly gray, as you can see in the second example in the figure. Luckily, one of the properties of Unsharp Mask is that it increases the amount of contrast between dark and light pixels. So, to bring the blacks and whites back from the dead, I set the Radius value inside the Unsharp Mask dialog box to the exact value I used in the Gaussian Blur dialog box — that is, 2.0. Using this value ensured that Unsharp Mask was able to correctly locate the blurred edges and boost their contrast. It's a great technique.

Figure 17-13:
After selecting the dark portions of the image, I embossed it (left), blurred it (middle), and sharpened it (right), creating a soft relief.

Emboss   Gaussian Blur   Unsharp Mask

Merging colors in flaky images

The last two filters I cover in this chapter — Facet and Median — average the colors of neighboring pixels to create areas of flat color. Both throw away detail, but they're great for smoothing out the imperfections in old, cruddy images such as the one that keeps popping up in this chapter.

Filter⇨Pixelate⇨Facet is a single-shot command that roams the image looking for areas of similarly colored pixels and then assigns the entire area a single color. In Figure 17-14, I started with the elder daughter from way back in Figure 17-2, before she was sharpened. In the middle example, I applied Filter⇨Pixelate⇨Facet. See how the image is now divided into a bunch of globby areas of color? To make the image clearer, I applied the Unsharp Mask filter to the far-right example, using an Amount value of 250% and a Radius value of 0.5.

Filter⇨Noise⇨Median averages the colors of so many neighboring pixels. To tell Photoshop the "so many" part, choose the Median command and enter a value anywhere between 1 to 100 (up from 16 in Version 5.5) into the Radius option box.

Figure 17-15 shows the result of applying various Radius values to the elder daughter. The top row shows the effects of the Median command; the bottom row shows what happened when I applied Unsharp Mask to each image. Notice how higher values melt away more of the image's detail. A Radius value of 3 makes the image gooey indeed; any higher value is pure silliness.

Original	Facet	Unsharp Mask

Figure 17-14: Starting with the original image (left), I applied the Facet filter (middle) and then reinforced the edges with Unsharp mask (right).

You can use Facet and Median to blur background images, just as I did earlier with Gaussian Blur. Or you can combine them with the Add Noise and Emboss filters to create special effects.

Keep in mind that the real beauty of these more specialized filters is in combining them and applying them to small, selected portions of your image.

Figure 17-15:
I applied the Median filter at three different Radius settings (top row) and then sharpened the results (bottom row).

Radius: 1   Radius: 2   Radius: 3

Median

Unsharp Mask

Chapter 18

Drawing Color from a Dreary Wasteland

*H*ere's a common scenario for you: You get some pictures or slides back from the photo developer — I'm talking regular photos here, not the digital kind — and one of them catches your eye. The color is great, the composition is fantastic, everyone's smiling; it ranks among the best pictures you've ever shot. It's not 100 percent perfect, but you figure you can fix the few glitches with Photoshop.

A few days later — after you've had the photo scanned to Photo CD — you open the image inside Photoshop, and your heart sinks to the pit of your stomach. The image is dark, colorless, and generally a big, fat disappointment. That little picture on the cover of the CD jacket looks better than this murky mess on-screen.

In a perfect world, this would never happen. The service bureau that scanned the image would have corrected the colors so that they would look the way they did in your photo. But in practice, even the best service bureaus let a few duds fall through the cracks, and some don't bother with color-correction at all. It's a pickle.

Take Color Plate 18-1, for example. The original slide looked something like the example on the right, but when I opened the image in Photoshop, the image appeared as shown on the left. Sure, it's an old slide — that's me in the striped shirt, so you know that a couple of years have passed — and the composition leaves something to be desired. (I have a fake tree growing out of my shoulder and my sister seems to be balancing a flower-adorned globe on her head.) But, come on, it didn't look this bad. I mean, are we auditioning for the remake of *20,000 Leagues Under the Sea* here or what?

If you run into a similar problem, never fear — you have cause to be optimistic. The colors may not look like much now, but chances are better than even that you have enough colors to get by. Though it may be hard to believe, your image very likely contains a few million colors; it's just that they're all squished toward the dark end of the spectrum. Your job is to bring these colors back to life.

Want proof? The image on the right side of Color Plate 18-1 isn't a different scan; it's just a color-corrected version of its neighbor on the left. In fact, I revived the color by using only two commands — Levels and Variations. I didn't touch a painting or editing tool; I didn't draw a selection outline; I didn't do anything to add colors to the image. I merely took the existing colors and stretched them across the spectrum.

Photoshop offers several color-correction commands, but you need only three of these — at the most — to get the job done. In this chapter, I show you how these miracle commands work and encourage you to ignore the rest. I also explain how to use adjustment layers, which let you do some of your color correcting on an independent layer, thereby providing you with extra flexibility and safety.

The Color-Correction Connection

The Photoshop color-correction commands are located in one central spot, under the Image➪Adjust submenu. Of these commands, only three should be of the least concern to you at this stage in your mastery of Photoshop: Levels, Auto Levels, and Variations.

Your friends — Auto Levels, Levels, and Variations

Choose Image➪Adjust➪Auto Levels or press Ctrl+Shift+L (⌘+Shift+L on a Mac) to automatically correct the contrast of an image. For example, Figure 18-1 shows a typical low-contrast image composed entirely of cheerless grays. The inset squares show the lightest and darkest colors in the image as well as some sample shades in between. If I apply the Auto Levels command, Photoshop automatically makes the lightest gray white and the darkest gray black and stretches out the colors in between. Figure 18-2 shows the result.

Figure 18-1:
What a dismal scene: Come to this gas station and get your tank filled with depression. The grim reaper will change your oil.

Unfortunately, Auto Levels doesn't always do the trick. Figure 18-2, for example, contains strong blacks and whites, but the grays appear overly dark (as witnessed by the shades in the inset squares). The solution is Image⇨ Adjust⇨Levels, which you can access from the keyboard by pressing Ctrl+L (⌘+L on a Mac). The Levels command takes some getting used to, but it lets you adjust the darkest and lightest colors as well as the medium gray. (I explain the command in detail later in this chapter, in the section "Leveling the Contrast Field.") Figure 18-3 shows the Gulf station running in tip-top condition, thanks to the Levels command. See how much clearer the details in the cars now appear?

Unlike Auto Levels and Levels, which serve grayscale and color images equally well, Image⇨Adjust⇨Variations is specifically designed to correct full-color images. (You can use the command on grayscale images, but it merely duplicates some of the options inside the Levels dialog box.) You can increase or decrease the intensity of colors or tint the image to remove a color cast. For example, if an image is too yellow, you can add blue to it, as in the first example in Color Plate 18-2. If the image is too blue, add yellow, as in the second example. In both cases, Variations preserves non-blue and non-yellow colors. Throughout, for example, the Christmas tree remains true to its natural color of pink.

Figure 18-2:
The Auto Levels command brings out some strong blacks and whites, but the grays remain dark and dreary.

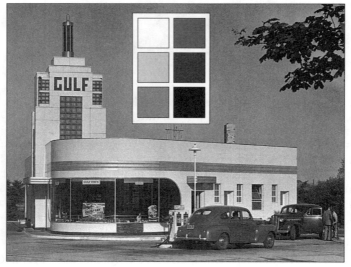

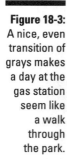

Figure 18-3:
A nice, even transition of grays makes a day at the gas station seem like a walk through the park.

Upcoming sections explain how to use Levels, Auto Levels, and Variations in detail. But just for the record, here's the general approach to take when color correcting an image in Photoshop:

1. **Apply the Auto Levels command.**

   Regardless of whether you're editing a grayscale or color image, this is a good first step.

   If you like what you see, you can skip all the other steps. If you think some more tweaking is in order, proceed to Step 2.

2. **Apply the Levels command.**

   Use this command to change the contrast of the image and to lighten or darken the medium colors.

   If you're editing a grayscale image, this command is the end of the line. If your full-color image looks a little drab, however, keep correcting.

3. **Choose the Variations command and select the Saturation radio button.**

   The options inside the Variations dialog box let you boost the intensity of colors in an image, as discussed in the section "Variations on a Color Scheme," later in this chapter.

   If the colors now look the way you want, press Enter (Return on a Mac) and get on with your life. Continue only if you want to tint the image with a certain color or remove a color cast.

4. **Still inside the Variations dialog box, select the Midtones radio button and adjust the colors in the image.**

   Note: The section, "Removing that color cast sure feels good," at the end of this chapter, tells all.

The other color correctors (boo, hiss)

The other color-correction commands in the Image⇨Adjust submenu range from useful but very complex to simple but completely inept. Just in case you're chock full of curiosity, here's the rundown:

- ✔ The **Curves** command is even more capable than the Levels command, enabling you to change every one of the possible 16 million colors to a different color. Unfortunately, this feature is also very difficult to use. You can get the full scoop on curves in *Photoshop Bible* (published by IDG Books Worldwide, Inc.).

- ✔ The **Brightness/Contrast** command is utterly and completely worthless. I'm serious. If you've never used it, don't start. If you have used it, stop — you're hurting your images.

✔ Avoid using the new color corrector, **Auto Contrast**, and stick with correcting contrast in an image by using the Levels command. Using the Levels command gives you more control.

✔ **Color Balance** is another loser. You keep thinking that it's going to produce some kind of useful result, but it never does. Worthless and irritating — what a combination.

✔ **Hue/Saturation** is good. It lets you change the color, intensity, and lightness of an image using three slider bars. However, the Variations dialog box provides these same controls and is easier to use.

✔ **Desaturate** is just the thing for draining the color from a selected area and leaving it black and white. But if you want to convert an entire image to grayscale, see Chapter 5.

✔ The **Replace Color** command is a combination of Select⇨Color Range and the Hue/Saturation command. What's the point?

✔ The **Selective Colors** command lets you modify a range of colors using CMYK slider bars. Not a terrible command, but not a particularly useful one either.

✔ The **Channel Mixer** command lets you redefine your channels by mixing them together. Very useful for repairing bad channels or special effects, but an advanced feature.

✔ The new **Gradient Map** command enables you to map any Photoshop gradient to the grayscale values in your image. You can produce some interesting special effects with this command.

✔ The other commands on the Adjust menu — **Invert, Equalize, Threshold,** and **Posterize** — are typically used for creating special effects. Invert, for example, makes all white pixels black and all black pixels white, creating a photo-negative effect. Fun to play with, but not the sort of tool you can use to brighten up a dingy gas station.

Leveling the Contrast Field

Not one image in this book — except the gloomy-looking Figure 18-1 — has escaped a thorough going-over with the Levels command. I consider this command to be one of the most essential functions inside Photoshop. In fact, if an image displays any of the following symptoms, you can correct it with Levels:

✔ The image is murky, without strong lights and darks, like the one in Figure 18-1.

✔ The image is too light.

✔ The image is too dark.

✔ The image is gaining weight, losing hair, and developing bags under its eyes.

Whoops, that last item sneaked in by mistake. If an image gains weight, loses hair, and develops baggy eyes, you have to send it on a three-week cruise in the Caribbean.

Leveling on a layer

Photoshop offers a feature to use in conjunction with the Levels command (and, in a roundabout way, the Auto Levels command): adjustment layers. Adjustment layers are just like the layers discussed in Chapter 15, except that you use them expressly to apply color-correction commands.

Another new layer is called a fill layer. You can use fill layers to add a layer of solid color, a gradient, or a pattern. Although you probably use adjustment layers more often, I cover both.

At any rate, adjustment and fill layers offer several advantages:

✔ The color-correction of adjustment layers affects all the underlying layers in the image. If you don't use an adjustment layer, the color-correction affects only the active layer.

✔ You can create as many different adjustment layers as you want. So, if you want a few layers to use one set of color-correction settings and the rest of the image to use another set, you just create two different adjustment layers. You can also create as many fill layers as you desire.

✔ Because the color-correction "exists" on its own layer, you can experiment freely without fear of damaging the image. If, at some point, you decide that you don't like the effects of the color-correction, you can edit the adjustment layer or just delete it entirely and start fresh. You can also edit or delete fill layers.

✔ You can blend adjustment and fill layers with the other layers using the Opacity and Blend mode settings in the Layers palette, just as you can with any layer. These features give you even more control over how your image appears.

To create an adjustment layer, do the following:

1. In the Layers palette, click on the layer that you want to color correct.

When you create an adjustment layer, Photoshop places it directly on top of the active layer in the Layers palette. This adjustment affects the layer or layers underneath, depending on what setting you choose in the New Adjustment Layer dialog box in Step 2.

If you select a portion of your image before creating the adjustment layer, the color-correction affects only the selected area across all underlying layers.

2. **Choose Layer⇨New Adjustment Layer and then select your desired adjustment. For this example, I chose Levels.**

   The New Layer dialog box appears. Here's a field guide to your options: If you want to give your adjustment layer a specific name, enter the name into the top option box.

   Although the Auto Levels command isn't available as an Adjustment Layer type, you can apply the Auto Levels command on an adjustment layer by choosing the Levels option as your Adjustment Layer type. The Levels dialog box has an Auto button that works just like the Auto Levels command.

   Skip the Opacity and Mode pop-up menus; if you want, you can change these settings later in the Layers palette. For now, skip the Group with Previous Layer check box. I cover this a little later in the chapter.

3. **Press Enter (Return on a Mac).**

   Photoshop adds the adjustment layer to the Layers palette and displays the Levels dialog box, which is explained in the next section.

Creating a fill layer is just as easy. Simply choose Layer⇨New Fill Layer and select from solid color, gradient, or pattern.

If you are wondering what that extra thumbnail is, shown in Figure 18-4, I'll give you a brief explanation. Photoshop now adds a layer mask to every adjustment or fill layer. In short, layer masks are like pieces of clear acetate that hover over the layer. You paint on them to selectively hide or display either the adjustment or fill effect, or in the case of regular layers, pixels. Applying black pixels on the layer mask hides, white pixels show, and any gray color in between displays or hides in varying degrees of transparency. In other words, to display the full strength adjustment or fill over the image, leave the layer mask white (the default). To remove the adjustment or fill over the image, paint the mask with black. To partially display the adjustment, paint the mask with gray. Any painting tool can be used on the mask, however, I recommend using the Airbrush, Paintbrush, or Gradient.

Remember that an adjustment or fill layer works just like any other layer in the Layers palette. You can vary the effects of the adjustment by playing with the Opacity slider and Blend modes; you can move the layer up or down in the Layers palette to affect different layers; and you can merge the layer with an underlying layer to permanently fuse the color-correction or fill to the image. (You can't, however, merge an adjustment or fill layer with another adjustment or fill layer.)

If you ever want to change the settings for an adjustment or fill layer, just double-click on the adjustment or fill layer icon in the Layers palette. You can also select the adjustment or fill layer and choose Layer⇨Layer Content Options. Photoshop redisplays the appropriate dialog box, where you can modify the settings. To delete the adjustment or fill layer, drag it to the trash icon in the Layers palette.

Clipping Group icon

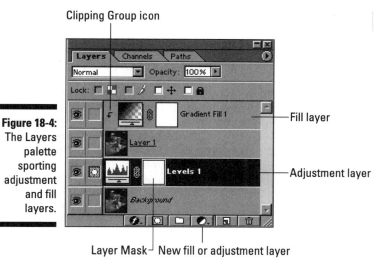

Figure 18-4:
The Layers palette sporting adjustment and fill layers.

Fill layer

Adjustment layer

Layer Mask — New fill or adjustment layer

To change the type of your adjustment or fill layer, choose Layer⇨Change Layer Content and select the new type of adjustment or fill you want.

You can flip back and forth between a view of your corrected image and your uncorrected image by clicking on the eyeball icon next to the adjustment layer name in the Layers palette. When the eyeball is present, the layer is visible, showing you the color-corrected image. When the eyeball is hidden, so is the layer, giving you a "before" view of your image. You can do the same with fill layers.

Before moving on to dissect the Levels command, let me give you a brief explanation on the Group with Previous Layer option I told you to skip earlier. If you check this box in the New Layer dialog box, the adjustment or fill layer will only affect the pixels of the immediately underlying layer. Any layers below that will be unaffected. This technique is referred to in Photoshop's higher circles as a *clipping group*. A clipping group is where you combine multiple layers into a group in which the lowest layer in the group masks the others. You can also create clipping groups with regular layers. In addition to selecting this option in the New Layer dialog box, you can also create a clipping group by selecting the adjustment or fill layer in the Layers palette and choosing Layer⇨Group with Previous or Ctrl+G (⌘+G on a Mac). Or simply press the Alt key (Option key on a Mac) and click on the horizontal line between the two layers. Notice that your cursor icon changes to an arrow with two circles and a small down pointing arrow and appears on the top layer after you click (see Figure 18-4). To remove the clipping group, simply Alt click (Option click on Mac) again or choose Layer⇨Ungroup or Ctrl+Shift+G (⌘+Shift+G on a Mac).

Making friends with the Levels dialog box

To apply the Levels command, you can create a new adjustment layer, as described in the preceding section, or choose Image⊏>Adjust⊏>Levels, or press Ctrl+L (⌘+L on a Mac). If you choose the command from the Image menu or press the keyboard shortcut, the color-correction is applied directly to the image and affects only the active layer.

Either way, the dialog box shown in Figure 18-5 appears. Luckily, you don't need to address all the options that inhabit this dialog box. So, before you break into a cold sweat or shriek at the top of your lungs (or do whatever it is you do when you see terrifying sights like Figure 18-5), let me try to distinguish the important options in this dialog box from the stuff you won't use in a month of Sundays:

Histogram

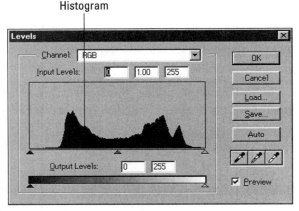

Figure 18-5: The complicated-looking Levels dialog box contains a lot of options that you don't need to worry about.

✔ The options in the Channel pop-up menu let you adjust one color channel in a full-color image independently of the other channels. These options are helpful if you know what you're doing, but they're not terribly important.

✔ The three Input Levels option boxes control the settings of the darkest, medium, and lightest pixels in your image, in that order. These options are important, which is why I cover them thoroughly in the next section.

✔ That black birthmark in the middle of the dialog box is called a *histogram.* It shows you how the colors in your image are currently distributed. It also rates the Seal of Importance.

✔ The slider bar beneath the histogram provides three triangles, one each for the darkest, medium, and lightest pixels in your image. These triangles are the most important options of all.

✔ The Output Levels option boxes and the accompanying slider bar let you make the darkest colors lighter and the lightest colors darker, which is usually the exact opposite of what you want to do. Mark these options Not Particularly Important.

✔ The OK and Cancel buttons are as important as always. One applies your changes, the other doesn't. No news here.

✔ Press the Alt key (Option key on a Mac) to change the Cancel button to a Reset button. Click on the button while pressing Alt (Option on a Mac) to reset the settings to the way they were when you entered the dialog box. Very helpful.

✔ Click on the Save button to save the settings in this dialog box to disk. Click on the Load button to later load and reapply them. Unless you're color correcting about 20 images in a row, all of which require exactly the same treatment, these buttons are about as important to your health and well-being as lava lamps. Ignore them.

✔ Click on the Auto button to automatically change the darkest pixels to black and the lightest ones to white, exactly as though you had chosen Image➪Adjust➪Auto Levels. The only time you need to use this button is when you want to apply the Auto Levels command on an adjustment layer, as discussed earlier. Otherwise, just choose the command from the Image➪Adjust menu or press Ctrl+Shift+L (⌘+Shift+L on a Mac) and save yourself some work.

✔ When you press the Alt key (Option key on a Mac), the Auto button changes to an Options button. I tell you about this feature only because I'm afraid that you may notice it for yourself when you press the Alt key (Option key on a Mac) to access the Reset button. But whether you notice it or not, the Options button is totally unimportant. And if you do notice it, don't muck with the settings that become available to you when you click on the button.

✔ The three eyedropper icons let you click on colors in your image to make them black, medium gray, or white. If I were you, I'd steer clear of these icons except to stamp them Not Important, Ditto, and Doubly So.

✔ The Preview check box lets you view the effect of your edits inside the image window. It's very important that you turn this option on.

Figure 18-6 shows the Levels dialog box as it appears after you strip it down to its most important components. As you can see, the Input Levels options — which include the three option boxes, the histogram, and the slider bar — represent the core of the Levels command. The other options are just icing on the cake.

Figure 18-6:
When you strip the Levels dialog box of its excessive regalia, it becomes far less daunting.

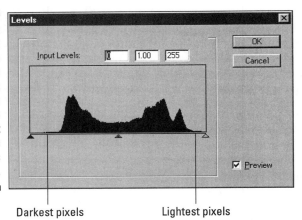

Darkest pixels   Lightest pixels

Brightness and contrast as they should be

The histogram in Figure 18-6 is a graph of the color in the uncorrected image in Figure 18-7. (I didn't even choose the Auto Levels command.) The graph is organized from darkest colors on the left to lightest colors on the right. The peaks and valleys in the histogram show the color distribution. If the darkest colors were black, the histogram would start on the far-left edge of the slider bar. If the lightest colors were white, it would continue to the far-right edge. But as it is, the left and right edges taper off into flatlands. This means that the darkest and lightest pixels in the image are not as dark or light as they could be.

If some of that information went a little over your head, not to worry. Some folks understand graphs, while other folks think that they're in a board meeting and start to nod off the second they see anything resembling a graph. Either way, remember that the histogram is provided for your reference only. All that matters is how you adjust the slider triangles underneath the histogram:

✔ To make the darkest pixels black, drag the left slider triangle to the right so that it rests directly under the beginning of the first hill in the histogram. Figure 18-8 shows the dragged triangle and its effect on the image.

✔ To make the lightest pixels white, drag the right-hand triangle to the left so that it lines up directly under the end of the last hill in the histogram, as in Figure 18-9.

✔ If you already chose the Auto Levels command or the Auto button in the Levels dialog box, you most likely won't have to change either the left or right slider because Photoshop has already done this automatically. (You may want to adjust the sliders slightly, but that's up to you.) Instead, just concentrate on positioning the middle slider, described next.

Figure 18-7:
Though they lived in a time when Photoshop was not available, these uncorrected characters still managed to find something to smile about.

Figure 18-8:
Dragging the first triangle affects the darkest pixels in the image.

✔ The most important triangle is the middle one. Called the *gamma point* — just in case you get stuck in an elevator with the guys from R&D and find yourself scraping for something to talk about — this triangle lets you change the brightness of the medium colors in your image. Drag to the right to make the medium colors darker. But more likely, you want to drag to the left to make the medium colors lighter, as demonstrated in Figure 18-10.

Figure 18-9:
The image lightens up when I drag the white triangle to the left.

Figure 18-10:
Dragging the middle triangle brings out the detail in an image.

The values in the three option boxes above the histogram update as you drag the slider triangles. The left and right values are measured in color levels. Just like the values in the Color palette — where you define colors (see Chapter 5) — 0 is black and 255 is white. So if the left value is 45, as it is in Figures 18-8 through 18-10, any pixel that is colored with a level of 45 or darker becomes black. The gamma value — the middle one — is measured as a ratio . . . er, forget it, it doesn't make any sense, and it matters even less. The point is, a value of more than 1 lightens the medium colors; a value less than 1 darkens them.

The old stock photo featured in Figures 18-7 through 18-10 is a wonderful example of a work of art that takes on new meaning the more you look at it. Three of the subjects are proudly displaying unlighted tobacco products, the fourth guy is using a paper cup for a megaphone, and all four have feathers in their caps (figure that one out). Meanwhile, you can see their shadows on the wall in back of them. Call me picky, but it sort of ruins the illusion that they might be outdoors enjoying a chilly sporting event.

If you want to see the effect of the Levels command on a full-color image, you need look no further than Color Plate 18-3. Nestled in this quiet corner of the book is a homemade Italian gate. Starting with the uncorrected image in the upper-left corner, I adjusted each of the slider triangles, eventually arriving at the much superior color balance shown in the lower-right image. It just goes to show you, Levels is bound to be good for any image.

If you notice a loss of color in your image after you apply the Levels command, don't worry. You can get that color back by using the Variations command, discussed in the next section.

Variations on a Color Scheme

One negative effect of the Levels command is that it can weaken some of the colors, particularly if you lighten the medium colors by dragging the gamma point in the Levels dialog box to the left. To bring the colors back to their original intensity, call on Image➪Adjust➪Variations.

The Variations command can also cure color casts, in which one color is particularly prominent in the image. A photograph shot outdoors, for example, may be overly blue; one shot in an X-rated motel room may be a shade heavy in the reds. Whatever color predominates your image, the Variations command can tone it down with elegance and ease.

Turning plain old color into Technicolor

To bolster the intensity of colors in your image — for what it's worth, color intensity is called *saturation* in image-editing vernacular — follow these pleasant steps:

1. **Choose Image➪Adjust➪Variations.**

   The enormous Variations dialog box erupts onto your screen, filled with about a million small previews of your image.

2. **Select the Saturation radio button in the upper-right corner of the dialog box.**

   Most of the small preview images disappear. Only five remain, as shown in Figure 18-11. The three previews in the middle of the dialog box represent different color intensities. The top two previews show the image as it appeared before you chose the Variations command and how it looks now, subject to the changes in the Variations dialog box.

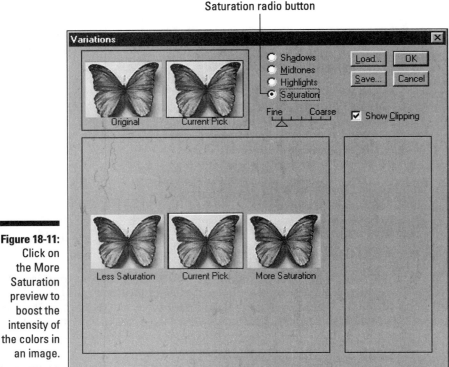

Saturation radio button

3. **Drag the slider triangle in the upper-right corner to the left, toward Fine.**

   This slider controls the extent of the changes made inside the Variations dialog box. If you drag the triangle toward Coarse, the changes become more drastic; drag it toward Fine, and they become more gradual. The setting is reflected inside the left and right previews in the middle of the dialog box. The changes become more subtle.

   Because color intensity is a very sensitive function inside Photoshop, it's best to set the slider to one of the first two notches so that you can make gentle, incremental changes.

4. To increase color intensity, click on the preview labeled More Saturation.

Clicking once increases the intensity by a gradual amount, owing to the slider bar setting. To add more intensity, click again. Each time you click, the Current Pick previews update — one in the middle and one at the top — to reflect your latest change.

If inconsistently colored pixels begin to emerge, Photoshop is telling you that these colors are outside the CMYK color range and will not print. Don't worry about it until the weird pixels take over a third or more of your image. (If you don't care whether the colors will print correctly or not, turn off the Show Clipping check box to view the pixels normally.)

If at any time you want to reset the Current Pick preview to the original image, just click on the preview labeled Original in the upper-left corner of the dialog box.

5. When you're satisfied with the increased color intensity, press Enter (Return on a Mac).

Photoshop applies your settings to the original image, just as they were shown in the Current Pick preview. No surprises with this dialog box.

Changes you make via the Variations dialog box affect only the active layer. Unfortunately, you can't apply the Variations command using an adjustment layer as you can the Levels and Auto Levels commands.

Color Plate 18-4 shows the difference between a butterfly whose splendor I completely destroyed using the Levels command and that same butterfly restored to its original luster and brilliance via the Variations command. To achieve this radical transformation, I set the slider bar inside the Variations dialog box to the second notch over from the left and clicked on the More Saturation preview a total of six times.

Removing that color cast sure feels good

Images are like people in that they hate to wear casts. When your image is encumbered by a color cast, it becomes uncomfortable and downright crotchety. Take the first image in Color Plate 18-5, for example. To the inexperienced eye, this image may appear happy and at peace with itself. But in truth, its life is a living heck, made miserable by a decidedly yellow color cast.

To remove the color cast once and for all, revisit the Variations command:

1. Choose Image⇨Adjust⇨Variations.

The Variations dialog box takes over your screen.

2. **Select the Midtones radio button in the upper-right corner of the dialog box.**

   This option lets you edit the medium colors in your image. (You can also edit the dark or light colors by selecting Shadows or Highlights, but these options produce extremely subtle effects and have little impact on your image.)

   After you select Midtones, the central portion of the dialog box fills with seven previews, as shown in Figure 18-12. These previews let you shift the colors in the image toward a primary color — green, yellow, red, magenta, blue, or cyan. As usual, the Current Pick preview in the center of the cluster updates to show the most recent corrections applied to the image.

   The three previews along the right edge of the Variations dialog box let you lighten and darken the image. But because they're less capable than the gamma point control in the Levels dialog box, you can feel free to ignore them.

3. **Click on one of the More previews to shift the colors in the image toward that particular color.**

   First, identify the color cast. Then click on the preview opposite to that color. In the case of the horse image from Color Plate 18-5, the cast is clearly yellow and, to a lesser extent, green. To eliminate the yellow cast, I clicked on More Blue. To eliminate the green cast, I clicked on More Magenta.

   Check out Color Plate 5-3, which shows that yellow ink filters out blue light and magenta ink filters out green light. This filtering means that yellow and blue are direct opposites, as are magenta and green. Such opposite colors are termed *complementary*. I'm not sure why. I guess it's like a marriage of opposites in which each spouse complements the other. If they don't kill each other first, of course.

4. **If you go too far toward one color, just click on the opposite color to step backward.**

   In Color Plate 18-5, for example, I clicked on the More Blue preview twice, clicked on More Magenta twice, and then clicked on More Blue again. But after some concerted soul searching, I decided that I had gone too far. The resulting image — shown in the bottom-right corner of the color plate — was too blue and too magenta. So I clicked on the More Yellow button to remove the last application of blue and clicked on More Green to remove the last application of magenta. The lower-left example in the color plate shows the result.

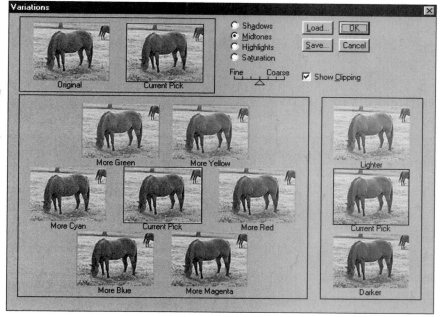

Figure 18-12:
Click on the
More Blue
preview to
add blue
and remove
yellow in an
image. Click
on More
Magenta
to add
magenta
and remove
green.

As when you adjust color saturation, you can vary the impact of the previews
on the image by dragging the slider triangle toward Fine or Coarse. The
images in Color Plate 18-5 were all created with the triangle set right in the
center, as it is by default.

If your image has more than one layer, your color-cast manipulations affect
only the active layer.

Chapter 19

Taking a Peek at Web Graphics

Despite (or perhaps because of) its extraordinary popularity as an online graphics creation tool, Photoshop attracted a lot of criticism in the past for its relatively paltry collection of Web-savvy features. Adobe used to tell Web designers that they were missing the point — Photoshop was for print graphics and ImageReady was for the Web. But most Web designers ignored this advice and continued to grouse, so Adobe did the right thing and caved.

In Version 5.5, Adobe's engineers started by expropriating a bevy of features from ImageReady 1.0 and hot-wiring them directly into Photoshop. Then midway into the process they said, "Oh to heck with it!" and tossed in ImageReady 2.0 for good measure. It's like a mad scientist who, after creating a half-man half-beast, decides the fellow isn't beastly enough and arms it with a pet wolverine. Now with Photoshop 6, Adobe adds in a few more Web features. And that pet wolverine went out and got its teeth sharpened even more and came back as ImageReady 3.0.

When to Turn to ImageReady

When you fork out your hard-earned dollars for Photoshop 6, you also get ImageReady 3.0. This may sound like a wonderful two-for-one deal, and to an extent it is, but it also makes for a lot of confusion. Most of ImageReady's capabilities are also built into Photoshop 6, and some of them work differently in ImageReady than they do in Photoshop. For example, GIF and JPEG file-saving options are located in the Optimize palette. As a result, telling the difference between a unique feature that warrants your attention and one that's merely an old horse decked out in a new saddle can be difficult.

My personal take on it is this: Stay inside Photoshop whenever possible and switch over to ImageReady only when you have to. If you need to create image maps, rollovers, and animations, you need to dive into ImageReady. Unfortunately, providing all the ins and outs of ImageReady would require a second volume of this book. I recommend turning to Adobe's documentation or picking up a third party book devoted exclusively to ImageReady. I'm not a betting man, but if my hand were forced, I'd say in the future there's a good possibility that Photoshop and ImageReady will be rolled into one big, mean, comprehensive image-editing machine.

And as if to say, "Yes, we know we should have rolled these two programs into one already — we're sorry," Photoshop 6 and ImageReady 3.0 are hot-linked to each other. To take the image that you're editing in Photoshop and open it up in ImageReady, click on the icon at the bottom of the toolbox. To switch back to Photoshop — and take your ImageReady edits with you — click on the icon at the bottom of the ImageReady toolbox.

If you've been working in Photoshop 6, you know what a memory hog it is. If you plan on having both Photoshop and ImageReady open at the same time, make sure you have beaucoup amounts of RAM at your editing disposal.

With that said, this chapter just deals with the Web features found within Photoshop. And it deals with them lightly at that. There are tons of books solely devoted to the fine art of Web design and production. These books provide every nitty, gritty detail you would ever want to know. IDG Books Worldwide, Inc., publishes a lot of Web design books, such as *Creating Web Pages For Dummies,* 5th Edition, by Bud Smith and Arthur Bebak, and *Roger C. Parker's Guide to Web Content and Design,* by Roger C. Parker. I recommend that you spend some of those hard-earned dollars you saved by not having to purchase ImageReady separately and pick up a book or two.

Web File Formats

As I mention in Chapter 6, to display your image on the Web, you must save your image in one of three file formats — PNG, GIF, or JPEG. Read on to find out the most important attributes and functions of each.

PNG: The new kid on the block

PNG stands for *Portable Network Graphics* and was originally designed to replace the popular GIF format. PNG is much more sophisticated than GIF — it supports 24- and 48-bit images, while GIF supports only 8-bit images. PNG can support RGB, Grayscale, or Indexed color image modes. You can also have varying levels of transparency in a PNG image, something both GIF and JPEG cannot do. The downside to PNG files is that the color images are often larger than GIFs or JPEGs because they contain more colors than GIF and do not have the advantage of JPEG's great compression scheme. Therefore, the PNG file format is good for small images, such as buttons and thumbnails with details. The biggest downside to PNG, however, is that it's still not yet widely supported by the browser world. In order to display a PNG in Netscape Navigator or Internet Explorer, you have to install a third party plug-in. And it's not really a good idea to make the visitors of your Web site download a plug-in, unless you're offering them something spectacular.

GIF: For Webbies only

Computer hacks are divided on how you pronounce GIF. Some folks swear that the proper pronunciation is with a hard "G" — as in one *t* short of a *gift.* Other experts insist that you say it with a soft *g,* so that the word sounds just like that famous brand of peanut butter. Regardless of which camp you decide to join, GIF is best used for high-contrast images, illustrations created in Photoshop or imported from a drawing program, screen shots, and text. The biggest drawback to GIF is that it can save images with only 256 colors or less (8-bit color). However, it's the format you want to use for simple — no computer programming skills required — animations, called *animated GIFs.* Create these easily by using shareware programs, such as GIF Builder, that are downloadable from the Web.

Using indexed color

If your image contains more than 256 colors, choose Image⇨Mode⇨Indexed Color to reduce the number of colors before you save in the GIF format. As shown in Figure 19-1, the Indexed Color dialog box has grown fairly significantly over the past couple versions of Photoshop, permitting you to lock down important colors, choose from more naturalistic palettes, and apply transparency. Here are all the options:

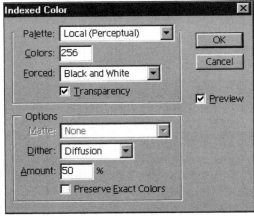

Figure 19-1:
The Indexed
Color
dialog box
controls the
appearance
of GIF
images.

✔ **Palette:** Photoshop offers a multitude of palette options. Here's a short briefing on each:

- **Exact:** If an image already contains less than 256 colors, the Exact palette appears by default. If this happens, leave it as is.

- **System (Mac) and System (Windows):** Use this palette only if you want to add a graphic to your system (when adding a desktop pattern or a file icon that will appear on your desktop).

- **Web:** This palette of 216 colors is the one used by browsers and is usually used for graphics that display on ancient 8-bit monitors. There are better palettes to use than Web.

- **Uniform:** The worst palette of the lot. Consists of a uniform sample of colors of the spectrum. Don't use it.

- **Local (Perceptual):** Perceptual is a variation on the Adaptive palette, which varies the reduced color palette to suit the image. But where Adaptive maintains the most popular colors, Perceptual is more intelligent, sampling colors that produce the best transitions. Use this palette with photographic images, where smooth transitions are more important than actual color values.

- **Local (Selective):** This palette is also a variation on the Adaptive palette, but better preserves Web colors. Use this palette when an image contains bright colors or sharp, graphic transitions.

- **Local (Adaptive):** Adaptive selects the most frequently used colors in your image. If an image contains relatively few colors and you want to keep the colors as exact as possible, apply this palette.

    Notice that you also have Master versions of the Perceptual, Selective, and Adaptive palettes. Local palettes are based on the image's color while master palettes are palettes created by ImageReady.

- **Custom:** This palette enables you to load a color look-up table from your hard drive or disk. Not used that often for Web graphics.

- **Previous:** This palette uses the last look-up table created by the Indexed Color command. Usually used when creating a series of high contrast graphics that need to maintain a consistent look. This pop-up menu offers two new options, Perceptual and Selective. Both are variations on the Adaptive option, which varies the reduced color palette to suit the image. But where Adaptive maintains the most popular colors, Perceptual is more intelligent, sampling the colors that produce the best transitions. The Selective option tries to maintain key colors, including those in the so-called 216-color "Web-safe" palette.

✔ **Colors:** For Color, start with the lower setting (such as 64), and see what happens to your image. Use the lowest number of colors that keeps your image reasonably intact. You may find that photographic images, especially those with a wide range of colors, require a higher setting than non-photographic images or photos with a limited color range. Photoshop has jettisoned the old Color Depth option box in favor of the lone Colors value. The idea is that scaling colors by an entire bit depth — 8-bit for 256 colors, 7-bit for 128, 6-bit for 64, and so on — isn't really necessary to achieve smaller file sizes, so you may as well free your mind and enter the exact number of colors you deem fit. Still, Color Depth was a valuable option, and I would have preferred to see it stay. Sacrificing an entire bit does sometimes make a difference, after all.

✔ **Forced:** Sometimes an adaptive palette can very easily upset extremely important colors. For example, the white background of an image might turn a pale red or blue, even if white was a predominant color. With this option you can lock in important colors so that they don't change. Black and White locks in black and white. Primaries protects eight colors — white, red, green, blue, cyan, magenta, yellow, and black. And Web protects the 216 colors in the Web-safe palette. Very helpful indeed.

✔ **Transparency:** If an image is set on a layer against a transparent background, selecting this check box maintains that transparency. Bear in mind, however, that transparency in a GIF file is either on or off; there are no soft transitions as in a Photoshop layer.

✔ **Matte:** The Matte option works in collaboration with the Transparency check box. (If there is no transparency in an image — that is, all layers cover one another to create a seamless opacity — then the Matte option is dimmed.) When Transparency is selected, the specified Matte color fills the translucent pixels in the image. When Transparency is turned off, the Matte color fills all translucent and transparent areas. To ensure smooth transitions, select the Matte color that matches the background color of your Web page.

✔ **Dither:** This option controls how Photoshop mimics the several million colors that you have asked it to remove from an image. The None option makes no attempt to smooth out color transitions, but results in smaller file sizes. Diffusion mixes pixels to soften the transitions between colors. The new Noise option mixes pixels throughout the image, not merely in areas of transition. And the Pattern option just plain sucks. (To find out why, consult the *Photoshop Bible,* published by IDG Books.) If you ask me, stick with Diffusion and the following option.

✔ **Amount:** This wonderful option controls the amount of dithering applied. When, and only when, Diffusion is active, you may modify the amount of dithering by raising or lowering this value. Lower values produce harsher color transitions but lower the file size. It's a trade-off. Keep an eye on the image window to see how low you can go.

✔ **Preserve Exact Colors:** This option preserves areas of flat color when Diffusion is selected. I prefer to leave this check box turned on. By doing this, colors in your image that are also in the palette are not dithered; therefore, lines, text, and other small details in your Web images have better on-screen quality.

Notice that you can preview the Indexed Color by making sure Preview is checked on. Using Preview enables you to experiment with the number of colors and dithering and prevents a lot of Edit to Undos.

If you apply the Indexed Color command with the Transparency check box turned on, Photoshop fills the transparent portion of the image with the familiar checkerboard pattern. What's unusual about this is that the file is flattened, as indicated by the single *Index* layer pictured in Figure 19-2. Furthermore, you cannot add new layers to the file, making an indexed image the only kind of Photoshop document that can accommodate transparency without layers.

Figure 19-2: An indexed image is unique in that it can accommodate transparency inside a flattened document.

Color table transparency

In the old days, you had to use File⇨Export⇨GIF89a Export to save a GIF image with transparent pixels. Now any GIF file can store transparency information. In fact, there's really no reason to go on using GIF89a Export. (See the next section for more information.)

After indexing the colors in an image, you can make all occurrences of one of those colors transparent using the Color Table command. Choose Image⇨ Mode⇨Color Table to display the dialog box shown in Figure 19-3 and then select the Eyedropper icon below the Preview check box. Now click on a color in the palette or in the image itself. Either way, that one color becomes transparent.

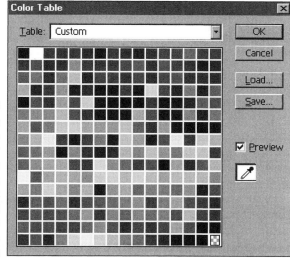

Figure 19-3:
Use the
Eyedropper
tool to
select a
color that
you want
to make
transparent.

The Color Table command suffers one limitation: You can make just one color transparent at a time. To make a second color transparent, you must press Enter (Return on a Mac) to exit the dialog box and then choose Image⇨Mode⇨ Color Table again.

Saving (and opening) GIF with transparency

As I mentioned earlier, there's really no reason to go on using the GIF89a Export command. Using this command is hard to script from the Actions palette (for more on Actions, see Chapter 21), you lose your work if you cancel midway through, and its functions are already built into the standard and easier-to-access GIF format.

Here's how to save a GIF image with transparency:

1. **Specify the transparency using the Indexed Color command.**

   You can make additional colors transparent using the Color Table commands if you like.

2. **Choose File⇨Save As.**

   Or press Ctrl +Shift+S (⌘+Shift+S on a Mac).

3. **Select the CompuServe GIF format.**

   You can find this format in the Format menu. On the Mac, be sure to add the three-character *.gif* extension, if it is not already there.

4. **In the GIF Options dialog box, select either Interlaced or Normal.**

   The Interlaced setting results in an image that appears gradually when it's downloaded, like a progressive JPEG image (coming up next). If you don't want your image to be downloaded in this way, choose Normal.

5. **Press Enter (Return on a Mac).**

   Photoshop saves the GIF file to disk.

When you open a GIF file that contains transparency, Photoshop displays the transparency as a checkerboard pattern. This goes both for GIF files saved the new way with the Save a Copy command and the old way with GIF89a Export. No more having to remember which colors are transparent and which are opaque — what you see is what you get.

JPEG: The compact format

I cover a lot of information on JPEGs in Chapter 6. JPEG is the one file format that is used for both print and Web graphics. What I delineated there is also applicable to Web images so I recommend taking a gander at Chapter 6 to brush up on the details.

When saving JPEG images, you don't have to monkey around with the Indexed Color or Color Table commands because JPEG supports the full 24-bit color spectrum. To recap, JPEG also uses lossy compression. (The compression ratio is fantastic, but pixels are deleted in the process.) For the Web, you want to use the JPEG format for continuous tone images, such as photographs or images with a wide range of colors.

If you read Chapter 6, forgive me for repeating myself, but I want to make sure that you're clear on the downside of JPEGs and lossy compression. Photoshop recompresses a JPEG image every time you save it — pixels are being deleted in order to squeeze down the file size. During a single edit session, this compression won't hurt because JPEG works from the on-screen

version. But, if you close, reopen, and resave it in JPEG format, some damage
occurs. Repeat this process over and over, however, and the damage
increases each time. So remember, apply all of your necessary edits to the
image, save in JPEG format, and leave well enough alone. If you need to edit
an image over a longer length of time, it is better to save it as native
Photoshop format. Then save it as a JPEG only after you have completed
your editing process.

When you save a JPEG image, you are greeted with the JPEG Options
dialog box, as shown in Figure 19-4. The options work as follows:

✔ **Matte:** Unlike GIF, JPEG does not support transparency. So if your image
   contains transparent areas, Photoshop needs to know what color to fill
   them with. Select the desired color from the Matte pop-up menu. Keep
   an eye on the background image to make sure you like the effect.

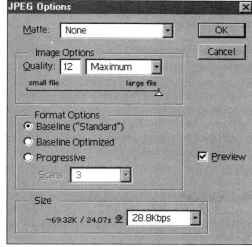

Figure 19-4:
Photoshop
offers a
multitude of
JPEG
options,
including
the ability to
measure the
download
speed for an
image.

✔ **Quality:** If you've ever seen the movie "This Is Spinal Tap," you may
   recall the scene in which lead guitarist Nigel Tufnel demonstrates how
   he can crank up the dials on his amplifier to 11, one beyond the standard maximum of 10. When asked, "Why not just make 10 louder and
   make 10 the top number?" Nigel blanks for a moment and finally con-
   cludes, "This goes to 11!" In that same vein, I present you with the
   Quality value, which tops out at 12 (it topped out at 10 in Version 5.0 and
   earlier). Why not simply make 10 better quality and make 10 the top
   number? You don't need a computer science degree to figure out the
   answer to that question: "This goes to 12!" Oh, and by the way, quality
   lets you choose the amount of compression applied to your image,
   which is directly related to the quality. The higher the compression, the
   lesser the quality and the smaller the file. You get it.

✔ **Format:** Choose Progressive to have your image gradually appear on-screen in full image passes. Specify the number of scans you want it to take to fully materialize. Leave it on Baseline ("Optimized") to have it appear in line-by-line passes. The Optimized option creates a smaller file size than the Standard option.

✔ **Size:** To help you determine the proper Quality setting to use, Photoshop tells you how long an image should take to download at various connection speeds. In Figure 19-4, for example, my image will take 24 seconds to download at 28.8Kbps. That's *way* too slow for a single image, so I need to lower the Quality setting.

Making Side-by-Side Comparisons

Not sure what settings to use when saving a GIF or JPEG file? Wouldn't it be nice to compare a bunch of different settings side-by-side to decide which group of settings provides the best trade-off between quality and size? A command permits you to do exactly that. You can compare different indexed palettes or JPEG compression settings. You can even compare GIF to JPEG. And at all times, the original image remains visible so that you don't stray too far.

The command at work here is Save For Web. This one command lets you index colors, add transparency, and save to the GIF or JPEG formats in one operation. So there's no need to use the Indexed Color or Color Table commands — in fact, Save For Web works best if you start from a full-color, RGB image.

Choose File⇨Save For Web or press Ctrl+Shift+Alt+S (⌘+Shift+Option+S on a Mac). Either way, Photoshop displays the large window in Figure 19-5. There's a lot going on here, but don't fret; most of the options duplicate functions that are discussed in this chapter.

When you first enter the Save For Web window, you have to decide which image you want to preview. Photoshop defaults to the 2-Up view, which shows the original image along with a copy with color indexing or JPEG compression applied, as it appears when opened in a Web browser. To compare multiple settings at a time — the real power of the window — click on the 4-Up tab in the top left corner of the window. Figure 19-5 shows this multiple view.

Next, click on the preview that you want to experiment with and modify the settings along the right side of the window. By default, the first preview shows the original image, untainted by compression settings. You probably want to leave that one alone. But the others you can change until your heart's content.

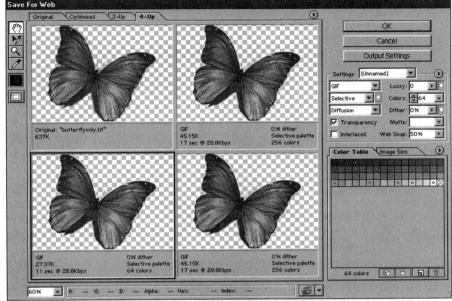

Figure 19-5:
Click on the
4-Up tab at
the top of
the window
to compare
the original
image to
three sets
of Web
compres-
sion
settings.

To get a closer view, you can zoom and scroll the previews using the Zoom and Hand tools. You can also change the zoom ratio by changing the value in the bottom left corner of the window. To preview a set of settings in your favorite Web browser, click on the button in the lower-right corner. Your image appears in your selected browser window.

There are a couple new tools in the Save For Web dialog box. The Slice Select tool enables you to select any slices your image may contain, enabling you to selectively optimize portions of your image. To select a slice simply click on it with the tool. To select multiple slices, Shift+click or drag across your desired slices. Double-clicking the slice displays the Slice Options box. The other new tool is the Toggle Slices Visibility button, which shows or hides your slice boundaries. For everything you need to know about slices, check out the section, "Slicing up buttons and other graphics" later in this chapter.

After that, it's just a matter of adjusting the various options along the right side of the window. These options change according to the file format that you select from the pop-up menu directly below the word Settings. There is one set of options for GIF and another for JPEG. I explain these in two separate lists. If you opt to use one of the two PNG formats (not advisable given the lack of support among browsers), then reference the GIF list for discussions of the options.

The GIF options

The following options appear when you select the GIF format. All options are organized in the order they appear. If the option is not named, I use the hint name that appears when you hover your cursor over the option. For example, hover over the Format pop-up menu to see the hint Optimized File Format.

- ✔ **Color Reduction Algorithm:** The pop-up menu controls how the colors are reduced from 16 million to 256 or fewer. As in the Indexed Color dialog box, you can choose from Perceptual, Selective, or Adaptive, all of which are covered in the section "Using Indexed Color" earlier in this chapter. You can also select a specific palette, such as Web, Black and White, Grayscale, Mac OS, or Windows.

- ✔ **Dithering Algorithm:** Select the kind of dithering you want to apply. No Dither results in a smaller file size, but Diffusion produces better transitions.

- ✔ **Transparency:** If a layered image contains empty checkerboard areas, you can keep them transparent by turning on this check box.

- ✔ **Interlaced:** This option results in an interlaced GIF file, in which the image fades into view as it is downloaded by the Web browser. I used to like this option — in theory, it permits Web surfers with slow connection speeds to get a sense of an image before it completely loads — but I've seen it create enough problems with Web browsers that I now steer clear of it.

- ✔ **Optimize Menu:** Click on the arrowhead to the right of the Settings option to display a menu of commands, as shown at the top of Figure 19-6. These commands let you save your settings for later use, delete settings that you saved, or automatically repopulate the views in the 2-Up and 4-Up modes with fresh alternative settings. But the best command is Optimize to File Size, which lets you forgo messing with the options and instead enter a target file size. After you click on OK, Photoshop automatically changes the settings to meet the target size. If you don't know whether you want to use GIF or JPEG, select the Auto Select GIF/JPEG radio button. The Use options enable you to optimize to that file size the current slice, each slice, or all of the slices.

- ✔ **Lossy:** Technically, GIF relies on "lossless" compression, meaning that no data is sacrificed when saving a file. But by cranking up the Lossy value, you can rearrange the pixels in an image so that they compress better. In my experience, values as high as 30 whittle away the file size, while causing very little damage to the appearance of an image. Higher values are rarely acceptable. Use this option prudently and keep an eye on the preview.

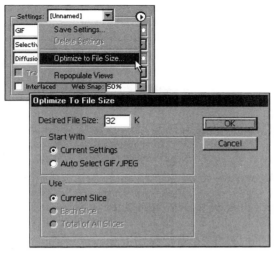

Figure 19-6:
To automate
the
proceedings,
choose
Optimize to
File Size and
enter a
target file
size into the
subsequent
dialog box.

✔ **Colors:** Here's where you specify the number of colors in an image. You can also select predefined bit depths using the pop-up menu.

✔ **Dither:** When the Diffusion option is active, use this value to specify the amount of dithering you want to apply. See the section "Using Indexed Color" for more information.

✔ **Matte:** When the Transparency check box is selected, translucent (partially transparent) pixels are filled with the Matte color you've selected. For example, if you select None for the Matte color, the translucent areas are converted to full transparency. If you select White for the Matte color, the translucent areas are filled with opaque white. When Transparency is off, both transparent and translucent pixels will be filled with the Matte color.

✔ **Web Snap:** This ingenious option replaces a specified percentage of colors in an image with members of the 216-color Web-safe palette. It's a way to hedge your bets — you can lock down some colors so that they're compatible with older 8-bit monitors and permit other colors to roam free so that the image still looks great on 24-bit screens.

✔ **Color Table:** Clicking on this tab shows all the colors in an image. Below the colors, you find four tiny icons. The first changes a selected color to the nearest Web-safe equivalent. The second locks the selected color so it can't be changed. The third adds a color selected with the Eyedropper to the palette. Here's how it works: Click on the original image preview (upper-left by default), select the Eyedropper, click on the color you want to add to the palette, switch back to the preview you want to change, and then click on the third Color Table icon. Finally, the fourth icon deletes the selected color.

Double-click on a color to display the Color Picker, with three Web-specific options spotlighted in Figure 19-7. Select the Only Web Colors check box to select exclusively from the 216-color Web-safe palette. Click on the cube icon to the left of the Custom button to replace a color with its nearest Web-safe equivalent. And if you're a hexadecimal geek (and proud of it!), you can enter the desired hexadecimal color value into the # option at the bottom of the dialog box.

✔ **Color Palette Menu:** When the Color Table tab is active, you can modify selected colors, sort colors, and load and save palettes by choosing commands from this menu. Just click on the arrowhead to the right of the tab.

✔ **Image Size:** If an image is physically too large to fit snugly on your Web page, you can make it smaller by clicking on the Image Size tab and fiddling with the Width, Height, and Percent values. These options work just like those offered by the Image Size command. For complete information, see Chapter 4.

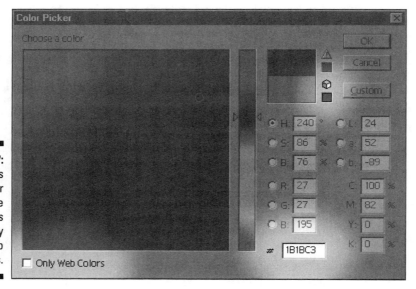

Figure 19-7: Photoshop's Color Picker adds three options specifically for Web designers.

The JPEG options

The GIF options make quite the list. Luckily, the number of options available when saving a JPEG image is much more modest, as shown in Figure 19-8. Here's how they work:

✔ **Compression Quality:** Select an option from the pop-up menu immediately below the word JPEG to set the image quality to one of Photoshop's familiar predefined settings.

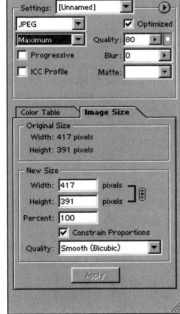

Figure 19-8: These options appear when you select JPEG as your file format.

✔ **Progressive:** This option is the equivalent of Interlaced for GIF images, displaying the image incrementally as it is downloaded by a Web browser. Again, for compatibility reasons, I'm inclined these days to turn this check box off.

✔ **ICC Profile:** This check box embeds a color profile with the JPEG image. The color profile adds about 3K to the file size, which means an extra second of download time at 28.8Kbps. And thanks to the fact that, as I write this, no Web browser can read a color profile without a special plug-in, the extra 3K goes wasted. Leave it off.

✔ **Optimized:** This option optimizes the lossless compression built into a JPEG image. It has so little impact on file size — often none whatsoever — I recommend you turn it off. (This option is unlikely to cause problems with Web browsers, but it may make the image incompatible with other image editors.)

✔ **Quality:** This option affects the quality of the compression. You can specify a setting by entering a value into the Quality option box or by using the sliders. Where the standard JPEG Options dialog box permits values between 0 and 12 (as discussed earlier in the "JPEG: The compact format" section), this value ranges from 0 to 100. I can hear Nigel now: "This goes to 100!"

✔ **Blur:** This is hands down Photoshop's most reprehensible and downright dangerous option. The idea is that JPEG's lossy compression scheme is better at compressing soft transitions than hard edges, so it can compress blurry images better than sharp ones. So by blurring an image, you reduce its file size without applying more compression. *But you also destroy the freakin' detail!* Believe me, you're way better off applying more compression than blurring the image. Leave this value set to 0.

✔ **Matte:** This is the upteenth time I explain the Matte option in this chapter, so I'm getting pretty sick of sounding like a broken record (and I'm sure you're not getting a kick out of hearing it again, either). Suffice it to say, if the image contains any transparency, this is where you tell Photoshop what color to fill it with.

The remaining option — Image Size — works just like it does when saving a GIF image. Please, don't ask me to run through that explanation again.

The Preview menu

Before you exit the Save For Web window, there's one last set of options I want to explain. At the top of the window, well to the right of the 4-Up tab, you see an arrowhead in a circle. Click on it to reveal the Preview menu, shown in Figure 19-9. The commands in this menu control the appearance and feedback provided by the image previews.

Figure 19-9:
Choose a
command
from the
Preview
menu to
change the
appearance
of a
selected
preview.

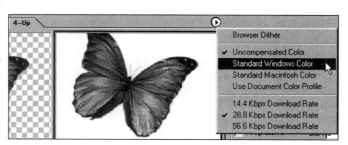

The commands are divided into three sections:

- ✔ **Browser Dither:** Select this option to see how a selected preview will look when displayed on an 8-bit monitor. This method is exceedingly useful for determining whether you need to go with a Web-safe palette or to gauge the performance of the Web Snap value.

- ✔ **Color Compensation:** Colors shift from one screen to the next and from the Mac to Windows. There's no way to predict exactly how an image will look on another screen, but you can use the four color commands to get a sense. By default, Uncompensated Color is active, so Photoshop makes no attempt at a prediction. Select Standard Windows Color or Standard Macintosh Color to see how the colors might look on another platform. The final color command, Document Color Profile, uses the ICC Profile of the document.

- ✔ **Download Rate:** The final three commands change the estimated download times listed below each preview. These commands are unusual in that they affect all previews, not just the selected one.

When you save your image via the Save for Web command, Photoshop saves your image as an ImageReady native file format. Gee, I guess you really should use these two programs together.

Working with Type

To make amends for past sins, where Adobe either disregarded treatment of text to be viewed on the Web or even caused it to look atrocious, Version 5.5 and now Version 6.0 have added quite a few type functions that Web designers desperately needed. Although the basics of creating and editing text are the same for both the Web and for print (check out the particulars in Chapter 16), there are some attributes that you should treat differently for text that is to be viewed online.

- ✔ **Faux Bold, Faux Italic, and Underline Font styles:** Faux Bold and Faux Italic let you apply bold and italic to fonts that lack such styles, such as Geneva, Monaco, and others. You can likewise make a bold font bolder, or further slant italic type. But as I stated in Chapter 16, it is best to use the fonts as they were designed by the typeface designer. Be aware that applying these faux styles can potentially distort the attractive proportions of the typeface. As far as Underline style goes, use it without worry. We know the vast quantity of online type that is underlined. This Underline style eliminates the need to use the Line or Pencil tool to draw underlines.

- ✔ **Fractional Widths:** If kerning, the space between two letters, is still giving you fits, try turning this option off. When type gets very small, the spacing between letters may vary by fractions of a single pixel.

Photoshop has to split the difference in favor of one pixel or the other, and 50 percent of the time the visual effect is wrong. You can turn the feature off and avoid the problem entirely.

The Fractional Widths option is handy when the default Metrics setting for kerning is not selected and the Anti-Alias option is set to None. Macintosh users will find it especially useful, particularly if you're working with preset screen font sizes, such as 9-point Geneva. For a detailed explanation on kerning, check out Chapter 16.

✔ **Anti-Alias:** You can tweak the anti-aliasing (softness) by selecting an option from the Anti-Alias pop-up menu in the Options bar or from the Type submenu under Layer. The first setting, None, turns the softening off and leaves hard, choppy edges, which is good for very small type. Crisp adds a slight amount of anti-aliasing, thus retaining sharp contrast. If you notice jagged edges, try applying the Smooth setting. If the antialiasing seems to rob the text of its weight, you can thicken it up a bit with the Strong setting. Crisp, Strong, and Smooth produce more dramatic effects at small type sizes, as shown in Figure 19-10. Let me add, however, that these anti-aliasing options can vary in their effect depending on the particular typeface and the size of that typeface. Nothing substitutes good old experimentation to find the best results.

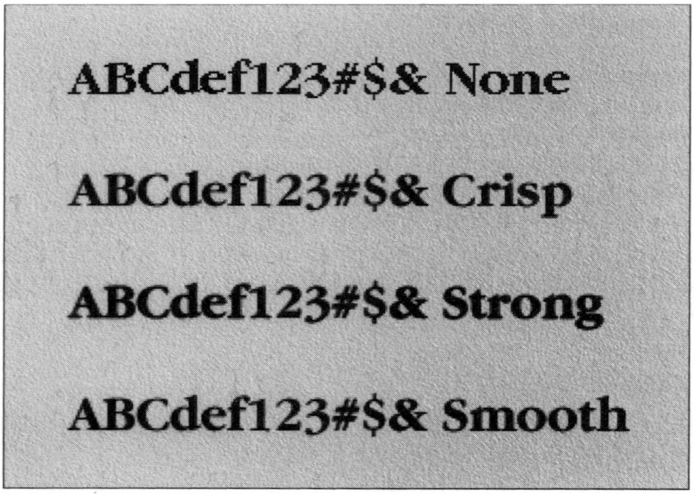

Figure 19-10:
The four anti-aliasing settings available in Photoshop 6.0.

ABCdef123#$& None

ABCdef123#$& Crisp

ABCdef123#$& Strong

ABCdef123#$& Smooth

Note that the faux bold, faux italic, and underline styles affect only the highlighted letters in the text entry area. Meanwhile, the Fractional Widths and Anti-Alias options affect all text on a layer, whether highlighted or not.

Using the Color Palette for Web Graphics

When creating graphics, such as spot illustrations, buttons, and backgrounds for the Web, you want to make sure the color sliders are set to RGB in the color palette (for a color refresher see Chapter 5). The only time you should use Web color sliders is if you are creating graphics to be viewed on ancient 8-bit (256 color) monitors. And this is getting to be a rarity today.

The Copy Color as HTML option in the Color palette pop-up menu is for you hard-core webbies who do your own HTML coding. By choosing this option, Photoshop converts the currently selected color to HTML code, for example color=#5604CC, and copies that code to the clipboard. You can then go into your HTML program of choice and choose Edit⇨Paste to bring in the code of the color.

Finally the last command in the Color palette pop-up menu is Make Ramp Web Safe. This option will allow only 256 colors to be displayed in the color bar at the bottom of the Color Palette. It is similar to selecting Web Safe Colors in the Color Picker dialog box. Again, like the Web Color sliders option, use these options only when creating graphics for old 8-bit monitors.

Slicing Up Buttons and Other Graphics

If you're like most Web designers I've talked to, you rough out your pages in Photoshop. If you don't, you should — it's a great way to work. Photoshop lets you assemble all the elements the way that you want them to appear on the final Web page. Using layers, layer styles, preset Actions (see Chapter 21), and all the nifty techniques you've found in this book, you can easily create an attractive splash page that you can then slice and dice out to later assemble in HTML.

That's right. I said slice and dice. Photoshop now provides a couple of new tools, which previously resided only in ImageReady.

Slices enable you to divide your image into rectangular chunks where you can then apply HTML links, rollovers, image maps, and animations. (The last three techniques mentioned have to be performed in ImageReady, however.) You can also, as we just covered, selectively optimize each slice for viewing on the Web. Photoshop offers two slicing tools, one for drawing the slicing boundaries and another for editing them. The two tools appear spotlighted in Figure 19-11. Here's how they work:

Figure 19-11:
Use the
Slice tool to
draw
rectangular
boundaries
around
buttons and
other page
elements.

> ✔ **Slice tool:** Use this tool to draw the slice boundaries. Draw a rectangle around the shape that you want to slice. Because images have to be rectangular in shape, it makes sense that all slices are rectangular. To select the Slice tool from the keyboard, press the K key, as in *kut*.
>
> ✔ **Slice Select tool:** Use this tool to select, modify, or move a slice. You can select this tool from the keyboard by pressing Shift+K.

When the Slice tool is active, you can temporarily access the Slice Select tool by pressing and holding Ctrl (⌘ on a Mac). Conversely, if the Slice Select tool is active, holding Ctrl (⌘ on a Mac) gets you the Slice tool.

Working with slices

As you draw slices around buttons, graphics, and other page elements, you will see the appearance of lined boxes with numbers in the top left corner. These are your slices. Photoshop then automatically fills in the gaps with spacer slices. In Figure 19-11, the blue boundaries are the so-called "user slices" drawn with the Slice tool; the dotted lines with gray labels are the spacers that Photoshop creates automatically. As you're working, you may find the spacers a bit confusing (I often do), in which case, just ignore them. You draw your slices and let Photoshop worry about its spacers.

Here are some other things to know about slices:

✔ Choose a style from the Options bar. Normal enables you to drag freely. Constrained Aspect Ratio lets you specify a height to width ratio. Fixed size lets you specify a particular height and width in pixels. After you select Fixed style, you don't need to drag. Just click.

✔ You can also create a slice from a layer. Select the layer in the Layers palette. Choose Layer➪New Layer Based Slice.

✔ To hide and show the slice boundaries, choose View➪Show➪Slices. You can also check off Show Slice Numbers in the Options bar to hide the numbers and only display the slice boundaries.

✔ To change the color of the slice boundaries, click on the Line Color drop-down menu in the Options bar.

✔ To select a slice, select the Slice Select tool and click on the slice. To select multiple slices, use Shift+click.

✔ To move a slice, place the Slice Select tool inside the slice and drag to a new position.

✔ To resize a slice boundary, grab a side or corner handle and drag with the Slice Select tool.

✔ To duplicate a slice, select the slice with the Slice Select tool and Alt+drag (Option+drag on a Mac) from inside the selection.

✔ To delete a slice, select the slice with the Slice Select tool and press the Backspace key (Delete key on a Mac). To delete all slices, choose View➪Clear Slices.

✔ To lock slices, choose View➪Lock Slices.

✔ To rearrange user slices, select the slice with the Slice Select tool and choose a stacking order option in the Options bar. Bring To Front makes the selected slice the topmost slice. Send To Back makes it the bottom-most slice. Bring Forward and Send Backward move the slice one level up or down.

✔ To turn one of Photoshop's automatic slice spacers (gray) into a fully editable user slice (blue), click on the spacer with the Slice Select tool and choose the Promote to User-Slice command in the Options bar. Then you can control the colors of the slice, assign a URL, and so on. If you're wondering where the opposite command is — Demote to Spacer — there's no point. Photoshop creates spacers on its own; it doesn't need or want your help.

Slice options

To specify how you want a graphic to be saved — whether to use GIF or JPEG, for example — select one or more slices and adjust the settings in the Save For Web dialog box. (For complete information, read the section "Making side-by-side comparisons" earlier in this chapter.)

To assign URLs, specify file names, and establish other attributes, you can turn to the Slice Options dialog box, pictured in Figure 19-12. These options affect how the image appears and responds in your browser. With your Slice Select tool, select your slice and click on the Slice Options button in the Options bar. Here's how the options work:

 ✔ **Type:** There are two types of slices — Image or No Image. You can either fill a slice with image data or with a solid color or HTML text. Photoshop won't display the No Image data. It must be previewed in the browser.

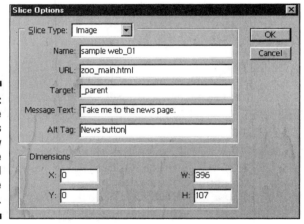

Figure 19-12:
The Slice options affect how your image acts and looks in the browser.

 ✔ **Name:** Photoshop automatically names the slices in the order they appear. If you want to override the automatic naming system, enter your slice names here (for Image slices only).

 ✔ **URL:** To turn the slice into a hotspot (the user clicks on the slice and is transported to a particular URL), enter the URL that the hotspot should link to. If the linked HTML page appears in the same folder as the page you're working on, a simple file name will suffice. For files inside folders, enter the path name. To link to an outside Web page, enter the full URL, such as `http://www.cityzoo.com` (for Image slices only).

✔ **Target:** If your page includes frames, enter the appropriate frame name into this option box.

✔ **Message:** Enter a message to appear at the bottom of the browser window when a visitor hovers the cursor over the button. The default message is the URL of the slice.

✔ **Alt:** To provide a text alternate for the hotspot, enter the text into this option box. This text also appears in place of the slice while the image is downloading or if the browser can't render the image.

✔ **Dimensions:** Lets you specify the position and dimension of the slice in relation to the entire image window.

✔ **Background:** This option only appears in the Save For Web dialog box. If a slice contains transparent areas, use the background option to select the color, if any, that should be used in place of transparency. It works like the Matte option discussed several times previously in this document.

For additional slice capabilities, and there are many, jump to ImageReady.

Creating a Web Photo Gallery

In addition to creating contact sheets and picture packages (described in Chapter 7), Photoshop offers another command under the File⇨Automate submenu, called Web Photo Gallery, that organizes multiple images onto a single page.

This feature, like contact sheet and picture package, is geared toward professional and aspiring photographers. This command assembles a folder of images into a Web site, complete with HTML pages and JPEG images. You specify the name of your page, the size of the thumbnails, and the size and compression of the larger gallery images. As shown in Figure 19-13, your Web page isn't going to win any design awards, but it's easy to navigate and it gets the job done. And if you know a little HTML, you can use the pages as a jumping off point for a more sophisticated site.

Here are the various options involved in creating a gallery:

✔ Choose a style: The various styles — Simple, Table, Horizontal Frame, and Vertical Frame — are displayed via the preview thumbnail in the dialog box.

✔ Choose settings under the various options:

  • **Banner:** This is the title that appears at the top of the Web page. Enter your site name, photo credits, and date.

- **Gallery Images:** This option establishes the settings for the individual image pages (the page that loads when the user clicks on the thumbnail). Specify the size of the border around each image. Choose whether to resize the images based on size and quality (for info on compression quality, see the section "JPEG: The compact format").

- **Gallery Thumbnails:** This option establishes the settings for the thumbnail index page. Specify the size of the thumbnails and the border around those images. And finally establish the captions that appear under each thumbnail.

- **Custom Colors:** This option enables you to choose a different color for all the various elements on your Web page.

✔ Specify your Source and Destination folders: Dump the images you want to appear in one Source folder and designate a new, empty folder for the Desintation folder.

✔ After you click on OK, Photoshop immediately displays the Web page in your Web browser. The HTML file and the JPEG images are saved in your destination folder.

Figure 19-13:
The Web Photo Gallery assembles your images into an index of thumbnails (rear) and a series of pages for the larger gallery images (front).

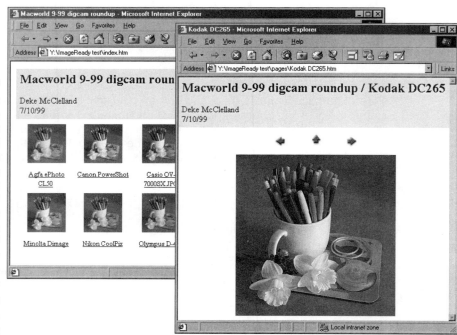

Part VI
The Part of Tens

The 5th Wave   By Rich Tennant

"That's a lovely photo of your sister. Now take her head off the body of that pit viper before she comes in the room."

In this part . . .

Some say that there's magic in the number three. Bears, pigs, Musketeers, and Stooges regularly cavort about in groups of three. But I say that the real magic is in tens. The Ten Commandments, the ten amendments to the Constitution that make up the Bill of Rights, and the ten ingredients in a Big Mac (if you count both all-beef patties and the three sesame seed buns) are items that you can count on the ten fingers of your hands (or the ten toes of your feet when you're at the beach). Top ten lists abound in newspapers, magazines, books, and late-night TV shows. And I say, why buck a trend? If everyone else is doing it, I for one am happy to mindlessly follow along.

But then I thought, "What ho, if there's magic in threes and in tens, why not do both?" So, that's what I did. This part contains three chapters, each of which contains ten factoids. Ten great shortcuts that you'll want to assign to memory, ten great ways to wreak havoc on a loved one's face, and ten things you can do with your image after you finish messing it up in Photoshop.

We're talking major number magic at work here, the kind of stuff that numerologists, fortune-tellers, and lottery fanatics would give their eyeteeth for. And this book costs you only $19.99, a number whose only claim to fame is that it's slightly cheaper than $20.

Chapter 20

Ten Tricky Techniques to Assign to Memory

- -

In This Chapter

▶ Hiding the Toolbox and palettes

▶ Changing an Option Box value

▶ Scrolling and zooming

▶ Changing the brush size

▶ Changing the opacity of a brush, layer, or floating selection

▶ Creating straight lines

▶ Adding to, subtracting from, and reselecting selection outlines

▶ Moving, nudging, and cloning

▶ Filling a selection

▶ Making, switching, and selecting layers

▶ Stepping through the History palette

- -

Some guy named Odell Shepard said, "Memory is what makes you wonder what you've forgotten." I don't know anything about this Odell fellow — he was just lucky enough to get picked up by one of those books of quotations that are supposed to make you sound like a halfway-intelligent human being without really trying. Not having met Odell — Odie, I call him — I can only guess that he was talking about that feeling you get (usually when you're in bed, trying to sleep, or when you're on the way home from work and it's too late to turn back) that you've forgotten something that's pretty much going to send your life spinning into a state of absolute chaos. In fact, I believe that feeling is known as the Odie Syndrome.

Well, I can't help you with every aspect of your life, but I can help you with Photoshop. Suppose, for example, that you wake up at 2 a.m. with the dreaded suspicion that you've forgotten an important Photoshop shortcut.

You'd just have to give up on your technological pursuits and take up beet farming. But thanks to this chapter, people like you can again live happy and productive lives because all of the most important Photoshop shortcuts are contained in these pages. A few minutes of reading, and order is restored.

Displaying and Hiding the Toolbox and Palettes

Tab

I'm ashamed to admit this, but there was a time when I wanted to view an image on-screen all by itself, without the Toolbox. I had no idea how to do it. I even called the Photoshop product manager and asked him how to do it. He told me it was impossible.

Naturally, he was wrong. It was possible then, and it's possible now. Just press the Tab key. The Toolbox, the status bar, the Options bar, and all the palettes disappear, leaving just you and the image. To bring the Toolbox, status bar, and palettes back, press Tab again. To make the Toolbox, status bar, and palettes flash crazily on-screen and off, press Tab over and over again until your finger gets numb. I'm not sure why you'd want to do this, but I like to spell out all the options.

If you want to hide the palettes but keep the Toolbox, the Options bar, and status bar visible, by the way, press Shift+Tab. Press Shift+Tab again to bring the palettes back.

If you have a dialog box open or an option in a palette is active (highlighted), Tab and Shift+Tab take you to the next option box or move you back one option box, respectively. But after you close the dialog box or press Enter (Return on a Mac) to apply the palette option, Tab and Shift+Tab control your palettes and Toolbox once again.

F6, F7, F8

Press F6 to hide or display the Color palette, and F7 to hide or display the Layers palette. To display the Navigator palette, press F8, which brings up the Info palette. Then click on the Navigator palette tab. Press F6, F7, or F8 twice to hide each of the above mentioned palettes (Color or Layers).

Changing an Option Box Value

Up arrow, down arrow

Enter a new value in the option box or use the up or down arrow key to raise or lower the value by 1. Press Shift+up arrow or Shift+down arrow to raise or lower the value by 10, respectively. Then press Enter (Return on a Mac) again to accept the new value.

Scrolling and Zooming

Spacebar

Press the spacebar to temporarily access the Hand tool. As long as the spacebar is down, the Hand tool is available. Spacebar+drag to scroll the image.

Ctrl (⌘)+spacebar, Alt (Option)+spacebar

To get to the zoom in cursor, press Ctrl+spacebar (⌘+spacebar on a Mac). Pressing Alt+spacebar (Option+spacebar on a Mac) gets you the zoom out cursor. This means that you can magnify the image at any time by Ctrl+spacebar+clicking (⌘+spacebar+click on a Mac). To zoom out, Alt +spacebar+click (Option+spacebar+click on a Mac). You can also Ctrl+spacebar+drag (⌘+spacebar+click on a Mac) to marquee an area and magnify it so that it takes up the entire image window.

Ctrl++ (plus), Ctrl+– (minus) (⌘++ (plus), ⌘+– (minus) on a Mac)

Another way to magnify or reduce the image is to press Ctrl++(plus sign) (⌘++(plus sign) on a Mac) to zoom in or Ctrl+–(minus sign) (⌘+–(minus sign) on a Mac) to zoom out.

Double-click on the hand icon

To zoom the image so that you can see the whole thing on your monitor, double-click on the Hand Tool icon in the Toolbox or press Ctrl+0 (⌘+0 on a Mac).

Double-click on the zoom icon

To restore the image to the 100% (Actual Pixels) zoom factor, double-click on the Zoom tool icon or press Ctrl+Alt+0 (zero) (⌘+Option+0 on a Mac).

Shift+Enter (Shift+Return on a Mac)

When you change the zoom factor by using the magnification box in the lower-left corner of the image window, press Shift+Enter (Shift+Return on a Mac) instead of Enter (Return on a Mac) after you enter a new zoom value. That way, the option box remains active after Photoshop zooms your image. If you need to further magnify or reduce your image, just enter a new zoom value from the keyboard. When you have the image at the magnification you want, press Enter (Return on a Mac) to finalize things.

This trick also works when you're using the magnification box in the Navigator palette.

Changing the Brush Size

Left bracket ([)

For the default round and fuzzy round brushes, press [(left bracket) to reduce the brush size in the following increments: 1 pixel increments to a size 10 pixel brush, 10 pixel increments to a size 100 pixel brush, 25 pixels to a size 200 pixel brush, 50 pixels to a size 300 pixel brush, 100 pixels to a size 900 pixel brush, and finally it jumps to the maximum of a 999 pixel brush.

Right bracket (])

For the default round and fuzzy round brushes, press] (right bracket) to increase the brush size by the same increments listed in the preceding "Left bracket([)" section.

Shift+[, Shift+]

Shift+[(left bracket) reduces the hardness of a brush in 25 percent increments. Shift+] (right bracket) increases the hardness in 25 percent increments.

Shift+Right-click (Shift+Control+click on a Mac)

To make the Brushes palette appear under your cursor, press Shift+Right+click (Shift+Control+click on a Mac) on your canvas.

Changing Opacity

1, . . . , 9, 0

To change the Opacity setting for a selected painting or editing tool, just press a number key — 1 equals 10% Opacity, 9 equals 90%, and 0 equals 100%. To enter a more specific value — say, 82 — just type the number quickly.

If a selection tool or the Move tool is active, pressing a number key changes the opacity of the active layer.

Creating Straight Lines

Shift+click

To create a straight line with any of the painting or editing tools, click at one end of the line and Shift+click at the other. Photoshop connects the two points with a straight line.

Click with Polygon Lasso, Alt+click (Option+click on a Mac) with regular Lasso and Magnetic Lasso

The Polygon Lasso creates straight-sided selections; you just click to set the first point in your selection and keep clicking to create additional points.

When working with the regular Lasso tool, you can temporarily switch to the Polygon Lasso by Alt+clicking (Option+click on a Mac). Alt+click (Option+click on a Mac) to set the first point in the selection and keep Alt+clicking (Option+click on a Mac) until you finish drawing the desired outline.

When working with the Magnetic Lasso, press Alt (Option on a Mac) and click with the mouse to get the Polygon Lasso. Release the Alt key (Option key on a Mac) and drag momentarily to reset to the Magnetic Lasso.

However, don't use this approach when you want to add or subtract from an existing selection marquee. When you have an active selection marquee, pressing Alt (Option on a Mac) subtracts from the selection instead of switching you between lasso tools. So use the Polygon tool to add or subtract straight-sided areas from a selection.

Click with the Pen tool

To create straight segments with the Pen tool, click at the beginning of the path to create the first anchor point and keep clicking until the path is complete. To end the path, press the Ctrl key (⌘ key on a Mac) to access the Direct Selection tool and click away from the path.

Alt+click (Option+click on a Mac) with the Freeform and Magnetic Pen tools

To create straight segments with the Freeform Pen, press the Alt key (Option key on a Mac), making sure to keep the mouse button pressed, and then click to create a point. Keep clicking until you finish drawing the straight segments. Press the mouse down, release the Alt (Option on a Mac) key, and continue dragging. The mouse returns to the Freeform Pen.

When working with the Magnetic option of the Freeform Pen, Alt+click (Option+click on a Mac) to set anchor points for the straight segments. To return to the Magnetic Pen, release the Alt key (Option key on a Mac), click again, and continue moving the mouse.

Adding to, Subtracting from, and Reselecting Selection Outlines

Shift+drag, Shift+click

To select an additional area of your image without deselecting the part that is currently selected, Shift+drag around the new area with a Lasso or Marquee tool or Shift+click with the magic wand. You can also press Shift and choose Select⇨Color Range.

Alt+drag, Alt+click (Option+drag, Option+click on a Mac)

To deselect an area of the selection, Alt+drag (Option+drag on a Mac) around it with a Lasso or Marquee tool or Alt+click (Option+click on a Mac) with the Magic Wand. You can also press Alt (Option on a Mac) and choose the Select⇨Color Range command.

Shift+Alt+drag, Shift+Alt+click (Shift+Option+drag, Shift+Option+click on a Mac)

To retain the intersection of the existing selection and the new outline you draw with a Lasso or Marquee tool, Shift+Alt+drag (Shift+Option+drag on a Mac) with the tool. To retain an area of continuous color inside a selection, Shift+Alt+click (Shift+Option+click on a Mac) with the Magic Wand.

Ctrl+Shift+D (⌘+Shift+D on a Mac)

To reselect your last selection, press Ctrl+Shift+D (⌘+Shift+D on a Mac).

Moving, Nudging, and Cloning

Ctrl (⌘ on a Mac)

To move selections and layers, use the Move tool. To temporarily access the Move tool when any tool is active, press and hold Ctrl (⌘ on a Mac). This shortcut doesn't work with the pen tools (all the various flavors), the Hand tool, the Slice and Slice Select tools, the Path Component Selection tool, the Direct Selection tool, or any of the shape tools.

Arrow

To nudge a selection one pixel, press one of the arrow keys with the Move tool selected. Or press Ctrl (⌘ on a Mac) and an arrow key with any tool except those I previously mentioned.

Shift+arrow

To nudge a selection 10 pixels, select the Move tool and press Shift with an arrow key. Or select any tool but the ones I previously mentioned and press Ctrl+Shift (⌘+Shift on a Mac) with an arrow key.

Alt+dragging, Alt+arrow, Shift+Alt+arrow (Option+dragging, Option+arrow, Shift+Option+arrow on a Mac)

To clone a selection and move the clone, Alt+drag (Option+drag on a Mac) the selection with the Move tool. You can also press Alt (Option on a Mac) with an arrow key to clone a selection and nudge it one pixel or press Shift+Alt+arrow key (Shift+Option+arrow key on a Mac) to clone and nudge 10 pixels.

With any other tool but, yes you guessed it, the ones I just listed, you can accomplish the same cloning feats by pressing and holding the Ctrl key (⌘ on a Mac) with the other keys. (Pressing Ctrl (⌘ on a Mac) temporarily accesses the Move tool, remember?)

Drag with a Selection tool

To move a selection outline without moving anything inside the selection, just drag it with a Marquee tool, Lasso tool, or the Magic Wand. You can also press the arrow key or Shift+arrow key to nudge the selection outline in 1-pixel and 10-pixel increments, respectively. This works with any tool except the Move tool, Slice, Slice Select tools, Path Component Selection tool, Direct Selection tool, or any of the pen tools.

Ctrl/Cmd with a shape tool

Pressing Ctrl (⌘ on a Mac) with any of the shape tools brings up the Path Component Selection tool, letting you quickly move shapes and lines.

Filling a Selection

Ctrl+Backspace (⌘+Delete on a Mac)

To fill a selection with the background color, press Ctrl+Backspace (⌘+Delete on a Mac). If the selection exists on the Background layer, you can also press Backspace (Delete on a Mac) to accomplish the same thing. However, if the selection is on a layer or is floating on the Background layer, pressing

Backspace (Delete on a Mac) wipes out the selection instead of filling it. So, pressing Ctrl+Backspace (⌘+Delete on a Mac) instead of Backspace (Delete on a Mac) to fill your selections is a good idea.

Alt+Backspace (Option+Delete on a Mac)

To fill any selection with the foreground color, press Alt+Backspace (Option+Delete on a Mac).

Shift+Backspace (Shift+Delete on a Mac)

Press Shift+Backspace (Shift+Delete on a Mac) to bring up the Fill dialog box, which lets you fill a selection with all kinds of stuff.

Ctrl+Alt+Backspace (⌘+Option+Delete on a Mac)

Press Ctrl+Alt+Backspace (⌘+Option+Delete on a Mac) to fill the selection with the source state identified in the History palette.

Making, Switching, and Selecting Layers

Ctrl+J, Ctrl+Shift+J (⌘+J, ⌘+Shift+J on a Mac)

To clone a selection and place the clone on a new layer, press Ctrl+J (⌘+J on a Mac). To cut a selection and place the selection on a new layer, press Ctrl+Shift+J (⌘+Shift+J on a Mac).

Alt+[, Alt+] (Option +[, Option+] on a Mac)

To activate the layer below the one that's currently active, press Alt+[(left bracket) (Option+[(left bracket) on a Mac). To activate the next layer up, press Alt+] (right bracket) (Option+] (right bracket) on a Mac).

Alt+right-click, Ctrl+Alt+right-click (Option+Control+click, ⌘+Option+Control+click on a Mac)

To activate the layer belonging to a certain image, Alt+right-click (Option+Control+click on a Mac) on that image with the Move tool. Or Ctrl+Alt+right-click (⌘+ Option +Control+click on a Mac) with any other tool except the Hand tool.

Ctrl+click (⌘+click on a Mac) on layer name

To generate a selection outline from the contents of a layer, Ctrl+click (⌘+click on a Mac) the layer name in the Layers palette. You can use any tool to do the job.

Stepping through the History Palette

Ctrl+Alt+Z, Ctrl+Shift+Z (⌘+Option+Z, ⌘+Shift+Z on a Mac)

To step backward one history state at a time, press Ctrl+Alt+Z (⌘+Option+Z on a Mac). To move forward one state at a time, press Ctrl+Shift+Z (⌘+Shift+Z on a Mac). Keyboard equivalents can be changed via the Edit➪Preferences➪General menu.

So Many Shortcuts, So Little Time

The preceding tips don't address all of the many Photoshop shortcuts. For some additional time-savers, be sure to check out the Cheat Sheets at the front of this book.

Chapter 21

Ten Amusing Ways to Mess Up a Loved One's Face

*N*ormally, we're all pretty fond of our loved ones. But on that one day when a loved one gets kind of pesky — or two days during leap years — it's nice to have Photoshop within easy reach. So, are you mad at your boyfriend for going to Paris with a childhood sweetheart? Just scan his face and while away the hours modifying it in a way he won't soon forget. Peeved at your sister for snagging all of Aunt Rowena's multimillion-dollar inheritance? Open Sis in Photoshop and distort her as you please. No need to get angry. Just warp your loved one's face, print it, and send it off to your local newspaper or tack it on neighborhood telephone poles.

But, alas, I'm one of those rare people who have never experienced anger or resentment. So instead, I'll take a stab at the absolute strangers shown in Figure 21-1, who, as I understand it, were actresses, captured in the moment of auditioning for a commercial. Although I'm not sure they were actually cast in parts, in tribute to their obviously stirring performances, I'm going to trod heavily upon them in the following sections.

Figure 21-1:
Two faces that cry out "Muck me up in Photoshop!"

Creating the Movie Starlet Glow

Here's how to create that soft face-flaw-forgiving glow that the movie stars of yesteryear were so fond of. Check out the magic in Figure 21-2:

1. **Select L̲ayer⇨Ne̲w⇨Layer via C̲opy or press Ctrl+J (⌘+J on a Mac).**

   This creates a layer which looks just like the background.

2. **Choose Fil̲ter⇨Blur⇨Gaussian Blur.**

   Select a pretty high radius. Try 5.0 pixels.

3. **Lower the Opacity in the Layers Palette to 70%.**

   This enables the original image to show through a bit to lessen the blurry effect.

4. **In the Layers palette, change the blend mode to lighten.**

   Doing this applies the glowy, blurry effect only to areas in the layer that are lighter than the underlying original image.

Figure 21-2:
Applying the
soft glow in
Photoshop
is a lot less
messy than
smearing
petroleum
jelly on the
camera
lens.

Turning the Face into a Button

Find out how to really push someone's buttons (see Figure 21-3) by following the easy steps below:

1. **Choose Layer➪New➪Layer via Copy or press Ctrl+J (⌘+J on a Mac).**

   You have a layer which is a duplicate of the background image.

2. **Choose Layer➪Layer Style➪Bevel and Emboss.**

   Here's where you want to play with the various settings to get the effect you want. I chose the following:

   - **Style:** Emboss (adds bevels to give the effect that the element is raised off the page)
   - **Technique:** Chisel Soft (provides a soft definition to the edge of the bevel)
   - **Depth:** 200% Up
   - **Size:** 50 px
   - **Soften:** 2 px

I left the Shading at the default settings. By the way, you can use the same method to create buttons for Web pages — a tad more practical use of this technique. Create buttons from selections made from images, patterns, gradients, or solid color.

Figure 21-3:
Here's a button just begging to be pushed.

Creating a Painted Masterpiece

So you say you're not artistic? Well, nobody will believe you when you show them a work of art like Figure 21-4.

1. **Choose Layer⇨New⇨Layer via Copy or press Ctrl+J (⌘+J on a Mac).**

   You're getting to be quite the pro at this command.

2. **Choose Filter⇨Blur⇨Gaussian Blur.**

   Set the radius to around 6.0 pixels.

Figure 21-4:
Just think of
what
Leonardo
could have
done with
some
Photoshop
filters.

3. **Set the Opacity to 80% and the Mode to Darken.**

   This enables the original image to peek through and applies the blurry effect only to areas in the layer that are darker than the underlying background image.

4. **Choose Filter➪Texture➪Texturizer.**

   Select your desired texture, scaling, relief, and light source direction. I chose Canvas, with a scaling of 150%, a relief of 4, and the light from the top left.

In addition to pictures of loved ones, this technique also works especially nicely with color landscape photos. So dust off the old travel snapshots and go to town. And if you think your masterpiece is deserving, add a frame around it by using the technique I describe in "Framing the Goofy Pose" later in this chapter.

Giving the Face a Bath

If you're only slightly piqued at your loved one, you may want to make the face appear under water, as shown in Figure 21-5. Here's how to submerge the image:

1. **Select the image any which way you want.**

   No special constraints this time.

2. **Choose Filter⇨Distort⇨Ripple.**

   There are lots of great face-mucking features under the Filter⇨Distort submenu. Check them out when you have a spare moment or two.

3. **Select Medium from the Size pop-up menu in the Ripple dialog box.**

   The Small option isn't enough, and the Large option is too much. As with the baby bear in the famous story — I believe Snow White and the three little pigs is the one — Medium is just right.

4. **Enter any old Amount value you want and press Enter (Return on a Mac).**

   In Figure 21-5, I applied an Amount value of 300 to the first image and 999 — the maximum setting — to the second image.

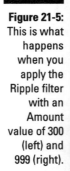

Figure 21-5:
This is what happens when you apply the Ripple filter with an Amount value of 300 (left) and 999 (right).

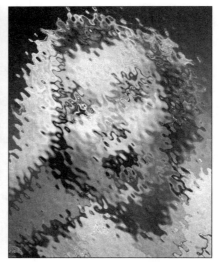

Stretching the Face This Way and That

Next, let's try out some manual distortion techniques? Figure 21-6 shows how to distort an image using Transform and Free Transform commands. The following steps tell you what the figure leaves out.

1. **Select something.**

   Again, select what you want. I can't make all the decisions for you. But you have to select something or you can't access the command I'm about to instruct you to use. If you want to apply the command to your entire image, press Ctrl+A (⌘+A on a Mac) or choose Select⇨All.

2. **Press Ctrl+H (⌘+H on a Mac).**

   Photoshop hides the selection outline. Otherwise, the outline just gets in your way.

3. **Choose Edit⇨Free Transform or press Ctrl+T (⌘+T on a Mac).**

   The Free Transform command surrounds the selection with a box and displays square handles on the sides and at the corners. With the Free Transform box, you can resize, rotate, skew, distort, and apply perspective effects to your selection.

Figure 21-6: The Free Transform command lets you bend, pull, rotate, and otherwise stretch a selection in whatever way you please.

To scale (resize) the selection, drag any handle. Shift+drag to scale proportionately, and Alt+drag (Option+drag on a Mac) to scale symmetrically around the center of the selection. To rotate the selection, move the cursor outside the marquee until you see a curved, double-headed arrow, and then drag. To move the selection, drag inside the marquee.

But to really have some fun, use the following techniques: Ctrl+drag (⌘+drag on a Mac) any handle to distort the image freely. Ctrl+Shift+drag (⌘+Shift+drag on a Mac) a side handle to skew the image. And Ctrl+Shift+Alt+drag (⌘+Shift+Option+drag on a Mac) a corner handle to apply perspective effects.

Be patient when working with the Transform command — Photoshop sometimes takes a while to generate the effects of your drags. If you don't like the outcome of a drag, just press the Esc key or press Ctrl+Z (⌘+Z on a Mac) to undo it. You can now also click the Cancel button (the X icon) in the Options bar.

4. **After you've distorted the image to your satisfaction, press Enter (Return on a Mac).**

   You can now also click the Commit button (the check icon) in the Options bar.

Figure 21-6 shows two lovely effects created by tugging this way and that on my crying woman. In the left example, I skewed and distorted the image, giving Miss Crocodile Tears shoulders that a linebacker would envy. In the right example, I Ctrl+Shift+Alt+dragged (⌘+Shift+Option+dragged on a Mac) to create an infant-looking-up-from-a-crib view.

The Edit⇨Transform submenu contains individual commands for distorting, skewing, scaling, rotating, and adding perspective to the image. When you choose one of these Transform commands, you get the transform box as you do when using Free Transform. Just drag the handles to apply the effect — no Alt, Ctrl, Shift key (Option, ⌘, Shift key on a Mac) combinations required. If you want to apply a different effect, you can choose the desired effect from the Edit⇨Transform submenu. I usually prefer the Free Transform command — it's one-stop-shopping for transforming.

You can choose the Flip Horizontal and Flip Vertical commands, also found in the Transform submenu, when you are in the process of transforming your image using the Free Transform command.

Applying the Nuclear Sunburn Effect

Phew, that's enough of that manual stuff. You're entitled to automation, and automation is exactly what you're going to get. This next effect takes a different approach. Rather than moving the pixels around, the Nuclear Sunburn effect relies on commands that change the pixels' colors. As you can see in Figure 21-7, the face takes on a kind of eerie luminescence.

Figure 21-7:
Choose the Solarize filter and the Auto Levels command (left) and then press Ctrl+I (⌘+I on a Mac).

1. **Select an image.**

   Make your selection as detailed or as imprecise as you like.

2. **Choose Filter⇨Stylize⇨Solarize.**

   Sounds like an exciting command, huh? Actually, by itself, Solarize is pretty dull. It makes the black pixels black, the medium pixels medium, and the white pixels black again. Big whoop. But have no fear, we're going to spruce things up a little.

3. **Choose Image⇨Adjust⇨Auto Levels.**

   Photoshop lightens the gray pixels and makes them white, as shown in the first example in Figure 21-7. The areas that were previously either dark or light are now dark; the medium areas are now light.

4. **Choose Image⇨Adjust⇨Invert or just press Ctrl+I (⌘+I on a Mac).**

   This command inverts the image, turning the black pixels white and the white pixels black, as in a photo negative. The finished result is shown in the second example of Figure 21-7.

Applying the Cubist Look

I create this effect with the 3D filter. This filter isn't the greatest; for example, it doesn't map all sides of the shape. But, hey, this isn't a 3D drawing program either! Take it for whatever it's worth. You can check it out in Figure 21-8.

1. **Select an image.**

   In this case, I used the lasso (see Chapter 12) to select the face and hand which now looks like it was surgically attached to her face. Ah, the wonders of modern plastic surgery.

2. **Double-click the Background in the Layers palette to convert it to a layer.**

3. **Choose Select⇨Inverse and then press Backspace (Delete on a Mac).**

   This gets rid of the background and leaves the area around the selection transparent.

4. **Choose Select⇨Deselect.**

5. **Choose Filter⇨Render⇨3D Transform.**

   A dialog box containing a small toolbox appears, enabling you to choose various mapping types — sphere, cube, or cylinder.

6. **Select the Cube tool in the Toolbox and drag a cube around the whole image.**

   You can resize the cube by dragging on the cube's handle with the white arrow. To move the cube itself, drag on a side of the cube.

7. **When the cube is positioned the way you want, select the Trackball tool (black circle with a curved arrow) in the toolbox and drag the cube to rotate it.**

8. **Use the Pan Camera tool (to the left of the Trackball) to move the image if needed.**

   You can also use the Field of View and Dolly sliders to adjust how large the image appears against the background.

9. **Press Enter (Return on a Mac).**

   Photoshop may take a couple of minutes to render the image, so be patient.

Stamping the Face in a Marble Haze

A fairly weak name for a wonderful effect. The following steps alternatively lighten and darken the image, utilizing a cloud pattern that ends up looking a lot like marble, as you can see in Figure 21-9.

1. **Select an image.**

2. **Choose Filter⇨Render⇨Difference Clouds.**

   Of the two Clouds filters, this one is the more exciting. It blends Photoshop-generated clouds with the selected image using the Difference mode. The first example in Figure 21-9 shows the result of this single-shot filter.

3. **Press Ctrl+F (⌘+F on a Mac) to reapply the Difference Clouds filter.**

   Photoshop blends the clouds with the image. Things are getting more mottled.

4. **Repeat Step 3 three times.**

5. **Choose Image⇨Adjust⇨Auto Levels.**

   Looking a little dark? Auto Levels brings the colors back to life.

6. **Apply the Unsharp Mask filter.**

   An Amount value of 50% and a Radius of 0.5 should bring back some of the detail. The second example of Figure 21-9 shows how the face now appears emblazoned on a dense, marble wall. At least, that's what the image looks like to me. Feel free to draw your own conclusions.

Figure 21-9:
The result of choosing the Difference Clouds command once (left) and five times (right).

Effecting a Total Molecular Breakdown

This technique reduces your image to a bunch of colored shapes and then blends them with the original image to form something truly other-worldly, as shown in Figure 21-10.

1. **Select an image.**

2. **Choose Filter⇨Pixelate⇨Crystallize, enter** 30, **and press Enter (Return on a Mac).**

   Nice words, Pixelate and Crystallize, but what do they mean? Like most of the commands under the Filter⇨Pixelate submenu, Crystallize subdivides the image into blocks of color. In this case, the blocks resemble little particles of stained glass, as in the first example in Figure 21-10.

3. **Choose Edit⇨Fade Crystallize.**

   The Fade command lets you mix the filter effect with the unfiltered original by using the same blending modes and Opacity slider you find in the Layers palette.

4. **Choose the Difference option from the Mode pop-up menu and press Enter (Return on a Mac).**

   Photoshop uses the stained-glass pattern to invert the face.

Figure 21-10: After applying the Crystallize command to my image, I used the Fade command to mix the new image with the original using the Difference mode (right).

 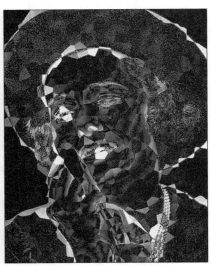

5. **Press Ctrl+L (⌘+L on a Mac) and use the options in the Levels dialog box to lighten the image.**

As things stand now, the image is way too dark to print. I lightened the image on the right side of Figure 21-10 by setting the three Input Levels values to 0, 2.30, and 170, respectively. Press Enter (Return on a Mac) to apply the changes.

6. **Apply the Unsharp Mask filter.**

   I used an Amount value of 100% and a Radius of 0.5, but I encourage you to sharpen according to your personal tastes.

Framing the Goofy Pose

Sometimes, you're lucky enough to dig up a photograph of your unruly loved one that's embarrassing all on its own — no special effects required. In that case, all you need to do is add a little finishing touch, such as the wood frame or vignette effect shown in Figure 21-11.

The Actions palette contains prerecorded macros (sets of commands) that apply the effects shown in Figure 21-11. Here's how to create the wood frame effect by using the Actions palette:

1. **Make sure your image is at least 100 pixels wide and tall.**

   If you aren't sure, choose Image⇨Image Size and check the dimensions. (For more info on sizing, see Chapter 4.)

2. **Choose Window⇨Show Actions to display the Actions palette.**

3. **Click on the right-pointing gray triangle next to the Default Actions folder to display a list of actions.**

   If the arrow is pointing down, the Actions will already be displayed.

4. **Select the Wood Frame-50 pixel action.**

5. **Choose Play from the Actions palette pop-up menu or click on the white triangle at the bottom of the Actions palette.**

   Photoshop automatically starts applying the steps to create a wood frame around your image.

6. **When you see the dialog box saying your image must be a minimum of 100 pixels wide and tall, press Enter (Return on a Mac).**

7. **If you see a dialog box stating that changing modes will affect layer compositing, choose Don't Flatten.**

   Photoshop creates the faux wood frame and places it on a separate layer.

Figure 21-11:
You can
easily create
a wood
frame of
vignette
effect using
the Actions
palette.

To create a rectangular vignette, as shown in the right-hand example in Figure 21-11, follow similar steps:

1. **Select the face with the Rectangular Marquee tool.**

2. **Select and play the Vignette (selection) action from the Actions palette.**

3. **When you see a dialog box, press Enter (Return on a Mac).**

   As Photoshop applies the vignette effect, a dialog box appears enabling you to apply more or less of a feather radius. Just press Enter (Return on a Mac) to accept the default settings. Photoshop creates the vignette and places it on a separate layer.

Photoshop places the wood frame or vignette effect on a separate layer. If you don't like what you see, drag the layer to the trash can icon at the bottom of the Layers palette. You can't undo the wood frame or vignette using Ctrl+Z (⌘+Z on a Mac) because Photoshop has actually applied a series of commands to create the effect. You can undo only the last command in the series, which doesn't get you back to your original image. You can, however, get your original back by using the trusty History palette (for more on the History palette see Chapter 11).

Well, that should do it. If you don't have the anger worked out of your system by now, I suggest counseling. Or better yet, you kids kiss and make up. That's what my mate and I always do.

Chapter 22

Ten Things to Do with Your Photoshop Masterpiece

*A*fter you finish creating your image in Photoshop, you may experience a hint of letdown. I mean, now that you're done with the image, what do you do with it? You can't just sit there and look at it on your screen for the rest of your life.

Well, that is an option, I suppose, but certainly not your only option. Photoshop is one of the key programs used by graphics professionals, and only a few of said professionals create images just to sit around and stare at them all day. More often, these images have specific purposes and are used in specific ways.

This chapter examines a few options. Some of them cost money, and some involve the use of other programs that I don't explain in this book. All of the following options provide food for future thought.

Printing and Dispersing

Just about everyone who has a computer also owns a printer. Assuming that you do too, make sure that the image fits onto a sheet of paper and print it out (refer to Chapter 7 if you need help). Then you can photocopy the image and hand it out to everyone you know or stick it in an envelope and mail it to your grandmother. Digital images are a welcomed gift any time during the year.

Framing Your Work of Art

Okay, the preceding option was obvious. This one isn't, and it's expensive to boot. If you've created just about the best-looking image you could possibly imagine, you can actually print it and frame it. The image needs to have a resolution of at least 150 ppi, and you probably want it to be fairly large to justify the expense (although many classic works of art are only a few inches tall). And, of course, the image should be full color, RGB. (See Chapter 5 for more on RGB and other color modes.)

Desktop color printers have improved by leaps and bounds in the past couple years. If you happen to own a decent desktop color printer, like one of the Epson or Hewlett-Packard models, you may be able to get a print of high enough quality to be frameworthy. I suggest investing in some nice, glossy paper. It costs anywhere from 50 cents to $2 a sheet. Many printer manufacturers make their own paper, which is specially formulated to work well with their particular printer. But if you can't find it, generic glossy paper works fine. Then just make sure to print in the highest resolution your printer offers. You may want to take a peek at the manual that came with your printer. You never know what kind of useful advice the manufacturer may offer.

If you don't own a decent color printer, call around to a few service bureaus in your neck of the woods and find one that can print to a dye-sublimation printer. A dye-sub printer creates images that look just like photographs — no little dots, like you see in newspaper photos, just smooth colors. You can't reproduce from dye-sub prints, but they look great. If you think your masterpiece deserves an even better print, look into Iris prints. They are a bit more expensive than dye-sub prints, but the quality is top notch. Images to be printed on an Iris printer should be 300 ppi and CMYK color. (See Chapter 5 for more on CMYK and other color modes.) Professionals use them for proofing to make sure that the colors in the printed image look the way they want.

A dye-sub printout will probably cost you from, say, $10 to $20. An Iris print will run $25 to $40. But provided the image looks good, the results for both prints can be fantastic.

When you go to get the image framed, make sure to ask for UV-protected glass, which also runs around $20 to $30. Most service bureaus spray Iris prints with UV spray to protect them. Dye-sub prints are very sensitive and can fade when exposed to direct or even indirect light, so hang the piece away from a window.

Placing the Image into PageMaker, InDesign, or QuarkXPress

Adobe PageMaker, Adobe InDesign, and QuarkXPress are three popular page-layout programs. They enable you to combine text and graphics to create multipage documents such as brochures, newsletters, reports, catalogs, magazines, and even books. This book, for example, was laid out entirely in QuarkXPress. (For more information on these three programs, check out *PageMaker 6.5 For Dummies,* Internet Edition, by Galen Gruman; and *QuarkXPress 4 For Dummies,* by Barbara Assadi and Galen Gruman, with John Cruise — both published by IDG Books Worldwide, Inc.)

If you want to use a Photoshop image in one of these programs, save it in the TIFF format with LZW compression. (See Chapter 6 for more on file formats.) Then import the file from disk into PageMaker or InDesign by choosing the Place command or Ctrl+D (⌘+D on a Mac), found under the File menu, or into QuarkXPress using the Get Picture command, Ctrl+E (⌘+E on a Mac), also found under the File menu. (Both commands are found inside the respective programs, not inside Photoshop.)

You can move the image on the page, run text around it, and print the final pages, all inside PageMaker, InDesign, or QuarkXPress. So, unless you want to further modify the image, you have no reason to return to Photoshop. Although you can change the dimensions and rotate or skew the image in PageMaker, InDesign, and QuarkXPress, it is always best to do this in Photoshop rather than in your page layout program. Your file prints much faster and has less potential for snafus.

Whatever you do, don't copy the image in Photoshop and paste it into PageMaker, InDesign, or QuarkXPress. When you copy the image, it is sent to the Windows Clipboard, which converts the image to the Windows Metafile format. And on the Mac, copying the image is the same as importing the image in the PICT format, and neither PageMaker nor QuarkXPress works well with PICT. Trust me, you won't be happy with the results of the conversion.

Placing the Image into Illustrator, FreeHand, or CorelDraw

Adobe Illustrator, Macromedia FreeHand, and CorelDraw are graphics programs like Photoshop, but instead of enabling you to edit images, they let you create smooth-line artwork. Information graphics, logos, maps, architectural plans, general artwork, and single-page documents, such as flyers and ads, are all projects ideally suited to Illustrator, FreeHand, and CorelDraw.

All three programs let you import images. In the case of Illustrator, save your Photoshop image in the Photoshop EPS format. Then import it from disk by choosing the Place command inside Illustrator. For FreeHand, go ahead and save the image as a TIFF file. Then choose the Import command or Ctrl+R (⌘+R on a Mac) from inside FreeHand. To import an image into CorelDraw, you can use either the TIFF or Photoshop EPS format. Place the image into your CorelDraw document by using the File⇨Import command or Ctrl+I (⌘+I on a Mac) inside CorelDraw.

After placing the image, you can combine it with smooth-line artwork or integrate it into a single-page document. The IDG Books Worldwide, Inc., production staff used Illustrator to label Figure 2-1 (see Chapter 2) and the other figures that required labels in this book. It's not possible to label the figures inside Photoshop — which is where they all originated — because small text in Photoshop is jagged and illegible. QuarkXPress, meanwhile, is great for creating long text documents but not so good at handling little bits of text here and there.

Here's how labeled figures such as Figure 2-1 got onto their respective pages:

1. **I saved the image in the TIFF format.**

   Then I copied the TIFF file to disk and sent it to IDG Books Worldwide, Inc., in Indiana.

2. **A member of the IDG Books crackerjack production staff placed the images into Illustrator.**

   A production artist then created all the labels and saved the Illustrator document in the EPS format. (See Chapter 6 for more on file formats.) EPS is the best format for smooth-line artwork and high-resolution text. It also retains the image.

3. **Inside QuarkXPress, another production artist imported the Illustrator EPS graphic.**

   The layout artist then positioned the EPS graphic and ran the text around it, as you see the page now.

4. **The final QuarkXPress document was saved to disk and shipped to the commercial printer.**

    The printer printed the pages and reproduced the pages onto the paper you're reading now.

How's that for a start-to-finish examination of how this process works? And, just in case you thought I was spilling out some trade secrets, just about every publisher creates books this way these days. It's a desktop world.

Pasting the Image into PowerPoint

Microsoft PowerPoint is a popular presentation program used for creating slides and on-screen presentations for board meetings, product demonstrations, and kiosks. Photoshop is a great tool for creating backgrounds for these presentations or refining head shots that may appear on the slides.

Because PowerPoint does most of its work on-screen, it's acceptable to transfer the image from Photoshop via the Clipboard. While inside Photoshop, just select the portion of the image you want to use, copy it by pressing Ctrl+C (⌘+C on a Mac), switch to PowerPoint, and paste the selection by pressing Ctrl+V (⌘+V on a Mac). If, however, your image looks less than desirable, try saving the image in a file format that PowerPoint accepts, such as TIFF, and then importing the file into PowerPoint.

However, this recommendation holds only if you're creating an on-screen presentation or plan to print the presentation on a non-PostScript printer. If you want to print overheads on a color PostScript printer, don't use the Clipboard to place the images into your presentation program. Instead, import the image into PowerPoint as a TIFF file.

As you can in page layout programs, you can move the image around, change the dimensions, and wrap text around it. If you plan on displaying the presentation on-screen, you want to give some thought to the file size of the image. For example, if you intend for the image to serve as a background for a presentation that takes up an entire 13-inch monitor, the image should be 640 x 480 pixels. A good size for a head shot may be 300 x 200 pixels. Experiment to find the file sizes that work best for you.

Making a Desktop Pattern

You know that pattern that appears in the background behind all the icons on your Windows desktop or at the Mac Finder? You can create your own custom background using Photoshop.

For PC users, here's what you do:

1. **Create your image.**

   If you want a single image to fill your entire screen, make the image the same size as the Desktop Area setting in the Windows Desktop Properties dialog box. To check the setting, right-click anywhere on the desktop, choose the Properties command to display the Display Properties dialog box, and click on the Settings tab. If the setting is 640 x 480, for example, make your image 640 x 480 pixels. Set the image resolution to 72 ppi.

2. **Save your image in the BMP format.**

   When you save the image, be sure the File Format is Windows.

3. **Right-click anywhere on the Windows desktop to display the Desktop Properties dialog box.**

   That's assuming that you don't already have the dialog box open from Step 1.

4. **Click on the Background tab.**

5. **Click on the Browse button in the Wallpaper section of the dialog box.**

   Windows displays a dialog box showing all your drives, directories, and files.

6. **Select your image in the dialog box and press Enter.**

   You should see your image name selected in the Wallpaper drop-down menu.

7. **Choose a Display option.**

   If you choose the Tile radio button, your image is repeated across the screen. If you choose the Center button, the image is centered on the screen.

8. **Click on Apply.**

   Windows applies your new wallpaper to your screen without closing the Display Properties dialog box. If you don't like what you see, you can change the Display option or choose another image to use as your wallpaper (wallpaper images must be in the BMP format). You can also play with the settings on the Appearance tab to change the color of the labels under your desktop icons so that they coordinate with the new wallpaper.

9. **Press Enter to close the dialog box.**

For Mac users, here's what you do:

1. **Go to the Apple menu and slide down to Control Panels and then slide over to Appearance.**

   These are the controls that affect the way your screen looks.

2. **Click on the Desktop tab at the top of the Appearance control panel.**

   This displays a window with a scroll bar that lets you scroll through various predefined patterns.

3. **Switch to Photoshop.**

4. **Open an image.**

5. **Crop it to 128 x 128 pixels.**

   Use Image⇨Canvas Size or the Crop tool. This file size — 128 x 128 pixels — is the maximum size of desktop patterns and pictures.

6. **Press ⌘+A, ⌘+C.**

   This selects the image and copies it.

7. **Switch back to the Desktop portion of the Appearance control panel.**

8. **Press ⌘+V to paste the image from the Clipboard.**

   If you get an insufficient memory error, you have to increase the amount of memory devoted to the Appearance control panel, like so: Quit the program. Double-click your System Folder and then your Control Panels folder. Select the Appearance icon and press ⌘+I to display the Info dialog box. Select Memory from the Show pop-up menu and enter a higher value in the Preferred Size option box. Close the Info dialog box and return to the Desktop portion of the Appearance control panel. Then press ⌘+V again.

   You can also use the Place Picture button in the bottom of the control panel. Click the button, navigate, and select your image. Then choose how you want to position or tile your image from the pop-up menu below the Remove Picture button.

9. **Click on the Set Desktop button.**

   The background fills with the pattern. Close the control panel.

Turning Your Face into a Mouse Pad

Now that more and more folks are acquiring the ability to produce digital images, copy shops such as Kinko's are offering a plethora of products on which you can print your image. You can get your favorite Photoshop image transferred onto a mouse pad, coffee cup, T-shirt, calendar, and a whole bunch of other items that are guaranteed to be a big hit come holiday gift-giving season. What employee wouldn't love to receive a mouse pad with your smiling face on it, after all? Check with your copy shop for information on any image size, resolution, or file format requirements you need to follow when preparing your image.

Engaging in Tag-Team Editing

Just because you're an electronic artist doesn't mean that you have to work alone. If you want to give another artist or a friend a whack at one of your images, copy it to disk and mail it off. Then have the associate or friend mail the disk back when he or she is done. Or, if you're hooked into the Internet or some other online service that offers e-mail, just send the file back and forth using e-mail.

You didn't have nearly this range of give-and-take editing options back in the days before computers. I mean, you can keep trading images for years. It's like a long-distance chess game — whoever comes up with the craziest editing trick wins.

Posting the Image over the Internet or an Online Service

America Online (AOL) electronic information services has Photoshop forums, and subscribers can connect to either service using a modem. You can then upload images to the forums to make them available to other subscribers. Remember, it takes time to upload and download images — so keep the images fairly small and save them in the JPEG or GIF format. (See Chapters 6 and 19 for more about these formats.)

Also, tons of Photoshop-related sites are on the World Wide Web, accessible to anyone with a modem and an account with an Internet Service Provider. If you do a search for the word Photoshop, you'll be surprised at the number of matches.

If you happen to have your own Web page — or know someone who does — you can also add your image to the page, thereby making it available to Web surfers worldwide. As discussed in Chapters 6 and 19, you can use JPEG or the GIF format to post images on the Web.

Just in case you haven't gotten enough of me through the course of reading this book, by the way, you can check out my Web page at the following URL: www.dekemc.com. It offers some Photoshop tips and tricks along with a bunch of other stuff, including lots of shameless self-promotion. But hey, what's the point of having a Web page if you can't brag a little, right?

Adding It to Your Private Collection

No one says that you have to produce artwork for public consumption. I do plenty of stuff just for my own amusement and edification. What you see in this book, for example, represents about half of what I came up with; the other images are working files, experiments, or just too hideous for publication.

So share the stuff you're proud of, keep the random experiments to yourself, and try to learn from your inevitable mistakes. Oh, yeah, and don't beat the computer when it crashes.

Index

Notes

Notes

Discover Dummies Online!

The Dummies Web Site is your fun and friendly online resource for the latest information about *For Dummies®* books and your favorite topics. The Web site is the place to communicate with us, exchange ideas with other *For Dummies* readers, chat with authors, and have fun!

Ten Fun and Useful Things You Can Do at www.dummies.com

1. Win free *For Dummies* books and more!
2. Register your book and be entered in a prize drawing.
3. Meet your favorite authors through the Hungry Minds Author Chat Series.
4. Exchange helpful information with other *For Dummies* readers.
5. Discover other great *For Dummies* books you must have!
6. Purchase Dummieswear® exclusively from our Web site.
7. Buy *For Dummies* books online.
8. Talk to us. Make comments, ask questions, get answers!
9. Download free software.
10. Find additional useful resources from authors.

Link directly to these ten fun and useful things at
http://www.dummies.com/10useful

For other technology titles from Hungry Minds, go to
www.hungryminds.com

Not on the Web yet? It's easy to get started with *Dummies 101®: The Internet For Windows® 98* or *The Internet For Dummies®* at local retailers everywhere.

Find other *For Dummies* books on these topics:
Business • Career • Databases • Food & Beverage • Games • Gardening
Graphics • Hardware • Health & Fitness • Internet and the World Wide Web
Networking • Office Suites • Operating Systems • Personal Finance • Pets
Programming • Recreation • Sports • Spreadsheets • Teacher Resources
Test Prep • Word Processing

HUNGRY MINDS
BOOK REGISTRATION

Register This Book and Win!

We want to hear from you!

Visit **dummies.com** to register this book and tell us how you liked it!

- Get entered in our monthly prize giveaway.

- Give us feedback about this book — tell us what you like best, what you like least, or maybe what you'd like to ask the author and us to change!

- Let us know any other *For Dummies*® topics that interest you.

Your feedback helps us determine what books to publish, tells us what coverage to add as we revise our books, and lets us know whether we're meeting your needs as a *For Dummies* reader. You're our most valuable resource, and what you have to say is important to us!

Not on the Web yet? It's easy to get started with *Dummies 101®: The Internet For Windows® 98* or *The Internet For Dummies®* at local retailers everywhere.

Or let us know what you think by sending us a letter at the following address:

For Dummies Book Registration
Dummies Press
10475 Crosspoint Blvd.
Indianapolis, IN 46256

™

BESTSELLING BOOK SERIES